NATIVE AMERICAN LITERATURES

An Encyclopedia of
Works, Characters, Authors, and Themes

NATIVE AMERICAN LITERATURES

*An Encyclopedia of
Works, Characters, Authors, and Themes*

Kathy J. Whitson

ABC-CLIO

Santa Barbara, California
Denver, Colorado
Oxford, England

Library of Congress Cataloging-in-Publication Data

Whitson, Kathy J.
    Native American literatures : an encyclopedia of works, characters, authors, and themes / Kathy J. Whitson.
        p.   cm.
    Includes bibliographical references (p.   ) and index.
    Summary: An encyclopedia of Native American literatures featuring articles on individual authors, on individual works, on important characters in works, and on terms and events of historical significance that figure in many of the works.
    1. American literature—Indian authors—Bio-bibliography—Encyclopedias.   2. American literature—Indian authors—Themes, motives—Encyclopedias.   3. Characters and characteristics in literature—Encyclopedias.   4. Indians of North America—Intellectual life—Encyclopedias.   5. Indian authors—United States—Biography—Encyclopedias.   6. Indians in literature—Encyclopedias.   [1. American literature—Indian authors—Encyclopedias.   2. Indians of North America—Encyclopedias.   3. Indian authors—Encyclopedias.]   I. Title.
PS153.I52W47   1999   810.9'897—dc21   98-49251

ISBN 0-87436-932-0

05 04 03 02 01 00 99   10 9 8 7 6 5 4 3 2 1 (cloth)

ABC-CLIO, Inc.
130 Cremona Drive, P.O. Box 1911
Santa Barbara, California 93116-1911

This book is printed on acid-free paper ∞.
Manufactured in the United States of America

For my mother and grandmother,
who gave me the love of learning.

Contents

Preface, xiii
Introduction, xv

NATIVE AMERICAN LITERATURES

An Encyclopedia of
Works, Characters, Authors, and Themes, 1

Preface

From "time immemorial," Native American cultures have celebrated their religion, rituals, and customs with song, poetry, and storytelling. The richness of their verbal art—from the sacred to the profane—is documented by many who study the oral tradition. With the arrival of the literate, Christian Europeans who first colonized North America came aggressive proselytization by Christian missionaries, who were eager to convert the Indians from their "paganism" and oral traditions to Christianity and literate traditions. In the Christian tradition, the primacy of the Holy Bible, the written *Word* of God, provided the imperative for the missionary efforts.

So it was that the earliest Native American writers were those early converts to Christianity such as Samson Occom, William Apess, George Copway, and Peter Jones. They wrote accounts of their conversions, tribal histories, travel literature, and other nonfiction prose.

At the same time, there was great interest in the lives of "famous" Indians or those who were present at well-known historical occasions. The individual life story was not a part of the cultural ethos of tribal, communal peoples, but white collaborators were anxious to tell the life stories of individual Indians. The first of these collaborative, and mediated, autobiographies was *The Life of Ma-ka-tai-me-she-kia-kiak, or Black Hawk*, published in 1833 after the Black Hawk War. Some others that followed were *Wooden Leg: A Warrior Who Fought Custer* (1931) and *Black Elk Speaks* (1932), the life story of a Lakota holy man who was present at the battle of Greasy Grass (the Little Bighorn) and at Wounded Knee.

With the advent of Boasian anthropology, autobiographies of "ordinary" Indians were sought after; some examples of these are Walter Dyk's *Left-Handed: Son of Old Man Hat* (1938) and Ruth Underhill's *Papago Woman* (1936). By this time, though, many literate Indians were desirous of presenting unmediated life stories of their own. Charles Alexander Eastman, Luther Standing Bear, and Zitkala-Ša all wrote their own autobiographies in the early part of the twentieth century. Autobiography remains a popular contemporary genre; probably the most sophisticated of the unmediated, literary autobiographies are N. Scott Momaday's *The Names* (1976) and Leslie Marmon Silko's *Storyteller* (1981).

In 1854, John Rollin Ridge's *Life and Adventures of Joaquín Murieta* became the first novel published by a Native American. Ridge also holds the distinction for the first volume of poetry (*Poems* in 1868) published by a Native American. Though both poetry and fiction had their hesitant beginnings in the nineteenth century, they did not flourish until the early twentieth century. The most prolific novelist of the 1920s was John Milton Oskison; his *Wild Harvest* (1925), *Black Jack Davy* (1926), and *Brothers Three* (1935) were widely read. By the 1930s, two more novelists, John Joseph Mathews and D'Arcy McNickle, were raising the standard of artistry in the Native American novel. Their respective novels, *Sundown* and *The Surrounded*, adumbrated the themes that continue to resonate throughout Native American fiction: the difficulty that the mixed-blood has living in two worlds and the necessity of returning to traditionalism.

In the last three decades of the twentieth century, the horizon has been dominated by the giants of the Native American novel, N. Scott Momaday, Leslie Marmon Silko, James Welch, and Gerald Vizenor. Though they continue to write and their work forms the basis of many courses in Native American literatures, they have been joined by a host of other novelists: Louise Erdrich, Michael Dorris, Paula Gunn Allen, Susan Power, Sherman Alexie, Linda Hogan, W. S. Penn, Gordon Henry, and Louis Owens, to name a few.

The Native American novel is generally marked by a highly poetic voice, just as the poetry is marked by a strong narrative voice. Indeed, nearly all of the contemporary novelists also are fine poets. Several gifted writers— Simon Ortiz, Joy Harjo, Wendy Rose, Ray Young Bear, and Luci Tapahonso—primarily write poetry but do write some fiction and essays as well. The richness of the crossover between the Native American prose writers and poets is unparalleled in the field of American literature, and there is every indication that the body of Native American literatures will only continue to grow in both volume and literary merit.

In the process of research, I had the support of many people, including Jayne Chiavario, Sarah Gohl, Kristi Howe, Sheri Roe, and Lisa Williams; Craig Howe of the D'Arcy McNickle Center for American Indian History; and the Faculty Status and Development Fund of Eureka College.

Introduction

Larry Evers has noted that "patterns of interest in American Indian oral literature have been cyclic" (Evers, 1983: 23–32). His observation is true of American Indian written literature as well. In the eighteenth century, interest in the American Indian was fanned by the publication of Samson Occom's *Sermon Preached at the Execution of Moses Paul, an Indian* in 1772. Occom's sermon became an immediate bestseller, the first for a Native American writer. Its strong temperance message contributed to its popularity, but certainly, so did the fact that this sermon was written and preached by a "product" of intense "civilizing" and "Christianizing." That Occom moved from the centuries-old tradition of orality to literacy and from "paganism" to Christianity in a generation was doubtless perceived as a moral victory by those who believed that Native Americans were without art and religion simply because they were without literacy.

By the mid-nineteenth century, other Native Americans began using the language of the conqueror to articulate their message, often a bifurcated one that simultaneously embraced the "civilizing" influence and regretted the loss of traditional ways. The works of William Apess, George Copway, and John Rollin Ridge reflect the tensions of living in two worlds.

The next wave of interest in Native American writers developed at the beginning of the twentieth century. Charles Alexander Eastman, Alexander Posey, Luther Standing Bear, Mourning Dove, Zitkala-Ŝa, and John Milton Oskison, among others, found an outlet for their voices as their works were published. In the 1930s, two important writers emerged and laid the groundwork for what has come to be known as the Native American Renaissance in the late 1960s. Building on the efforts of those who came before, John Joseph Mathews and D'Arcy McNickle moved the Native American novel to a place of artistic merit that demanded literary response rather than mere anthropological interest.

Thus the stage was set for N. Scott Momaday's 1968 publication of *House Made of Dawn*, a Pulitzer Prize winner and literary masterpiece that in turn opened the floodgates of literature from a burgeoning Native American literary community. The significance of Momaday's accomplishment and subsequent recognition is profound; Paula Gunn Allen has said that *House Made of Dawn* provided hope for Native American writers and suggested that she "wouldn't be writing now if Momaday hadn't done" *House Made of Dawn* (Allen 1987).

The term "Native American Renaissance" is somewhat deceptive, suggesting as it does that Native American literature flourished at times in the historical past and then died out, to be born again in 1968 with *House Made of Dawn.* It is more accurate to recognize that since literacy was overlaid on an already sophisticated body of "oral literature," there has been a continuous outpouring of literary art by Native Americans. What *has* moved in cycles is the response to that literature from the non-Native publishing and reading worlds. However, since Momaday's external validation through the Pulitzer Prize, the cycle of interest has been sustained and, indeed, has grown larger decade by decade. The number of very fine Native American writers seems to increase almost daily, and finally their works are making their way to the literature sections of bookstores and away from the anthropology sections.

The interest in multiculturalism at the public school and collegiate levels is both a blessing and a bane to Native American (and other minority) writers. On the one hand, their works are receiving more attention in the classroom than ever before; on the other hand, their works are often placed in courses in such a way as to relegate them to second-class status. An unfortunate message that comes with the placement of such literature in minority literature classes is that the works do not deserve to be included in the canon of "regular" American literature, that they have moved in through a kind of literary affirmative action.

A close look at the literature being written by the best Native American authors easily belies that assumption of inferiority. This volume closely examines the literature produced by Native Americans from the eighteenth century, when American Indians were beginning to write in English, to the present. The great body of oral literature produced and still being produced is not the focus of this volume. It is undeniable, however, that the written literature of Native Americans is greatly indebted to the long-standing oral literature that undergirds and is integrated into every aspect of their tradition and culture.

Native American Literatures, emphasizing the plural of the word *literatures,* indicates that there is no one literature of Native Americans, just as there is no one group of people called *Native Americans*. The term *Native American* (or *American Indian*) is merely one of hegemonic convenience attributed to the indigenous peoples of the North American continent by those who understood or cared little for the diversity of peoples whose lives were disrupted by the European conquest.

With well over three hundred separate cultures populating the continent at the time of the European conquest, each culture with its own language, history, religion, customs, and bodies of oral literature, it would be ludicrous to assert that there is one monolithic Native American literature. It is more accurate and culturally sensitive (and absolutely indispensable when dealing with oral literatures) to recognize the distinctions between Lakota and Hopi and Chickasaw and Mohawk, for example. Even with the movement from oral to written art and with the homogenizing influence of a common English language, it is necessary to recognize that Navajo literature cannot be read and understood with the same lens that one would use for reading Ojibwa literature.

That so great a body of Native American literatures exists is startling to many outside the field, and in no way does this volume attempt to be comprehensive. What *Native American Literatures* does attempt to do is provide summary and interpretive information on those texts that would most likely be read and studied by high school students and college undergraduates. The volume features four kinds of articles: on individual authors, on individual works, on important characters in works, and on terms or events of historical importance that figure in many of the works. For example, the cross-references allow the reader to move from an article on the author Zitkala-Ŝa to an entry on her *American Indian Stories* to an entry on Indian Boarding School. An extensive bibliography allows readers to continue their own research of the literature.

NATIVE AMERICAN LITERATURES

An Encyclopedia of
Works, Characters, Authors, and Themes

A

Abel

Abel is the protagonist of N. Scott Momaday's first novel, *House Made of Dawn* (1968). Abel is a mixed-blood Jemez Pueblo man who returns from World War II with a strong dislocation from his tribal identity. Though exacerbated by his war experience, the loss of identity and cultural estrangement that Abel feels started long before he left the reservation. Abel has never known his father, and his mother and brother, Vidal, both died when he was young. He was raised by his maternal grandfather, Francisco, whose secure sense of tribal identity is problematic for the young Abel, but by the end of the novel, Francisco's grounding is one of the primary factors that allows Abel to reintegrate into the cultural ethos.

In the first section of the book, "The Longhair," Abel returns to the Jemez Pueblo and tries to reintegrate into that society but cannot. He walks into the canyon, reestablishing his connection to the earth and sky, and "tried to pray, to sing, to enter into the old rhythm of the tongue, but he was no longer attuned to it." The narrator diagnoses Abel's problem as the inability to articulate his thoughts in his native language. "Had he been able to say it, anything of his own language," Abel would "once again have shown him whole to himself; but he was dumb. Not dumb . . . but *inarticulate*."

Abel finds work splitting wood for Angela St. John, the wife of a Los Angeles doctor. Angela has come to the pueblo for the local baths; she is in need of spiritual healing as well, and her brief affair with Abel, though it does not heal him, offers her some measure of restoration.

Abel comes back to the pueblo near the time of two ceremonies that serve to bind the community together—the Feast of Santiago with its *corre de gaio*, or rooster pull, and the fiesta of Porcingula, with its Pecos bull ceremony. Abel participates in the *corre de gaio*, and for the first time since his return home, does not wear his military uniform. Father Olguin, the local parish priest, presents background information on the Feast of Santiago that helps to contextualize the rooster pull. In the ceremony, riders race up to a rooster that has been buried in the ground. Only the head sticks out, and the rider, as he swoops by, is to grab the rooster from the ground. Abel makes "a poor showing, full of caution and gesture." It is the albino Indian who is able to pull the rooster from the ground. He then completes the ceremony by choosing another participant and flailing him with the rooster until the bird is dead. He chooses Abel and finds in him an unwilling participant. When Abel later kills the albino in the desert during the fiesta of Porcingula, it is not to seek revenge for the humiliation of the rooster pull, but because Abel senses that the albino is a witch, palpable evil, who must be destroyed.

The scene in which Abel kills the albino reveals the act as passionless, a kind of ritual dance of death. Abel and the albino had been in the bar, and "then they were ready, the two of them. They went out into the darkness and rain." The albino attacks Abel, and "sick with terror and revulsion," Abel feels the "quick, uneven blowing at his ear, and felt the blue shivering lips upon him, felt even the scales of the lips and the hot slippery point of the tongue, writhing." Abel plunges a knife into the albino and after a struggle, kills him. Working in his fields, Francisco senses that Abel has killed the albino, and as the ceremonial dance goes on in the background, he sighs "Abelito."

The second section of the novel starts with a description of "a small silversided fish that is found along the coast of southern California." These fish "hurl themselves upon the land and writhe in the light of the moon. . . . They are among the most helpless creatures on the face of earth." In the characteristic dissociative narrative structure of the novel, the section stands alone, apparently a mere descriptive passage. Later, though, after the section that records Tosamah's sermon, the narrative voice asks, "Why should Abel think of the fishes?" The reader realizes that Abel too has seen the fishes, that they hold some metaphoric relationship for him, and that he is now lying in a ditch in a cold rain. It is six years after his trial and imprisonment for the killing of the albino, and Abel is in Los Angeles, having been beaten nearly to death by the cop Martinez.

In Los Angeles, Abel has trouble adjusting. He doesn't fit into the larger white society, nor does he fit with the Native American community as exemplified by the congregation of Tosamah's church. Tosamah disparagingly calls Abel a "longhair"—that is, a Native American unwilling to abandon the ways of the reservation and accommodate to white culture. Although Abel does feel a distance from his native culture, he feels no affinity to the white or urban culture of Los Angeles. He is taken by

a relocation officer to a job site where he meets Benally, who befriends him and takes him into his own home. Abel also establishes a tenuous romantic relationship with his social worker, Milly.

But he is no more at home or centered in Los Angeles than he has been anytime since his return from the war. A set of rebukes hasten his return to the Jemez Pueblo. In a social gathering, Tosamah taunts Abel until he lunges drunkenly at the preacher. Tosamah ridicules Abel, who is deeply but quietly hurt by the incident. Benally sees this blow as the beginning of the end. The second and more dramatic event is Abel's beating by the cop Martinez. One night, after fighting with Benally, Abel storms from the apartment vowing revenge on Martinez for striking his hands with a nightstick some time earlier. The incident ends badly for Abel, and he is beaten nearly to death. After a time of recovery in the hospital, including a visit from Angela St. John, Abel returns to Jemez Pueblo.

Back home, Abel finds Francisco near death. In a series of six monologues at dawn, Francisco attempts to pass on meaningful information to Abel, information that will help to locate him in his culture. Abel patiently cares for Francisco until his death, and then he makes arrangements for his burial. When the time came, Abel "knew what had to be done." He prepared the body in the ceremonial way and then went to participate in a ceremonial run:

> He was alone and running on. All of his being was concentrated in the sheer motion of running on, and he was past caring about the pain. Pure exhaustion laid hold of his mind, and he could see at last without having to think.

Abel is on the threshold of healing; he is participating in a ritual that will center him in his culture. He has heard the testimony of his grandfather, and he begins to sing: "There was no sound, and he had no voice; he had only the words of a song. And he went running on the rise of the song." (Evers 1985; Hirsch 1983; Momaday 1968; Oleson 1973; Owens 1992a)

See also The Albino; Benally, Ben; Father Olguin; Francisco; *House Made of Dawn*; Martinez; Milly; St. John, Angela; Tosamah, John Big Bluff.

The Absence of Angels

The Absence of Angels (1994) is the first novel of William S. Penn, Nez Perce, Osage, and English mixed-blood writer and educator. It is the story of a young mixed-blood, urban boy, Albert (Ally) Hummingbird, who is growing up with a distant father and a mother who is spiraling toward insanity. Ally has two sisters; Pamela spends most of her time in a closet, and Elanna visits the local cemetery, leaning against a gravestone talking to her dead grandmother. Ally finds his own way of dealing with his dysfunctional family. He talks to his paternal grandfather with an imaginary telephone. At times the "reception" is clear, but at other times, Ally is unable to connect with his grandfather.

By marrying a white woman and taking a job in the petrochemical industry, Ally's father has decentered himself culturally. As a result, Ally feels connected to himself and his family only when he is back on the reservation with his grandfather. The connection between Ally and his grandfather starts at Ally's birth, when the doctor predicts that he will not survive. It is his grandfather who recognizes that Death is lingering about the baby's bed; he "walked Death to the mission, where he left Him chained like a rabid dog beside the mission door." The grandfather declares, "The boy has it and won't let go." Ally does take hold of life and survives.

His childhood and journey through adolescence are marked by all of the typical coming-of-age ordeals. With the exception of the times he and his friends spy on two counselors having sex, he spends a miserable time at summer camp. He plays the requisite games of Cowboys and Indians with neighborhood children until he grows sensitive about always killing the Indians; then the games change to Bombs Away. He learns that his playmate, Tommy, is homosexual. As he grows older, he experiments with alcohol and sex and builds a police record of petty offenses. All the while, he maintains respect for his grandfather and draws his own strength from what he imagines his grandfather would say.

Death comes to his family once again when Ally's sister Pamela suffers a miscarriage and then hemorrhages to death. With Pamela dead and Elanna in Crete for two years of study, Ally's solitude grows. He stills feels some connection to his grandfather, though "he was becoming more a memory and less a presence." Ally starts his freshman year of college virtually alone. His parents have divorced, and his mother grows ever more disassociated from her family.

Ally finds a stable, parental relationship with one of his professors, Proctor Thompson, and his wife. At the same time, he develops a friendship with two students, David and Sara. These relationships provide a safety net as once again Death comes seeking him. Ally learns that his terrible headaches stem from a brain tumor that must be removed. He recovers from his surgery just in time to be present at the death of his beloved grandfather. The novel ends with an affirmation of life and love as Ally and Sara commit themselves to each other. (Krupat 1996; Penn 1994)

See also Penn, William S.

Adare, Adelaide

When Adelaide Adare climbs into the plane of The Great Omar and flies away from the Orphan's Picnic, abandoning her three children, she sets into motion the plot of Louise Erdrich's *The Beet Queen* (1986). Three years into the Great Depression, Mr. Ober, Adelaide's married lover and the father of her children, dies in an accident that looks suspiciously like suicide. Adelaide is pregnant with their third child when Mr. Ober dies, and when the baby is born, she refuses to name it. Their money runs out, and when Adelaide steals silver spoons from her landlady, the family is asked to leave.

Adelaide has a sister named Fritzie Kozka in Argus, North Dakota, and though she sends a postcard to Fritzie—"I think about the children every day. How are they?"—she never visits or sends for them. The narrative reveals glimpses of Adelaide through the years, always in desperate straits. One scene reveals her suffering in a hospital after a plane crash and another with her mind deteriorating in her late middle age.

She does send her daughter Mary two sewing machines through the years, saying, "If Mary learns how to sew, she'll always have a skill to fall back on." Mary never acknowledges either gift. (Erdrich 1986; Rainwater 1990; Towery 1992; Wong 1991)

See also Adare, Karl; Adare, Mary; *The Beet Queen*; Kozka, Pete and Fritzie; Kozka, Sita; Miller, Jude.

Adare, Dot

See Nanapush, Dot Adare.

Adare, Karl

In Louise Erdrich's *The Beet Queen* (1986), Karl is "a tall fourteen" with a mouth that is "sweetly curved" and skin "fine and girlish" when he and his sister Mary hop a boxcar on their way to Argus, North Dakota. Their quiet life in Prairie Lake came to an end when the man who was their mother's lover and their father died. Karl, always jealous of his mother's affections, is delighted to hear of Mr. Ober's death.

Karl and Mary are separated from each other in Argus when a dog attacks them. Karl runs back to the train, hides in a boxcar, and ultimately finds his way back to Minneapolis. On the boxcar he has his first homosexual experience with a young man named Giles St. Ambrose. Karl is so moved by the experience that he says to Giles, "I love you." Giles responds, "it wasn't anything. It happens." The sensitive Karl feels rejected by Giles's dismissive reply and jumps out of the moving boxcar.

With broken feet and pneumonia, Karl is found by Fleur Pillager, a Chippewa cart woman, and is nursed back to health. When he is well, Fleur drops him off at a church, and the nuns take him to the orphanage at Saint Jerome's in Minneapolis. He spends a year there before entering the seminary for a brief time.

Though "in love with the picture of [him]self in a slim black cassock," Karl discovers that he is better suited to the life of a traveling salesman. Years later, he goes back to Saint Jerome's, at another Orphan's Picnic, in his new clothes and with new money, to leave contemptuous greetings with the fathers. He sees a young man working the fishing booth and knows it is his brother Jude, kidnapped 16 years earlier. He judges him to be "cheerfully pious and self-important, a raffler of door prizes, a shiner of the priests' shoes," and decides "he disliked his brother as intensely now as he had long ago." He does not leave before telling Jude that he is a "piece of crap."

Karl's life on the road allows him to meet Wallace Pfef at a convention in Minneapolis. Karl sells Pfef on the idea of the air seeder, the sugar beet, and his first homosexual experience. Wallace provides Karl with another draw to the town of Argus, where his sister Mary lives. Karl does visit Argus later and for two weeks is devoted to Pfef. He also meets Mary's friend Celestine James, however, and begins a relationship with her, fathering her child. When the baby is born, Karl marries Celestine. Always the transient, however, Karl goes back on the road and doesn't see his daughter again until she is 14. He does send occasional gifts to Dot, samples of whatever line he is presently selling.

By the time Karl grows weary of the road, his rootlessness, and his longing for all that he'd left behind, Dot is a young woman and in the running for Beet Queen at the Argus Sugar Beet festival. Karl takes a hard look at himself and says, "I give nothing, take nothing, mean nothing, hold nothing." With a new sense of purpose, he quits his job and goes to Argus to see Dot crowned as Beet Queen. He arrives just in time to see Dot dunk Wallace Pfef in the dunk tank. He notices that Wallace is hurt and rescues him, the first step toward their reconciliation. (Bak 1992; Erdrich 1986; Owens 1992a; Rainwater 1990)

See also Adare, Adelaide; Adare, Mary; *The Beet Queen*; James, Celestine; Kozka, Sita; Miller, Jude; Nanapush, Dot Adare; Pfef, Wallace; Pillager, Fleur.

Adare, Mary

In Louise Erdrich's *The Beet Queen* (1986), Mary Adare is 11 years old, "so short and ordinary" and with a name that is as "square and practical as the rest of her," when the book opens. When her mother gets into a plane and flies off from the Orphan's Picnic, leaving her three children, Mary feels a stab of satisfaction: "For once she had played no favorites between Karl and me, but left us both." The children go home and cry, but Mary reacts differently: "When that was done, however, I acquired a brain of ice." She goes to her Aunt Fritzie's in Argus, North Dakota, and decides to "be essential to them all, so depended upon that they could never send me off." In addition to earning her keep with solid work, Mary tries to pay her own way with the contents of the blue velvet box that had belonged to her mother. In a humiliating scene, she learns that it holds nothing of value when she pries it open.

Mary garners instant respect in Argus when she goes headfirst down the frozen slide on the playground at school. She crashes on the bottom, and her face makes an imprint that the nuns hail as a miracle, for in it they see the face of Christ. Mary herself sees only the face of her absent brother, Karl.

Mary does indeed develop a frozen heart where her mother is concerned. When Adelaide sends Fritzie a postcard asking about the children, Mary writes back in Fritzie's hand, "All three of your children starved dead." The extraordinary events of her young girlhood have an effect on Mary, who is "pigheaded, bitter, moody," and prone to "fits of unreasonable anger." She also grows unbending and unwilling to take risks, even for love. Mary makes an attempt to flirt with Russell Kashpaw, but when it doesn't take after one "date," she abandons the idea, vowing, "I would never go out of my way for romance again. Romance would have to go out of its way for me." Instead, she devotes her considerable energies to running the butcher shop and becoming an eccentric character. Still, in the quiet of the night, Mary dreams of a lover that she never finds.

When Celestine and Karl become a short-lived couple, Mary feels a sense of double loss.

However, their daughter Dot gives Mary another outlet for her strong and possessive love. Mary's obsessive love for Dot often estranges Celestine and always spoils Dot. Mary is judged "ruthless" by Wallace Pfef, a local entrepreneur and family friend, and he further suggests that she is responsible for the unraveling of her cousin Sita's mind. (Bak 1992; Erdrich 1986; Owens 1992a; Towery 1992; Wong 1991)

See also Adare, Adelaide; Adare, Karl; *The Beet Queen*; James, Celestine; Kashpaw, Russell; Kozka, Pete and Fritzie; Kozka, Sita; Miller, Jude; Nanapush, Dot Adare; Pfef, Wallace.

Agent Parker

In D'Arcy McNickle's *The Surrounded* (1936, 1978), Agent Horace Parker is the Indian agent more concerned with saving his skin than faithfully discharging his duties. Though he "liked his job and he liked his Indian wards," he has grown callous to their needs. He has learned that "if an agent wished to remain in the Service, he had to keep his record clear." So, when Archilde Leon and his mother return from a hunting trip in the mountains with the dead body of Louis Leon, Parker takes the cautionary measure of jailing Archilde even though there are no charges against him. Parker holds Archilde for over a month until an inquiry is over.

Parker shows up in an even more unfavorable light at the end of the novel, when he and Sheriff Quigley track Archilde, Elise La Rose, and Archilde's nephews, Mike and Narcisse. He scolds Archilde, "You had everything, every chance, and this is the best you could do with it!" And when Mike and Narcisse slip away from him, Parker exclaims, "It's too damn bad you people never learn that you can't run away." (McNickle 1936, 1978)

See also La Rose, Elise; Leon, Archilde; Leon, Catharine; Mike and Narcisse; Quigley, Sheriff Dave.

Aho

Aho is the paternal grandmother of N. Scott Momaday, and she is a subject in his personal memoir, *The Names* (1976), and in his cultural autobiography, *The Way to Rainy Mountain* (1969). The introduction to *The Way to Rainy Mountain* is given over to the story of Aho and how, on the occasion of her death, Momaday decides to make the journey that the Kiowas had made, from their ancestral origin in the western country of Montana to Rainy Mountain in the southern plains of Oklahoma.

Aho also appears in *House Made of Dawn*, when Momaday interpolates her story whole cloth into the novel by way of Tosamah. (Momaday 1968; Momaday 1969; Momaday 1976)

See also *House Made of Dawn*; Mammedaty; Momaday, N. Scott; *The Names*; *The Way to Rainy Mountain*.

The Airplane Man

The Airplane Man is an enigmatic character in James Welch's *Winter in the Blood* (1974). He is found only in the central section of the book, that section given over to chaos and surrealism. Like the narrator, he remains nameless and is on a quest. Though the narrator is running *toward* something, the Airplane Man is running *away* from something. He is a fugitive from the law, and he asks the narrator to drive him to Canada to escape from the FBI. He explains that he "took a little something that wasn't exactly [his]—absconded, you might say." The narrator asks if he shouldn't be in hiding, and the Airplane Man replies, "I am. I'm hiding in Montana; what better place to hide?" Again, the Airplane Man's situation parallels the narrator's in part, for he too has been in a long period of hiding from his past, from the memories of the death of Mose.

The Airplane Man, though in hiding, attracts all manner of attention to himself by his talkative eccentricity. He sits at the bar and plays chances at punchboard, winning a purple teddy bear and boxes of chocolate-covered cherries. His chatter is so disconnected and full of improbabilities that it is only when the Airplane Man is arrested that the narrator realizes that perhaps he was telling the truth. (Owens 1992a; Welch 1974, 1986)

See also Mose; Nameless Narrator; *Winter in the Blood*.

The Albino

In N. Scott Momaday's *House Made of Dawn* (1968), the albino Indian suggests the presence of evil. He participates in the rooster pull and is successful where Abel is not. He first shows the rooster to Angela St. John and then rides over to Abel and flails him with the rooster. The albino participates in the ceremonial act "with only the mute malice of the act itself, careless, undetermined, almost composed in some final, preeminent sense."

That the albino represents evil is certain, and when Abel kills the albino, it is with the same "mute malice" and composure with which the albino kills the rooster. When he is tried for murder, Abel thinks, "It was not a complicated thing, after all; it was very simple. . . . A man kills such an enemy if he can." But Abel's response to the presence of evil is wrong. He attacks evil rather than turning from it as his grandfather does when the albino watches him in the cornfield. (Momaday 1968)

See also Abel; Francisco; *House Made of Dawn*; St. John, Angela.

Alexie, Sherman

Sherman Alexie (Spokane/Coeur d'Alene) was born in October 1966, and grew up on the Spokane Indian reservation in Wellpinit, Washington. Alexie attended Gonzaga University and earned a bachelor's degree from Washington State University in 1991. An enrolled member of the Spokane tribe, he has rocketed into public attention since the publication of his first book, *The Business of Fancydancing* (1992). He quickly added several volumes of poetry: *First Indian on the Moon* (1993), *Old Shirts and New Skins* (1993), and *The Summer of Black Widows* (1996). His collection of short stories, *The Lone Ranger and Tonto Fistfight in Heaven* (1993), was a citation winner for the PEN/Hemingway Award for best first book of fiction. His two novels, *Reservation Blues* (1995) and *Indian Killer* (1996), have received praise as well.

Alexie has recently moved into other ventures; he has written the screenplay for a movie, *Smoke Signals*, based on "This Is What It Means

Sherman Alexie, 1995. (Courtesy of Sherman Alexie)

to Say Phoenix, Arizona," a story from *The Lone Ranger and Tonto Fistfight in Heaven.* He is just finishing the screenplay for the movie version of *Indian Killer* and has plans to direct the movie. A work in progress, *The Sin Eaters,* is a novel in which scientists discover that the cure for cancer "involves the bone marrow of Indians." (Purdy 1997; Witalec 1995)

See also *The Business of Fancydancing; Indian Killer; The Lone Ranger and Tonto Fistfight in Heaven; Reservation Blues.*

Allen, Paula Gunn

Paula Gunn Allen is a registered member of the Laguna Pueblo tribe but values the many cultures and nationalities contributing to her identity. Her father is of Lebanese-American ancestry and her mother is of Laguna-Sioux ancestry. The confluence of cultures gives Allen a singular place from which to write. She is a poet, novelist, leading critic of Native American literatures, and an educator.

Her childhood in Cubero, New Mexico, included a Catholic school education and the

images that would provide the thematic bedrock of all her work: "the land, the family, the road." These are Allen's "sources," her "home." Allen describes herself as a very religious person who cannot "abide" the politics of the Catholic Church. She says,

Sometimes I get in a dialogue between what the Church taught me, the nuns taught me, what my mother taught me, what my experience growing up where I grew up taught me. Often you can't reconcile them. I can't reconcile them.

For all the irreconcilable differences of her Euroamerican and Laguna heritages, Allen capitalizes on the "mediational capacity that is not possessed by either of the sides." The mixed-blood can "bridge variant realities" and pollinate both traditions. She further says, "you must accept all your identities; they are yours, and nobody has the right to take them away from you. You have to be a lot smarter to manage two cultures or five cultures than you do to manage one."

In college, Allen married and had two children; when the marriage ended in divorce, Allen went back to the university and began studying writing. She says, "a writer's job is to be as accurate a receiver as you can be. It is hard work." She credits N. Scott Momaday with providing hope for many Native American writers: "I wouldn't be writing now if Momaday hadn't done [*House Made of Dawn*]. I would have died."

A strong feminist, Allen suggests that pre-Columbian Native American cultures were all gynocratic; she says, "I have never found a patriarchal culture in Native America, North or South. Never." Her 1986 volume, *The Sacred Hoop: Recovering the Feminine in American Indian Traditions,* is a collection of 17 essays from a feminist point of view. She has edited several volumes of writing by Native American women, including *Spider Woman's Granddaughters* (1989) and *Grandmothers of the Light* (1991).

Allen's strength as a writer is in her poetry; her 1982 volume, *Shadow Country,* and *Skin and Bones* (1988), a collection of poetry she wrote from 1979 to 1987, have garnered praise. Her novel, *The Woman Who Owned the Shadows* (1983), is a more uneven performance, though it focuses on racism and sexism, themes central to Allen's artistic design.

Allen received her bachelor's degree and master of fine arts from the University of Oregon and a doctorate from the University of New Mexico. Since 1990, she has been teaching in the English department of the University of California at Los Angeles. She is the recipient of many awards, including the Native American Literature prize in 1990 and the American Book Award for her anthology *Spider Woman's Granddaughters*. (Allen 1987a; Allen 1987b; Allen 1990; Ruppert 1994)

See also *The Woman Who Owned the Shadows.*

Almanac of the Dead

Leslie Marmon Silko's *Almanac of the Dead* (1991), an enormous accomplishment, taking over ten years to write, is a book that sprawls across 500 years of conquest, colonization, and crimes against humanity. The book is both a historical account and a prophetic warning to the colonizers that the vanquished people of the Americas will not always be vanquished. The book is built on the premise that the ancient Maya, Aztec, and Inca peoples foretold the coming of the Europeans and also foretold the disappearance of all things European. Tucson is the epicenter of the novel, and all evil sprawls from and coagulates there.

The book is remarkably biblical in its breadth and rhetorical purposes. It is part history, part prophecy, part poetry, part myth, part apocalypse, and part spiritual handbook. Though the story line is circuitous and convoluted, it nonetheless points in the sure direction of its ending. Silko pushes the reader to the edges of the social order; she forces the reader to view the oppressed and the oppressors. Though at times the drugs and violence and unspeakable crimes seem to pull the reader under, the overriding message of the novel is an optimistic one. The discomfort experienced by the reader may be in part due to the inevitable realization that wherever there is tyranny, all people share in the guilt.

In a novel in which there are over 70 major characters and centuries of violence of every kind, there are some stabilizing structural devices. The book opens and closes with the same set of characters—the twin sisters, Lecha and Zeta, and their companions, Seese and Sterling. There are two sets of twins who anchor the novel in North and South America. Lecha and Zeta live in Tucson; Tacho and El Feo, twin brothers, are Mexican Indians living near the Guatemalan border.

The novel opens in Tucson at the ranch of Zeta and Lecha, where Zeta and Ferro, Lecha's son, have been living and creating a base for their gun- and drug-smuggling operation. Lecha has returned home after many years of being a TV psychic. She is presumably suffering from cancer and comes to the ranch with Seese, her nurse and secretary, set upon transcribing the notebooks that were given to her and Zeta by their grandmother Yoeme. The notebooks are the almanac of the title, and they are of inestimable importance, for they encode the stories of the peoples of the Americas. They have been passed on since the time of the European invasion of the continent, and "the people knew if even part of their almanac survived, they as a people would return someday."

As keeper of the almanac, Lecha is just one of the many characters in the book who is working to bring about the time when indigenous peoples of the Americas will come together as a great marching army and repossess the land. These characters are divided in their methods, however. Some, such as Tacho and El Feo, advocate peaceful marching and trust in the ancient spirits of the land; others, such as Angelita (also known as the Meat Hook) and the Barefoot Hopi, advocate violence.

Though the major prophecy of the novel is that all things European will pass away from the continent, the book is not necessarily anti-European. The message of the book is anti-Destroyers. Silko relates, "Hundreds of years before the Europeans had appeared, sorcerers called Gunadeeyahs or Destroyers had taken over in the South." When the European Hernán Cortés came to the Americas, he found in Montezuma a like mind. They were both "members of the same secret clan," the Gunadeeyah clan, those Destroyers and sorcerers who grew excited at human sacrifice and human blood. The coming together of these two Destroyers opened the floodgate of destruction in the Americas.

Though crimes against humans dominate the novel, crimes against "Mother Earth" are just as heinous. The result of "what the white man had to offer the Americas: poison smog in the winter and the choking clouds that swirled off sewage treatment leaching fields and filled the sky with fecal dust in early spring." The message of the sacred macaws who guide the revolution through their intermediary, Tacho, is that tribal people must "retake ancestral land all over the world." The "earth's spirits" want "her indigenous children who loved her and did not harm her."

A common thread throughout the novel is the prevalence of characters who are disconnected from family or any stable connections that might root them. Seese ran away from home at age 16; Sterling is exiled from his reservation; Root, Lecha's biker boyfriend, is estranged from his family; and Ferro has been abandoned by his own mother. Another permutation of the pattern is the disconnection of the people from the earth. The earth has been polluted, mined, blasted, and bombed, and the weapons of destruction are ever increasing in number and potency. It is little wonder, then, that without connection to family or the sustaining earth, many of the novel's characters are involved in crimes against humanity and nature.

The novel ends with a confirmation that the peoples' army of the South will be moving North, reclaiming the continent. As one character says, "We don't believe in boundaries. Borders. Nothing like that." According to Silko, "History was the sacred text. The most complete history was the most powerful force." In providing the stories and histories of indigenous peoples of the Americas in *Almanac of the Dead*, Silko has made a major contribution to the powerful force of truth. (Cheuse 1991; Jaimes 1992; Silko 1991; Tallent 1991)

See also The Barefoot Hopi; Beaufrey; Blue, Bingo; Blue, Leah; Blue, Max; Blue, Sonny; Calabazas; Clinton; El Feo; Eric; Ferro; General G.; Iliana; Jamey; La Escapia, Angelita; Las Casas, Bartolomeo de; Lecha; Liria; Martinez-Soto, Alegria; Menardo; Monte; Mosca (Carlos); Paulie; Rambo (Roy); Root; Sarita; Silko, Leslie Marmon; Sterling; Tacho; Tiny; Trigg, Eddie; Weasel Tail, Wilson; Yoeme; Zeta.

American Indian Stories

American Indian Stories is the 1921 mixed-genre volume by Zitkala-Ša (Gertrude Simmons Bonnin). The volume opens with three autobiographical essays that were written and published while Zitkala-Ša was teaching at the Carlisle Indian Industrial School. The first, "Impressions of an Indian Childhood," introduces "a wild little girl of seven" who is at ease in her life, full of "freedom and overflowing spirits." Though she is later lured from the prairie to gain an education in the East, her training at her mother's hand is its own education, one appropriate to her culture and place. Her mother teaches her of the losses that the Dakotas have suffered at the hands of the encroaching whites, but she also learns the old legends of the Sioux, including the Iktomi (trickster) tales. In her mother's home, she learns to locate and gather roots, grains, and fruits; to do intricate beadwork; to respect her elders; to practice the art of hospitality and gift giving; and to worship the Great Spirit. These idyllic days are interrupted by the appearance of missionaries who are recruiting Indian children to go east to the land of "red apples" for an "American" education. Drawn by an overwhelming curiosity and not yet "an ambition for Letters," young Gertrude Simmons left the home of her mother to travel to Wabash, Indiana. The decision forever altered the life of Simmons, as the next essay, "The School Days of an Indian Girl," reveals.

The anticipatory joy of the children leaving the prairie to travel on the "iron horse" soon

Gertrude Bonnin, or Zitkala-Ša, in full dress in July 1930, shortly after publishing American Indian Stories. *(Washington State University Libraries)*

evaporated. During the train ride, the children encountered their first experiences with social difference and ultimately prejudice, as the white women and children on the train stared and poked at them. Their arrival at the school brought only further humiliations and bewildering changes. Their hair was cut—an unbearable humiliation, for in their culture only cowards had their hair cut by another—and their clothes were taken and replaced by stiff, uncomfortable, "civilized" clothes. When Gertrude refused to submit to the haircut, she was captured and tied onto a chair. As she felt the cold blades of the scissors against her neck and heard the cutting of her braids, she realized that then "[she] lost [her] spirit."

The essay recounts other adjustments that the children were forced to accept, all of which moved them further from their own culture but did not place them comfortably in white culture either. The "wild little girl" of the prairie has become "only one of many little animals driven by a herder." After three years of regimentation, Simmons was allowed to return home for a visit. The visit turned into several years of inarticulate unhappiness. During this time, she says, "I seemed to hang in the heart of chaos, beyond the touch or voice of human aid." What she felt was the inevitable displacement caused by the overlay of the white educational, spiritual, and ideological system onto her own still-forming Siouan pattern of culture. The resulting liminality—being at the threshold of two worlds but firmly placed in neither—shaped and directed the rest of her life. Back home on the prairie with her mother, she no longer felt connected to her mother or her former way of life. When she left again for school, it was with the hope that "it would bring [her] back to [her] mother in a few winters, when [she] should be grown tall, and there would be congenial friends awaiting [her]."

The rift between her and her mother did not heal, and Simmons stayed in the East to continue her education at Earlham College in Indiana. Often, however, she longed to be back in harmonious relationship with her mother in the West rather than "remaining among a cold race whose hearts were frozen hard with prejudice."

Zitkala-Ša's third autobiographical essay, "An Indian Teacher among Indians," begins with her experiences at the Carlisle Indian Industrial School in Carlisle, Pennsylvania. By this time she was firmly convinced that she would direct her life's energies "in a work for the Indian race." Working from the inside of the system proves just as disheartening, however, as being a subject of its efforts. She is discouraged to learn that many of her colleagues are the dregs of white society—opium eaters, drunkards, and abusive personalities. She comes to see more surely than ever that what she has gained in the white world's education has been at a dear cost. She says, "For the white man's papers [the Bible] I had given up my faith in the Great Spirit. For these same papers I had forgotten the healing in trees and brooks. On account of my mother's simple view of life, and my lack of any, I gave her up, also. I made no friends among the race of people I loathed. Like a slender tree, I had been uprooted from my mother, nature, and God." On a trip home, she is somewhat reconciled to her mother, and as the essay ends, Simmons resigns from the Indian school.

The next essay in the volume is a polemic against Christianity. Originally published as "Why I Am a Pagan" and retitled here as "The Great Spirit," the essay is Simmons's reaffirmation of her culture and the sacredness of the Great Spirit. On a visit home, she listens respectfully to a Christian preacher, "though he mouth[s] most strangely the jangling phrases of a bigoted creed." But the dogma holds no sway over her; she prefers "excursions into the natural gardens where the voice of the Great Spirit is heard in the twittering of birds, the rippling of mighty waters, and the sweet breathing of flowers."

In the next section of *American Indian Stories*, Zitkala-Ša (for she is now going by her self-christened name) moves away from strict autobiography into fiction. In her most recognized short story, "The Soft-Hearted Sioux," Zitkala-Ša assumes the narrative voice of a young Sioux who returns to his tribal group

Singing class at the Carlisle Indian Industrial School, 1901. (Cumberland County Historical Society)

after living among the Christians in an eastern boarding school setting, not unlike the one she herself had been in. Nine years in a mission school where he hunted only for the "soft heart" of Christ thoroughly disengaged him from the role he would have assumed only a generation earlier—that of a "warrior, huntsman, and husband." In the tenth year of his schooling, he is sent back to his tribe "to preach Christianity to them." He returns to his village a stranger to his family, his people, and their ways. He finds that his father is sick and is being treated by a medicine man. In a fit of righteous anger, fearful that the medicine man would "ensnare [his] father's soul," he forces the medicine man to leave. The young man is unable to effect a spiritual or physical cure for his father and only alienates the village in his attempts to do so. Neither is the young man able to hunt for food for his father, who is starving; he has lost all skills that would serve him well in the hunt. Finally, at the point of death, his father bids him kill from a herd of domestic cattle that is

"two hills eastward." Predictably, the young man kills the cow too late to save his father and, furthermore, is arrested for the theft of a white man's property. The story ends with the young man in jail, dramatically trapped between the values of two conflicting ways of life. Though predictable and stylistically imperfect, with its heavy dose of sentimentality, the story effectively portrays the crisis of generations of Indians who were stripped of much of their own culture and given so little access to the white culture in return.

Another of the short stories, "A Warrior's Daughter," is significant for its portrayal of a young woman who takes on the role of a warrior in order to save her lover who has been captured by the enemy. "The Trial Path" relates the story of two inseparable friends and a fit of anger that results in the slaying of one. The story is rich with information concerning revenge and forgiveness in the Sioux culture. "A Dream of Her Grandfather" is a short vignette that validates the spiritual connection of a young girl and her grandfather. In "The Widespread Enigma Concerning Blue-Star Woman," Zitkala-Ša grows more political in her purpose as she chronicles a story of greed and betrayal set in the days following the 1887 Dawes Allotment Act. The final selection in the volume, "America's Indian Problem," is not a story at all but a political tract calling for citizenship for Native Americans and accountability in the Bureau of Indian Affairs.

Despite the large-print edition republished by the University of Nebraska's Bison Books, the volume of stories is not children's fare; it is a serious work of art by a gifted writer struggling for a voice from the margins of two languages and two worlds. (Cutter 1994; Fisher 1979; Zitkala-Ša 1921)

See also Indian Boarding School; Zitkala-Ša.

Amos

In James Welch's *Winter in the Blood* (1974), Amos is a duck who has significance for the narrator. When the narrator and his brother Mose were young boys, their father won five ducks while "pitching pennies at the fair." The boys built a small pond for the ducks by digging a hole in the ground and putting a washtub in it. They filled the tub with water to the lip and let the ducks swim. One day when they went to town, the water level lowered and four of the ducks drowned because they could not get out of the tub. Only Amos survived. The duck becomes symbolic of survival and is connected to the narrator in his adulthood when he dreams of Amos with an "orange leg cocked at the knee." Both the duck and the narrator share an injured leg.

But Amos is significant beyond this correlation to the narrator. When the narrator is establishing his identity by reclaiming memory, he and his mother share stories of the past. Teresa tells him that they ate the duck for Christmas dinner. In the mind of the narrator, he remembers eating a turkey for dinner. Teresa explains that the turkey was killed by a bobcat. Again the narrator misremembers. He thinks that his father killed Amos, but his mother counters, "Your father wasn't even around!" As the realization sinks in that his mother killed the duck out of necessity because of her largely absent husband, the narrator comes to a new understanding of his parents. (Owens 1992a; Thackery 1985; Welch 1974, 1986)

See also First Raise, John; First Raise, Teresa; Mose; Nameless Narrator; *Winter in the Blood.*

The Ancient Child

The Ancient Child (1989) is the second novel of N. Scott Momaday, the Kiowa writer and artist whose first novel, *House Made of Dawn* (1968), won the Pulitzer Prize for fiction. Like that first novel, *The Ancient Child* is infused with Navajo and Kiowa myth. When Momaday was in the process of writing *The Ancient Child*, he described his intent in an interview:

> The novel that I'm working on now is really a construction of different myths. I've taken a Kiowa myth to begin with and am bringing it up to modern times. . . . my main character, Set, is the reincarnation of a boy who figures in Kiowa mythology, a boy who turns into a bear.

The Kiowa myth is the tale of seven sisters and their brother who are out playing together. The seven sisters are being chased by the boy when they discover that he has metamorphosed into a bear as he runs after them. In terror, they climb a tree straight into the sky where they become the seven stars of the Big Dipper. The tree turns into stone and becomes the great sacred landmark of the Kiowa, Tsoai, the "rock tree."

The novel is actually stretched on the frame of two bear myths, the Kiowa myth mentioned above and a second myth of the Ancient Child. A child comes into a Piegan camp and makes himself at home. He speaks a bubbling, happy language, but it is one that the Piegan cannot understand. They are drawn to the mysterious boy and feel honored by him and protective of him. They are greatly grieved when he disappears from their camp the following morning.

To help them know how to respond to the disappearance of the child, a wise man of the village explains that perhaps the child was not a human child at all but a bear cub.

The two bear myths are significant to the work, for they signal the major thematic concern of the main character, Locke Setman—transformation. The novel is essentially the journey of Setman, called Set, to an awareness of, and participation in, his cultural destiny. He has been separated from his cultural moorings since the death of his mother at childbirth and of his father in a car accident when Set was only seven. Set—then called Loki—is sent to an orphanage, the Peter and Paul Home, where his most significant human contact is with the enigmatic Sister Stella Francesca. After some time, Set is adopted from the home by Bent Sandridge, a philosopher and academic who has retired from his profession. Under the kindly guidance and tutelage of Sandridge, Set's life assumes some measure of normalcy. He goes on to art school and begins a successful life as an artist, though his early successes are diminished by his more recent artistic compromises. At midlife and mid-career, Set is increasingly dissociated from his art and from himself.

He receives a mysterious telegram calling him to the deathbed of his dead father's grandmother, Kope'mah. Though he feels no sense of connection to his father's family, he answers the telegram by flying to Oklahoma to his father's home. There he meets a distant cousin, Jessie Mottledmare, and her husband, Milo. He also meets Grey, a more distant cousin who has recently come to Oklahoma from Navajo country. Grey, the daughter of a Navajo mother and a Kiowa father, has journeyed to Oklahoma some two years before the narrative opens, searching for a connection to her father's people. There she is received with special regard by the old medicine woman, Kope'mah, her great-grandmother, and with generous tolerance by Jessie and Milo Mottledmare. For two years she nurses Kope'mah and learns of the old Kiowa ways and of the powers of the medicine woman.

Insofar as the novel is the story of Set's journey to his mythic past, it is also the story of Grey's journey to her cultural present. Set is cut off from his Kiowa past and must recover it; Grey lives in the imaginary past of the legendary Billy the Kid. She is invested with visionary powers, but she is using them in a nonproductive way. She must leave behind the visions of Billy the Kid and move into her powers as a contemporary medicine woman. Momaday gives repeated stylistic signals to the reader to show the progress each is making in his or her quest. As Set moves into his past so that he might understand it and claim it, the text signals, "And Set remembered." When Grey moves into an imagined life with Billy the Kid, the text signals, "Never had Grey to quest after visions." The signals reinforce the importance of the two necessary ingredients of personal wholeness—memory and vision. Set must recover his personal and cultural memory, and Grey must realign her vision. Ultimately their paths merge, and it is Grey who enables Set to complete his journey. Before that can happen, though, Set must endure a time of pain and separation that becomes the preparation for his final growth.

Set returns to his home in San Francisco, to the vacuous art world that is giving him less and less satisfaction. There is a hollowness to his life that is exacerbated by the sudden death of his adoptive father. Set enters a time of depression, what his friends call a nervous breakdown. He is hospitalized, and his doctor cautions Lola Bourne, his lover:

> Be careful. This man is preoccupied with the thought of being a bear. He wants to be cared for because he has been wounded. But he is trapped in some acute awareness of himself. He is dangerously self-centered.

Unknown to Set and Lola, Grey is working toward his healing with a ceremony. She is aided by Jessie and Milo Mottledmare and the supernatural guidance of Kope'mah, who continues to instruct Grey even after her death. Caught in a destiny that he can neither explain nor escape, Set returns to Oklahoma with the help of Lola. There he is delivered into the care of Grey, where he feels perfectly safe and at peace. Under Grey's care, Set and Grey and Dog, her horse, set out to drive to Navajo country, where they join Grey's mother's family. Once there, Set and Grey marry; Set settles into a daily routine of running, painting, and resting. He slowly comes to a state of wholeness and health. Grey is pregnant with their child when Set goes on a vision quest. He follows the instructions of Kope'mah and travels to the foot of Tsoai, the rock tree of the Kiowa legend that is intertwined into the very heart of the text and of Set's experience. The story ends with Set's identification with the bear. He enters the myth and becomes the boy who chases his sisters to Tsoai. It is by this growing into the bear myth that Set gains a cultural identification that centers him. (Momaday 1989; Owens 1992a; Velie 1994; Wiget 1994)

See also Bourne, Lola; Grey; Momaday, N. Scott; Sandridge, Bent; Setman, Locke.

The Antelope Wife

In her last several novels, Louise Erdrich has been spinning tales around a familiar group of characters. *The Antelope Wife* (1998) is a departure from this pattern, as Erdrich introduces a new cast of passionate and sometimes dysfunctional Ojibwa (Anishinabe) characters. The story opens with the historical origins of the Roy and Shawano families. Scranton Roy is a cavalry soldier involved in a raid on a peaceful Ojibwa village, and he is sickened by the violence he is executing. When he kills an old woman with his bayonet, he sees in her his own mother, and he runs from the scene. He spies a dog running with a child tied to its back. On the child's cradleboard hangs a necklace of blue beads. Roy follows them, and after two days of wariness, the dog finally sidles up to Roy. He takes the child from the dog's back and tries to feed it, but it is too young to accept adult food. In an act of unlikely desperation, Roy opens his shirt to the rooting baby, and she feeds at his breast.

Scranton Roy never returns to his cavalry company; he lives with the child in relative isolation until the girl, now called Matilda, grows

to school age. When Matilda is six, Roy marries the schoolteacher, Peace McKnight. Meanwhile, the Ojibwa child's mother, Blue Prairie Woman, mourns for her lost child. For six months, she eats nothing but leaves and dirt and grows more and more distant, always dreaming of the dog and her child. The village elders have the namer dream Blue Prairie Woman a new name so that she might "return to the living." She is named Other Side of the Earth, for it is as if she has gone there in search of her absent child. She gives birth to twins, Mary and Zosie, but leaves them in the care of their grandmother as she leaves to search for her lost daughter. She finally finds the house of Scranton Roy and waits outside in the darkness until her daughter senses her presence and follows her. Matilda Roy leaves a note for her parents: "She came for me. I went with her." But there is a sickness in the house of Scranton Roy, and his wife is suffering from it. Other Side of the Earth contracts it and dies within 24 hours. The seven-year-old Matilda is left with her mother's lifeless body, singing the song that her mother sang all the while she was dying. The song attracts a herd of antelope, and they stand around her and "bend to her," drawing the child into their care: "When they walk, she walks, following, dried berries in a sack made of her dress. When they run, she runs with them. Naked, graceful, the blue beads around her neck."

The narrative then moves to contemporary times and a group of characters who are all connected to the events set into motion by Scranton Roy in the century before. The four primary characters are Rozin and Richard Whiteheart Beads, who are in an unhappy marriage; Klaus Shawano, erstwhile business partner of Whiteheart Beads and kidnapper of an antelope woman, Sweetheart Calico; and Frank Shawano, a baker who is the lover and later the husband of Rozin.

Rozin is a descendant of Blue Prairie Woman through the twins that the distraught woman gave birth to before leaving on her fatal mission to find her first daughter. Those twins were named Mary and Zosie, and in each subsequent generation, there was a set of girl twins named Mary and Zosie. The naming pattern is disrupted in Rozin's generation; her twin is named Aurora, and dies at age five. Rozin names her twin girls Cally and Deanna and comes to regret it: "Bad choice. I broke more continuity, and they suffered for it, too. Should have kept the protection."

Deanna too dies in childhood, the result of an aborted suicide attempt by her father. When Richard Whiteheart Beads learns that his wife is having an affair with Frank Shawano and that she plans to leave the marriage, he decides to asphyxiate himself in his truck. Deanna senses that her father is leaving without her and slips into the truck while Richard has gone back into the house for a drink of whiskey. Richard returns to the truck to find that he has locked it; not knowing that Deanna is under some coats behind the seat, he lets it run through the night. After Deanna's death, Rozin does leave Richard, but she does not go to Frank either. She takes Cally and goes to live with her mother and aunt, Zosie and Mary.

Richard Whiteheart Beads has been in the landfill and garbage business with Klaus Shawano but leaves Klaus holding the bag when authorities bust them for illegal practices. After the failure of their business and the failure of Whiteheart Beads's marriage, both men reach bottom and live on the street.

Klaus fares no better in his relationship with the woman he loves than does Richard Whiteheart Beads. In his days as a trader on the powwow circuit, Klaus sees a beautiful woman and immediately falls in love with her. He seeks the help of Jimmy Badger, a medicine man, so that he might attract the attention of the beautiful woman. Badger warns Klaus that the woman is an antelope woman, the descendant of a girl who ran with the antelopes long ago. Even though Badger further warns, "Our old women say they appear and disappear. Some men follow the antelope and lose their minds," Klaus will not be dissuaded. He kidnaps the woman and takes her back to Minneapolis with him. For a while he keeps her tied to his wrist with strips of cloth called sweetheart calico. The

beautiful woman never speaks and becomes a respected curiosity to others in the community. When Klaus's life deteriorates and he becomes a street person, his brother Frank accepts responsibility for the care of the woman now called Sweetheart Calico.

Years pass before Frank Shawano and Rozin reestablish their relationship, though their love has continued unspoken all the while. They make plans to marry, and on their wedding day, Whiteheart Beads disrupts the wedding with yet another suicide attempt. Though his attempt at the wedding is unsuccessful, he shows up at the hotel where Frank and Rozin are beginning their honeymoon; he shoots himself in their hallway and dies later in the night.

It is not until the end of the novel that Erdrich takes the reader back to the nineteenth century and Scranton Roy and clarifies the tangled relationships between the contemporary characters. Blue Prairie Woman, an antelope woman, married a Shawano man and gave birth to three daughters. The first child was saved from the cavalry raid because the antelope warned Blue Prairie Woman to put her child on the dog so she might escape. The other two daughters were the first twins named Mary and Zosie. For the rest of his life, Scranton Roy is troubled by the images of the woman he killed during the raid. When he is an old man, being cared for by his grandson Augustus, Scranton Roy returns to the "village and the people he had wronged." His grandson is with him and immediately falls in love with one of that generation's Mary and Zosie twins. He trades all he owns and "hanks of red beads . . . the old ones of highbush red, white centers, glowing glass" for the girl.

Augustus Roy marries Zosie Shawano, and the family lines are connected. The "whiteheart beads" Roy traded into the Ojibwa community become favorites of the women and decorate the blanket of a child who is "named for the decoration it loved. Whiteheart Beads." By the time of the contemporary generation, Rozin carries the Roy and Shawano blood, marries a Whiteheart Beads, and later marries a Shawano. The complexities are pure Erdrich. She leaves the reader with the questions, "Who is beading us? . . . Who are you and who am I, the beader or the bit of colored glass sewn onto the fabric of this earth?" (Erdrich 1998)

See also Erdrich, Louise.

Apess, William

William Apess (sometimes recorded as "Apes") was born in 1798 to a mixed-blood Pequot father and a full-blood Pequot mother, but his parents parted when the child was only three years old. He became the unfortunate subject of one of his grandmother's alcoholic rages when he was around four years old and was nearly beaten to death. Only the intervention of an uncle saved his life. He was placed with a kind white family, the Furmans, around age five, and they raised him in a Christian atmosphere. While with them, he attended school for six winter sessions and began to feel the pull of the Gospel upon his heart. When he was ten, Furman sold his indenture, and Apess lived with two other families until he was 15. At age 14, Apess felt again the call of God and yielded his life to the Gospel through Methodist preaching. Though he was offended by the racial bigotry of the Methodists, he could not deny that he heard the voice of God. He reports, "On the 15th day of March, in the year of our Lord, 1813, I heard a voice saying unto me, in soft and soothing accents, 'Arise, thy sins that are many are all forgiven thee; go in peace and sin no more.' There was nothing very singular, save that the Lord stooped to lift me up, in my conversion."

Because his "skin [was] of a different color," Apess was excluded from the careful spiritual nurturing usually given converts, and he soon relapsed to his "former state." Now acquainted

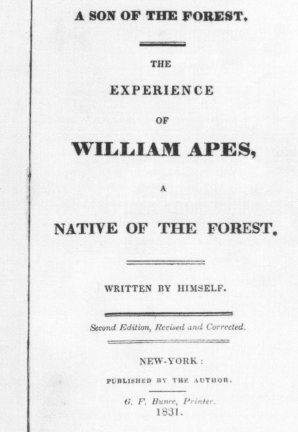

A SON OF THE FOREST.

THE

EXPERIENCE

OF

WILLIAM APES,

A

NATIVE OF THE FOREST.

WRITTEN BY HIMSELF.

Second Edition, Revised and Corrected.

NEW-YORK:

PUBLISHED BY THE AUTHOR.

G. F. Bunce, Printer.
1831.

The title page and engraving opposite in William Apess's A Son of the Forest, *1831. (Archives & Manuscript Division of the Oklahoma Historical Society)*

with "wicked and silly youths," he ran away and joined a militia as a musician and "experienced all the horrors of war" in several campaigns of the War of 1812. After being discharged from the army, he returned to the home of his earliest days among the Pequots. There he moved from his "backsliding state to the worship of God"; he united with the Methodists and was baptized. He began preaching and was ordained in 1829. Also in 1829, he published his autobiography, *A Son of the Forest,* which gives account of his childhood and conversion to the Christian faith. His autobiography was the first to be written in English by an American Indian.

Apess followed his autobiography with *The Experiences of Five Christian Indians of the Pequot Tribe* (1833), a collection of brief conversion autobiographies, and *Indian Nullification of the Unconstitutional Laws of Massachusetts, Relative to the Marshpee* [sic] *Tribe: Or, the Pretended Riot Explained* (1835), an account of the Mashpee conflict and his part in it. When Apess visited the Mashpee in 1833, they were struggling with the state government over the issue of self-governance. The Mashpees adopted Apess into their tribe and followed his leadership in what came to be called a "revolt." Apess wrote several documents for the cause, and largely through his efforts, the Massachusetts governor, Levi Lincoln, consented to grant most of their demands.

Apess's *Eulogy on King Philip* (1837) is the last tract he wrote. In it, he criticizes the Puritans for their treatment of the Native Americans and suggests that the anniversary of the Pilgrim landing, December 22, should be a day of mourning for Native Americans.

A newspaper obituary in New York noted the untimely and alcoholic death of Apess at 41. (Apess 1833; Dannenberg 1996; O'Connell 1996; Peyer 1994; Wiget 1985)

Auntie

Auntie is a character in Leslie Marmon Silko's novel *Ceremony* (1977, 1986). She is a charac-ter who is ashamed of her Indianness, and she seeks solace and acceptance through her associations with the Catholic Church rather than through family and tribal connections. She takes a perverse pleasure in the shame that her family causes her; "she never let them forget what she had endured, all because of what they had done." She takes care of Tayo when he returns from the hospital because "she needed a new struggle, another opportunity to show those who might gossip that she had still another unfortunate burden which proved that, above all else, she was a Christian woman."

The first in her series of burdens is the birth of her sister's illegitimate child, Tayo, and then her sister dies, which inconveniences her with raising Tayo. Though Tayo is raised alongside Rocky, his cousin, the aunt makes known very definitely that he is a disgrace to the family and that she is a martyr for taking him in. She gives Rocky preferential treatment and makes sure that Tayo notices the distinction. Her behavior borders on cruelty; she tells Tayo painful stories about his mother, and she refuses to allow him even to see a picture of his mother.

She urges her son Rocky to assimilate into white culture and to abandon the old ways, hoping that he will be successful in and accepted by the white world. Rocky and Tayo both join the army and are sent to the Philippines, where Rocky is wounded and finally dies before he can fulfill his mother's dream. Auntie cannot forgive Tayo for living through the war when her son died.

For all of her negative qualities, one can feel a degree of sympathy for Auntie. She hides deep within her the guilt for allowing her sister to fall into wicked ways. Tayo senses that Auntie is imprisoned behind a wall of pain that causes her to behave the way she does; he hears it, "like fingernails scratching against bare rock, her terror at being trapped in one of the oldest ways." She is locked in shame, guilt, and the pain of loss and cannot escape. (Silko 1977, 1986; Swan 1992)

See also *Ceremony*; Rocky; Tayo.

B

The Barefoot Hopi

The Barefoot Hopi is a character in Leslie Marmon Silko's *Almanac of the Dead* (1991). He "feels" messages from the earth through his bare feet and preaches the message that all the dispossessed in the Americas will rise up against their oppressors. The Barefoot Hopi was imprisoned for shooting a helicopter of voyeuristic tourists out of the sky as they were trying to watch the Snake Dance at old Oraibi. The Hopi travels around the world raising money and political support for the "return of the land to indigenous Americans." He visits the camp of the Homeless Army and meets with its leaders, Rambo and Clinton, in Tucson before going to the International Holistic Healers Convention, where he attracts a huge following. (Silko 1991)

See also *Almanac of the Dead*; Clinton; Mosca (Carlos); Rambo (Roy).

Barthelme, Painter

In James Welch's *The Death of Jim Loney* (1979, 1987), Barthelme is a cop who has come to Harlem, Montana, to escape his life of broken love in California. In this way his character parallels that of Loney's girlfriend, Rhea Davis. Like Rhea, he is unhappy and lonely, and the only fantasy in which he can imagine happiness in Montana is if he can have her. Barthelme is on duty the night that Jim Loney leads the police to Mission Canyon. Barthelme serves an important narrative function in that he provides Welch with a mouthpiece for the interpretation of Loney's actions. (Welch 1979, 1987)

See also Davis, Rhea; *The Death of Jim Loney*; Loney, Ike; Loney, Jim.

Bearheart: The Heirship Chronicles

In 1990, Gerald Vizenor's *Darkness in Saint Louis Bearheart* (1978) was republished as *Bearheart: The Heirship Chronicles* by the University of Minnesota Press. With its postmodern trickster discourse, the novel is simultaneously a departure from the body of contemporary Native American novels and a return to traditional storytelling. The structure of *Bearheart* features a novel-within-a-novel; old Bearheart opens the novel with the proclamation, "The bear is in me now." Bearheart is in the offices of the Bureau of Indian Affairs as they are being attacked by members of the American Indian Movement (AIM). He is confronted by a young militant Indian woman, Songidee migwan, who takes his "hairship book" from the filing cabinet and reads it. As she begins to read, Bearheart laughs, "ha ha ha haaaa."

The interior story begins with the lineage of Proude Cedarfair, the leader of the pilgrim band. He is the fourth Proude Cedarfair to "have celebrated the sacred cedar trees." The First Proude Cedarfair "claimed a large circle of cedar trees which bordered the *misisibi*, the great river," and the cedar "became his source of personal power." A government surveyor names the circle a "circus, a civil and sacred parish, a circular arena of cedar wood." The Second Proude Cedarfair served in World War I, and while he was gone, he "turned the sovereign cedar nation over to the women of the circus." Second Proude felt inadequate to live up to the image of his brave father and lost much of his life to drink and dissolution. However, when the government instituted a new system of governance under the Indian Reorganization Act, Second Proude "stopped drinking to save his cedar nation." He organized the "Allied Tribal Circuses" and commanded them in a successful war against the government.

Third Proude "was a warrior diplomat" who "abhorred violence more than evil and corruption." His son, Fourth Proude, is "the last leader of the cedar nation"; he is a "ceremonial diplomat" who has "learned from his father how to please with silence and smiles."

During the time of Fourth Proude, the federal government is once again anxious to claim the cedar circus, this time because of the depletion of energy sources. The government is "not capable of negotiating trades or developing alternative fuels. The nation ran out of gasoline and fuel oil. Electrical power generating plants closed down. Cities were gasless and dark. Economic power had become the religion of the nation." The rapacious government has set its eye on the cedar circus as an energy source, and sends representatives to drive out or kill Proude Cedarfair.

Fourth Proude first confounds the government agents who come to the circus and then escapes with his wife Rosina Parent. They begin a journey west to New Mexico, to the fourth world. Along the way, they are joined by many others until they resemble a bawdy group of Chaucerian mixed-bloods moving from adventure to adventure. Their first stop is the "scapehouse" of the 13 sensitive women poets who live for orgasmic pleasures and eat their pets. In this time of gasoline wars and energy crisis, they have a vehicle that was left to them by a "rich friend" who died in "an ecstatic passing." They give the car to the pilgrims, and one of their guests, Benito Saint Plumero, goes with them. Sister Eternal Flame sends the dog, Pure Gumption, along with the pilgrims because she is fearful that someone will eat Gumption.

As they travel along, listening to the radio, Proude Cedarfair and Rosina hear for the first time public service announcements indicating the state of crisis: "All citizens will be issued bionic residential identification cards during the coming month. No citizens will be permitted to travel without government authorization. Citizens found cutting or selling federal timber will be executed." Proude responds, "We are not citizens."

They continue along the weed-covered asphalt roads and pick up a hitchhiker, Zebulon Matchi Makwa. They enter the town of Big Walker, where no more than three tribal people can be on the streets at the same time, lest they be killed. When the pilgrims realize their danger, they start acting as if they are the first car in a parade. However, they slow down too much and are covered with white people who were gathering their wood rations. By the time the car makes it to the top of the hill, the tires have exploded, the body is scraping the asphalt, and all of the pilgrims have slipped out of the car. The white people crush each other in the press of the crowd. In their attempt to siphon off gasoline, they set the fuel line on fire and a huge knot of them go up in flames. The pilgrims slip away into the darkness of the trees and find Belladonna Darwin-Winter Catcher.

Joined by Belladonna Darwin-Winter Catcher, the pilgrims next come upon "a cream colored house with chartreuse shutters and a white cross on the front door." Inside lives the "Sacred Order of Gay Minikins," former priests. The priests don't have much to eat, but they share what they have. Proude Cedarfair is invited to share a story. He tells of a shaman crow, a "child girl," a mongrel, and four puppies. In the course of the tale, the child girl teaches her human family how to "love both animals and themselves." Proude ends the story by telling the group that "Pure Gumption is a healer and cedar shaman. Private Jones is a tribal clown and trickster." The pilgrims don't realize until they leave that they have been served human flesh by the gay minikins.

The pilgrims cross the Camp Ripley Military Reservation, spend a night at the Charles Lindbergh house, and progress to the Cathedral of Saint Paul, where they meet more pilgrims. By now they are joined by Inawa Biwide, Bishop Omax Parasimo, Justice Pardone Cozener, Sun Bear Sun and Little Big Mouse, Lilith Mae Farrier and her two boxers, Doctor Wilde Coxwain, and Pio Wissakodewinini. The enlarged group of pilgrims gets hold of a postal truck and makes its way to What Cheer, Iowa, where they gamble for their lives with Sir Cecil Staples, the "monarch of unleaded gasoline." Until this point in the narrative, the group of pilgrims has been steadily increasing; from What Cheer, Iowa, on, the group will diminish one by one.

Lilith Mae is chosen to go against the gambler; she loses and sets herself and the boxers on fire. Proude Cedarfair is the next gambler, and he wins. The Evil Gambler is killed, and the group of pilgrims take off in their postal truck with just a little gas left. When their gas runs out, they walk until they come to an abandoned farmhouse. There they stop and bury Lilith and her boxers. Benito Saint Plumero (Bigfoot) also buries his beloved bronze statue there, vowing to return when there is once again gasoline.

The farther they walk, the more people they encounter on the road, including "hundreds of cripples, whole communal families of people with similar disabilities." It is among the cripples that Little Big Mouse loses her life. The journey becomes ever more dangerous as the pilgrims meet starving crowds. Cannibalism becomes a genuine fear, and the travelers stay close together for protection.

The pilgrims witness a paradigm shift as oral traditions become the currency of the road. As they travel,

Families welcomed the good tellers of stories, the wandering historians of follies and tragedies. Readers and writers were seldom praised but the traveling raconteurs were one form of the new shamans on the interstates.

As they continue their travels, the pilgrims visit the Bioavaricious Regional Word Hospital, where the staff has had "solid funding for the past decade to examine words where and when [they] find them in conflict." The goal of the word *hospital* is to fix the meaning of words and disallow the fluidity of language. Justice Pardone and Doctor Wilde decide to fall away from the party of pilgrims and stay at the word hospital. The rest of the pilgrims make their way to Ponca City, Oklahoma, where they visit the Ponca Witch Hunt Restaurant and Fast Foods. There, "food fascists" hang "witches out for a week or two and then cut them down and into pieces for takeout orders." The pilgrims decide to liberate the witches, and Bishop Parasimo wears one of his metamasks to pull off the liberation. In the rescue, Matchi Makwa is killed, but two witches escape and join the pilgrims.

The pilgrims have been on the road for two months when they make their way to the enclosed city of Orion. In Orion, run by hunters as the constellation-based name suggests, the pilgrims are given hospitality in exchange for a story. Belladonna Darwin-Winter Catcher tells the story, but it is fraught with clichés about the nature of Indianness, and she is rewarded with a poison cookie. She dies as a result of her inability to imagine Indianness beyond the plastic definitions of those who espouse Vizenor's hated "terminal creeds." After her death, Proude Cedarfair delivers the twins in her womb, the result of a terrible rape. The twins are dead and are buried along with Belladonna.

The remaining pilgrims continue on their journey. Bishop Parasimo is killed by lightning. Proude Cedarfair secures passage on the Freedom Train to Santa Fe with a medicine bundle. They are soon made prisoners on the freedom train, however. By the end of the story, Proude

Cedarfair and Inawa Biwide make their way magically to the fourth world, where they enter as bears. Rosina, too, achieves a transcendence as she finds bear tracks in the snow and follows them to the rim of the mesa. (McClure 1997; Monsma 1997; Owens 1992a; Rigel-Cellard 1997; Velie 1982; Vizenor 1978, 1990)

See also Biwide, Inawa; Cedarfair, Proude; Coxwain, Doctor Wilde; Cozener, Justice Pardone; Darwin-Winter Catcher, Belladonna; Farrier, Lilith Mae; Parasimo, Bishop Omax; Saint Plumero, Benito; Staples, Sir Cecil; Sun Bear Sun and Little Big Mouse; Wissakodewinini, Pio.

Beaufrey

In Leslie Marmon Silko's *Almanac of the Dead* (1991), a book filled with evil characters, Beaufrey is one of the most evil of all. He is "in partnership with a rare book seller in Buenos Aires with a complete line of dissection films and video tapes for sale." In addition to his pornographic and snuff films, he runs an import-export business trading drugs and guns. He hates women and finds particular relish in live films of female circumcisions, late-term abortions, sex change operations, and dissections. Among the numbers of young boy lovers he keeps around are Eric and David, with whom he is particularly obsessed. He simply tolerates the presence of Seese, David's other lover. When she gets pregnant the first time, Beaufrey persuades her to abort the baby. When she is pregnant for the second time and refuses to abort the baby, he finds a way to turn the situation to his own good. He arranges the abduction of the child and uses him in a live snuff film. He tells David the baby is dead from "natural causes" as a result of Seese's poor genes. He scares Seese away from San Diego by having terrorists attack her apartment. He leaves her with money and a kilo of cocaine, sure that she will kill herself and save him the trouble.

Beaufrey was a precocious child whose interest in crimes and pictures of brutal crimes goes back to his earliest memories. His childhood hero was Albert Fish, a cannibal and child molester. "Survival of the fittest" is one of his signature comments on nearly any situation. After David dies in a horse-riding accident, Beaufrey takes pictures of his broken body, realizing that such photos would make a fitting coda to David's series of photographs documenting Eric's suicide. (Silko 1991)

See also *Almanac of the Dead*; David; Eric; Monte; Seese.

The Beet Queen

The Beet Queen (1986) is the second novel written by Louise Erdrich and is the third chronological novel in her North Dakota tetralogy. The novel incorporates some of the Chippewa characters from her earlier family saga, *Love Medicine* (1984, 1993), but also introduces a set of Euroamerican characters in the small town of Argus, North Dakota. Karl and Mary Adare provide the nexus through which the other characters meet and interact. The two come as children to Argus from Minneapolis on a boxcar during the Great Depression, having just been abandoned by their mother and separated from their kidnapped infant brother. On the way to their aunt's butcher shop, they are attacked by a large dog; they both run, but in different directions, and they too are separated.

Mary continues on to her aunt Fritzie's, and Karl runs back to the boxcar, which establishes the metaphor for his rootless, wandering life. Mary, 11 years old, is welcomed into the Kozka family by her aunt and uncle, though her cousin Sita resents every kindness shown to her. Sturdy and tenacious, Mary takes root in Argus and obliterates all memory of her mother from her mind, erasing the day of the carnival when Adelaide took off in the plane of a barnstormer and left behind three children. Mary takes her place working in the butcher shop, determined "to be essential to them all, so depended upon" that she would never be sent away. Karl finds his way back to Minneapolis, where he is taken in at a Catholic orphanage and "turned out worse than their wildest dreams." He becomes a traveling salesman, always changing locations, companies, and products. Their lives do not intersect again for over 20 years, when Karl comes to Argus looking for Mary and instead finds Celestine James working in the butcher shop. Celestine quickly becomes his second lover from Argus. A year earlier, Karl had met an Argus businessman and booster, Wallace Pfef, at a crop and livestock convention, and they had a brief affair. Now Karl and Celestine stay together long enough to create a child, break Pfef's heart, and calcify Mary's disdain for her brother. Karl leaves Celestine, and when her labor begins during a blizzard, Celestine makes it only to the home of her neighbor, Pfef, before she delivers her daughter. The child is named Wallacette Darlene, after Pfef, but Mary quickly creates the nickname Dot for her.

Karl and Celestine marry after the birth of their daughter, a mere formality, but never live together. Dot now becomes the center of attention for Celestine, Mary, and Wallace. The fierceness of Mary's love for Dot creates a silent competition between her and Celestine, her friend and coworker. As the years go by, Mary becomes more and more eccentric, and Karl drifts into Dot's life with occasional and inappropriate gifts. Their cousin Sita begins a mental and emotional unraveling that takes her through two marriages, a failed business, a stay in the mental hospital, and finally death by overdose. Wallace redirects his obsessive love for Karl into business and agricultural empires. He introduces the sugar beet to the local farmers and changes the physical and economic landscape of Argus. Only Celestine, grounded in her motherhood, maintains any kind of normalcy in her life. Dot, doted upon by too many people, becomes willful and surly, hanging with the wrong kind of crowd in high school. Pfef sees an alternative to Dot's sure path to destruction. He determines that she needs a boost in her self-esteem and goes into a year-long plan to organize a sugar beet festival in Argus. He rigs the election so that Dot wins the contest for Beet Queen.

On the day that Dot is to be crowned queen, all points of the plot converge. Karl realizes that he has nothing to show for his life and that he longs for family, and he starts driving to Argus in the hopes that he will arrive in time to see the coronation ceremony that Celestine has written him about. Jude Miller, the kidnapped sibling of Karl and Mary, finally learns from his adoptive mother that he has family in Argus, and he too makes his way there. Celestine and Mary go to pick up cousin Sita for the ceremony and find her dead, caught in a tree at the front door. They buckle her into the front seat of the van and go into town for the ceremony, intending to deliver her to the funeral home after the coronation. Dot hears that her election was rigged, and she goes after Pfef, finds him at the dunk tank, and douses him. Karl watches Pfef fall into the water and realizes that he is hurt; he plunges into the water after Wallace and revives him and their 20-year-old love affair. Dot is soothed by her patient mother, but not before she, like Adelaide so long ago, takes off in a plane at the festival. She helps seed the clouds for a rain to end the drought, and the novel ends with the rains gently falling.

Erdrich's ability to weave a story is again on display in this complicated novel of grasping, hopeless, and desperate love. (Bak 1992; Erdrich 1986; Meisenhelder 1994; Owens 1992a; Rainwater 1990; Towery 1992; Walsh and Braley 1994; Wong 1991)

See also Adare, Karl; Adare, Mary; *The Bingo Palace*; Erdrich, Louise; James, Celestine; Kashpaw, Russell; Kozka, Pete and Fritzie; Kozka, Sita; *Love Medicine*; Miller, Jude; Nanapush, Dot Adare; Pfef, Wallace; Pillager, Fleur; *Tracks*.

Benally, Ben

Ben Benally is a character in N. Scott Momaday's *House Made of Dawn* (1968); he is the narrator of the third section of the novel, "The Night Chanter." Ben is a relocated Navajo man who is attempting to assimilate into the white, capitalistic culture of Los Angeles. Whereas Abel is inarticulate and cannot speak his language or pray, Ben is still connected enough to his culture to do so. He meets and befriends Abel and talks of the "Beautyway," "Bright Path," and "Path of Pollen"—traditional Navajo healing ceremonies—with him. In Tosamah's peyote prayer service, Ben prays, "Look! Look! There are blue and purple horses . . . a house made of dawn. . . ."

Ben meets Abel when Abel is released from prison and the relocation officer takes Abel to work at the factory where Ben works. Ben immediately takes an interest in Abel and shows him around work, offers to share his lunch, and even lets Abel stay with him in his apartment. Ben says of Abel, "We were kind of alike, though, him and me." But in a fundamental way, they are not alike. Ben tries to believe that assimilation is the best way for Native American peoples to survive. He says, "A man with a good job can do just about anything he wants," but he lives in a broken-down apartment without even private bath accommodations. He praises Los Angeles,

> Once you find your way around and get used to everything, you wonder how you ever got along out there where you came from. There's nothing there, you know, just the land, and the land is empty and dead. Everything is here, everything you could ever want. You never have to be alone.

And yet Ben is alone and unhappy.

His friendship with Abel is threatened as Abel deteriorates; finally they fight, and Abel storms out of the apartment and is gone for three days. When Abel returns badly beaten, it is Ben who calls the ambulance and who locates Angela St. John so that she might help Abel. When Abel goes back to Jemez Pueblo, it is with the beginnings of a healing that started with Ben's Night Chant ceremony. (Evers 1985; Hirsch 1983; Momaday 1968; Raymond 1983; Schubnell 1985)

See also Abel; *House Made of Dawn*; St. John, Angela; Tosamah, John Big Bluff.

Benoit

In Linda Hogan's *Mean Spirit* (1990), Benoit is "the legal husband, by white law, of Sara Blanket." He is half-white, part French, and because his mother was French, "that meant he would

have been outside the tribe without an Osage Indian wife." He marries the partially paralyzed Sara to take care of her, and he gets tribal recognition in return. Though there is no romance between them, Benoit and Sara love and regard each other deeply. Benoit has another, concurrent relationship with Lettie Graycloud. Benoit and Lettie are involved in an affair "that would have been misunderstood by the townfolks who didn't know a thing about love without possession." Contrary to the opinions of others, "Lettie and Sara were friends, doubly bound together by their mutual love for Benoit."

After the murder of his sister-in-law, Grace Blanket, Benoit's house is blown up and his wife killed. Benoit is immediately arrested for Sara's murder. His case never comes to trial, but he is kept in jail for months. He is allowed to leave the jail for one night to marry Lettie. Their happiness is short-lived, however, for the morning after Benoit is returned to the jail, he is found hanging in his cell. Though the official story claims suicide, there is plenty of suspicion that he has been murdered. The "hammered silver conchos and coins" have been stripped from his belt, and the first witness faintly remembers that Benoit's hands were tied. Quite possibly, it is his vow to solve the murders that costs him his life. (Hogan 1990)

See also Blanket, Grace; Blanket, Sara; Gold, Jess; Graycloud, Lettie; *Mean Spirit*.

Betonie

In Leslie Marmon Silko's *Ceremony* (1977, 1986), Betonie is the mixed-blood Navajo medicine man whose ceremony brings health to Tayo and ultimately to the Laguna Reservation. He lives in the foothills north of the ceremonial grounds in Gallup, New Mexico, looking down on the city dump and the Indian shantytown by the railroad tracks and the river. When Tayo wonders why Betonie lives with the constant reminders of the losses and degradation of his people in view, Betonie says, "It is the town down there which is out of place. Not this old medicine man." Betonie's hogan is built in the traditional way, though it is filled with an unusual combination of traditional and nontraditional items. Curing bundles of roots, twigs, sage, and mountain tobacco are nestled in Woolworth shopping bags; the hogan is crowded with stacks of newspapers, old calendars, and piles of telephone books from cities all over the United States. Betonie explains, "All these things have stories alive in them"; because the times have changed, the ceremonies must change, and even nontraditional items must be incorporated into the ceremonies. "At one time," he says, "the ceremonies as they had been performed were enough for the way the world was then. But after the white people came, elements in this world began to shift; and it became necessary to create new ceremonies . . . things which don't shift and grow are dead things." Betonie cautions Tayo not to imagine that all white people are bad, though; they are simply being manipulated by witchery.

With his helper, Shush, Betonie begins the lengthy healing ceremony for Tayo. Tayo is placed in the center of a white corn sand painting and is given a basket of prayer sticks to hold. He is given a ritual cut on the head before Betonie moves him through five ceremonial hoops. While Tayo sleeps and dreams, Betonie tells the story of his own grandfather, Descheeny. It was Descheeny who, two generations ago, started the ceremony in which Betonie and Tayo presently play a part. In his final act in the ceremony, Betonie draws a configuration of stars. He says, "Remember these stars . . . I've seen them and I've seen the spotted cattle; I've seen a mountain and I've seen a woman." With the help of Betonie, Tayo is equipped to undertake his part of the healing ceremony. (Bell 1979; Jahner 1979; Lincoln 1983; Owens 1992a; Silko 1977, 1986; Wiget 1985)

See also *Ceremony*; Ku'oosh; Silko, Leslie Marmon; Tayo; Witchery.

Betty and Veronica

In Sherman Alexie's *Reservation Blues* (1995), Betty and Veronica are two "wannabes," white women who "wore too much Indian jewelry. . . . Turquoise rings, silver feather earrings,

beaded necklaces." They own a New Age bookstore in Seattle, which they close down when they hear rumors of the Indian band, Coyote Springs. They become Coyote Springs groupies, singing along with them in their early practice days and aspiring to be backup singers for the band. The two women start sleeping with Victor and Junior, and the other members of the band are outraged by their pushiness. Chess, a female member of the band from the Flathead reservation, says that Victor and Junior are "betraying their DNA" by sleeping with Betty and Veronica. Thomas is just as disapproving of the co-opting women: "All they talk about is Coyote this and Coyote that, sweatlodge this and sweatlodge that. They think Indians got all the answers."

After Coyote Springs comes back from Seattle with their prize money, Victor and Junior drink up most of theirs and get into a fight with Michael White Hawk, a local bully. The fight turns into a general brawl with even Betty and Veronica getting pushed around and hit. The two women finally wonder what they are doing on the reservation. They feel threatened when the old women on the reservation spit in their shadows as they walk along. Chess confronts them, "Can't you handle it? You want the good stuff of being Indian without all the bad stuff, enit? Well, a concussion is just as traditional as a sweatlodge." They decide to leave the reservation and return to Seattle, where they sign a deal with Sheridan and Wright, two recording executives (whose names are taken from historical figures) for Cavalry Records. Sheridan believes that Betty and Veronica will meet the market that longs for the Indian experience without all the risks of a real Indian band. He sells them to his employer: "We don't need any goddamn just-off-the-reservation Indians. We can use these women. They've been on the reservations. They even played a few gigs with Coyote Springs. . . . They really understand what it means to be Indian."

Betty and Veronica send Thomas a demo copy of their first recording, which he listens to and destroys because its message is one that validates cultural theft:

And my hair is blonde
But I'm Indian in my bones
And my skin is white
But I'm Indian in my bones
And it don't matter who you are
You can be Indian in your bones.
(Alexie 1995)

See also Builds-the-Fire, Thomas; Joseph, Victor; Polatkin, Junior; *Reservation Blues*; Warm Water, Chess and Checkers.

Big Mom

In Sherman Alexie's *Reservation Blues* (1995), Big Mom is a character of mythic proportions. She is a "part of every tribe," is of an undetermined age, and is the subject of "a million stories" that are "stretched back more than a hundred years." She lives on top of Wellpinit Mountain and is a "musical genius" who has been the "teacher of all those great musicians who shaped the twentieth century." It is to Big Mom that Robert Johnson goes for healing.

Big Mom has the ability to see and know private things. She knows the real names of Chess and Checkers; she knows that Victor was sexually abused by a priest when he was a boy. She tells him to forgive the priest: "That will give you power over him, you know. Forgiveness is magic, too." When Big Mom hears that Coyote Springs has an audition in New York, she writes Thomas a note and invites them to her home on the mountain so that she might help them get ready. Big Mom starts the band's instruction by playing "the loneliest chord that the band had ever heard" on a guitar "made of a 1965 Malibu and the blood of a child killed at Wounded Knee in 1890."

Big Mom is a powerful spiritual being with a self-effacing humor. She has been seen walking across the water of Benjamin Pond, and she performs an antimiracle of feeding the hungry with the power of "mathematics." When people refuse to believe in her, Big Mom simply looks like a "tiny grandmother without teeth or a life . . . some dried old apple sitting on a windowsill." Michael White Hawk and Victor Joseph both refuse to accept her teaching, and both fall prey to the dangers that she could have saved them from: alcohol, violence, and poverty of the spirit. (Alexie 1995)

See also Builds-the-Fire, Thomas; Father Arnold; Johnson, Robert; Joseph, Victor; Polatkin, Junior; *Reservation Blues*; Warm Water, Chess and Checkers.

Billy, Joe

Joe Billy is a young Creek Indian in Linda Hogan's *Mean Spirit* (1990) who goes to seminary in Boston and marries a white woman. He comes back to Indian Territory "determined to save and serve his own Indian people." His father, Sam Billy, was a medicine man for "twenty-three years before he converted to the Christian faith." As Joe Billy watches the world around him coming apart, he grows more and more attracted to Indian spirituality. His wife Martha, blond, frail-looking, adapts to Indian ways too and steps into the Indian world with the energy of "a convert to another faith." Though Joe Billy is himself reverting back to the traditional ways, he wishes that his wife did not feel so negatively about her own white people that she "wouldn't even look for the good that lived in so many of the townspeople." She has so fully assimilated into Indian ways that "she gave not even a single glance backward at her past."

Joe Billy starts spending more and more time with the bat medicine bundle that had belonged to his father before his conversion. When his wife asks about the bundle, he says, "It's the older world, wanting out." Billy realizes he can learn from the bats because "they are a race of people that stand in two worlds," just as the Indians do. As Joe Billy and his wife grow more in tune with traditional ways, they join the settlement of the Hill Indians, leaving the world of Christianity behind. (Hogan 1990)

See also Horse, Michael; *Mean Spirit*.

The Bingo Palace

The Bingo Palace (1994) is the final volume in Louise Erdrich's North Dakota tetralogy that began with *Love Medicine* (1984, 1993), *The Beet Queen* (1986), and *Tracks* (1988). The novel features the narrative voice of Lipsha Morrissey, the likable and sometimes dim hero of *Love Medicine*. Perhaps because of *The Bingo Palace*'s much-touted relationship to the earlier novels, the book suffers from a strained and self-conscious intertextuality, but it does provide the typical Erdrichian blend of sharp insight, surrealistic humor, and lavish metaphors ripe with the flavors of Chippewa and contemporary American culture.

Many familiar characters from the earlier novels make minor appearances in *The Bingo Palace*: Albertine Johnson, Russell Kashpaw, Lulu Lamartine, Marie Kashpaw, Gerry Nanapush, Fleur Pillager, and even the ghostly June Morrissey Kashpaw. The heart of the story belongs to three characters from previous books, though now more fully developed—Lipsha Morrissey, Lyman Lamartine, and Zelda Kashpaw Johnson—and the newcomer to Erdrich's North Dakota series, Shawnee Ray Toose. The plot centers on Lipsha's need once again for a love medicine, but this time for himself. He is madly in love with Shawnee Ray, the erstwhile girlfriend of Lyman Lamartine. Zelda is set on keeping Lipsha out of the picture and pushes the on-again, off-again relationship of Shawnee and Lyman. Lyman, a slick and moneyed reservation entrepreneur, is the reputed father of Shawnee's young son Redford and seems to have the jump on Lipsha in the love game. What neither counts on is the strong will of Shawnee herself. Though she and Redford are living with Zelda, who daily exerts her grip on the two, Shawnee is ultimately strong enough to resist all of those who want something from her. The two men strain for her love, and Zelda uses her to construct a family portrait that will otherwise never be. In Zelda's mind, Shawnee will become the loving, surrogate daughter that her own natural daughter, Albertine, refuses to be, and Redford will be the grandchild that Albertine does not supply for her.

In a parallel plot, Lyman has his eye on grander business and political schemes. He in-

tends to create a bingo palace that will draw people from miles around. He is in the process of wrangling deals to secure the area at "the far end of Matchimanito Lake." Shawnee realizes, and Lipsha comes to understand during a vision quest, that the land at Matchimanito Lake should never be violated by Lyman's "gambler's paradise." The land is "a spirit place," the homeland and burial grounds of the tribe's greatest medicine men and women, the Pillagers.

In the narrative tendrils that thread out from the main stories, Lipsha is given and twice loses the ceremonial pipe that had belonged to his grandfather Nector Kashpaw; Lyman gambles away his fortune; Lipsha wins a customized van at a bingo game and then has it nearly destroyed by rednecks on a vendetta; Shawnee Ray goes to college; Redford is taken from his extended family by the grasping Zelda; Lulu orchestrates a prison transfer for her son, Gerry Nanapush; Gerry escapes with the help of Lipsha and the spirit of June and her blue Firebird; Lipsha meets Fleur, his great-grandmother; Lipsha and Lyman go on a vision quest; and Zelda has a heart attack that forces her to realize that she must seek the only love of her life, Xavier Toose. And of course, Lipsha wins the heart of Shawnee Ray and saves Matchimanito Lake from Lyman's outlandish plans for a bingo palace.

Although *The Bingo Palace* is not the strongest stake in the narrative tent that Erdrich pitches across the North Dakota landscape, it certainly secures the flapping ends of earlier stories that she has tantalized us with in the earlier volumes of the tetralogy. (Erdrich 1994)

See also *The Beet Queen*; Erdrich, Louise; Johnson, Albertine; Johnson, Zelda Kashpaw; Kashpaw, June Morrissey; Kashpaw, Marie Lazarre; Kashpaw, Nector; Lamartine, Lulu Nanapush; Lamartine, Lyman; *Love Medicine*; Morrissey, Lipsha; Nanapush; Nanapush, Gerry; Pillager, Fleur; Toose, Shawnee Ray; Toose, Xavier; *Tracks*.

Bird

In James Welch's *Winter in the Blood* (1974, 1986), Bird is the horse of the nameless narrator. He figures significantly in the main remembered event of the novel—the death of Mose, the older brother of the narrator. The narrator and his brother were rounding up a herd of cattle and returning them to the home corral to winter when a calf ran away from the group. As a well-trained cattle horse, Bird took off after it, catching his rider off-guard. In the never fully explained confusion that followed, Mose tried to warn his surprised brother of an oncoming car, but he himself was struck by it instead. The responsibility and damaging guilt that the narrator feels for the accident are inextricably tied to the blame he places, perhaps unknowingly, on Bird.

Near the end of the novel, after the death of his grandmother, the narrator comes to a place of understanding that allows him to forgive Bird for his part in the death of Mose. He says, "Now old machine, I absolve you of your burden" and follows with an encomium to Bird as a kind of universal horse, a beast of mythic and heroic proportions. He continues:

> You are no longer a cow horse. No, don't think it was your fault—when that calf broke, you reacted as they trained you. I should compliment you on your eyes and your quickness. I didn't even see it break, then I felt your weight settle on your hind legs and the power. . . .

In forgiving Bird, the narrator also releases himself from 20 years of unproductive guilt. "'What use,'" the narrator begins to say, and he cries "for no one but [his] soul as though the words would rid it of the final burden of guilt."

Following the pivotal scene with Bird, the narrator rides the horse to the camp of Yellow Calf, where once again Bird figures into an important turning point for the narrator. The pieces of information that the narrator has tacitly gathered for years, beginning with his first trip with his father to meet Yellow Calf, start to come together in a pattern. As Yellow Calf relates the story of the winter that the Blackfeet starved, the narrator pauses to think for a moment. In that moment of quiet, "Bird farted." In a scene of typical Welchian humor, where the seriousness of a moment is under-

cut by scatology, the narrator experiences an epiphany:

> And it came to me, as though it were riding one moment of the gusting wind, as though Bird had had it in him all the time and had passed it to me in that one instant of corruption.

The narrator realizes that Yellow Calf is his biological grandfather, and the knowledge gives him a place to locate his own cultural identity.

Bird and the narrator leave Yellow Calf and return home, but as they round the bend of a slough, the narrator hears the bawl of a calf. Again a cow horse, and in a scene that replicates the one on the day of Mose's death, Bird "lope[s] straight for the corral, his ears forward and his legs stiffened." The narrator and Bird struggle to pull the calf's mother from the slough, but Bird is too old for the strain and goes down. Though Bird dies, his death happens at a time when the narrator is finally at peace with the horse and with himself. (Ballard 1991–1992; Sands 1978; Thackeray 1985; Welch 1974, 1986)

See also First Raise, John; Mose; Nameless Narrator; *Winter in the Blood*; Yellow Calf.

Biwide, Inawa

In Gerald Vizenor's *Bearheart: The Heirship Chronicles* (1978, 1990), Inawa Biwide is "the one who resembles a stranger." Biwide is an orphan "rescued by the church from the state and the spiritless depths of a federal reservation housing committee"; he is 16 years old when the band of pilgrims come to the cathedral where he lives. Proude Cedarfair recognizes his spiritual powers and tells his wife, "Inawa Biwide has the old nights in him. He knows the darkness and how to live alone." Biwide leaves the cathedral with the pilgrims when they go.

When the group reaches the Palace of the Governors in Santa Fe, Biwide is tortured because he will not reveal how the sacred crows came to express their disgust with the governors. His ears are cut off, and his eyes are plucked out. However, he learns "to see with birds," and because of his spiritual purity, he is able to reach the final destination of the pilgrim journey. (Velie 1982; Vizenor 1978, 1990)

See also *Bearheart: The Heirship Chronicles*; Cedarfair, Proude.

Black Elk Speaks

Black Elk Speaks (1932, 1988) is arguably the most well-known Native American autobiography. Just 50 years after the massacre at Wounded Knee, John G. Neihardt went to South Dakota and met one of the witnesses to the Ghost Dance, the event that ignited the infamous massacre. Neihardt was anxious to meet an old medicine man who might give more than just the facts of the experience; he was interested in "something to be experienced through intimate contact." Recommended to Black Elk, a *wichasha wakon* (holy man) and second cousin to Crazy Horse, Neihardt welcomed the chance to meet him. Neihardt's visit was received with an overwhelmingly positive response; Black Elk said, "[Neihardt] has been sent to learn what I know, and I will teach him." Neihardt took his opportunity to question Black Elk about "great battles, high moments in Sioux history," but realized that "it was increasingly clear that [Black Elk's] real interest was in 'the things of the Other World.'" What resulted is what Vine Deloria, Jr., calls "a North American bible of all tribes," one of the only holy books to emerge in the twentieth century.

It is impossible to discuss *Black Elk Speaks* without considering the voice of the recorder and editor, John Neihardt. Neihardt is responsible for imposing a "literary" style on the words of Black Elk, and careful studies of the manuscripts show that he made significant changes in the text. Nonetheless, the vision of Black Elk comes through the layers of translation and editing.

Black Elk opens his story with the account of White Buffalo Woman and how she brought the sacred pipe to the Lakota people. She promised that they would "multiply and be a good nation," and then the beautiful woman became a white bison and galloped away. After this necessary cultural context is identified and expressed, Black Elk proceeds with the story of his own birth and early memories. In telling of the Lakota confrontation with U.S. soldiers at Powder River, in present-day South Dakota, he introduces a pattern of collaboration that is present throughout the book. He appeals to his friend Fire Thunder to tell his version of the battle. This pattern is very much in keeping with storytelling in the oral tradition. Witnesses are present to validate and corroborate the story.

In the summer of his fourth year, Black Elk first begins to hear voices. He says, "It was like somebody calling me, and I thought it was my mother, but there was nobody there. This happened more than once, and always made me afraid, so that I ran home." When he was five years old, he had his first vision. From the clouds in the north, two men came "headfirst like arrows slanting down"; they sang a sacred song, and "the thunder was like drumming." They wheeled close to young Black Elk and then became geese and were gone. "I did not tell this vision to any one," Black Elk says. "I liked to think about it, but I was afraid to tell it."

The next important vision occurred when he was nine. One evening while eating dinner, he heard a voice: "It is time; now they are calling you." He grew weak and ill, and the next day the two men came "from the clouds, headfirst like arrows slanting down." He recognizes them as the men in his first vision years ago. While the young Black Elk lay dangerously ill for 12 days, he received a detailed vision from the six Grandfathers. The Grandfathers looked "older than men can ever be—old like hills, like stars." He is aware that the six Grandfathers are the "Powers of the World," of the four directions and of the earth and the sky. He is given the "power to make live" and the "power to destroy." Black Elk understands that the powers he is given are not for personal gain but for the health of the nation. The Sixth Grandfather tells him, "my power shall be yours, and you shall need it, for your nation on the earth will have great troubles." The complexity and

A class of Roman Catholic catechists from the Rosebud and Dakota reservations in South Dakota, July 1911. "Nicholas" Black Elk is the sixth from the left. (The Newberry Library)

power of the vision were so great that Black Elk knew he had seen more than he could tell and that he understood more than he saw. A result of the vision was Black Elk's immediate sense of isolation, the painful aloneness of a private vision. He was unable to articulate the vision and was fearful that he would not be understood or given credibility. Whirlwind Chaser, a medicine man, is aware that something has happened to the young boy. He tells Black Elk's father, "I do not know what it is, but there is something special for him to do, for just as I came in I could see a power like a light all through his body."

Black Elk is different after his visionary experience, and as he tries to participate in all of the activities that would be normal for a young Lakota boy, he has a "queer feeling." When he plays with other boys the hunting games that serve as training for the life of a hunter and warrior, his sense of kinship with the animal kingdom is so great he cannot bring himself to shoot a bird or squirrel. This "queer feeling" comes to him at other times as well and serves as a sign to others that his vision has bestowed certain powers on him. One day when he is out hunting deer with his father, he receives inner knowledge of just where to find the deer.

The event serves as a turning point for his father, who is coming to a certainty about Black Elk's powers. On another occasion, after his band moves to Grandmother's Land (Canada) for a while to avoid contact with the impinging whites, he provides inner information to his uncle to aid in a buffalo hunt.

Though he senses that his powers are growing, he is still confused about his duty to the vision. He is certain that the vision is not for him alone, but for the good of the tribe. At the same time, he is watching serious threats to the integrity and fabric of the Lakota nation being mounted by the U.S. government. Gold has been discovered in the Black Hills, and the rush to the hills incurs treaty violations. Battles between the Lakota and the government escalate and then culminate in the "rubbing out of Long Hair" (Custer) and the murder of the charismatic Lakota leader, Crazy Horse. Black Elk notes that "we remembered and they forgot" about the treaties. Clearly, the time is ripe for the meaning of Black Elk's vision to be revealed.

Now 17, he becomes very fearful, hearing voices in the thunder around him and in the birds and animals; he cannot get along with people any longer, and he begins to wonder if he is crazy. Finally, "so afraid of being afraid of everything," he reveals his vision to an old medicine man, Black Road. Black Road says that he must perform the horse dance for the people. He assures Black Elk that "the fear will leave you; but if you do not do this, something very bad will happen to you."

The performance of Black Elk's vision provides happiness and healing for many people. Black Elk notices that "even the horses seemed to be healthier and happier after the dance." He himself is freed from his fears and "everything seemed good and beautiful now, and kind." The reprieve from torment is only temporary, however. Soon Black Elk realizes that though individuals have benefited from the reenactment of his visions, his nation has not been freed from oppression. He wishes that his vision "had been given to a man more worthy." He continues to be faithful to the vision, though, and performs the dog vision with the help of *heyokas*, or sacred clowns, and later the elk vision. His healing powers grow, and he is becoming known as a powerful holy man. Still, he is discouraged and says, "when I thought of my great vision, which was to save the nation's hoop and make the holy tree to bloom in the center of it, I felt like crying, for the sacred hoop was broken and scattered."

By his twenty-third summer (1886), he hears of a traveling show run by Buffalo Bill and of the call for a band of Oglalas to go with the show. He decides to go in the hopes that he "might learn some secret of the Wasichu [white man] that would help [his] people somehow." The experience does not yield the benefits Black Elk hopes for; he is terribly dislocated and lonesome and has visions of home. When he does return after three years in the eastern United States and Europe, he finds his people in a more hopeless condition than when he left, and his own healing powers greatly diminished.

He returns to the reservation and finds much excited talk about the vision of the Paiute holy man, Wovoka, called "Jack Wilson" by the Wasichus. He is at first puzzled by the similarity of Wovoka's vision to his own but is willing to learn what he can from Wovoka and his spiritual movement, the Ghost Dance. The power

of the movement alarms the U.S. government, and in an attempt to squash it, a devastating blow is dealt the Sioux—the massacre at Wounded Knee in 1890. Black Elk was at the battle and recognized that "something else died there in the bloody mud, and was buried in the blizzard. A people's dream died there."

Black Elk was born in 1863 and died in 1950 after witnessing great changes in the life of the Lakotas. His own life is a study in outward contradictions. In 1904, he was baptized as Nicholas Black Elk at the Holy Rosary Mission near what is now Pine Ridge, South Dakota. By the time he narrated his life story as a "holy man of the Oglala Sioux" to John Neihardt, he had been a catechist in the Catholic faith for a quarter of a century. In view of the pressures exerted on Native Americans by missionaries and by the U.S. government, which made the practice of native religions illegal, Black Elk's "conversion" can perhaps best be understood as subversion rather than capitulation. (Allen 1986; DeMallie 1984; Lincoln 1983; Lone Hill 1996; Neihardt 1932; Rice 1994; Wiget 1985)

See also Native American Autobiography.

Blaeser, Kimberly

Born in 1955, Kim Blaeser is an enrolled member of the Minnesota Chippewa tribe. Of mixed ancestry (Anishinaabe and German), Blaeser is a strong new voice in Native American poetry. She grew up on the White Earth Reservation in northwestern Minnesota, the family home of another famous Anishinaabe writer, Gerald Vizenor. She earned both her master's and doctoral degrees at Notre Dame University and now teaches English and Comparative Literature at the University of Wisconsin at Milwaukee.

Blaeser's first volume of poetry, *Trailing You*, received positive attention and won the North American Native Authors First Book Award and the Diane Decorah Award for Poetry. Blaeser addresses issues of identity, authenticity, and ownership of Indianness in her work. In "American Indian Voices: I Wonder If This Is an Indian Poem," she resists the stereotype that Indians "shouldn't have much to do with clock

Kim Blaeser, 1998. (Courtesy of Kimberly M. Blaeser)

time / and more to do with spiritual things than with religion." She asserts that "Indian voices do talk about a lot of Indian stuff / like ricing and fry bread and bingo, / But they talk about computers and car pooling, too."

"Downwinders" is a powerful poem about all of the experimentation that has been done on those who live "downwind and downstream," of the detonation of the nuclear bomb on Bikini Atoll, of the electrical shock (rather than Novocain) given to Indian children at the dentist's office. She thinks of the Indian land that was "ripped open in searches for its gold heart / its copper bosom / its coal black eyes," and she is aware of the irony that in America, "'Some of us are more equal than others.'"

Blaeser's political poetry has a controlled edge, a wisdom that should be heard. She also can write with delicate lyricism as "learning, at last"; "This Cocoon"; "Two Haiku"; and other poems illustrate.

In addition to being a poet, Blaeser is earning a solid critical reputation as her book-length study, *Gerald Vizenor: Writing in the Oral Tradition,* attests. Of her writing, Blaeser says, "In both my creative and scholarly work I hope to explore the way writing can cross the boundaries of print, seeking not to report but to engender life, seeking to understand and enact the ways of survival." (Blaeser 1994)

Blanket, Grace

In Linda Hogan's *Mean Spirit* (1990), Grace Blanket is a character raised among the Hill Indians and sent to the community below so that she might learn the ways of the white people. Her mother is Lila Blanket, a "river prophet" who hears the river's warning that engineers will dam the river. Grace is taken in by the Graycloud family. After she graduates from school, Grace goes to work at Palmer's store in town and shows no indication that she will be the one to be "the salvation of the Hill Indians." Her younger twin sisters move to town with her. Molene dies several years later, and Sara "caught the same paralyzing illness" and stays in town thereafter. When the reservation is divided into allotments, Grace and Sara, "in total ignorance, selected dried-up acreages that no one else wanted." Only later is oil discovered beneath their land.

Grace grows locally famous "as a basketmaker and as an oil-rich Indian who was given to catting around. She had a sweet disposition, a mind of her own, and a fondness for men and drink." One Sunday morning before church, as she is gathering willows for baskets, she is shot and killed. The men responsible place a gun in her hand and pour whiskey all over her body so as to suggest suicide. After her burial, her grave is robbed, the body is stolen, and the objects placed in the coffin for her journey to the other world are taken. Grace is survived by her daughter Nola, who is immediately in danger of the same fate. (Hogan 1990)

See also Benoit; Blanket, Nola; Blanket, Sara; Graycloud, Belle; Graycloud, Moses; *Mean Spirit.*

Blanket, Nola

Nola is the daughter of Grace Blanket in Linda Hogan's *Mean Spirit* (1990). She is more like the Hill Indians than her mother, "a gentle child who would wander into the greenwood forest and talk to the animals." Though her mother does not fulfill the expectations of Lila Blanket, the "river prophet," Nola is "the river's godchild."

After her mother's murder, Nola is slow to recover and sleeps with her eyes wide open. She is cared for by the Graycloud family and by four "runners," men who come down from the hill country to guard her. The runners show up at the four corners of the Graycloud house after Grace's murder, saying that the screech owls told them to come. Not long after her mother's death, Nola is forced by the Indian Affairs official to go back to school under the threat that she will be sent to boarding school in Custer, Oklahoma, if she does not go. She finally consents but refuses to wear the school uniform and wears her traditional clothes instead. Nola becomes a "hero to most of the other children. Her anger and defiance spoke for all of them."

Though she is taken care of by the Grayclouds, the courts determine that Nola needs a legal guardian and appoint a Mr. Forrest in that role. The Indians are wary of guardianships, for the legal role is being used as a front for white guardians to siphon off the riches generated by oil on Indian lands. And, indeed, Forrest does abuse his powers to profit from Nola's wealth.

Though Forrest is unfair in his dealings with Nola, his son Will is genuinely in love with the young girl and persuades her to marry him. When the ornamental bride falls off the cake at the wedding, it seems like an omen, though, and Nola grows increasingly fearful in her marriage. By the time she is pregnant, she is decidedly afraid of Will, believing that he means only harm toward her. When she learns that his father is mismanaging her money, she becomes even more convinced that Will is involved. That Will is spending time with a young white woman does not help his case, and in a moment of great distress, Nola shoots and kills him. The four watchers outside her house lift her up from his body and carry her to the hills. There she gives birth to a girl whom she names Moses, after Moses Graycloud. She is also reunited with Belle Graycloud, who had disappeared into the hills after an attempt on her life. It is Belle who decides that Nola should not be told of Will's innocence. She says, "Think of how she would feel to have killed an innocent man she loved." (Hogan 1990)

See also Blanket, Grace; Forrest, Will; Graycloud, Belle; Graycloud, Moses; *Mean Spirit*.

Blanket, Sara

In Linda Hogan's 1990 book *Mean Spirit*, Sara Blanket is the younger sister of Grace Blanket and the wife of Benoit. Sara and her twin sister, Molene, arrive in the town of Watona several years after Grace has graduated from high school and gotten a job at Palmer's store in town. Both twins suffer from a "paralyzing illness"; Sara recovers, but Molene does not. Sara is paralyzed afterward, and her marriage to Benoit is one of convenience and mutual respect. Sara gains a caregiver from the arrangement, and Benoit, a mixed-blood, gains tribal recognition as an Osage man. Sara is killed when her house is blown up by conspirators seeking the oil fortune of the Blanket sisters. (Hogan 1990)

See also Benoit; Blanket, Grace; Graycloud, Lettie; *Mean Spirit*.

Blue, Bingo

Bingo is the younger son of Max and Leah Blue in Leslie Marmon Silko's *Almanac of the Dead* (1991). He runs the exclusive dealerships of vending machines and pinball machines in El Paso, just as his brother Sonny runs the businesses in Tucson. Whereas Sonny is ambitious and wants to expand his business, Bingo is content to live quietly in his huge house outside El Paso, surrounded by his illegal alien sexual partners and plenty of cocaine. Bingo has always felt emotionally separated from his family and only learned about his father's mob connections when his college roommate placed an article from *Time* on his bed, making the connection explicit. Bingo has always depended on Sonny to get him out of any problems that he might have. (Silko 1991)

See also *Almanac of the Dead*; Blue, Leah; Blue, Max; Blue, Sonny; Mosca (Carlos).

Blue, Leah

Leah Blue is the wife of the retired mobster Max Blue in Leslie Marmon Silko's *Almanac of the Dead* (1991). When they move to Tucson from New Jersey after Max's nearly fatal shooting, she begins a business of her own, buying up real estate all over the area. She intends to create a water community, "a city of the twenty-first century, Venice, Arizona." She is not interested in the environment, but thinks that the real estate business is "to make profits, not to save wildlife or save the desert." To pump the water she needs, she buys a deep-well rig from some Texans and counts on Max's pressure on the local judge to block the suit of some Nevada Indians who try to abort her plans. Through her companies "Blue Horizons" and "Blue Waters," she is willing to endanger the local water table in an effort to increase the attractiveness of her water community.

She uses her own sexual powers and the implied threat of her husband's "assassination franchise" to manipulate anyone in her way. She takes Trigg, her chief rival in the real estate business, as a lover in order to funnel his ideas and plans away from him. (Silko 1991)

See also *Almanac of the Dead*; Blue, Bingo; Blue, Max; Blue, Sonny; Trigg, Eddie.

Blue, Max

In Leslie Marmon Silko's *Almanac of the Dead* (1991), Max Blue is the mobster who "retires" to Tucson after he is shot and must leave New Jersey. He runs his "assassination franchise" from the golf course, where he holds court each day with all of the powerful people in the city.

Because of a plane crash when he was younger, he feels an impinging sense of mortality, but after he is shot outside a New Jersey cleaners, he is never the same. He loses all interest in sex and feels his emotional bonds with his family diminish. He prefers to call the death contracts he arranges "assassinations" because he insists that all deaths are political. In a fitting end for a man who runs a business such as his, Max is killed by a bolt of lightning while on the golf course. His death by "natural causes" supports one of the themes of the novel, that "it was the earth who possessed the humans and it was the earth who disposed of them."

See also *Almanac of the Dead*; Blue, Bingo; Blue, Leah; Blue, Sonny.

Blue, Sonny

Sonny Blue is a character in Leslie Marmon Silko's *Almanac of the Dead* (1991). He resents the insignificant role his father gives him in the family business, that of tending the food vending machines and pinball machines in Tucson. Dissatisfied with the small-time job, he starts a cocaine-smuggling business on the side. Soon his business is encroaching on the business of local smugglers, Ferro and Calabazas.

He expands his business to Mexico and begins dealing with Menardo. Sonny presents Menardo with a bulletproof vest that will prove to be his undoing. Before long, Sonny is sleeping with Menardo's wife, Alegria.

Sonny and his brother Bingo live in the inviolable world of Mafia protection. But when Mosca, a local hoodlum, hears from the spirit in his shoulder that he should get the Blue brothers, Sonny's bubble of paid protection bursts in a scene of comic irony. Mosca decides to shoot Sonny during a drug deal at the Yaqui Easter Dance. When Mosca's aim is off and he kills a bystander instead of Sonny, Sonny pulls his gun and attracts the attention of the police who brutally beat him. Mosca gets away with the money from the drug deal, and Sonny is seen as a bungler by his father and others in the smuggling community. (Silko 1991)

See also *Almanac of the Dead*; Blue, Bingo; Blue, Leah; Blue, Max; Calabazas; Ferro; Martinez-Soto, Alegria; Menardo; Mosca (Carlos).

Body Indian
See Geiogamah, Hanay.

Bone Game
Louis Owens's 1994 novel *Bone Game* incorporates several characters from his second novel, *The Sharpest Sight* (1992). Cole McCurtain is now a middle-aged professor of Native American literature at the University of California at Santa Cruz. He is recently divorced and has just moved to California from a position at the University of New Mexico. His life is coming apart at the seams, and he is unable to stop the

disintegration. He is drinking on the job and is experiencing nightmarish dreams that leave him emotionally frayed.

Cole dreams of a priest who was killed and mutilated in 1812, and he is awakened by the unfamiliar name *Venancio Asisara!* On the sixth night of the same disturbing dream, he gets up from bed and sees someone outside his window. The figure is naked, with his body painted in two halves. One side of the body is painted black and the other white; in his open palms, the man holds "an object the size of a marble, one pale and one dark." Cole recognizes the man as the evil, mythic "gambler" and shoots out the window at the figure; but upon inspection, he finds nothing there, not even footprints. On campus the next day, Cole McCurtain hears of the killing and dismemberment of a woman student.

He does not yet realize the crisis he is in, but his Uncle Luther and "Grandmother" Onatima in Mississippi are aware of his distress. His daughter is also aware that something is wrong, and she shows up unannounced at his house, ready to keep an eye on him. Meanwhile, we are introduced to three more characters, any one of whom might be involved in the continuing murders of young women or in Cole's dreams of the "gambler." Alex Yazzie is a young Navajo academic who befriends Cole and becomes involved with Cole's daughter, Abby. Robert Malin is Cole's teaching assistant, an intense young graduate student given to quoting Edgar Cayce, "the sleeping prophet" who said that "the earth speaks to us in dreams." Paul Kantner is an older, hulking student who disapproves of the behaviors of the undergraduates. Robert and Paul both attach themselves to Abby, creating suspicion about their motives.

Owens maintains the suspense and creates a truly frightening situation that would end disastrously if not for the intervention of Cole McCurtain's family. His father, Hoey, and Uncle Luther drive cross-country to help ward off the magic of his nightmares and confront the "gambler." Onatima flies to California ahead of them just in time to save Cole's daughter from being attacked by the prowling, painted "gambler"

figure. Onatima recognizes that the danger is not simply physical but that evil spiritual forces are at work. Before leaving Mississippi, she had dreams of "a painted man in a clearing between tall trees, his body half black and half white."

Before Cole can be freed of his nightmares and the danger that is surrounding him, he must be prepared spiritually. Only unwillingly and through the agency of his friend, Alex Yazzie, does Cole experience a sweat lodge and peyote service that begin his healing. When Onatima arrives, she cautions Cole that the person in his dreams "seems to have a great deal of power."

In the dramatic conclusion of the story, both Paul Kantner and Robert Malin are revealed to be murderers, and both die in their separate attempts to harm Abby. The psychopathic Kantner has been killing young women, but it is Robert who has assumed the powers of the historical character Venancio Asisara, the Indian who killed and mutilated the priest in 1812. The narrative reveals:

Venancio will never die, will wander between worlds, his hate too strong for death, the violence of his people's life taken by the invaders become a mark upon the very earth. Venancio will inhabit the earth.

When Robert is shot by Abby, the spirit of Venancio separates itself from his dead body and attempts to draw Abby into his game of death. Cole reaches the scene just in time to warn Abby and break the gambler's spell. The gambler smiles at Cole and says, *"Eran muy crueles"* (They were very cruel) before shifting into the shape of a bear at the edge of the forest. (Krupat 1996; Owens 1994)

See also Owens, Louis; *The Sharpest Sight.*

Boudinot, Elias

Elias Boudinot was born in the eastern Cherokee Nation around 1802 and was named Buck Watie or Gallegina (Kiakeena). He enrolled in a Moravian mission school in 1811 and quickly distinguished himself as a student. A representative of the American Board of Commissioners for Foreign Missions invited him and two other students to study in Cornwall, Connecticut, at the Foreign Mission School. Buck Watie's family agreed, and in 1818, he went east to the school. Along the way, the group stayed with Elias Boudinot, a former member of the Continental Congress and the American Bible Society. Young Watie was impressed enough with Boudinot that he enrolled at the Foreign Mission School with a new name.

Encouraged by his schoolwork and his 1820 confession of faith, Boudinot's teachers arranged for him to attend Andover Theological Seminary, but poor health prevented his attendance. In 1826 he married the daughter of a white physician of Cornwall; the marriage was viewed as an affront to propriety and was even called "criminal" by those connected with the Foreign Mission School.

By 1825, Boudinot was involved in the work of the Cherokee Nation. He encouraged adoption of the Christian faith and the assimilation into white ways. He participated in a fundraising tour in 1826 in order to purchase a

Front page of the first issue of the bilingual Cherokee Phoenix, *the first Native American newspaper. Elias Boudinot served as its editor. (Courtesy American Antiquarian Society)*

printing press and type for Sequoyah's new Cherokee syllabary. Boudinot became the first editor of the bilingual *Cherokee Phoenix*, the first Native American newspaper. He also worked with Samuel Austin Worcester, a missionary, on translations of scripture and Christian hymns.

Boudinot's early political activity focused on Cherokee land rights and resisted the idea of Cherokee resettlement. In time, however, Boudinot came to favor negotiation with the government and signed the Treaty of New Echota, which mandated removal of eastern Indian tribes to Oklahoma Territory, a journey later called the Trail of Tears. For his actions, which were not received favorably by the Cherokees, Boudinot and his cosigners—Major Ridge and John Rollin Ridge—were assassinated by Cherokee loyalists in 1839.

Boudinot's major literary contributions are his work with the *Cherokee Phoenix*, his translation of the religious tract *Poor Sarah or The*

Portrait of Elias Boudinot taken from the frontispiece of In Memoriam: Elias Cornelius Boudinot, *1891. (Reproduced from Boudinot,* In Memoriam: Elias Cornelius Boudinot, *1891)*

Indian Woman, and his *An Address to Whites, Delivered in the First Presbyterian Church on the 26th of May, 1826*. This latter work is an argument that stresses the intelligence and humanness of Indians and their ability to become "civilized." (Parins 1994; Perdue 1996)

Bourne, Lola

In N. Scott Momaday's *The Ancient Child* (1989), Lola Bourne is the "beautiful and ambitious" woman who plays an important part in the growth of the main character, Locke Setman. Bourne is a musician and patron of the arts who recognizes Setman's talent and buys one of his paintings, "Night Window Man." She says of the piece, "It is deeply disturbing, and I like it, and I want it."

The scene where Bourne buys the painting adumbrates the essential tension of the novel. Set, too, is drawn to and disturbed by the painting, but he cannot articulate why. He asks Lola to help him understand the painting. Lola looks at the man in the painting and says, "I think he's about to be transformed." Her analysis prefigures Set's transformation and his need for external help in achieving that transformation.

Set and Lola become friends and lovers, but when Set goes through a debilitating depression after the death of his adoptive father Bent Sandridge, even Lola cannot help him. She recognizes her part in the larger pattern of Set's health, however, and takes him to Oklahoma, where she delivers him into the care of Grey, a young Kiowa/Navajo Indian, who is essential to the next stage of Set's transformation. (Momaday 1989)

See also *The Ancient Child*; Grey; Sandridge, Bent; Setman, Locke.

Bruchac, Joseph

Joseph Bruchac was born in 1942 and is of Abenaki descent. He is a poet, storyteller, and critic. He was raised largely by his Indian grandfather, who ran a general store. Though his grandfather lived in denial of his Indian heritage, Bruchac's great-uncle revealed the connection to him. Bruchac prefers to be called *metis*,

a person of mixed blood. He explains, "In English it becomes 'Translator's Son.' It is not an insult, like *half-breed*. It means that you are able to understand the language of both sides, to help them understand each other."

Bruchac was educated at Cornell University, Syracuse University, and Union Graduate School, where he earned a doctorate in comparative literature. At Cornell, he was a heavyweight wrestler. When he studied at Syracuse as a creative writing fellow, a teacher told him his prose was too poetic, and he smashed his typewriter and burned all of his work. His despair was premature; as a critic and editor, Bruchac has become a major voice in the field of Native American literatures and is a fine writer himself. His writing is "informed by several key sources. One of these is nature, another is the native American experience."

With the *Greenfield Review*, Bruchac started a journal dedicated to publishing the work of minority writers. The effort blossomed into the larger enterprise of the Greenfield Review Press, which has published many volumes by Native American writers. In addition to publishing, Bruchac has contributed significantly to the field of Native American literatures by editing several important anthologies, including the still useful 1983 volume, *Songs from This Earth on Turtle's Back*. His anthology *Breaking Silence: Contemporary Asian Poets* won a 1984 American Book Award.

Bruchac says, "I believe that poetry is as much a part of human beings as is breath—and, like breath, poetry links us to all other living things and is meant to be shared." Some of his own many volumes of poetry include *This Earth Is a Drum* (1977), *Entering Onondaga* (1978), *Ancestry* (1980), *Near the Mountains: New and Selected Poems* (1987), and *Long Memory and Other Poems* (1989). (Bruchac 1987; *Contemporary Authors* 1995b, vol. 147; Lerner 1994)

Builds-the-Fire, Thomas

A character in Sherman Alexie's 1995 novel *Reservation Blues* and his earlier collection *The*

Lone Ranger and Tonto Fistfight in Heaven (1993), Thomas is the reservation storyteller and misfit, full of wisdom and silences, yet bullied by his two best friends, Victor Joseph and Junior Polatkin. The three young men have a tangled and wrenching past and a present that works in spite of obvious dysfunctions.

The story opens when Thomas, in his characteristic kindness, offers a ride to a black man, Robert Johnson, standing at the crossroads of the reservation. Thomas takes him to Big Mom, and Johnson leaves his guitar in Thomas's blue van. Thomas carries the guitar around very carefully and even gives it a place of honor in his living room. He has it with him at the Trading Post one day when Victor and Junior drop by to bully him. Victor smashes the guitar, and when Thomas starts to use the broken pieces the next day for wood to smoke some salmon, he finds that the guitar has fixed itself. The guitar begins to speak to Thomas and to play itself. It tells Thomas that he and Victor and Junior are starting up a band: "Y'all need to play songs for your people. They need you."

And so the band Coyote Springs is formed with Thomas as the lead singer and bass guitarist. Of the three friends, Thomas is the most rooted in his tribal culture, and not coincidentally, he is the only one who survives. Thomas has always used his gift of storytelling to understand life and to help others: "He wanted the songs, the stories, to save everybody." It is a gift that is largely ignored on the reservation, however, and he knows "that his stories never healed anything." Still, Thomas values his gift because "his stories came from beyond his body and mind, beyond his tiny soul." When Chess tells Thomas the story of the death of her brother, Backgammon, he feels that he's "just met the only Indian who told stories like his." Thomas, who has always been "marked by loneliness," has finally found someone who can love and be loved by him. When Chess kisses Thomas for the first time, both are ennobled by it: "She kissed him like he was a warrior; she kissed him like she was a warrior."

As Coyote Springs moves in and out of troubles, it is Thomas who anchors the band.

He begins writing songs for them to perform because "Buddy Holly wasn't a Spokane Indian." Thomas is an acute observer of human nature, and in his journal he writes a parody of the Ten Commandments that is so ripe with truth that it cuts in its comic brilliance. In his musings about the Catholic Church, he suggests, "Maybe we got it all backwards and you get into heaven because of hate."

After the band disintegrates, Thomas leaves the reservation with Chess and Checkers and goes to Spokane. (Alexie 1995)

See also Betty and Veronica; Big Mom; Father Arnold; Johnson, Robert; Joseph, Victor; The-man-who-was-probably-Lakota; Polatkin, Junior; *Reservation Blues*; Warm Water, Chess and Checkers.

The Business of Fancydancing

Sherman Alexie's *The Business of Fancydancing* (1992) is a volume of stories and poems that takes a bracing look at life on the reservation for the contemporary Indian. The look is often painful, often ironically comic, but always imbued with survival and hope. It is difficult to view the pictures that Alexie draws of racism, poverty, alcoholism, and loss, knowing that change will be slow or absent altogether. The narrator of the first story, after watching his father being harassed by a state trooper, says, "I'm so damn tired." He pushes the van that has run out of gas and waits "for something to change." The reader is left with the distinct feeling that nothing will ever really change for the Indians, who must live in HUD houses and eat government commodity food. The promises of past treaties have worn ironically thin, and no one believes that the condition of Indians will improve. Nonetheless, there is an undercurrent of survival permeating the volume. The survival will not be vouchsafed by governmental promises and handouts but by the resilience of cultural values, the power of story, and the enduring strength of family, however damaged it may become.

Alexie notes the fascination of the American public with the *idea* of Indianness and their distaste at the *presence* of Indians in his poem

"13/16." In the poem, a young white boy asks the persona if he is a "real Indian" and then carves his initials into a totem pole. The poem is rich with the image of white culture defacing and rewriting Indian history. For the young white boy, Indian authenticity is desirable, necessary, and even exotic. But on the same night, the 11 o'clock news reports the death of an Indian, "a member of some tribe or another." When Indians become real, they are best reduced to anonymity.

"Evolution" is another poem in which Alexie makes a political point that the Indian is valued most in our culture when he or she becomes artifact. In the poem, Buffalo Bill opens a pawn shop, buying everything that the Indians bring in, from the "full-length beaded buckskin outfit / it took Inez Muse 12 years to finish" to the very skeletons of the Indians. When "the last Indian has pawned everything / but his heart, Buffalo Bill takes that for twenty bucks" and closes the pawn shop. He reopens it as "The Museum of Native American Cultures."

Not all of Alexie's poems and stories are sharpened on past and present grievances, though. His "Morphine and Codeine" is a powerful look at the pain of both a parent dying with cancer and the pain of the family member who watches the process of death. The first stanza establishes the longing of the family member to take the pain "down to the hospital cafeteria / for lunch, while you watched television / for an hour or two, able to laugh cleanly." The poem moves to the memory of the persona as he was injured and carried to safety in the arms of the parent. He wishes that the painkiller given to him at that time could be given now and take away the pain that morphine and codeine can no longer touch.

"Sudden Death" is a wistful poem about a father who is trapped in his moment of failure in 1956 when he missed an important field goal. He is waiting still for "God and 1956 / to pick him up, carry him on their shoulders." "Reservation Love Song" is a wonderful love poem that promises "old blankets / to sleep with in winter / they smell like grandmother."

The collection ends with "Gravity," the story of a father-son reunion. The returning son finds that both he and his father have experienced hardships and losses in the years that they have been apart. The father affirms that it is good to have the son return, and they go to the basketball court as they have so many times before. "How much you got left?" the son asks the father, and with an acknowledgment of years of waiting "for something to change," the father replies, "Just as much as you."

Alexie's volume has plenty left for the reader willing to take an honest look at the painful but hopeful lives of the characters he puts before us. (Alexie 1992)

See also Alexie, Sherman; *Indian Killer*; *The Lone Ranger and Tonto Fistfight in Heaven*; *Reservation Blues*.

Calabazas

Calabazas is a character in Leslie Marmon Silko's 1991 novel, *Almanac of the Dead*. He is a Mexican Indian, an older clan brother of Zeta and Lecha, twin sisters and principal characters in the novel, and he too is involved in the smuggling business. Calabazas is from a Sonoran mountain village but now lives in Tucson. During World War II, he smuggled tires and spools of copper wire but later moved to smuggling cocaine in the hollowed-out shells of pumpkins. Whereas Zeta begins to smuggle guns and explosives, he prefers to limit himself to drugs. Calabazas objects to trafficking in guns, explosives, and human cargo because they necessarily imply a connection to politics, which he wants to avoid. His only, albeit passive, political concern is the 500-year ongoing war for the American continent. Though skeptical of the message of the coming revolution, he attends the International Holistic Healers Convention and comes to trust the Barefoot Hopi and Wilson Weasel Tail, two healers and prophets. As a young man, Calabazas falls in love with Liria, but he is tricked into marrying her older sister, Sarita, by their father. He continues his affair with Liria throughout their lives but still feels sheepishly betrayed when he learns that Sarita has been the lover of the local priest for many years. He keeps in-laws and cousins on his pay-roll to avoid worrying that his family members might betray him in some way. (Silko 1991)

See also *Almanac of the Dead*; The Barefoot Hopi; Lecha; Liria; Mosca (Carlos); Root; Sarita; Weasel Tail, Wilson; Zeta.

Carter, John and Julia

In Mourning Dove's *Cogewea, the Half-Blood* (1927, 1981), John and Julia Carter are the brother-in-law and sister of the main character, Cogewea. John, a middle-aged white man and rancher of some success, marries Julia when she is just a 16-year-old girl. It is to their home that Cogewea returns after her graduation from Carlisle Indian Industrial School. "Good natured and amiable," John is a father figure to Cogewea, and it is Julia who encourages the romance between Cogewea and Densmore. In her encouragement of Densmore's suit, Julia reflects an accommodationist position. It is not that she is ashamed of the "Red race," but she determined it would "be better to draw from the more favored and stronger, rather than to fall back to the unfortunate class so dependent on their conquerors for their very existence." (Mourning Dove 1927, 1981)

See also Cogewea; *Cogewea, the Half-Blood: A Depiction of the Great Montana Cattle Range*; Densmore, Alfred; LaGrinder, Jim; McDonald, Mary; The Stemteema.

Cedarfair, Proude

Before Jordan Coward goes to the cedar circus and demands Proude's cedar trees and threatens his life, Proude Cedarfair is content to live in his ancestral home, making ceremonial objects and cedar incense for shamans and religious leaders. When there is no longer any way to peacefully resist the federal government, which demands the cedar trees as an energy source, Proude and his wife leave the circus and become the leaders of a pilgrim band in Gerald Vizenor's *Bearheart: The Heirship Chronicles* (1978, 1990).

They are followed by seven clown crows, for Proude has the wisdom to understand the "silence and languages of animals." Along the way, they are joined by many mixed-bloods who are either running from something or searching for something. Without asserting any power, Proude becomes the leader of the group. When it seems that they will be destroyed by the Evil Gambler in What Cheer, Iowa, it is Proude who risks his own life and wins their freedom. In another instance, Proude is able to decoy their enemies by giving them a fake medicine bundle.

The pilgrims all shun him, thinking he has desecrated the medicine bundle by giving it to whites, but he bears their mistaken anger in silence.

Because his behavior is pure and his motives are spiritual, Proude completes the journey to the fourth world when many of the other pilgrims fail. (Vizenor 1978, 1990)

> See also *Bearheart: The Heirship Chronicles*; Biwide, Inawa; Darwin-Winter Catcher, Belladonna; Farrier, Lilith Mae; Staples, Sir Cecil.

Ceremony

Ceremony (1977, 1986) is the title of Leslie Marmon Silko's first novel, the story of Tayo, a mixed-blood Laguna, who returns to the reservation from World War II still suffering from "shell shock," or what might now be called post-traumatic stress disorder. The illness that plagues Tayo is not a singular experience, however. It has also come over the Laguna Reservation in the form of a drought and over the nation and world in the form of the rampant blood-lust of the nuclear age.

The setting of Leslie Marmon Silko's Ceremony, *the Laguna Pueblo, as it appeared in 1880. (Courtesy Museum of New Mexico)*

Silko's novel is aptly named *Ceremony*, for the process that Tayo must go through to restore order to his personal and communal world is a traditional ceremony. Paula Gunn Allen, another contemporary Laguna mixed-blood writer, describes the nature of a ceremony in native cultures:

> The purpose of a ceremony is to integrate; to fuse the individual with his or her fellows, the community of people with that of the other kingdoms, and this larger communal group with the worlds beyond this one. . . . But all ceremonies, whether for war or healing, create and support the sense of community that is the bedrock of tribal life. This community is not made up only of members of the tribe but necessarily includes all beings that inhabit the tribe's universe.

In carrying out the ceremony, Tayo has help from several others, especially from the Navajo medicine man, Betonie. Tayo is successful in his ceremony, and the novel ends with order restored to him, the Laguna community, and for the time being, the world.

Silko's achievement in *Ceremony* goes far beyond the skillful telling of Tayo's story. In both style and content, the novel reflects the oral tradition of the Laguna culture. Charles Larson praises her for the "rich use of traditional ritual, folklore and myth, the evocation of life on the Laguna Pueblo Reservation," and Frank MacShane acknowledges that Silko's "achievement lies partly in the way she has woven together the European tradition of the novel with American-Indian storytelling." Her success with *Ceremony* firmly establishes Silko as a novelist of the first rank. (Allen, 1986; Larson 1977; MacShane 1977; Silko 1977, 1986)

See also Betonie; Descheeny's Wife; Emo; Harley; Helen Jean; Ku'oosh; Montaño; Ts'eh; Night Swan; Rocky; Silko, Leslie Marmon; Tayo; Witchery.

Claiming Breath
Diane Glancy's 1992 volume *Claiming Breath* won the 1991 North American Indian Prose Award and is a mixed-genre memoir that chronicles a year in her life. The major concerns of that year are her divorce; the illness and death of her mother; and her own attempt to establish an identity as mother, ex-wife, daughter, mixed-blood, and writer.

During the year of which she writes, she is on the road, moving from point to point in her job as the artist-in-residence for the state arts councils of both Oklahoma and Arkansas. The traveling between places serves as a metaphor for her position as a mixed-blood, always negotiating the differences in her two cultures. The opening page of the text provides a physical representation of what it is like for Glancy to be caught in the middle. Her words are centered in the middle of the page, trapped in a column of print. Because she is "not fully a part of either" culture, Glancy writes "with a split voice." Glancy feels the greatest tension between cultures in her religious life. She appreciates the old ways of her Cherokee ancestors, but values her Christianity: "If I got anything from the white man, it's the Christian faith." She even goes so far as to suggest that the "sacred hoop of the Indian nation was broken because it wasn't the sacred hoop of God."

Glancy wants "to explore the breakdown of boundaries between the genres," and *Claiming Breath*, with its hybridized format of poetry, essay, and memoir, certainly does so. In this way, the book is indebted to N. Scott Momaday's *The Way to Rainy Mountain*. In her playfulness with language, the trick of merging phonetic and orthographic representations of words, she echoes the talents of Gerald Vizenor. She provides a lovely definition of writing: "word-cloth over disembodied meaning." That she sometimes falls short of that endeavor is forgivable, given that she often does achieve her goal. (Glancy 1992)

See also Glancy, Diane; Vizenor, Gerald; *The Way to Rainy Mountain*.

Clara
In Michael Dorris's *A Yellow Raft in Blue Water*, Clara is the much younger sister of Ida's mother. Clara comes to stay with Ida's family on their

Montana reservation when her mother is sick. Ida adores her aunt and is shocked to realize that Clara and her father are having an affair. When Clara becomes pregnant, she and Lecon, Ida's father, devise a scheme in which Ida would accept responsibility for the child. Clara says of Ida, "Everyone's aware she's after Willard Pretty Dog . . ."; she promises to "be here for the baby. Only outside the house will it be hers." At the convent, Clara plays upon the sympathies of the nuns, and they are "enraptured" to hear her story, that she is a victim, "an innocent lamb, abused like a martyr by a rampaging beast of a man." When the baby is born, the plan falls apart because Clara is charmed by Denver and decides to give the child away and stay in the city. Clara says of the baby, "She isn't even *pretty*; she's all nose." Ida fights for the baby, Christine, and returns with her to the reservation.

Three years later, Clara returns to the reservation; she has married and divorced a white man, has had many failed job experiences, and is now ready to move to another city to get a fresh start. When she decides to take Christine with her, Ida and Father Hurlburt join forces to keep Christine in Ida's care. Clara is forced to leave without the child, and only twice more does Ida allow her to see Christine. Ida and Christine visit Clara when she is dying, but no one shares the information that she is Christine's birth mother. (Dorris 1987)

See also Father Hurlburt; George, Ida; Pretty Dog, Willard; Taylor, Christine; *A Yellow Raft in Blue Water*.

Clinton

Clinton is a character in Leslie Marmon Silko's *Almanac of the Dead* (1991). He works with Rambo in the Army of the Homeless. He holds the theory that the conflict in Vietnam was "designed to stop the black man in America"—to keep American cities from being burned to the ground by socially and politically disenfranchised blacks. He waits for the best time to take power in the United States. Meanwhile, he reads and makes tapes that he will play on the air when he seizes radio stations. His messages are a "call to war" and will tell people that "all

around them lay human slavery, although most recently it had been called by other names." He believes that the gods of Africa also inhabit the Americas and that indigenous peoples of America have a profound connection to the African Americans. With Rambo, he kills Trigg, a thug who commits murder and sexual crimes in his organ-harvesting business, as the first step in their attempt to bring judgment on the oppressors and to realign existing power structures. (Silko 1991)

See also *Almanac of the Dead*; Rambo (Roy); Trigg, Eddie.

Cogewea

Cogewea is the main character in the 1927 novel *Cogewea, the Half-Blood,* by Mourning Dove. Drawn with the inescapable limitations of a character in a dime novel, Cogewea nonetheless shows some complexities that save the character from pure cliché. She is concerned with the liminal position she occupies as a mixed-blood and laments, "Regarded with suspicion by the Indian; shunned by the Caucasian; where was there any place for the despised breed!"

Her mother died when Cogewea was quite young, and her white father, Bertram McDonald, went to Alaska with the gold rush and has not been heard from in 14 years. Cogewea was sent to Carlisle Indian Industrial School and graduated with high honors at age 21. Now, back home at her sister and brother-in-law's ranch, Cogewea is liked and respected by the rangers. The ranch foreman, Jim LaGrinder, is in love with her, but she cannot favor him with more than a brotherly affection. Instead, she falls in love with Alfred Densmore, an Easterner on the scam for quick money. Her sister Mary, her grandmother, and Jim are all able to see the deception that Densmore is playing upon Cogewea, but she is blind to the knowledge and resistant to their warnings.

Though she suffers from blindness in love, Cogewea is a sharp and sensitive woman in other regards. She is thoroughly aware of the pressures that are being put on the traditional ways of her people; she longs to be "an authoress" so that she might place on record the "threads in the woof of her people's philosophy." She is aware that the great roundup of buffalo from the range betokens a similar fate for native peoples. When she sees the head of a buffalo mounted on the wall of her brother-in-law's home, she cannot look at it "without a pang of regret. The fixed glassy eyes haunted her, as a ghost of the past." Furthermore, she is able to see the political ramifications of the European conquest of America. She suggests, "Viewed in its proper light the coming of the May-flower was, to my people, the falling of the star 'Wormwood'; tainting with death the source of our very existence." Her recognition of the injustices inherent in a racist society is revealed at the Fourth of July picnic where she enters and wins both the "squaw" race and the "ladies" race but is denied the prize in both. She confronts the judge and accuses him of "disbursing *racial* prizes regardless of merit or justice."

Even throughout her dalliance with Densmore, Cogewea aligns herself with her Indian heritage. She insists that when she and Densmore marry it be in the way of her people, and she confirms, "I will *never* disown my mother's blood." After Densmore betrays her, she only agrees to marry Jim LaGrinder when she hears the intermediary voice of the Great Spirit announcing that Jim is "The Man!" Her choices are now guided by traditional wisdom rather than personal impulse. (Larson 1978; Mourning Dove 1927, 1981; Owens 1992a)

See also Carter, John and Julia; *Cogewea, the Half-Blood: A Depiction of the Great Montana Cattle Range*; Densmore, Alfred; LaGrinder, Jim; McDonald, Mary; The Stemteema.

Cogewea, the Half-Blood: A Depiction of the Great Montana Cattle Range

Mourning Dove is best known for her novel *Cogewea, the Half-Blood* (1927, 1981), thought to be the first novel by a Native American woman. Mourning Dove wrote the book with the close editorial assistance of her mentor, Lucullus Virgil McWhorter, an amateur historian and Indian advocate of the Pacific North-

west. Her text, from conception to fruition to publication, had a tortured history of delays and disappointments, and without McWhorter's help, the novel might never have reached the public. Mourning Dove had completed a draft of *Cogewea* in 1912, two years before she met McWhorter. But during the winter of 1915–1916, Mourning Dove stayed with McWhorter's family and with his help revised the novel. By 1922, the novel was still not published, and in frustration, McWhorter continued to revise the novel.

In spite of McWhorter's essential part in delivering *Cogewea*, it was not without cost. Charles Larson notes the "confusing voice" in the novel. Alanna K. Brown acknowledges that "*Cogewea* is a very disjointed novel, difficult to read because both rich and banal literary movements are juxtaposed." Paula Gunn Allen says that Mourning Dove "was caught between the contradictory imperatives of her editor's desires and tastes and her knowledge of how an Okanogan story should go." Allen further suggests that the result is "a maimed—I should say martyred—book." Mourning Dove herself wrote McWhorter on June 4, 1928, and expressed surprise at his final editorial changes: "I have just got through going over the book *Cogeawea* [sic], and am surprised at the changes that you made. . . . I felt like it was some one [sic] elses [sic] book and not mine at all. In fact the finishing touches are put there by you, and I have never seen it."

The text that has come to us is flawed, to be certain, but it does show some narrative skill and certainly indicates a promise that, under other circumstances, might have been nurtured to a more perfect end. *Cogewea* is the story of a young mixed-blood woman who is very aware of the complications that surround her as a result of her mixed blood. After graduation "with high honors" from Carlisle Indian Industrial School at age 21, she returns to the West and lives with her sister and white brother-in-law rancher on the Horseshoe Bend Ranch. Cogewea is "a lover of nature," and "the wild appealed to her." She is at home on the ranch, surrounded once again by loving family, her

Okanogan culture, and the free-spirited company of the ranch hands. Jim LaGrinder, the foreman of the ranch and a "half-blood" himself, is in love with Cogewea. She respects Jim, but loves him only as a brother, and this situation establishes the primary conflict of the novel. Another suitor, Alfred Densmore, is hired as a ranch hand, and even though his cowboy talents pale in comparison to Jim's, he catches the interest of Cogewea. Jim is certain that his standing as "the best rider of the Flathead" should win him some favor with Cogewea. That recognition alone will not secure her affections for him, and both are long in learning just what it is that constitutes their love for each other. Meanwhile, Cogewea is becoming more attracted to Densmore in spite of the warnings of Jim and of her beloved grandmother. It becomes obvious to them and to the narrative audience that Densmore is a blackguard intent only in stripping Cogewea of her property and money before abandoning her, at best, or killing her, at worst. He presses for a quick marriage, and finally wins her approval for an elopement. He confesses that he is short of money, and that should she provide the necessary cash, he will repay her twofold. Cogewea takes $1,000 from her account to finance the honeymoon, but Densmore immediately reveals his scheme and beats her, ties her to a tree, and absconds with the money. Jim is alerted to Cogewea's danger and rescues her. In the "two snows" that follow her abandonment and rescue, Cogewea realizes that she does love Jim. They profess their love for one another, and on the same day, they learn that Cogewea has inherited a fortune from the gold claim of the father who abandoned her family 14 years earlier. Jim has proven himself worthy of Cogewea, however, for he professed his love without knowing that she had considerable wealth; in this way, he becomes the opposite of the scoundrel Densmore and is deemed a proper mate for Cogewea.

Though the novel is a melodramatic dime Western with a formulaic plot and predictable characters, it is significant for the author's portrayal of a female protagonist and for the pre-sentation of identity issues that would continue to dominate Native American literature for the rest of the century. (Allen 1986; Brown 1994; Fisher 1981; Larson 1978; Mourning Dove 1927, 1981; Owens 1992a)

See also Carter, John and Julia; Cogewea; *Coyote Stories*; Densmore, Alfred; LaGrinder, Jim; McDonald, Mary; Mourning Dove (Christine Quintasket); *Mourning Dove: A Salishan Autobiography*; The Stemteema.

Cook, Marlis

Marlis Cook is a woman who "scared women, snowed men." In Louise Erdrich's *Tales of Burning Love* (1996), Marlis is the fourth wife of Jack Mauser and the only one of his five wives to bear a child. She is the epitome of the survivor, a woman who uses the system to defeat the system. She is virtually homeless, living on a sheet of black plastic under the trailer owned by her brother's former wife. She has made a living of finding accidents and stepping into them so she can sue, and she realizes that she has been warming up for the big accident of her life. When she enters a store that is undergoing renovation, she grabs an electrical cord and is electrocuted. Jack Mauser is there shopping, and he gives her mouth-to-mouth resuscitation. She recovers with a tic in her eyelid and tries to sue him. Jack visits her and asks her to drop the case, but she refuses to cooperate. In a burst of anger, Jack jumps on her and rubs her face, massaging the twitch out of her eyelid. Marlis is shocked, thinking it is "both disgusting and cool" that Jack has cured her with his touch. "It could be abuse," she thinks. "Then again, some places you would pay for it." Because her nerve damage is healed, she reluctantly drops the lawsuit. A few weeks later, she is at a bar and sees Jack again, though he doesn't recognize her. She joins in his celebrating—he has just received a loan check from his banker—and before the day ends, they leave the bar together for a motel. Thus begins a month-long spree of deceit and blackmail that ends in marriage and Marlis's pregnancy. When Jack won't tell Marlis what she wants to hear—that he loves her and the baby—she realizes that she was only "a stopping place, a way station on the road to somewhere else" for Jack.

Their relationship is over, but Marlis does benefit financially from her time with Mauser. She keeps half of the check she took from him on their first night together, and she convinces him to pay for her training as a blackjack dealer at the casino. She starts working for Lyman Lamartine at his B&B casino, and on the night of Jack's funeral, the other widows find her there to discuss the disposition of Jack's ashes. The four women leave the casino together when Marlis gets off work, and they are all together in the blizzard that threatens their lives. In the hours when the four women tell the stories of "burning love," Marlis and Candice reveal that they are lovers.

Though Marlis is a self-avowed manic-depressive, and though she has all the earmarks of a low-class character, she is not without intelligence and her own kind of depth. She wonders, for example, "how water stays together, lets people in and lets them out." Once she has a measure of financial security and stability in her relationship with Candice, Marlis settles into a more mature pattern. (Erdrich 1996)

See also Lamartine, Lyman; Mauser, Eleanor Schlick; Mauser, Jack; Nanapush, Dot Adare; Pantamounty, Candice; *Tales of Burning Love.*

Elizabeth Cook-Lynn, 1998. (Eastern Washington University)

Cook-Lynn, Elizabeth

Elizabeth Cook-Lynn was born in 1930 at the Government Hospital at Fort Thompson, South Dakota. She is a member of the Crow Creek Sioux tribe and the granddaughter of writers. Her grandmother wrote in Dakota for Christian newspapers in the mid-nineteenth century, and her father and grandfather contributed to the writing of an early Dakota dictionary. Cook-Lynn says, "Ever since I learned to read, I have wanted to be a writer." She spent much of her childhood reading but never found any reading material about her own people. As a college student, she was shocked to take a history course about the westward movement that failed to address the presence of Indians. Those erasures of her heritage caused her first to choose silence, but her feelings changed to mistrust and finally anger toward the dominant culture. She writes now as "an act of defiance born of the need to survive."

Cook-Lynn holds a bachelor's degree in journalism from South Dakota State College and received a master's degree in education, psychology, and counseling from the University of South Dakota in 1971. In 1985, she founded the *Wicazo Sa Review*, an Indian studies journal, which she continues to edit. She is professor emeritus at Eastern Washington University, where she taught for over 20 years.

Her work includes *Then Badger Said This* (1977), a collection of poetry, myth, personal history, and cultural history not unlike N. Scott Momaday's *The Way to Rainy Mountain.* Other works are *See the House of Relatives* (1983), a chapbook of poems; *The Power of Horses and Other Stories* (1990), short fiction; and *From the River's Edge* (1991), a novel. (Cook-Lynn 1987; Ruppert 1994; Witalec 1995)

See also *The Way to Rainy Mountain.*

Copway, George

George Copway, or Kah-ge-ga-gah-bowh, was born in 1818 in Canada, near the mouth of the Trent River. An Ojibwa (Anishinabe), both of his parents were converted Christians, and he recognized early that he would follow a career in the church. He became a "model Indian convert," serving as an interpreter. When he was 17 years old, the Methodist missionaries promoted him to the role of preacher. As a reward for his diligent missionary work, he was given entrance into the Ebenezer Manual Labor School near Jacksonville, Illinois. By 1840, when he married a young Englishwoman, Elizabeth Howell, Copway's process of assimilation was outwardly confirmed. Working within an institutionalized religious system proved difficult for Copway, however, and there were frequent complaints of his headstrong and impetuous behaviors. He also encountered difficulties in the handling of church funds and was eventually accused of embezzlement. Unable to repay the money, Copway spent some time in prison and was expelled from the ministry by the Canadian Conference of the Wesleyan Methodist Church.

At age 29, at least partially separated from his Ojibwa identity and severed from his Christian calling, Copway reinvented himself by becoming an author and lecturer. His first volume, an autobiography with the lengthy title *The Life, History, and Travels of Kah-ge-ga-gah-bowh (George Copway), A Young Indian Chief of the Ojebwa Nation, A Convert to the Christian Faith, and a Missionary to His People for Twelve Years*, was published in 1847 and had gone through seven printings by 1848.

The success of the book fed an equally successful lecture circuit, and soon Copway had earned a national reputation and was enjoying the adulation of public figures such as Henry Rowe Schoolcraft, Henry Wadsworth Longfellow, Washington Irving, and James Fenimore Cooper. Cooper even went so far as to provide financial support for Copway's future projects. Copway followed his autobiography with a second volume, *The Traditional History and Characteristic Sketches of the Ojibwa Nation* (1850), a tribal history. Both the history and autobiography are marked by a bifurcated narrative voice. On the one hand, Copway supports the idea of the Indian as an innocent, natural man; on the other hand, he expresses the need for

Frontispiece illustration from George Copway's The Life, History, and Travels of Kah-ge-ga-gah-bowh, *1847 (Reproduced from Copway's* The Life, History, and Travels of Kah-ge-ga-gah-bowh, *1847)*

the Indian to abandon ways of darkness and embrace Christianity.

Copway's fame was short-lived. By 1850, his followers were falling away, his lectures were poorly attended, and the newspaper he had begun, *Copway's American Indian*, folded after only three months of circulation. He suffered a further tragedy when three of his four children died between August 1849 and January 1850. By 1851, he was bankrupt and in unstable mental health, and his marriage was deteriorating. Copway never again regained the fame, or even respectability, that he once had. The defrocked Methodist minister returned to Canada in 1858 and declared himself a "pagan" who desired baptism in the Catholic Church. He died in 1869, just days before his first communion. (Copway 1847; Copway 1850; Ruoff 1994; Smith 1988; Smith 1996)

Coward, Jordan

In Gerald Vizenor's *Bearheart: The Heirship Chronicles* (1978, 1990), Jordan Coward is the "elected president of the reservation government." However, he is nothing more than a pawn in the schemes of the federal government, which uses him to give the message to Proude Cedarfair that he must surrender his property. Coward knows that he is being manipulated for the crimes of the government, but he does not have the moral courage to resist. Proude Cedarfair prefers to avoid the evil that Coward represents, and in his impotent rage, Coward wishes that Proude's cedar trees would be "cut into little sticks and burned in the federal offices of the bureau of public remorse." (Vizenor 1978, 1990)

> See also *Bearheart: The Heirship Chronicles*; Cedarfair, Proude.

Coxwain, Doctor Wilde

Doctor Wilde Coxwain is the lover of Justice Pardone Cozener in Gerald Vizenor's *Bearheart: The Heirship Chronicles* (1978, 1990). Coxwain is "the arm wagging tribal historian." Along with Cozener, Coxwain elects to stay at the word hospital rather than travel on to the fourth world with the pilgrims led by Proude Cedarfair. He values the aid of the government, which will "care for us and feed us here," over his own spiritual journey. (Vizenor 1978, 1990)

> See also *Bearheart: The Heirship Chronicles*; Cozener, Justice Pardone.

Coyote Stories

Coyote Stories by Mourning Dove was originally published in 1933 and has been reprinted in 1990 by Bison Books, an imprint of the University of Nebraska Press. Mourning Dove was first encouraged to collect the "stories and traditions of her people, the Interior Salish," by Lucullus Virgil McWhorter, her early mentor and collaborator on her novel *Cogewea*. Though McWhorter turned the primary editorial responsibilities for the volume of Indian legends over to his friend Heister Dean Guie, who worked for the Yakima newspaper, he remained involved in the project, even to the extent of reading and commenting on the correspondence between Mourning Dove and Guie. The relationship between Guie and Mourning Dove was often strained by their divergent intentions for the volume. Guie wanted to "produce suitable bedtime reading for children" by "abbreviating and bowdlerizing the stories," while Mourning Dove wanted to highlight "Indian themes and concerns." Guie's intentions for the volume won out; Mourning Dove indicates in her introduction to the volume that the legends are "for the children of another race to read."

In his "Foreword," Chief Standing Bear confirms the importance of the legends as "our books, our literature, and the memories of the story-tellers were the leaves upon which they were written." He further emphasizes, "These legends are of America, as are its mountains, rivers, and forests, and as are its people. They belong!"

The 28 tales are of the Animal People, who were "here first—before there were any real people." Of these Animal People, "Coyote was the most important because, after he was put to work by the Spirit Chief, he did more than any of the others to make the world a good place in which to live." Most of the stories focus on Coyote and reveal one or both of his salient roles, the bungling fool and the cultural hero.

In "The Spirit Chief Names the Animal People," Coyote oversleeps and must keep the name that no one else wants, *Sin-ka-lip'*. The Spirit Chief gives Coyote special work to do in preparation for the coming of the "real people" and gives him special powers. To Coyote's twin brother, Fox, is given the power to bring Coyote back to life should he be killed. Spirit Chief also points out to Coyote that he has two inescapable natures, one to do good and one to do foolish and mean things. "That you cannot help. It is your way," Spirit Chief tells him.

Coyote does provide help to the Animal People. In one tale, he helps Fox get his wife back from Whale Monster; in another, Coyote fights several monsters and diminishes them in size and power. He saves children from being eaten by Owl-woman; he is responsible for the gift of flint to his people so that they might hunt; he gives his people the gift of the black moss food.

Coyote's careless behavior causes any number of misfortunes. In one instance, Coyote offends the buffaloes, and they refuse to come across the Rockies so that Coyote's people might hunt them. He makes an ineffective sun-god because he looks down at all the people do and spies on them. Though Coyote often gets into trouble, he usually gets back out of trouble. In "Coyote Juggles His Eyes," the only real loss he suffers is inconvenience and humiliation. And as is evident in "Coyote Imitates Bear and King-fisher," the traditional bungling host story, Coyote is willing to pay for his adventures with personal humiliation.

Mourning Dove's volume contains several animal stories that do not feature Coyote. The delightful etiological tales explain how turtle got his tail, why skunk's tail is black and white, why spider's legs are long, why marten's face is wrinkled, and more. It would be a mistake to view these stories simply as explanations for physical phenomena. As Chief Standing Bear explains in the "Foreword," the stories are "closely related to the lives of the people" and carry "lessons and morals for daily guidance."

Mourning Dove's collection received positive reviews and was in a second printing by 1934. The achievement of Mourning Dove and her collaborator McWhorter is recognized by Alanna Brown, who notes, "they preserved an essential part of Indian culture, and they made that culture imaginatively comprehensible to the dominant Euroamerican population." (Brown 1996; J. Miller 1990a; J. Miller 1990b; Mourning Dove 1990)

> See also Cogewea; *Cogewea, the Half-Blood: A Depiction of the Great Montana Cattle Range*; Mourning Dove (Christine Quintasket); *Mourning Dove: A Salishan Autobiography.*

Cozener, Justice Pardone

In Gerald Vizenor's *Bearheart: The Heirship Chronicles* (1978, 1990), Justice Pardone Cozener is an illiterate tribal lawyer, one of the "overpaid tribal officials who fattened themselves overeating on expense accounts from conference to conference." Along with his homosexual lover, Doctor Wilde Coxwain, Cozener is at the cathedral when Proude Cedarfair arrives, and they join with the pilgrims. When the pilgrims reach the Bioavaricious Regional Word Hospital, Pardone and Coxwain decide to stay on in the word hospital because the "word wards reminded them of their first meeting and love among the mind farmers." (Velie 1982; Vizenor 1978, 1990)

> See also *Bearheart: The Heirship Chronicles*; Cedarfair, Proude; Coxwain, Doctor Wilde.

Cree, Kennedy (Foxy)

Foxy Cree is the cousin of Rayona Taylor, the principal character in Michael Dorris's *A Yellow Raft in Blue Water* (1987). Though his mother is Pauline, the sister of Aunt Ida, Foxy is merciless in his open contempt for the biracial Rayona. Father Tom Novak tries to initiate a friendship between Foxy and his cousin, but the attempt fails. Nonetheless, when Foxy needs Rayona's help, he is not embarrassed about requesting it.

When Rayona shows up at the Fourth of July rodeo, Foxy is the first familiar face she sees. He is drunk and greets her with hostility: "We thought you was dead, or gone back to Africa." Foxy knows that because he is drunk, he will be disqualified from his event as well as from all the remaining rodeos of the summer. He coerces Rayona into taking his place in the bronco riding, but when she wins the hard-luck buckle and reveals her identity, Foxy is appropriately humiliated. (Dorris 1987)

> See also Father Tom Novak; Nickles, Dayton; Taylor, Rayona; *A Yellow Raft in Blue Water.*

D

Darwin-Winter Catcher, Belladonna

When Belladonna Darwin-Winter Catcher joins the pilgrim group in Gerald Vizenor's *Bearheart: The Heirship Chronicles* (1978, 1990), she tells Proude Cedarfair that she has been raped by three white men and is three months pregnant.

She is the daughter of Old John Winter Catcher, a "man of great Lakota visions," and a white mother, Charlotte Darwin. Darwin was a journalist covering the occupation of Wounded Knee when she met Winter Catcher. Belladonna was conceived and born at Wounded Knee.

When the pilgrims reach the enclosed city of Orion, Belladonna gives a talk on "tribal values." When she is asked, "What does Indian mean?" she responds with stereotypical and reductive "definitions." The one who has asked the question tells her that "Indians are an invention." She is given a poison sugar cookie dessert for her speech, "the special dessert for narcissists and believers in terminal creeds." After she dies, Proude delivers her dead twins by cesarean. (Owens 1992a; Velie 1982; Vizenor 1978, 1990)

See also *Bearheart: The Heirship Chronicles*; Cedarfair, Proude.

David

In Leslie Marmon Silko's *Almanac of the Dead* (1991), David is a minor character with both a male (Beaufrey) and a female (Seese) lover. Before Beaufrey took him in and arranged for his connections to the art gallery, David worked for "an exclusive Malibu escort service" as a "live-in stud." From his employers he learned photography, and he made the move from "art object to artist." His greatest "artistic" achievement is his show that features the dead body of Eric moments after he commits suicide. David is complicit with Beaufrey in the first kidnapping of his child, Monte. After that kidnapping, David and Beaufrey go to Colombia to allow things to die down after the stir caused by the kidnapping and the Eric series. Spurred into jealous carelessness, David starts riding a high-strung mare and soon dies in a fall from the horse. Beaufrey takes photos of David's mangled body in a gruesome irony. (Silko 1991)

See also *Almanac of the Dead*; Beaufrey; Eric; Monte; Seese.

Davis, Rhea

Rhea Davis is the girlfriend of Jim Loney in James Welch's *The Death of Jim Loney* (1979,

1987). She is a Texan temporarily transplanted in the Big Sky country of Montana. She has recently graduated with a master's degree from Southern Methodist University and is led to Montana to teach on the slim thread of information given her by one former professor, who stressed the great opportunities in summer theater and the lovely mountains. Rhea left the home of her millionaire parents in Dallas, broke an engagement, and went north to escape "complications" in her life.

Rhea's dissatisfaction with her own life and her indecision about the future is perhaps the impetus for her relationship with Jim Loney. When Kate wonders why Rhea is attracted to her brother, Rhea admits that he was only a toy at first, but that she has grown to love him. She tells Loney, "I love your dark skin and your dark hair, your noble dark profile."

Rhea has written to Kate reporting that Loney is "suffering a crisis of spirit," that for two months he has sat in his house, leaving only for wine and cigarettes. She tells Kate that she is worried that she cannot do much to help him. When she gets a letter back from Kate, she realizes that Kate wants to take Loney to Washington, D.C., with her. Jealousy now splinters the two women. Rhea wants to be the one to "save" Jim, but when she imagines taking him back to Dallas to meet family, she knows it would be a disaster. She begins a fantasy of taking him away to Seattle where "there are options there, maybe even kind of salvation."

Loney chooses not to go to Seattle with Rhea, and they break off their relationship. She tells her high school principal that she is leaving Harlem, Montana, over the Christmas break. On the evening she resigns, she sits drinking with her friend Colleen and wonders, "Whatever am I going to do with myself?" (Owens 1992a; Welch 1979, 1987)

See also Barthelme, Painter; *The Death of Jim Loney*; Loney, Jim; Loney, Kate.

Davis, Sam

A character in John Milton Oskison's *Wild Harvest* (1925), Sam Davis has unusual vision-ary powers. He works for Billy Dines on his ranch in "Indian Territory," but he spends much time away from the ranch on his evangelistic tours. When he feels "led by the Spirit," he leaves the ranch for the open road and the direction of the Lord. It is Davis who has visions that foretell the injury of Billy Dines, the troubles of Chester Forest, and the shooting of Tom Winger. More importantly, he has a vision that reveals the location of the gun used by Dick Brothers in the shoot-out with Chester Forest. Once the gun is found and entered as evidence, Forest is acquitted of the "murder" of an unarmed man. (Oskison 1925)

See also Dines, Billy and Susan; Forest, Nancy; *Wild Harvest*; Winger, Tom.

The Death of Jim Loney

James Welch's second novel, *The Death of Jim Loney* (1979, 1987), has received less attention than his first striking success, *Winter in the Blood*, but it is a careful work that has all the artistic integrity of Welch's earlier novel. The opening chapter provides an overview of the book. The football game that is on the line parallels the struggle that is going on in Loney's life. Just as Loney is a spectator at the game, he is often a mere spectator in his own life. His character is initially defined by passivity, though he takes an active role in determining his future toward the end of the novel. Like most of the characters in the novel, Jim Loney is trapped in a malaise that he recognizes and wishes to escape, but he cannot find the answers that will allow him to make peace with himself and his past. He chooses instead to embrace death, where there are "No lost sons, no mothers searching."

The quietness and ordinariness of the plot reflect the interior struggle that is going on in Loney. The book is not about action but about reflection. We move with Loney into the world of his cryptic dreams and incomplete memories. He feels the dreams are sent to him from his mother's side of the family, but he cannot interpret them. He can neither fill in the gaps of his memories nor come to understand them.

Loney attempts to reconstruct his past and thus define his present and future by gathering information about his parents and the woman who took care of him for a brief while in his childhood. What he does learn is not enough to offset the feeling that he does not belong to either of his worlds, Gros Ventre or white. Perhaps more than any other mixed-blood in fiction, Loney is trapped on an unstable threshold that prohibits entrance into either world.

Loney does participate in one act that determines the course of his life and of the novel. With characteristic indifference, he agrees to go on a hunting trip with a high school friend, Myron Pretty Weasel. Loney mistakes Pretty Weasel for a bear and kills him. This action shifts the balance of Loney's life toward a purposeful plan for his death. Through the agency of his father, he alerts the authorities that he has killed Pretty Weasel; he then leads them to Mission Canyon on what he arranges to look like a manhunt, but what in actuality is an assisted suicide. Welch says of Loney's action, "I think in some ways it's probably the only really positive thing that he does, and it's positive by being an act that he has created."

Responses to Loney's death range from an affirmation that he is acting in a traditional Gros Ventre manner when he announces his intent to die and that the action connects Loney to his traditional heritage to the assertion that his action is the final result of complete personal disintegration. Whatever the case, Welch's novel is nonetheless a celebration of the human spirit and a parable about the losses concomitant with abandonment and despair. (Coltelli 1990; Lincoln 1983; Owens 1992a; Sands 1986; Scheckter 1986; Welch 1979, 1987)

See also Barthelme, Painter; Davis, Rhea; Loney, Ike; Loney, Jim; Loney, Kate; Pretty Weasel, Myron; Welch, James.

Deloria, Ella Cara

Ella Deloria was born in 1889 on the Yankton Sioux reservation in South Dakota, the daughter of the Reverend Philip Deloria, one of the first native Episcopal priests. She grew up on the Standing Rock Reservation, where her father served at the St. Elizabeth's mission. There she grew in both her cultural traditions and her Christian education. She attended St. Elizabeth's mission school and All Saint's School in Sioux Falls before winning a scholarship to Oberlin College. Deloria attended Oberlin for two years before transferring to Columbia University in New York to earn a degree in education.

After her graduation, Deloria taught for several years and took care of her ailing parents. In 1923, she went to the Haskell Institute in Lawrence, Kansas, as an instructor in physical education. By 1927, she was working with anthropologist Franz Boas of Columbia University. Her time was spent between South Dakota, where she did fieldwork, and New York, where she worked with Boas in the production of ethnological and linguistic texts. Her work includes *Dakota Texts* (1932), a bilingual collection of Sioux tales; *Dakota Grammar* (1941) with Boas; and *Speaking of Indians* (1944), an account of Siouan values. By 1944, her novel *Waterlily* was also completed in first draft but was not published until 1988, 17 years after Deloria's death.

Though she did not have an anthropology degree, Deloria's contribution to the field is significant; her linguistic and translation work as well as her ethnographic collections contribute to the rich body of material on Plains Indians. (Allen 1983; Deloria 1996; DeMallie 1988; Picotte 1988; Ruoff 1990)

See also *Waterlily*.

Densmore, Alfred

In Mourning Dove's *Cogewea, the Half-Blood* (1927, 1981), Densmore is the white "tenderfoot" who comes to the West looking for an opportunity to dishonor and defraud a woman. When he gets a job at the Horseshoe Bend Ranch, Cogewea becomes the object of his evil intentions. Decidedly a villain from his first appearance in the novel, when he arrives at the ranch he wonders, "Where were those picturesque Indians that he was promised to meet? Instead, he had been lured into a nest of half bloods, whom he had always understood to be the inferior degenerates of two races."

In their usual ritual, the cowboys on the ranch challenge the tenderfoot to ride a bronco. Densmore reluctantly accepts the challenge and is thrown and breaks his arm. The event is propitious because it places Densmore in Cogewea's care, where he can woo her. In the process, he almost falls in love with her but talks himself out of it: "I like the girl only as any pleasing chattel. As a game, she affords amusement, but hardly a dividend. The Brownie will be forgotten when I return to civilization." Meanwhile, Celluloid Bill and Rodeo Jack continue to make sport of Densmore by telling him that Cogewea is a wealthy woman. Densmore believes the cowboys, but they are unaware of the danger that they create for Cogewea. Densmore grows more determined to bilk Cogewea and plans a "light marriage ceremony—acquirement of property title—accidental drowning while pleasure boating—fatal shooting accident while hunting—sudden heart failure—or safer still—the divorce court."

Densmore finally convinces Cogewea to withdraw money from her account and to elope. As soon as they are some distance from the ranch, Densmore takes Cogewea's gun and her money and then leaves her tied to a tree. When Cogewea is rescued by Jim LaGrinder, she convinces him not to pursue Densmore. The novel ends with Densmore living in a "cheap boarding house in an eastern city" where he reads a newspaper account of the "settling of the great McDonald mining estate" and of the marriage of Cogewea and Jim LaGrinder. (Larson 1978; Mourning Dove 1927, 1981; Wiget 1985)

See also Carter, John and Julia; Cogewea; *Cogewea, the Half-Blood: A Depiction of the Great Montana Cattle Range*; LaGrinder, Jim; The Stemteema.

Descheeny's Wife
A young Mexican girl with hazel eyes, the fourth wife of Descheeny is the grandmother of Betonie in Leslie Marmon Silko's *Ceremony* (1977, 1986). She comes to Descheeny through a group of Navajo hunters who found her in a

tree. Their horses grew skittish at her presence, and when a blue lace shawl fell from the tree, the hunters brought her down from the tree. Her quiet defiance frightened them, and she "stared at them with hazel green eyes that had a peculiar night shine of a wolf or bobcat." Eager to be rid of her, they leave her with the old medicine man Descheeny, who decides to return her to her Mexican people. But she is unwilling to return, and Descheeny takes her in as a wife. He soon realizes that she "had come for his ceremonies, for the chants and the stories they grew from."

Both she and Descheeny have an acute awareness of the witchery that surrounds them, and they "plotted the course of the ceremony" that would bring its end. She tells him, "It cannot be done alone. We must have power from everywhere. Even the power we can get from the whites." The ceremony they chart is one in which they must "depend on people not even born yet. A hundred years from now." Thus they establish the chain of healing that moves through them to their grandson Betonie and then from him to Tayo. With her hazel eyes and blue shawl, she is also connected to another link in the chain, Night Swan. (Lincoln 1983; Silko 1977, 1986)

See also Betonie; *Ceremony*; Night Swan; Tayo.

Dial, Evelyn and Sky
In Michael Dorris's *A Yellow Raft in Blue Water* (1987), the Dials are an unassuming couple who help Rayona Taylor, the main character, when she is in need. Without his father's approval, Sky left the United States for Canada during the Vietnam War. The Conoco station that he now runs was left to him by his father in an act of unspoken forgiveness. Evelyn is a cook at Bearpaw Lake State Park, and she helps get a job for Rayona. The two allow Rayona to live with them and accept rent only to preserve Rayona's pride.

Rayona is overwhelmed by their kindness, but in their good-hearted simplicity, the Dials expect no return. They are so willing to help Rayona repair her relationship with her mother that Sky even closes his station on the Fourth of July, the most profitable day of the summer. (Dorris 1987)

See also Taylor, Christine; Taylor, Rayona; *A Yellow Raft in Blue Water*.

Dines, Billy and Susan

Susan and Billy Dines are the kindly aunt and uncle of Nan Forest, the main character in John Milton Oskison's *Wild Harvest* (1925). Susan is the older sister of Nan's father, Chester Forest, a well-meaning but inept farmer. She has raised Chester from his early childhood, and now she is helping raise his daughter, Nan. The Dineses are a stabilizing influence in Nan's life. Uncle Billy joins in a partnership with Nan to get her hay crop cut and properly stored. When Billy is hurt in a wagon accident, Nan must secure the haying services of Harvey Stokes. This encounter leads to the courtship and eventual engagement of the two. Aunt Susan takes the place of Nan's mother and is most often seen in the novel in instances of comfort and nurture. (Oskison 1925)

See also Forest, Nancy; Stokes, Harvey; *Wild Harvest*.

Dorris, Michael

Michael Anthony Dorris was born in 1945, an only child whose father was killed at the end of World War II. Though he spent "childhood vacations on reservations in Montana and Washington with his father's Modoc relatives," he was raised by his mother, three aunts, and two grandmothers. Dorris gives credit to them for helping develop one of his writerly strengths—the vision and perspective of strong women. But Dorris did not start his career as a writer.

After earning degrees from Georgetown (bachelor's degree in English and classics) and Yale (master's of philosophy in anthropology), he began teaching in 1971 at Franconia College in New Hampshire. It was a signal year for Dorris, marking the beginning of his professional career and his first year as a single, adoptive parent. While doing anthropological fieldwork in Alaska in a tribal culture that had

Michael Dorris, 1989. (Louise Erdrich)

no personal pronoun for "I," Dorris realized, "In a world of 'we,' I was an 'I,' with no essential responsibilities or links outside myself." That feeling was the genesis of his desire to become a parent. He made contacts that resulted in the placement of a three-year-old Sioux boy with him.

In 1972, Dorris joined the anthropology faculty of Dartmouth College and became chairman of their Native American Studies Department. By 1979, Dorris had adopted two more children, another boy and a girl, and progressed professionally to promotion and tenure at Dartmouth. In that year Dorris also became reacquainted with Louise Erdrich, a poet and former student at Dartmouth, when she came to Dartmouth to give a poetry reading. They married two years later and began a celebrated literary partnership that was intensely collaborative. Their working relationship went beyond the editing of each other's work to the actual joint planning of a book; their collaboration reached its most intense period when they not only coedited and planned a project but actually cowrote *The Crown of Columbus* (1991). *The Crown of Columbus* and *Route Two* (1991), a travel memoir, are the only books that carry both of their names as writers.

Artistically, Dorris moved beyond his collaborative role when he conceived and wrote *A Yellow Raft in Blue Water* (1987). The germ of the novel is an experience Dorris had 25 years earlier when, as a young boy, he swam to a yellow raft in the lake of a state park. On the raft he talked with a Jewish-Polish man, a concentration camp survivor, and "realized that I was a more serious person than I'd been when I swam out. I'd actually grown." Dorris says, "he talked to me as if I were an adult." Initially the main character in *Yellow Raft* was a young man named Raymond, but Dorris didn't want to write a "boy's coming-of-age story," so he changed the character to a young girl, Rayona. Rayona's experience with Babe the bronco at the Fourth of July rodeo also grows from a real experience in Dorris's life. He relates, "I got thrown off the same horse three times at the Montana State High School Rodeo, and just like Rayona, I thought if you get thrown off, you get back on."

Yellow Raft achieved considerable praise for a first novel and launched a second phase of Dorris's career. Next he focused his attention on a project that emerged from his personal life, a study of fetal alcohol syndrome. His first adoptive son suffered from the condition, and Dorris reveals their painful and poignant story in *The Broken Cord* (1989). The book won major awards, including the National Book Critics Circle Award for Best Nonfiction Book in 1989 and *Choice*'s Outstanding Academic Book in 1990, and helped initiate action by the Senate on the issue of fetal alcohol syndrome. The book also received strong criticism from several places; see, for example, Katha Pollitt's "A New Assault on Feminism" from *The Nation* and Elizabeth Cook-Lynn's review in *Wicazo Sa Review*. *The Broken Cord*, the award-winning movie, went into production just after its subject, Dorris's son, died from injuries suffered when he was hit by a car.

In 1989, Dorris resigned from his full-time faculty position at Dartmouth so that he might write full-time. In addition to *The Broken Cord* and *The Crown of Columbus*, other major works include *Morning Girl* (1992), a historical volume for young readers that won the Scott O'Dell Award; *Working Men*, a collection of stories in 1993; *Paper Trail*, a collection of academic and personal essays (1994); *Guests* (1994) and *Sees Behind Trees* (1996), both young adult novels; and *Cloud Chamber* (1997) and *The Window* (1997), both of which are at least tangentially concerned with the character Rayona from *A Yellow Raft in Blue Water*.

Michael Dorris's life and prolific career came to a tragic end on April 11, 1997, when he committed suicide in a Concord, New Hampshire, motel. An earlier attempt on March 28, 1997, was unsuccessful and resulted in a brief stay at a psychiatric hospital. Dorris and his wife, Louise Erdrich, were in the midst of a reportedly difficult divorce at the time. Days after the suicide, allegations of child sexual abuse became public. Dorris's suicide note read, "To whomever finds me, sorry for the inconvenience. I was desperate. I love my family and my friends and will be peaceful at last." (Chavkin and Chavkin 1994; Croft 1994; Dorris 1989; Lyman 1997; Passaro 1994; Robins 1994; Schumacher 1994; Streitfeld 1997a; Streitfeld 1997b; Wong 1994)

See also Erdrich, Louise; *A Yellow Raft in Blue Water*.

E

El Feo

El Feo is the twin brother of Tacho in Leslie Marmon Silko's *Almanac of the Dead* (1991). When El Feo and Tacho were born in the coastal area of Mexico, their family sent El Feo to the mountains to live with adoptive parents as a reminder to the mountain people that they are related to the coastal clans. Though he works with his lover, Angelita La Escapia, in the struggle for the return of all aboriginal lands, he does not share her ideological or political fervor. (Silko 1991)

> See also *Almanac of the Dead*; La Escapia, Angelita; Las Casas, Bartolomeo de; Tacho.

Emo

A character in Leslie Marmon Silko's *Ceremony* (1977, 1986), Emo is a veteran of World War II who returns to the Laguna Reservation having swallowed the lies of "witchery." Emo earned a Purple Heart at Wake Island but has not been able to abandon the lessons of killing he learned in the war. He still wears a GI haircut and recites tales of the power he had in the uniform of the United States Army. These stories center around killing, sleeping with white women, and drinking. Emo's war experience has so distanced him from his culture that he scorns even the land: "Look. Here's the Indians' mother

earth! Old dried-up thing!" Emo's insensitivity toward the sacredness of the land fuels the anger of Tayo, the main character.

Though they shared a common experience in the war, Emo is the antithesis of Tayo. Tayo tries, unsuccessfully, to counter Emo's attraction to evil and witchery by fighting him and cutting him in the stomach with a broken beer bottle. The animosity between the two is heightened, and Emo seeks the death of Tayo by the end of the novel. Instead, he kills Harley in a ritual torture to illustrate his intention toward Tayo. He later kills Pinkie, though the FBI calls it an accident. Emo goes to California when the Laguna elders banish him from the community. (Nelson 1988; Owens 1992a; Silko 1977, 1986; Wiget 1985)

> See also *Ceremony*; Harley; Silko, Leslie Marmon; Tayo; Witchery.

Engel, Ruby

Ruby Engel is the stock temptress character in John Milton Oskison's Western romance, *Wild Harvest* (1925). Driven by jealousy, she cannot bear to see anyone else have what she wants. She sows seeds of dissension throughout the community, making a special effort to keep Nan Forest from forming relationships with any of the eligible men. She calls Nan a "hayseed" and creates doubt in the mind of Tom Winger about his attraction to her. She further schemes to get Tom drunk at the Fourth of July picnic, and then she parades by Nan, acting as if she and Tom were a couple. By the end of the book, she is discredited and leaves the community to go to Denver for a job with a friend. (Oskison 1925)

See also Forest, Nancy; *Wild Harvest*; Winger, Tom.

Erdrich, Louise

Karen Louise Erdrich was born in Little Falls, Minnesota, on June 7, 1954, and grew up in Wahpeton, North Dakota, where her parents taught in the Indian boarding school. She is the first of seven children, a detail of significance since the welter of family—and extended family—voices is never absent from her fiction. Erdrich is of German-American extraction through her father and Ojibwa (Anishinabe) heritage on her mother's side of the family. Though her Ojibwa heritage is a rich repository from which she writes, both sides of Erdrich's family history inform her work.

In 1972, Erdrich left North Dakota for Dartmouth College, where she was in the first coeducational class at that institution. There she received early recognition as a writer of promise, and after graduation in 1976 went on to earn a master's degree in Creative Writing at Johns Hopkins University in 1979. From 1979 to 1980, she worked as communications director and editor of *The Circle*, a Native American newspaper in Boston, and wrote a textbook for the Charles Merrill Company. In 1981, she returned to Dartmouth College to give a poetry reading and became reacquainted with a former professor, Michael Dorris. They began a personal and literary correspondence and were married in 1981.

With Dorris, who had adopted three children as a single father, Erdrich had three daughters. Along the way, she published both a first volume of poetry and a first novel in 1984. *Jacklight* received praise for its intensely lyric and mythic voice. The volume falls into three primary sections: poems of a contemporary

Louise Erdrich, 1998 (© Michael Dorris)

Ojibwa sensibility, poems reflecting the European immigrant life, and myths. Her novel *Love Medicine* (1984) garnered even more praise and won a host of awards, including the National Book Critics Circle Award for Best Work of Fiction, the Sue Kaufman Prize for Best First Fiction, and the Virginia McCormick Scully Award for the Book of 1984 Dealing with Western Indians.

Erdrich has sustained her meteoric beginning with another volume of poetry, *Baptism of Desire* (1989), five more novels, a volume of nonfiction, a children's book (*Grandmother's Pigeon*, 1996), and a joint novel (*The Crown of Columbus*, 1991) with Michael Dorris. Three of the subsequent novels, *The Beet Queen* (1986), *Tracks* (1988), and *The Bingo Palace* (1994), join with *Love Medicine* to become what is now known as Erdrich's North Dakota tetralogy. When viewed as parts of a greater whole, these novels present a complex web of characters joined by blood and relationship and separated by passions and rivalries. Erdrich's vision is nothing less than epic in this sweeping, multigenerational tetralogy.

For years, Erdrich and Dorris maintained an intense collaboration. From conception to editing, with the exception of the actual drafting, the writing process was shared; they brought this arrangement to a fuller, and less satisfying, partnership in *The Crown of Columbus*. This novel and a travel essay entitled *Route Two* (1991) are the only volumes where the two writers share full authorship.

Erdrich's 1995 *The Blue Jay's Dance* reveals another side of her art. The nonfiction volume is a rich and luminous examination of the twin creative processes of birth and writing. It also shows Erdrich's fine eye for nature writing. With *Tales of Burning Love* (1996), Erdrich returns to fiction and some of the same characters who people her tetralogy. Dot Adare Nanapush returns as the main character and continues to mature. The presentation of this character—from her birth and demanding childhood in *The Beet Queen*, to her defiant late adolescence and protective young motherhood in *Love Medicine*, and now her wiser early middle age—is one of Erdrich's finest delineations of character. Sister Leopolda also enjoys a final (perhaps) reprise as the fanatic nun.

Erdrich's latest novel, *The Antelope Wife* (1998), is a departure in that it presents new characters. Otherwise, it continues in the vein of her powerful prose and mythic vision.

An enrolled member of the Turtle Mountain Chippewa, Erdrich attributes her gift of storytelling to her family and the rich stories that were shared around the table and back on her grandparents' reservation allotment. Of her maternal grandfather and former tribal chairman Pat Gourneu, she says, "He's a kind of legend in our family. He is funny, he's charming, he's interesting. He, for many years, was a very strong figure in my life. I guess I idolized him. . . . I always loved him and when you love someone you try to listen to them. Their voice then comes through."

As a young writer, Erdrich initially resisted the voice of the Chippewa side of her family. She says, "I just didn't feel comfortable with it for a long time. I didn't know what to make of it being so strong. It took a while to be comfortable and just say, 'I'm not going to fight it.'" She learned that "a writer can't control subject and background. If he or she is true to what's happening, the story will take over." In the years since she first started writing, however, she has gained admirable control over all of the voices that emerge. (Chavkin and Chavkin 1994; Erdrich 1985; Erdrich 1987; Erdrich 1991).

See also *The Antelope Wife*; *The Beet Queen*; *The Bingo Palace*; Dorris, Michael; *Love Medicine*; *Tales of Burning Love*; *Tracks*.

Eric

Eric is a character in Leslie Marmon Silko's 1991 novel, *Almanac of the Dead*, another of the many people caught up in the web of Beaufrey, a violent narcissist. He is David's photographic model and lover, though David often spurns him. He enters into a friendship with Seese, David's other scorned lover, and the two manage to find some moments of normalcy in the chaotic frenzy of lies, drugs, and pornographic sex that surround them. With a master of fine arts degree in art history from Columbia University and a conservative religious West Texas background, Eric does not fit the profile of the lost souls that are trapped by Beaufrey. Eric cannot find peace in the emotional maelstrom where he dwells, and he finally commits suicide. Even in his death, though, he is abused and exploited, for David turns his suicide into a photographic suite and profits from the tragedy. (Silko 1991)

See also *Almanac of the Dead*; Beaufrey; David; Monte; Seese.

Faces in the Moon

Betty Louise Bell's first novel, *Faces in the Moon* (1994), is a story about storytelling. Bell opens the novel, "I was raised on the voices of women. Indian women." The voices that crowd the beginning of the novel begin to delineate themselves, and there emerge the voices of a young narrator, Lucie; her mother, Gracie; her aunt, Rozella (Auney); her great-aunt, Lizzie; and the absent voice of her grandmother, Hellen.

Lucie has an ambivalent relationship with her mother: tolerance sparked with hatred, but always with the desire for understanding. Her mother is a hard-edged woman whose life has been marked by poverty, loss, and abuse. Gracie is unable to give Lucie the sustaining love and responsible parenting that the young girl needs. When Lucie is four, her mother's latest husband, J.D., rapes the young girl and then demands that Gracie get rid of the child or risk losing him. Gracie sends her daughter away to live with her aunt Lizzie and uncle Jerry. Although the action is a rejection on one hand, it is the best thing that can happen to the young girl. With her great-aunt and great-uncle, Lucie finds a steady and affirming love.

Not only does Lucie's physical and emotional life improve, but the lengthy stay with Lizzie offers her the chance to hear another side of the family narrative. Lucie adjusts the ungenerous versions of the stories she has heard from her mother and aunt about Aunt Lizzie and Uncle Jerry. She also learns the story of her grandmother, Hellen, the beautiful young woman who began the cycle of mother-daughter enmity when she was unable to adequately provide for Gracie and Rozella.

The event that governs the present tension of the novel is the hospitalization and death of Lucie's mother. The remaining action of the story largely comes as remembrance of past conversations and events. Through the reconciliation of memory and the present, Lucie comes to some understanding of her mother. She finds a notebook in which her mother has written her life story. Lucie reads the notebook and sits in the quiet of her dead mother's house, "wanting to decipher, to understand, to know what she had wanted me to know." Then she burns the notebook in the kitchen sink and realizes, "I did not hate her then."

When Hellen died and left her two daughters, she told them she would be watching over them from the moon. Gracie explains to Lucie, "Used to be we believed Indians went to the moon when they passed on." Now, after the death of Gracie, Lucie says, "I cannot look at the moon without searching it for mothers, known and unknown."

Also on the night of her mother's death, Lucie finds something else in her mother's papers that sticks in her mind for several years.

She finds the death certificate of her grandmother, Hellen Evers Jeeter. The certificate is incomplete in that it lists "Unknown" for the date and place of her birth, and "None" as the name of her father. From the oral traditions of her family, Lucie knows very well the name of Hellen's father. When she returns to Oklahoma several years later, she is determined to deal with the keepers of official records and complete the history of her grandmother. In doing so, she is taking the first step to break the three-generation cycle in her family in which the father is not named. Gracie and Rozella, Hellen's daughters, know only that they are the children of "some no-account traveling Scotch preacher who never married their mother." Lucie listens patiently at the edges of conversations, but never learns who her father is. So in putting right the record of who Hellen's father is, Lucie interrupts the cycle of incomplete heritage. When Lucie goes to the Oklahoma Historical Society and meets with an uncooperative librarian, she confronts him: "I am your worst nightmare: I am an Indian with a pen." She leaves him with a last piece of advice she has heard over and over from the mouths of her storytelling foremothers: "Don't mess with Indian women." (Bell 1994; Krupat 1996)

Farrier, Lilith Mae

In Gerald Vizenor's *Bearheart: The Heirship Chronicles* (1978, 1990), Lilith Mae is one of the pilgrims who are journeying to the fourth world with Proude Cedarfair. She was a teacher on the White Earth Reservation but left that job in disgrace. She innocently starts feeding scraps to reservation mongrel dogs, and soon she has attracted many dogs. She loads her van with dog food and travels around the reservation feeding all the strays. In doing so, she becomes the object of many obscene jokes concerning the dogs in the back of her van.

Three school officials rape her while she is at a conference, but the community rumors demand her firing for having sex with them. The only ones faithful to her in this ordeal are two brown boxers whom she both loves and

hates. She takes comfort in their faithfulness and has allowed them to learn to "take care" of her sexually; at the same time, she hates the dogs because they remind her of her sexually abusive stepfather.

Lilith Mae meets up with Proude's group at the cathedral and continues with them on their journey. When the group reaches the Evil Gambler, it is Lilith who is chosen to gamble with him. She loses, but before he can kill her, she immolates herself and the faithful boxers. (Owens 1992a; Velie 1992; Vizenor 1978, 1990)

See also *Bearheart: The Heirship Chronicles*; Cedarfair, Proude; Staples, Sir Cecil.

Fast Horse

In James Welch's 1986 novel, *Fools Crow*, Fast Horse is the childhood friend of White Man's Dog whose early promise of leadership and tribal standing is diminished as a result of two events during a raiding party on the Crow. Once they start the journey, Fast Horse announces that he has had a dream in which Cold Maker, the Blackfeet winter god, asks him to find and move a rock that has fallen over and blocked a spring on the side of Woman Don't Walk Butte. In the vision, Cold Maker says, "If you do this for me, I will make your raid successful." He also warns him that if he cannot find the spring and remove the rock, he must not continue on the raid or the whole party will be punished. He further asks Fast Horse to sacrifice two prime bull robes and cautions him, "It will go hard on you if you do not do this." Though Fast Horse fails to find and dislodge the rock over the spring, he continues on the journey. But what he does once he enters the camp of the Crows endangers the mission as much or more than his disobedience. Though the raiding party was instructed to work under the cloak of silence, Fast Horse rushes into the Crow camp and shouts: "Oh, you Crows are puny, your horses are puny and your women make me sick! If I had time I would ride among you and cut off your puny woman heads, you cowardly Crows." Through his boasting, Fast Horse endangers the raiding party and causes Yellow Kidney to be captured and tortured.

Fast Horse's father, Boss Ribs, is the keeper of the beaver medicine bundle, the most powerful medicine bundle of the Pikunis, and both father and son assume that the power and responsibility will one day be passed to Fast Horse. But after Fast Horse returns from the Crow raid, he changes and grows distant; "he had become an outsider within his own band." The beaver medicine loses meaning for him, he scoffs at Cold Maker, and he challenges Cold Maker to let him die. He "grew bitter and he hated his people and all they believed in." When Yellow Kidney returns to the Lone Eaters, Fast Horse's fate is sealed. To save himself from the vengeance of Yellow Kidney or the face-losing banishment by the chiefs, Fast Horse banishes himself; he goes to join another renegade, Owl Child.

Fast Horse is not a man of moral courage, and his association with Owl Child only entrenches him in a spirit of rebellion. When Boss Ribs sends Fools Crow after Fast Horse to give him another chance to reintegrate into the band of Lone Eaters and to learn the beaver medicine, Fast Horse refuses in profound bitterness.

Fast Horse's last act is bittersweet. One day when he and Owl Child are on a raid, he stumbles across the dead, frozen body of Yellow Kidney in a war lodge. He finally acknowledges his responsibility in Yellow Kidney's capture and mutilation, and in an act of repentance and respect, he takes the body of Yellow Kidney back to the edge of the Lone Eaters' camp. He realizes that "he was not one of them now; nor was he with Owl Child and his gang." He turns his horse toward the north, where there are "many men alone up there." (Barry 1991–1992; Murphree 1994; Owens 1992a; Welch 1986)

See also *Fools Crow*; Owl Child; White Man's Dog; Yellow Kidney.

Father Arnold

"Are you there?" is the favorite prayer of Father Arnold, an idealistic yet frustrated young priest on the Spokane Indian Reservation in Sherman Alexie's 1995 novel, *Reservation Blues*. He came

to the reservation "to save them all" but finds instead that he is falling into sin as he falls in love with Checkers Warm Water. He asks the bishop for reassignment but is refused, so he decides to leave the priesthood. On the day he is packing his van to go, Big Mom invites him to share in the graveside ceremony for Junior Polatkin, saying: "you cover all the Christian stuff; I'll do the traditional Indian stuff. We'll make a great team." Encouraged by Big Mom, Father Arnold stays in the ministry. She also takes him to Checkers so that they might bring their tangled relationship to a satisfying end. Father Arnold asks Checkers for forgiveness and tells her, "I knew how to pray with discipline. I can do it again." (Alexie 1995)

See also Big Mom; Polatkin, Junior; *Reservation Blues*; Warm Water, Chess and Checkers.

Father Damien

Father Damien is the "the new priest, just a boy really," in Louise Erdrich's *Tracks* (1988) who comes to the reservation when the previous priest died of the consumption that was ravaging the Indians. He arrives at the door of old Nanapush and Fleur Pillager just when they are nearly dead from starvation. From the beginning of his association with the Ojibwa (Anishinabe), he exhibits sensitive behavior and a respectful attitude toward his parishioners. Nanapush comes to respect him, though he does not embrace Christianity. Father Damien realizes that he can help the Ojibwa by keeping them aware of their vulnerabilities concerning their land. He is aware, when others aren't, that white encroachment onto reservation lands is increasing at an alarming rate. He urges Nanapush to seek a role in reservation politics to stop the encroachment. (Erdrich 1988)

See also Nanapush; Pillager, Fleur; *Tracks*.

Father Duncan

In Sherman Alexie's novel, *Indian Killer* (1996), Father Duncan is a Spokane Jesuit priest who baptizes John Smith. Father Duncan and John establish a relationship through John's early years, and the eccentric priest would "tell him secrets and make him promise never to reveal them." When John is six, Father Duncan takes him to the Chapel of the North American Martyrs, and the experience creates a sense of disequilibrium for both. John is confused by the pictures of Indians and Jesuits dying, unable to determine who is being martyred. When he presses Duncan for an explanation, the priest is "afraid to answer the question. As a Jesuit, he knew those priests were martyred just like Jesus. As a Spokane Indian, he knew those Jesuits deserved to die for their crimes against Indians."

A year later, the increasingly disoriented priest is sent to Arizona for retirement. After only one week there, Father Duncan walks into the desert and disappears. Throughout his life, John is visited by Father Duncan in his dreams and continues to imagine Duncan in the desert, talking to him. The voice of Duncan in John's head contributes, in part, to John's own disorientation and possible schizophrenia. (Alexie 1996)

See also *Indian Killer*; Smith, John; Smith, Olivia and Daniel.

Father Dunne

Father Dunne is the priest in Linda Hogan's *Mean Spirit* (1990) who moves his church to the woods after the building is destroyed by a tornado. In touch with nature for the first time, he starts moving toward the native ways. He ultimately abandons his connections with Catholic hierarchy and wanders through the countryside followed by a herd of pigs. He becomes known as the "hog priest" and tells Michael Horse that he has come to realize that "the life spirit lived in hogs and chickens as well as inside churches and cathedrals."

Father Dunne is sympathetic to the Indians who are trying to solve the rash of murders, and though he will not directly violate the confidentiality of the confessional, he does write a cryptic note in the dirt in front of the cave where Michael Horse and Stacey Red Hawk are staying. His information provides the first real lead for Red Hawk.

As Father Dunne continues to wander in the countryside, he learns a lesson that he feels is imperative to share with the Indians. He is bitten by a rattlesnake one day, and in realizing his fear of death, he comes to an understanding of the snake's point of view. He learns that the snake is his "sister." When he acknowledges their connectedness, the "sting and venom went away" from his leg. He gathers the Indians to reveal his wisdom about the snake, and the response of a child who is scolded for rudeness reflects the feelings of the Indians. The child says, "Yes, so what new thing did you learn?" (Hogan 1990)

See also Horse, Michael; *Mean Spirit*; Red Hawk, Stacey.

Father Grepilloux

A character in D'Arcy McNickle's *The Surrounded* (1936, 1978), Father Grepilloux is the parish priest who has given his life to the Christianizing of the Salish people. Though not the founder of the mission, he has been there longer and with greater influence than any other missionary. It is to Father Grepilloux that Max Leon appeals when he makes an effort to understand his wife and sons. The priest becomes his steadfast friend, arguing for tolerance and understanding, urging Max to send his son Archilde away to Europe to study music.

Grepilloux has kept a daybook of his experiences with the Salish, and he shares his early impressions with Max. He says that it was "not difficult to teach" the Salish because "they wanted to know the right Faith, their hearts were inclined." However, by the time Grepilloux dies at an advanced age, Max comes to realize that, however unwittingly, the priest too is culpable in the despoiling of the land and the people. Whatever understanding Father Grepilloux has of the losses that the Salish have suffered, it is imperfect, for he tells Max that still, "they have God." (McNickle 1936, 1978)

See also Leon, Archilde; Leon, Catharine; Leon, Max; *The Surrounded*.

Father Hurlburt

It is Father Hurlburt who, in Michael Dorris's *A Yellow Raft in Blue Water* (1987), befriends his parishioner Ida George and supports her in her decision to raise Christine. Father Hurlburt realizes more than Ida does the difficulties that she will encounter in giving up a chance at a life of her own in exchange for familial duty. Though he stresses that Ida is choosing to "keep this secret forever," he does not force his opinion on her; he allows her to make and stand by her choice.

When Father Hurlburt comes to the reservation, people are a bit fearful of him. He gains a "reputation for secrecy"; he is a "wall through which gossip didn't pass, and so was both feared and safe. People needed him for what he couldn't tell, and dreaded what he knew." Ida gets a glimpse of Father Hurlburt that allows her to see him as "the man within the priest," and she recognizes "a sadness about him, a lostness." This revelation establishes an immediate bond between the two. The priest begins a long-standing friendship with Ida, going to her home every Thursday night; he helps her with her schooling, which has been cut short by motherhood, and she teaches him the language of the reservation.

Three years later, when Christine's birth mother Clara comes to the reservation and tries to take the child, it is Father Hurlburt who steps in and produces a fabricated, but apparently legal, birth certificate that names Ida as the mother. Their friendship continues to grow, and when Ida is pregnant with her son Lee, her sister Pauline asks if the father is Father Hurlburt. Pauline's question causes Ida to realize that Father Hurlburt "was the only man [she] didn't want to lose."

Forty years later, save for his relationship with Ida, Father Hurlburt is still an outsider on the reservation and has a drinking problem. (Dorris 1987)

See also Clara; George, Ida; George, Lecon; George, Lee; Taylor, Christine; *A Yellow Raft in Blue Water*.

Father La Frambois

In Susan Power's 1994 novel, *The Grass Dancer*, Father La Frambois is the nineteenth-century priest who tries to convert Red Dress to Christianity. He visits her Dakota band each year,

spending time teaching her to read, write, and speak English, sure that she is a possible convert. He tries to rename her "Esther," but she refuses the new identity until it is to her advantage. In a dream, Red Dress is instructed to go to Fort Laramie. She does so and introduces herself as Esther to signify that she is Christian, a necessary protective deception.

Red Dress tries to explain to Father La Frambois why the Dakota will not accept Christianity, that to embrace "another import" from Europe would be degrading. He is shocked at her explanation, and Red Dress realizes that in his mind, they were "already a degraded people, whom he intended to elevate, single-handedly, into the radiant realm of civilization." (Power 1994)

See also *The Grass Dancer*; Red Dress.

Father Olguin

The parish priest in N. Scott Momaday's *House Made of Dawn* (1968), Father Olguin serves as a link between several parts of the narrative. He is the first lens through which we see Angela St. John, and through his reading of the journals of Fray Nicolas we learn of the generations in Jemez Pueblo previous to the present in the novel. Like several other characters in the novel, Father Olguin suffers from imperfect vision. He has one bad eye with an eyeball that is "hard and opaque, like a lump of frozen marrow in the bone."

When he first meets Angela St. John, he has a stirring of interest in her that is not unlike lust, but he soon reins it in. He comes back from a visit with her and drives into the town so distractedly that he nearly crashes into a baby on a cradleboard.

When Abel, the main character, is on trial for killing the albino, it is Father Olguin who speaks on Abel's behalf. He tries to help the court understand that what Abel has done is not viewed as murder by his culture. Father Olguin understands that Abel has responded to the presence of evil—manifest in the albino—in a way appropriate to his culture. To Abel, the albino represents the evil of witchcraft, and the health of the community depends on the purgation of such an evil. Abel acknowledges that "he would kill the white man again, if he had the chance. . . . A man kills such an enemy if he can."

Father Olguin is an important character for several reasons. He interprets the events of the pueblo to the outsider Angela St. John and thus simultaneously orients the reader into the culture; he provides the link between Angela St. John and Abel; and he opens the past generations of the pueblo to the reader through his reading of the journal of his predecessor, Fray Nicolas. (Evers 1985; Momaday 1968; Raymond 1983)

See also Abel; The Albino; Francisco; *House Made of Dawn*; St. John, Angela.

Father Tom Novak

In Michael Dorris's *A Yellow Raft in Blue Water* (1987), Father Tom is the young priest on the reservation trying desperately to fit in. Father Hurlburt introduces the main character, Rayona Taylor, to him, and she knows that "it's just a matter of time until Father Tom decides I'm his special project." She is put off by his looks and by his ways and says, "Father Tom is the last one on the reservation I want to know, but he's the only one that wants to know me."

Father Tom is unwittingly the butt of jokes; one youth, under the pretext of teaching him "Indian," has Father Tom shouting in church, "I smell like dogshit!" Little wonder the reservation youth don't like him; in his first meetings with Rayona, he tries to talk with her about wet dreams and sex. She fends him off by acting as if he is speaking of "medicine dreams." Father Tom invites Rayona to the Teens for Christ Jamboree in Helena but tries to seduce her. She is repelled by his "skin as pale as peeled potatoes." The priest tells Rayona that they have experienced "an occasion of sin." He quickly looks for a way to protect himself, should Rayona tell anyone of his advances. He gives her money, puts her on a train for Seattle, and goes back to the reservation without her. At the last minute, he hands her a gaudy beaded medallion so "people will know you're an Indian."

When Rayona comes back to the reservation some months later, he is unnerved and tries to protect himself by procuring the pain medication that Rayona's mother, Christine, can no longer legally obtain. (Dorris 1987)

See also Father Hurlburt; Taylor, Christine; Taylor, Rayona; *A Yellow Raft in Blue Water*.

Feather Woman

A figure in Blackfeet mythology, Feather Woman plays a significant role in James Welch's 1986 novel, *Fools Crow*. In the mythic story, So-at-sa-ki, Feather Woman, is "married to Morning Star and lived in the sky with him and his parents, Sun Chief and Night Red Light." She and Morning Star have a son, Star Boy. Though she had been warned not to, one day while digging turnips, she digs the sacred turnip. The violation results in her banishment from her husband and her home with his family in the sky. She returns to earth with her son and joins her former family. The reunion is a happy one, though Feather Woman soon longs for her husband. She watches him appear in the sky each morning, but she can never be with him. Before long, she dies of a broken heart. Her son returns to his father, accompanies him in the morning sky, and is instrumental in the origin of the Sun ceremony of the Blackfeet.

When Fools Crow learns from a dream that he is to take a seven-day journey, his destination is the home of Feather Woman. In a shimmering blur between reality and the spirit world, Fools Crow watches Feather Woman paint daily on a yellow skin. Each evening, the skin appears to be empty. But when Fools Crow leaves her world, Feather Woman allows him to see the message of the skin. There he sees the events that will befall his tribe, the Lone Eaters, and all of the Pikunis. Feather Woman tells him that he can use the knowledge on the skin to help his people, to prepare them for what is to come. She tells him, "Much will be lost to them, but they will know the way it was. The stories will be handed down, and they will see that their people were proud and lived in accordance with the Below Ones, the Underwater People—and the Above Ones." (Welch 1986)

See also *Fools Crow*.

Ferro

Ferro is a character in Leslie Marmon Silko's *Almanac of the Dead* (1991). He is the son of Lecha, who is translating the almanacs of the title, and was abandoned by her when he was only a week old. He is raised by his aunt Zeta but seems to have real feelings for neither his aunt nor his mother. He is 30 years old at the time of the story and helps Zeta run her gun- and drug-smuggling business. He is assisted by Paulie, his lover. When he gets involved with another lover, Jamey, an undercover cop, he is so distracted by him that he cannot keep up with his work. As a result, Sonny Blue, who is the son of a local mobster, starts to make in-roads into the drug-smuggling business. Ferro wants to retire from the smuggling business to get into the pinup calendar business with Jamey.

After Jamey is killed by the Tucson police, Ferro vows revenge and builds a car bomb, which he explodes at the police headquarters. The attack is also designed to announce that "Tucson wasn't United States territory any-more." The bombing brings quick reprisal from the police, and the ranch is attacked. (Silko 1991)

See also *Almanac of the Dead*; Blue, Sonny; Jamey; Lecha; Paulie; Zeta.

First Raise, John

John First Raise is the father of the nameless narrator in James Welch's 1974 novel, *Winter in the Blood*. First Raise is known for his ability to fix broken machinery, "one dollar to kick it and nineteen to know where." He also knows how to drink with the whites in town and often does. On the night that he froze to death, he was drinking in town with the white men, and he walked into a storm that was more powerful than he. He froze in a borrow pit with a hand outstretched, pointing homeward. This cryptic sign is one of only a few that he left his

son in his own search for identity. The narrator must learn the truth of his father's signpost: home is where he will be healed. The second, and perhaps even more important, memory left the narrator by his father is the trip to visit Yellow Calf, the narrator's biological grandfather. Another memory that is burned into the narrator's mind is the breakfast that First Raise cooked for him and his brother, Mose, the morning that they went to bring in the cattle, the day of Mose's death. The kind of warmth and love that First Raise creates for his sons is unequaled by the meager emotion that their mother, Teresa, can muster.

But First Raise is not entirely adequate in his role as father, especially after Mose is killed. The narrator knows that he and his brother "meant something to him although he would never say it . . . and after Mose got killed, he never showed it." After the death of Mose, First Raise started spending more and more time away from home: "He never really stayed and he never left altogether. He was always in transit." Teresa remembers his wandering with bitterness: "He was a wanderer—just like you, just like all these damned Indians."

First Raise was a dreamer too, but one who could never put his dream into action:

Every fall, before the first cold wind, he dreamed of taking elk in Glacier Park. He planned. He figured out the mileage and the time it would take him to reach the park, and the time it would take to kill an elk and drag it back across the boundary to his waiting pickup. . . . He had everything figured out, but he never made the trip.

First Raise is trapped in stasis and cannot move beyond the level of planning. Sadly, that he freezes to death in a borrow pit is an appropriate end for a man locked in stasis and frozen emotionally. First Raise is a character with "winter in the blood." Still, the narrator mourns the death of his father and realizes that he was "good to be with." The narrator remembers, and now appreciates, that his father took him to meet

Yellow Calf and thereby initiated the first link in the chain of events that helped him to understand that the old man was his grandfather. (Owens 1992a; Welch 1974, 1986)

> See also First Raise, Teresa; Mose; Nameless Narrator; *Winter in the Blood*; Yellow Calf.

First Raise, Teresa

Teresa is the mother of the nameless narrator in James Welch's novel, *Winter in the Blood* (1974, 1986). She is similar to Auntie in Silko's *Ceremony* in that she is unable to establish a relationship with her son that will anchor him in his culture. The narrator says, "I never expected much from Teresa and I never got it. But neither did anybody else." Her husband, John First Raise, has frozen to death ten years before the action of the novel begins, and although she is able to begin a new life with Lame Bull, her son is not yet reconciled to his loss. Teresa is a landowner, and Lame Bull marries into property as well as a relationship; this circumstance causes her son to question Lame Bull's motives. But Teresa seems well satisfied with Lame Bull. She is a Catholic and has maintained a drinking relationship with the priest from Harlem, the one "who refused to set foot on the reservation."

Teresa is an embittered woman who seldom has a word of encouragement for anyone. When she and her son are speaking of her husband, she says, "You must have him mixed up with yourself. He always accomplished what he set out to do." Of Amos the duck, she says, "He was lucky. One duck can't be smarter than another. They're like Indians." But for all her unpleasantness, she is a dutiful daughter who takes good care of her mother. When the old woman dies, Lame Bull and the narrator sit and drink in the kitchen, but Teresa goes to the bedroom to be alone in her grief.

By the end of the novel, when the narrator comes to learn who his grandfather is, the reader comes to realize who Teresa's father is. She is the daughter of Yellow Calf, and one wonders if she is aware of this information and how it may have shaped her. That part of the story is not accessible to the reader, however. (Owens 1992a; Welch 1974, 1986)

> See also Amos; Auntie; First Raise, John; Lame Bull; Nameless Narrator; *Winter in the Blood*; Yellow Calf.

Foghorn
See Geiogamah, Hanay.

Fools Crow
See White Man's Dog.

Fools Crow

Fools Crow (1986) is the third novel of Blackfeet/Gros Ventre writer James Welch. The historical novel is a departure from the contemporary settings in Welch's earlier novels, *Winter in the Blood* (1974, 1986) and *The Death of Jim Loney* (1979, 1987). While *Fools Crow* was still in progress, Welch described his novel in this way:

> I'm working with the whole southern Blackfeet, the Pikuni people, and in this historical novel, I'm telling it from their point of view, from the inside of their cultural point of view. And I'm sort of examining their lives, and also the lives of the encroaching people, the whites, but never from the white point of view; it's always from the Indian's.

The novel chronicles the year 1870 in the lives of the southern Blackfeet people, focusing particularly on the band of the Lone Eaters at the time when the main character, White Man's Dog, is coming of age. Louis Owens calls the novel "the most profound act of recovery in American literature." Indeed, what Welch has accomplished in *Fools Crow* is remarkable. He has re-created the cultural milieu of the nineteenth-century Blackfeet from an *insider's* point of view, and he has created a novel that, although embedded in historical fact, is not subordinated to the history—that is, the *story* about very human characters is not lost in the attempt to authenticate historical experience.

An Edward Curtis photograph of a medicine man packing up the Ceremonial Bag and Tipi-cover on a Blackfeet reservation around the turn of the century. (Courtesy Museum of New Mexico)

In writing *Fools Crow*, Welch confronted inescapable narrative constraints. As Paula Gunn Allen says, "conflict-based plots require a tragic outcome if the relationships between Indian and white are represented with historical accuracy." But although *Fools Crow* does depict the historical truth of the attempted genocide of the Blackfeet peoples, the novel's primary conflict is not between the Indian and white cultures; it centers around the choices that two major characters—White Man's Dog and Fast Horse—make. Concerning his narrative choices, Welch says:

> What you try to do is create fictional stories that coincide with historical fact. It's important for me to know what all the facts were of that particular time so I can tell my fictional story and not abuse the facts too much. It's a tricky process. I was more concerned with the characters and how they related to each other, how they related to the encroaching settlers, the soldiers, and what the dialogue was like than with the straight historical facts of that particular time.

Fools Crow is essentially a novel about choices that human beings make and how the consequences of those choices play out in a society in which each human being is intimately connected to all parts of the world around him or her. Though the protagonist of the novel is White Man's Dog (later called Fools Crow), all of his growth and actions are set in contrast to those of Fast Horse, his childhood friend. The novel opens with the plans for a horse-taking raid on the Crows, and both White Man's Dog and Fast Horse are going to participate in it. Whereas White Man's Dog is uneasy, fearful that his string of bad luck will adversely affect the raid, Fast Horse is brash and boastful. Yellow Kidney, an experienced and respected warrior, is going to lead the raid, and he recognizes that "in spite of his unlucky reputation, there was a steadiness, a calmness in White Man's Dog" that he liked. Yellow Kidney is not so sure about Fast Horse but takes him along because he has great respect for the father of the young man.

In the course of the journey, Fast Horse is involved in two behaviors that have serious outcomes. First, he does not obey the stipulations of a dream vision that Cold Maker, the Blackfeet winter god, has required of him. Second, he enters the camp of the Crows and breaks the silence and secrecy of the mission with a loud boast. His boast triggers a series of events that reverberate throughout the novel. The first and most dramatic of these events is that Yellow Kidney is captured in the heart of the Crow camp and is dealt with severely. He is exposed to "the white-scabs disease" (smallpox), is shot in the thigh, and is tortured by having each of his fingers cut off one by one. He is then tied to a scrawny horse and sent out of the camp into a driving snowstorm. Yellow Kidney finally wanders into Cheyenne country, where his hands and smallpox are treated by a medicine woman. When, against all odds, Yellow Kidney returns to the camp of the Lone Eaters, Fast Horse's boasting and cowardice are recognized as the cause of Yellow Kidney's injuries.

While Fast Horse moves further and further away from community approval, White Man's Dog is honored for his responsible behavior in the raid, and he continues to gain the respect of his tribal group. The two friends are irrevocably separated when Fast Horse banishes himself and joins the renegade band of Owl Child.

With the character conflicts and contrasts firmly in place, Welch allows the historical realities of the Blackfeet in 1870 to move to the foreground of the novel. Smallpox is once again ravaging the Pikuni, and many die; the Lone Eaters and other bands of the Pikuni engage in many discussions with each other and with the "seizers," the U.S. soldiers, over the dispensation of the northern plains. The historical inevitabilities impinge on the story, and one of the most striking scenes of the novel is when Fools Crow comes upon a small group of survivors fleeing from the Massacre on the Marias, in present-day Montana. After seeing to their safety, Fools Crow goes to the ruined camp to investigate. The horrors he finds there in the camp of Heavy Runner sicken him. The camp has been burned and destroyed; bodies of infants and elders lie in the snow, still smoldering from the fire. Heavy Runner himself has been killed even though he met the soldiers with a piece of paper signed by officials of the U.S. government saying that "he and his people were friends to the Napikwans [whites]." As Fools Crow attempts to absorb the horror, one by one, a few survivors straggle out of hiding. They recount the tragedy, and in an impotent gesture, Fools Crow tries to hearten them by reminding them, "We must think of our children." In the next moment, he realizes the ultimate tragedy: "They had no children."

The tragedies that have befallen the Pikunis are mitigated by the coming of spring and the hope for continuance and survival reenacted in the timeless cycles of the earth. The Lone Eaters ceremonialize spring with worship, prayer, and dance. The baby boy of Fools Crow and Red Shield has been born; Mik-api will soon hand the Thunder Pipe over to the next generation of healers, quite possibly to Fools Crow; the rains come to water the earth; and somewhere in the midst of a devastating immediate past and a doubtful future, the present seems "as it should be." (Allen 1986; Ballard 1991; Barry 1991–1992; Bovey 1991; Murphree 1994; Owens 1992a; Robbins 1990; Sands 1987; Welch 1986)

See also Fast Horse; Heavy Runner; Heavy Shield Woman; Kills-close-to-the-lake; Mik-api; Owl Child; Red Paint; Rides-at-the-door; Running Fisher; Three Bears; Welch, James; White Man's Dog; Yellow Kidney.

Forest, Nancy

Nancy Forest is the protagonist of John Milton Oskison's *Wild Harvest* (1925). After the death of her mother and the inability of her father to manage the family homestead in Indian Territory, Nan becomes the mainstay of her family. Her father is more interested in reading dime novels than he is in farming the land, and Nan must remind him to do his chores. The role-reversal allows Nan to become the focus of the novel, and her father's inefficacy provides the motivation for the plot development. When her father is arrested for a murder in Texas, Nan takes over the responsibility of the farm in order to raise the money to pay for his lawyer and provide for their needs in his absence. She abandons her desire for an education in St. Louis and her dream to become a professional elocutionist. She is wise far beyond her mere 15 years, and she soon gathers the respect of the entire community for her capabilities. She also gains the attentions of several young men in the area—Tom Winger, Jack Hayes, and Harvey Stokes. Her early romance with Tom turns sour when Ruby Engel schemes against them. In the course of time, she is courted by Harvey Stokes and eventually consents to marry him. At the time, she feels she is in love with him, but later realizes that Stokes's attractiveness is the result of his kindly intentions toward her father. Stokes has promised to put Chester Forest in charge of his haying machinery business. Nan feels that her responsibility for her father is being shared by capable hands. But the longer they are engaged, the more jealous and possessive he becomes. It is only when Tom Winger is shot by Jack's brother Buster Hayes while he is attempting to protect Stokes from revenge that Nan realizes the essential character of each of her suitors. Nan then breaks her engagement with Stokes.

Sometime later, at a Christmas Eve program at the local schoolhouse where Nan now teaches, Harvey Stokes comes to claim her. When she refuses him again, he tries to shoot her. Nan is only grazed, but in the ensuing fight over the gun, Stokes is accidentally shot and killed by Tom Winger.

Nan marries Tom Winger, and in a gesture that echoes a thematic concern of the novel, "their impulsive, fervent kiss sealed their dedication to the land they loved." (Oskison 1925)

See also Davis, Sam; Dines, Billy and Susan; Engel, Ruby; Stokes, Harvey; *Wild Harvest*; Winger, Tom.

Forrest, Will

Will Forrest is an unfortunate young man who falls in love with Nola Blanket in Linda Hogan's *Mean Spirit* (1990). He is unfortunate in that he truly loves Nola, but his father disapproves. Not only does the elder Forrest disapprove, but he is involved in the schemes to strip the Indians of their oil riches. Will marries Nola, but because of his father's actions, Nola is distrustful of him. Their marriage ends tragically when Nola shoots and kills Will. (Hogan 1990)

See also Blanket, Nola; Graycloud, Belle; *Mean Spirit.*

49
See Geiogamah, Hanay.

Francisco
Francisco is the grandfather of Abel, the protagonist in N. Scott Momaday's *House Made of Dawn* (1968). After the death of Abel's mother and brother, Francisco raises him. An old man in the novel, Francisco is the illegitimate child of the former parish priest, Nicolas. Francisco puts on the habiliments of Catholicism but does not live a life of purity and devotion so as to satisfy the old priest, Fray Nicolas, or the priest that follows, Father Olguin. Francisco is one of the townspeople of whom the narrator speaks when he says, "they still pray in Tanoan to the old deities of the earth and sky and make their living from the things that are and have always been within their reach. . . . They have assumed the names and gestures of their enemies, but have held on to their own, secret souls. . . ." In his journal, Fray Nicolas writes of Francisco,

"He is evil. . . . He is one of them & goes often in the kiva & puts on their horns & hides & does worship that Serpent which even is the One our most ancient enemy."

It is his rootedness in his own culture that makes Francisco the moral compass of the novel. He has taken part in the ceremonial races of the past; "twice or three times, perhaps," he has played the part of the bull in the Pecos bull ceremony. He is aware of the rhythms of the sun and the earth; he is conscious of spiritual evil when it surrounds him. One day, as Francisco is hoeing corn, he is "suddenly conscious of some alien presence close at hand." He finishes his work, blesses the corn, and leaves the field. He is followed out of the field by the "nearly sightless eyes" of the albino who has been watching him throughout the day. Francisco's response to the presence of evil is quite different from Abel's, who, when confronted with the albino, kills him.

In the end, however, Francisco helps Abel come to a spiritual wholeness. On his deathbed, for six straight mornings, he rises up to speak. He speaks "six times in the dawn, and the voice of his memory was whole and clear and growing like the dawn." By the seventh dawn he has died, but his gift of story and memory moves Abel to psychic and spiritual health. (Lincoln 1983; Momaday 1968; Owens 1992a; Wiget 1985)

See also Abel; The Albino; Father Olguin; *House Made of Dawn.*

G

Geiogamah, Hanay

Born in Lawton, Oklahoma, in 1945, Hanay Geiogamah (Kiowa-Delaware) is the foremost Native American dramatist. His best-known plays, *Body Indian*, *49*, and *Foghorn,* have been collected in *New Native American Drama: Three Plays.*

Geiogamah holds a bachelor's degree in theater and drama from Indiana University and has been active throughout his career in the theater. In 1972, he began the Native American Theatre Ensemble (NATE), an all-Indian acting troupe. The first play the troupe performed was Geiogamah's *Body Indian* in New York at La Mama Experimental Theater Club. Geiogamah has also served as artistic director of the American Indian Dance Theatre, which he cofounded. His contributions to the theater are matched by his contributions to academic life. He has taught at Colorado College and the University of California at Los Angeles and has been managing editor of the *American Indian Culture and Research Journal.*

Geiogamah's *Body Indian* is a moving drama that centers around the character Bobby Lee and his friends. The action opens on the day Bobby receives the lease money from his allotment of land. He intends to use the money to enter an alcohol rehabilitation program but loses it at the hands of his friends. All of the characters in the apartment Bobby visits are drinking or drunk, and in the course of the evening, all of them steal from Bobby. By the end of the play, he has no money left, and even his artificial leg has been pawned for alcohol. The play is about more than alcohol abuse and its devastating effect on the Native American community, however; it is also about the necessity of community members providing support for each other in the face of a hostile external world. When the internal community fails, the individual is alone indeed.

Foghorn, the second play in the collection, takes its title from the foghorns that blasted the Indians who occupied Alcatraz in 1969. The play is a collection of scenes, all of which sound a note of warning to Native Americans that their identity has been shaped and defined by others whose purposes are thoroughly self-serving. Though the play makes a strong political point (over and over again), the message is illuminating rather than quarrelsome. In his "Author's Notes" to the play, Geiogamah calls for "playful mockery rather than bitter denunciation."

The third play in the collection, *49*, was first performed by the Native American Theater Ensemble at Oklahoma City University in 1975. The play takes its title, primary setting, and action from the 49 celebrations that follow powwows, Indian fairs, or tribal celebrations. Geiogamah explains,

Forty-nines always take place at night; really good ones go on until sunrise and after. More young people are involved than older ones, and thus the scene is charged with the energy of hundreds of youths.

Forty-nines feature the activities of most social events—singing, drinking, and sexual flirtations.

The central character of the play is Night Walker, a shaman who has spiritual powers over time and place, and who thus connects the past (circa 1885) and present settings of the play. Amid the threatening presence of sadistic policemen who are determined to break up the 49, Night Walker speaks to the young people: "You must lead our clan / To a time of understanding / When a man will not hurt a man / By killing his way of living."

Weaving Woman also instructs the young people, encouraging them to create beauty. A young girl tells Weaving Woman that ways are changing, that they cannot design blankets when they have no sheep to grow wool. Weaving Woman replies, "A design can live and grow for many years before it is placed on the loom. You can always see it . . . when you close your eyes."

Anthropologist Alice C. Fletcher, far left, served as a special allotting agent on the Nez Perce Reservation in Idaho, 1890–1893. (Idaho State Historical Society #63-221.24)

When the police force a conflict at the end, the young people "form an elaborate barricade with their bodies" and stand peacefully and respectfully. Night Walker recognizes that his message of pride and solidarity has taken hold, and he praises the gesture of the young people by saying, "A beautiful bird is flying!" (Geiogamah 1980; Huntsman 1980; Johnson 1994; Ruoff 1990)

The General Allotment Act (Dawes Act) of 1887

The General Allotment Act, commonly known as the Dawes Act after its sponsor Senator Henry Dawes of Massachusetts, was enacted on February 8, 1887, in response to demands that Indian reservations be allotted in severalty to individual Indians and that tribal relations be broken. Each head of a family would receive one-quarter of a section (160 acres), and all other persons over the age of 18 would receive one-eighth of a section (80 acres).

The purpose of the act was to "civilize" the Indians by making them farmers rather than hunters and to allow parcels of reservation land to be sold by individual owners. Once the tribe no longer held ownership of the land, it was far easier for land-hungry settlers to gain access to the land. Generally, the Dawes Act was disastrous for the Indians. The dissolution of tribally owned lands contributed to the erosion of tribal values and the loss of much land. (Hoxie 1996; Prucha 1990)

General G.

A character in Leslie Marmon Silko's *Almanac of the Dead* (1991), General G. performs official military duties along the border for the Mexican army. He also works as the head of security for Universal Insurance Corporation and does consultant work for the Guatemalan government. Furthermore, he has connections with the CIA.

He is fully aware of the explosive political situation in Mexico and says, "No one can be trusted. A great storm is gathering on the south-

INDIAN LAND FOR SALE

GET A HOME
OF
YOUR OWN
❁
EASY PAYMENTS

PERFECT TITLE
❁
POSSESSION
WITHIN
THIRTY DAYS

FINE LANDS IN THE WEST

IRRIGATED
IRRIGABLE
GRAZING
AGRICULTURAL
DRY FARMING

In 1910 the Department of the Interior Sold Under Sealed Bids Allotted Indian Land as Follows:

Location.	Acres.	Average Price per Acre.	Location.	Acres.	Average Price per Acre.
Colorado	5,211.21	$7.27	Oklahoma	34,664.00	$19.14
Idaho	17,013.00	24.85	Oregon	1,020.00	15.43
Kansas	1,684.50	33.45	South Dakota	120,445.00	16.53
Montana	11,034.00	9.86	Washington	4,879.00	41.37
Nebraska	5,641.00	36.65	Wisconsin	1,069.00	17.00
North Dakota	22,610.70	9.93	Wyoming	865.00	20.64

FOR THE YEAR 1911 IT IS ESTIMATED THAT 350,000 ACRES WILL BE OFFERED FOR SALE

For information as to the character of the land write for booklet, "INDIAN LANDS FOR SALE," to the Superintendent U. S. Indian School at any one of the following places:

CALIFORNIA: MINNESOTA: NORTH DAKOTA: OKLAHOMA—Con.   SOUTH DAKOTA: WASHINGTON:
Hoopa.   Onigum.   Fort Totten.   Sac and Fox Agency.   Cheyenne Agency.   Fort Simcoe.
COLORADO: Fort Yates.   Shawnee.   Crow Creek.   Fort Spokane.
Ignacio.   MONTANA: OKLAHOMA: Wyandotte.   Greenwood.   Tokoa.
IDAHO: Crow Agency.   Anadarko.   Lower Brule.   Tulalip.
Lapwai.   NEBRASKA: Cantonment.   OREGON: Pine Ridge.
KANSAS: Macy.   Colony.   Klamath Agency.   Rosebud.   WISCONSIN:
Horton.   Santee.   Burlington.   Pendleton.   Sisseton.   Oneida.
Nadeau.   Winnebago.   Muskogee.   Roseburg.
Pawnee.   Siletz.

WALTER L. FISHER,
Secretary of the Interior.

ROBERT G. VALENTINE,
Commissioner of Indian Affairs.

Not Afraid of Pawnee, a Yankton Sioux, on an advertisement by the U.S. Department of the Interior offering surplus lands for sale in 1910–1911. (Library of Congress, #USZ62-812911)

ern horizon." He resents Marxists in the government and the military, and he calls Indians "savages." (Silko 1991)

See also *Almanac of the Dead*; La Escapia, Angelita; Menardo.

George, Ida

In Michael Dorris's *A Yellow Raft in Blue Water* (1987), Aunt Ida is a formidable character who does not become understandable until the third section of the novel, when she is given a narrative voice. She has suffered misunderstanding for two generations but gives every indication that she will share her story not only with the reader but with Rayona, her granddaughter.

Ida begins her narrative with the cryptic announcement, "I never grew up, but I got old." As her story unfolds from her teenage years forward, the mystery is revealed. When Ida is 18, her mother grows dangerously ill, and her mother's younger sister comes to their home to

help. Her Aunt Clara is close to her own age, and immediately Ida idolizes her young aunt and feels an emotional connection to her. She even reveals to Clara her secret romantic longing for the most popular young man on the reservation, Willard Pretty Dog.

Clara has not only won the devotion of Ida, but of Ida's father as well. The two become involved, and soon Clara is pregnant. In order to save face in the community, her father very selfishly asks Ida to say the baby is hers and that the father is Willard Pretty Dog. Ida acknowledges later: "'Yes,' I said, when I should have said no." But she does agree to the plan, and she and Clara go to a convent in Denver. There Ida becomes a scrub girl to pay for her board, while Clara is pampered. The nuns are certain that Clara has been raped, and they pour all of their attention on her. Clara gladly accepts victim status, basks in their attention, and even agrees to give the baby away. It is only through Ida's intervention that the baby is not put up for adoption.

When Ida returns to the reservation with the baby that the nuns named Christine, the burden of her complicity in the scheme doubles. Not only does Ida suffer the disapproval of the community, but Clara now threatens to take the baby away. Father Hurlburt is sympathetic to Ida and helps her get a birth certificate to prove that she is Christine's mother. Though the document now protects Ida's claim to the child, she still worries that Clara will return and try to "steal Christine back." Ida insists that Christine call her Aunt Ida, fearful that any real acknowledgment would be tempting fate. All the time that Christine is growing up, she believes that Ida loves her too little, never realizing that Ida holds her at a distance because she loves her so much.

Time passes; Ida's mother dies, and her father has "run off somewhere in his shame." The threat that Clara poses to Christine diminishes, and Ida starts to make a life for herself. She manages her money wisely and makes improvements to her property. Her only true friend is Father Hurlburt, and they establish a Thursday night visit that is a personal salvation to both. When Ida hears that Willard Pretty Dog has returned from World War II with severe injuries and damaged self-esteem, it is Father Hurlburt who arranges a meeting between the two.

Willard comes over for dinner, and the two recognize a kinship in their brokenness. Ida tells him the story of her life. She correctly senses that "unhappiness was the only thing that Willard valued, and as I admitted mine, I put myself in his broken hands." That night they become lovers, but Ida makes the mistake of protecting Willard's self-esteem at the risk of her own. Ida is smarter than Willard, but she never corrects him or asks him a question she thinks he can't answer. She pampers him and pumps up his sagging ego. Meanwhile, Willard is having reconstructive surgeries, and when he emerges from his final surgery looking handsome again, his mother encourages him to leave Ida and find someone more appropriate. Willard responds, "Ida may not be beautiful. She may not be very smart. But when no one else cared for me, she was there." Ida immediately cuts off the relationship, unwilling to accept his dutiful love and unwilling to walk into a constructed lie and be forever bound by its merciless demands.

For all the absences in her relationship with Christine, Ida makes sure that Christine always knows and values her intellect. She says, "I wanted her to see me smart, to know she could be that way herself in front of any man."

When Ida gives birth to Willard's son, she names him Lee and raises him as if he and Christine were brother and sister. Lee too calls her "Aunt Ida," and neither he nor Christine ever learn the secrets of their origins. (Dorris 1987; Owens 1992a)

> See also Clara; Father Hurlburt; George, Lee; Pretty Dog, Willard; Taylor, Christine; Taylor, Rayona; *A Yellow Raft in Blue Water*.

Drawing in charcoal of Wovoka "Jack Wilson" on 1 January 1892. (Nevada State Museum)

commits adultery with his wife's sister, Clara, and then asks his own daughter to accept responsibility for the child they have made, who is later named Christine. His attempt to save face, no matter what the cost to others, backfires, for after Clara and Ida go to Denver to wait out the pregnancy there, Lecon and his wife fight constantly. His "fear of scorn and disappointment lost its power" over Lecon, and his behaviors become unguarded. He finally dies in Minot in an accident after leading a prodigal life there. Ida says of him, "He existed without boundaries, and I never again met, even for an hour, the man who raised me." When her son is born years later, she dutifully names him after Lecon but calls him Lee to establish some distance from her disappointing father. (Dorris 1987)

> See also Clara; George, Ida; George, Lee; *A Yellow Raft in Blue Water*.

George, Lecon

Lecon George is the scoundrel father of Ida George in Michael Dorris's *A Yellow Raft in Blue Water* (1987). He breaks the family when he

George, Lee

In Michael Dorris's *A Yellow Raft in Blue Water* (1987), Lee George is the brother of Christine

Taylor. Unlike Christine, he is the biological child of Ida, but he too calls her Aunt Ida. He is never told that Willard Pretty Dog is his father, and the only thing he gets from Pretty Dog is his good looks.

From his childhood on, Lee is a favorite on the reservation. He "spoke the old language with the grandmothers and had clean English for his teachers in school." He hoop-dances at pow-wows and wins "Best Newcomer." His easy grace and respect for his culture earn him the nickname "the Indian JFK." But in his role as public idol, many people lay a claim to him, especially his sister Christine. By his teenage years, he and his best friend, Dayton Nickles, are talking of Red Power, and Lee tells Christine that he is "not going to fight a white man's war."

Christine insists that "the only way people around here are going to have an ounce of respect for Lee is if he serves his country." Lee succumbs to Christine's pressure and cuts his braid and enlists in the army. He is sent to Vietnam and is soon missing in action. The next report on Lee announces that he is dead. (Dorris 1987)

See also George, Ida; Nickles, Dayton; Pretty Dog, Willard; Taylor, Christine; Taylor, Elgin; Taylor, Rayona; *A Yellow Raft in Blue Water*.

The Ghost Dance

The Ghost Dance movement swept the western plains during the late nineteenth century. The movement reached its moment of greatest intensity in 1889 when Wovoka, a Paiute, experienced a vision of restoration for the Indian people. Black Elk explains Wovoka's vision of a new world coming:

> It would come in a whirlwind out of the west and would crush out everything on this world, which was old and dying. In that other world there was plenty of meat, just like old times; and in that world all the dead Indians were alive, and all the bison that had ever been killed were roaming around again.

Mass burial of Lakota Indians after the slaughter at Wounded Knee in South Dakota, 1 January 1891. (Nebraska State Historical Society)

The vision came at a critical time for the Plains Indians, especially. The U.S. government, intent on opening the West for settlement and squashing any Indian resistance with military force, was quickly destroying any opportunity for the Indians to live in their traditional ways. The attractiveness of Wovoka's vision was compelling, and he gained many zealous followers.

The Ghost Dance, with its revival of pride and hope for the disillusioned Indians, tragically led to the massacre at Wounded Knee in 1890. The government grew edgy at the reports of Indians dancing to bring back their ancestors. The dancers wore "Ghost Dance shirts" that they believed would protect them from harm. However, the shirts proved ineffective against the bullets of the federal soldiers on December 29, 1890, when over 200 Lakota men, women, and children were killed. (Hittman 1996; Neihardt 1932, 1988)

See also *Black Elk Speaks.*

Glancy, Diane

Diane Glancy is a contemporary poet, novelist, essayist, playwright, and professor of literature. She was born in Kansas City, Missouri, in

Diane Glancy, 1998. (Jim Turnure)

1941 to a working-class family and moved about quite a bit as a child. She earned a bachelor's degree from the University of Missouri in 1964, a master of arts degree from University of Central Oklahoma in 1983, and a master of fine arts degree from the University of Iowa Writer's Workshop in 1988. She presently teaches at Macalester College in St. Paul, Minnesota. Glancy has worked as artist-in-residence for the states of Oklahoma and Arkansas. She served as the poet laureate for the Five Civilized Tribes from 1984 to 1986.

Glancy's work is often controlled by the image of being split: she says, "I have the feeling of being split between two cultures, not fully belonging to either one." Her father's part-Cherokee heritage and her mother's German-English heritage add to this feeling, perhaps best defined in her phrase, "I'm a cultural bridge."

Language is the mediator for Glancy between her two cultures. Even as a child she recognized her "hunger for words," and she now acknowledges that "poetry is the medicine bundle I carry. Not a pouch around my neck on a cord, but a feeling within." While language mediates between her two cultures, it is her Christian faith that provides the bedrock of her existence. Still, the connection between language and religion is strong. She says, "I think I am a Christian because of the words in the Bible. The sturdiness of them."

Glancy has published several volumes of poetry, including *One Age in a Dream* (1986), *Offering* (1988), *Iron Women* (1990), and *Lone Dog's Winter Count* (1991). Her nonfiction work includes *Claiming Breath* (1992) and *The West Pole* (1997); her works of fiction are *Trigger Dance* (1990) and *Firesticks* (1993). (*Contemporary Authors* 1992a, vol. 136; Glancy 1987; Glancy 1992; Glancy 1996; Witalec 1995)

See also *Claiming Breath.*

Gold, Jess

Jess Gold is the sheriff in Linda Hogan's *Mean Spirit* (1990). He is a part of the conspiracies to rob the Indian people of their oil riches, and he will not stop even at murder. He is directly responsible for the murder of his Indian deputy, Willis, and is implicated in the hanging death of Benoit. His schemes are long-term and patient. Gold is responsible for the lengthy stay of Benoit in jail; while Benoit is thus out of the way, Gold starts to court Benoit's lover, Lettie Graycloud. Gold then arranges for Benoit to leave the jail for one night to marry Lettie. When Benoit is found hanged in his cell the next day, Gold is one step closer to the great riches that have come from Grace Blanket to her sister Sara and then to Sara's husband, Benoit.

Gold also learns of the oil that has been discovered on Belle Graycloud's land, and he tries to murder her. Her hive of bees is stirred up in the process, and Gold is stung to death in an act of poetic justice. Belle survives the bullet from Gold's gun when it glances off a meteorite pendant she wears around her neck. (Hogan 1990)

See also Benoit; Blanket, Grace; Blanket, Sara; Graycloud, Belle; Graycloud, Lettie; *Mean Spirit.*

Grand Avenue: A Novel in Stories

Grand Avenue (1994) is the first novel of Pomo writer Greg Sarris. Largely told by several first-person female narrators, the collection of stories spans four generations of two branches of a family that have been ruptured by distrust and suspicion. Sarris opens his volume with a story narrated by Jasmine, a young girl, "thirty pounds too big and even more dull-faced than [her] mother." The last story is told by an old woman, Nellie, a basket-weaver and healer. She is approached by a young relative from the estranged side of the family who wants to learn to weave baskets. Nellie teaches her eager student but is also compelled to tell stories as she works. She begs Alice to talk as well: "Talk. It's important to talk. . . . We got to get it out. The true stories can help us."

Sarris's volume is a collection of the "true stories" that "can help us." Between the stories of Jasmine and Nellie are generations of voices, of tangled stories all pouring forth from the

cousins who live together on Grand Avenue, an "in-town reservation." The characters are all descended from a matriarch, Juana Maria, and her two children, Juana and Maria. Were it not for the genealogy sketched out at the beginning of the book, the tangled relationships would be exceedingly difficult to unravel. Furthermore, Sarris has a narrow narrative register, and it is often difficult to discern one voice from another. Though his attempt at first-person female narrative is admirable, Sarris is strongest when using the voice of men. He is most effective with the voice of Steven Pen in the story "Secret Letters." Pen fathers a child when he is young but does not help raise the boy. When he finally meets his 11-year-old son, Steven does not confirm their relationship but is reluctant to let Tony out of his life again. Thus begins an artful dance of crossing paths that ends with charges of molestation and, finally, reconciliation.

Grand Avenue is concerned with jealousies over love, healing songs, and the power to "poison"; with revelations about absent mothers and fathers; with coming of age; and with race relations. In "The Magic Pony," Ruby, who lives with her "half-cracked" mother, is just as doomed as the foundered pony she tries to save from the slaughterhouse. Ruby burns the slaughterhouse barn in her final attempt to rescue the pony, and the story ends with the young girl being taken to "juve." Ruby tells her cousin Jasmine that the pony is safe: "He's free. He flew away." When Ruby is seen next, she is in a "tight red dress," "with lipstick and done-up hair," living on the fringes of prostitution.

"The Progress of This Disease" is narrated by Anna Silva and tells the story of her 14-year-old daughter's slow death by cancer. The extended family in the story seems obsessed with the workings of "poison" and the mystery surrounding Aunt Sipie's death. "Slaughterhouse," a coming-of-age story narrated by Frankie, refracts the same theme as did "The Magic Pony": a sensitive young character empathizes with a doomed character but is unable to save her. Here, Frankie is challenged by his teenage friends to enter the slaughterhouse and see what goes on there. In the hours before the requisite darkness, Frankie visits the object of his adolescent crush, Ruby. With his awkward eagerness, Frankie gets his hand caught in Ruby's blouse, and she pushes him away angrily, saying: "It's no use. You're like all the rest. It's all the same. Mama's right." Hours later when Frankie enters the slaughterhouse and sees the very adult gathering in which Ruby is wobbling "like she was just learning how to walk or had had too much of Smoke's wine," Frankie feels "dead inside." He considers rescuing Ruby but reasons, "it was no use. Things was bigger than me."

In "Waiting for the Green Frog," Nellie Copaz tells how she was given the power of singing and healing by a green frog: "One day a song hit me, just as if someone hit me with a stick, on the side of my neck. And the pain spread until it was singing in my throat. That was my first song."

The next story, "Joy Ride," is narrated by Anna's husband, Albert Silva. It is a story of passages, of emotional markers that shape his life: his first sexual experience, the death of his brother in Vietnam, the suicide of his father, and the revelation that his mother was black.

In "How I Got to Be Queen," a mother's neglect and a sibling rivalry set the stage for the story. Alice and her sister, Justine, are left in charge of their two young brothers while their mother works at a canning factory and parties afterward. Justine escapes the drudgery, flirts with danger, and leaves Alice to take care of the household. When Justine provokes a neighbor girl, the situation threatens to turn ugly; a mob gathers outside their house, and Alice breaks it up with a gunshot into the air. Alice gains the respect of the crowd: "Alice you're the queen now. Nobody's going to mess with you, girl."

"Sam Toms's Last Song" is a third-person narrative that opens on the one-hundredth birthday of Sam Toms. The consuming problem of his old age is finding someone who will take care of him. He lives for a time with his great-grandson, Ernesto, from whom he steals crack cocaine in order to pay for his hot meals and laundry. When the two are busted, Toms moves in with his great-granddaughter, Linda. He soon grows tired of her and decides to move in with Nellie, "a distant cousin of some sort who lived just up the street." He goes uninvited to Nellie's house with his suitcase and some money, determined to move in. He puts some money in her basket, and when she asks, "What else you got, old Indian man?" he sings every song he knows. Nellie is a rival healer to Sam Toms, and she catches his songs in her basket and takes them from him. She returns his money, calls a cab, and sends him home to Linda.

"The Indian Maid" is the story of Zelda, a young Indian girl trained at the Sherman Indian School to be a maid. In her first job out of school, she is humiliated by a woman she cares for, and she leaves the position, taking with her an opal ring as exchange for the abasement she has borne. When Zelda finally gets back to the reservation, she "slept and dreamed like never before." She never reveals the dream to her children but tantalizes them with its possibilities. The focus of the story shifts from Zelda to Stella, her youngest daughter, who must balance the legacy of the dream and the ring with a newfound knowledge of her mother.

The volume ends with "The Water Place," a story that resolves many of the novel's antagonisms. The offspring of Juana and Maria have been hostile for generations, but healing begins here when Alice comes to learn basket-weaving from Nellie. Alice introduces herself in the old-time way: "Alice. My mother is Mollie. Mollie *Goode*. Her mother was Sipie *Toms*." Nellie serves Alice cookies and milk and is surprised when the girl accepts them from a "suspected poisoner." In gratitude for the acceptance, Nellie helps Alice with her problem—the unhappiness in her home. This leads not only to the happiness of Alice's mother Mollie but also to the easing racial tensions in the neighborhood and the passing of the healing gift of song to Alice.

Grand Avenue has been adapted into an HBO movie that aired in 1996. Sarris wrote the movie script and served as co–executive producer. (Sarris 1994; Schneider 1996)

The Grass Dancer

The Grass Dancer (1994) by Susan Power won the PEN/Hemingway Award for first fiction and was a national best-seller. The novel has its chronological roots in the story of Red Dress and Ghost Horse, mid-nineteenth-century Sioux lovers who are separated by her premature death. The primary narrative, however, is the story of two women, Anna (Mercury) Thunder and Jeannette McVay, and their equally dangerous approaches to understanding traditional Dakota culture. Jeannette McVay is a white anthropology student who comes to the reservation to "record the funeral" of the Siouan culture. Anna Thunder is a Dakota woman who misuses her inherited powers, motivated by a complicated dual desire for revenge and to correct white ethnocentric anthropological assumptions. Both women set into motion events that have a lasting effect on at least two generations of the Wind Soldier and Thunder families. In her determination to "close the unhappy circle" of the love between Red Dress, her ancestor, and Ghost Horse, the ancestor of Calvin Wind Soldier, Anna claims Calvin as her lover. Calvin is happily married, though, and resists her advances. Anna Thunder then works a spell on Wind Soldier and Evelyn Many Wounds, the sister of his wife, until they are involved in an adulterous affair and produce a son, Duane. Jeannette McVay, too, is complicit in the larger design. She has been cheating on her lover, and one night he leaves a bar in a drunken rage and is responsible for the vehicular deaths of Calvin and Duane Wind Soldier.

When Jeannette McVay first comes to the reservation, she stays for a time in the home of Anna Thunder, and her eagerness to hear Anna's stories drives a further wedge between Anna and her daughter Crystal. Though she solicits Anna's stories, she is unable to believe them on a literal level; she makes the mistake of hearing the stories as superstition and dreams. It is not until Anna causes the adultery between Calvin and Evelyn that the truth of her power dawns on Jeannette. Frightened by Anna's power, Jeannette leaves her home the next day. Anna secretly punishes her by sprinkling "loose reservation soil" in her loafers so that Jeannette will "find herself incapable of leaving the reservation."

The troubles that Anna Thunder and Jeannette McVay set into motion in one generation continue to work their slow poison in the next. Harley Wind Soldier is the posthumous son of Calvin Wind Soldier, and his life is shaped by the absence of his father and the silence of his mother. Lydia Wind Soldier believes that she is responsible for the death of her husband and his son because she uttered harsh words as they left the house before their fatal drive. She vows never to speak again, and her son Harley is born into a silence and emptiness that define him as negative space.

When Crystal Thunder escapes from her mother by getting pregnant and marrying a white man, Anna demands "a soul for a soul," and whisks Crystal's child away from her. She raises Charlene as compensation for the loss of Crystal, and as Anna falls deeper and deeper into the lure of her powers, Charlene's life grows more and more unbearable.

It takes a visit from the spirit of Red Dress to both Harley and Charlene to reestablish balance in their lives. Charlene is also helped by Jeannette McVay, who tells her who and where her mother is. Charlene leaves the reservation, hoping that the power of her grandmother is "like a television signal: fading at a distance, dribbling away to nothing." (Dorris 1994; Niemann 1995; Power 1994)

See also Father La Frambois; Lundstrom, Crystal Thunder; Lundstrom, Martin; Many Wounds, Evelyn; Many Wounds, Margaret; McVay, Jeannette; Pumpkin; Red Dress; Reverend Pyke; Small War, Herod; Thunder, Anna (Mercury); Thunder, Charlene; Wind Soldier, Calvin; Wind Soldier, Harley; Wind Soldier, Lydia.

Graycloud, Belle

Belle Graycloud is a major character in Linda Hogan's *Mean Spirit* (1990). She is the strong spiritual and maternal figure who holds the community together in the time of crisis. Belle wears a meteorite on a leather thong around her neck, a gift from Osage Star-Looking that is her prized possession. The meteorite holds talismanic properties for Belle but also saves her life when, in the height of the oil wars, she is the object of attempted murder. The meteorite deflects the bullet, and Belle lives.

Belle is slight of stature but is "a giant on the inside, and hard to reckon with." On at least two occasions, Belle's values conflict with white society, but she stands firm in her beliefs. On a trip to town to sell eggs, Belle notices a truck filled with the bodies of golden eagles. Eagle hunters have killed 317 eagles to sell to "taxidermy shops in New York, London, and Philadelphia." Belle sees the eagles as "a tribe of small, gone people, murdered and taken away," and she flies into a rage against the hunters and is arrested. In another instance, when the sheriff tries to kill the bats in Sorrow Cave, Belle guards the entrance and protects the bats, which are sacred to the Osage. Sheriff Jess Gold tells her, "You can't go losing your head over every bird and snake"; he continues to chastise her, saying, "Violence never solved anything." Belle's response reveals a sad truth: "You're wrong about that. Around here violence solves everything."

Belle's militant resistance and the news that oil has just been discovered on her property make her the target of violence. One day while she is working with her bees, she is shot by the sheriff, Jess Gold; only her meteorite saves her life. In order to protect her, the Graycloud family pretends that she has indeed died. They stage a funeral and then send her to safety with the Hill Indians. (Hogan 1990)

See also Benoit; Blanket, Grace; Gold, Jess; Graycloud, Floyd; Graycloud, Lettie; Graycloud, Louise; Graycloud, Moses; *Mean Spirit*; Stink, John.

Graycloud, Floyd

In Linda Hogan's *Mean Spirit* (1990), Floyd Graycloud is the son-in-law of Moses and Belle Graycloud, a white man who is so attracted to Indian ways that he takes the Graycloud name upon his marriage to Louise. He makes his money as a moonshiner and always remains on the fringes of full acceptance by the commu-

nity. At one point, even Lettie, his sister-in-law, and Belle wonder if Floyd is involved in the murders. He earns some respect when he faithfully fulfills his promise to take care of John Stink's dogs when Stink, a tribal elder, is believed dead. (Hogan 1990)

See also Graycloud, Belle; Graycloud, Lettie; Graycloud, Louise; Graycloud, Moses; *Mean Spirit*; Stink, John.

Graycloud, Lettie

Lettie Graycloud is the daughter of Moses and Belle Graycloud, the Indian couple who provide the spiritual center of Linda Hogan's *Mean Spirit* (1990). She is the lover of Benoit, who is falsely arrested for the murder of his wife, Sara Blanket. When Benoit is jailed by the sheriff, Jess Gold, Lettie becomes the object of Gold's attentions. It becomes evident that Gold is using Benoit and Lettie to get to their money. He allows Benoit to leave jail for one night so that he and Lettie can marry. The next day, Benoit is found dead in his cell, and Lettie, as heir to Benoit's wealth, is all the more attractive to Gold.

After Sara's murder and Benoit's arrest, Lettie begins seeking spiritualists for answers. She uses her Ouija board and even travels to New Orleans to find a fortune-teller. She goes to a spiritual meeting held at Ona Neck's home and is told by Lionel Tall to dig in the center of Sara's cornfield, where she will find some clue. She finds very little there except a key to Floyd Graycloud's car, and she wonders if he is complicit in the murders.

She gradually moves through her pain and finds some measure of comfort in her friendship with Stacey Red Hawk. (Hogan 1990)

See also Benoit; Blanket, Sara; Gold; Jess; Graycloud, Belle; Graycloud, Floyd; Graycloud, Louise; Graycloud, Moses; *Mean Spirit*; Red Hawk, Stacey.

Graycloud, Louise

Louise Graycloud is a character in Linda Hogan's *Mean Spirit* (1990), the daughter of Moses and Belle Graycloud and the wife of

Floyd Graycloud. At the beginning of the novel, Louise rejects "everything Indian" and has said "'I love everything European.'" In this way, she does not fit the portrait of her very traditional Osage family. But when Belle and Moses are jailed for protecting the bats at Sorrow Cave, Louise comes to bail them out. She and her mother come to an understanding, and Louise confesses, "Mama, I am proud of you." (Hogan 1990)

See also Graycloud, Belle; Graycloud, Floyd; Graycloud, Lettie; Graycloud, Moses; *Mean Spirit*.

Graycloud, Moses

In Linda Hogan's *Mean Spirit* (1990), Moses Graycloud is a respected traditional Osage who advocates for the rights of his people. He, along with Michael Horse, writes letters to the president of the United States about the murders in Indian Territory. Though his wife, Belle, is more actively militant, Moses too is willing to take action. When Belle is nearly killed by Sheriff Jess Gold's bullet, Moses agrees to Stacey Red Hawk's plan to stage a funeral for Belle. And when John Tate kills his wife, the sister of Moses Graycloud, Moses avenges her death by killing Tate. His actions, and his family's wealth once oil is discovered on their land, endanger him and his family. Their only safety is to move to the settlement of the Hill Indians and disappear from the community of Watona. (Hogan 1990)

See also Gold, Jess; Graycloud, Belle; Horse, Michael; *Mean Spirit*; Red Hawk, Stacey; Tate, John; Tate, Ruth.

Grey

A main character in N. Scott Momaday's *The Ancient Child* (1989), Grey is the great-granddaughter of Kope'mah, the Kiowa medicine woman. She is Navajo from her mother's side of the family and maintains the integrity of both cultures in her life. She was raised in the Navajo world of her mother but travels to Oklahoma as a teenager to live with the people of her Kiowa father. There she is taken in by Kope'mah and is taught the ways of the medi-

cine woman. Grey lives deep within her own interior fantasy about Henry McCarty, better known as Billy the Kid. With an active imagination and a voracious reading habit, Grey manufactures a series of fantasies about herself and Billy the Kid; she becomes his lover, his confidante, his jailbreaker. The fantasies she engages in are preparatory to her powers as a medicine woman—or at least, they indicate the capability of Grey as a vehicle for medicine power.

The story of the novel is just as concerned with the growth of Grey as with that of Locke Setman. Grey's growth is more natural and less traumatic, though, for she is grounded in both the Navajo and Kiowa cultures. Early in the novel, Kope'mah whispers to Grey, "The bear is coming." The message is unconnected to anything that Grey has heard from Kope'mah, but that night she dreams of sleeping with a bear. With this message, Kope'mah sets into action the major plot machination of the novel—the coming of Set into his bear medicine. Grey will play an integral part in the healing of Set, and as she moves into her role as healer, she slowly leaves the fantasy world she has created around Billy the Kid. When Grey meets Set for the first time, she says, "The grandmother, Kope'mah, wants me to give you back your medicine. It belongs to you. You must not go without it." Before Set leaves for San Francisco, Grey hands him the bundle of bear medicine.

Grey continues to grow in her medicine powers even after the death of Kope'mah. She visits the grave of Kope'mah every day and learns from her spirit. Jessie and Milo Mottledmare, the couple who took her in when she arrived, recognize the transformation that is coming over Grey, and they treat her with quiet respect. Grey herself is aware that she is changing: "Her fantasies were still dear to her. But in fact she was aware that her destiny was singular and that she must accept certain very serious responsibilities."

She continues to sense the presence of the old grandmother; she wears the grandmother's moccasins, aprons, and shawls. In the grandmother's room, she makes masks and wears them; she puts on the power of the mask and feels it grow in her. All of these behaviors are positioning Grey for her most significant act, the healing of Set. With the help of the Mottledmares and Kope'mah's spirit, Grey prepares a healing ceremony for Set. Her own vision has now shifted from fantasies about Billy the Kid to Set. She sees a "man in confusion and pain, a man severely wounded in his intelligence, verging upon collapse, a man in danger of losing possession of himself." She sets her will to wait for his return, and it is her ceremony and strength of will that draw him inexplicably back to Oklahoma from San Francisco. From there, Grey takes Set to Lukachukai, her home in Navajo country. With her Navajo family, both Grey and Set grow into wholeness and health. They marry, and Grey is soon pregnant with their child. (Momaday 1989; Owens 1992a; Velie 1994)

See also *The Ancient Child*; Setman, Locke.

H

Hale, John

In Linda Hogan's *Mean Spirit* (1990), Hale is "a lanky white man" who's been a "rancher in Indian Territory for a number of years before he invested in the oil business. He was known as a friend to the Indians." Hale uses the reputation he has built to extort great wealth from the oil-rich Indians. The monstrosity of his deeds grows until he is the major player in the deaths of many Indians in the territory. In one instance, he runs an insurance scam on an older Indian named Walker. Walker owes Hale some money that he cannot repay, so Hale takes out an insurance policy on Walker and then collects soon after, when Walker shows up dead. In another scheme, Hale convinces his mistress, China, to marry John Stink so that he might get Stink's money. Because the white people don't know that Stink has been declared dead, Stink's death certificate foils Hale's plan.

Hale is finally charged with first-degree murder and pleads "not guilty." In the courtroom, "Hale sat tall, almost self-righteous; his circle of stolen money and power had built him far beyond human feeling and, it seemed, far above the law." The case ends in a mistrial, but the Osage Indians gather $20,000 to pay federal agents to conduct a private investigation. As soon as the mistrial is declared, Hale is again arrested by federal agents. As a result of this second trial, Hale is sent to prison. (Hogan 1990)

See also *Mean Spirit*; Red Hawk, Stacey; Stink, John.

Harjo, Joy

Joy Harjo is a Muskogee Creek poet, scriptwriter, editor, filmmaker, and musician. She was born in Tulsa, Oklahoma, in 1951, a premature birth. She says, "I was kept alive on a machine for the first few days of my life until I made a decision to live." She holds a bachelor's degree in creative writing from the University of New Mexico and a master of fine arts in creative writing from the University of Iowa; she has held several professorships and presently teaches at the University of New Mexico at Albuquerque. Harjo entered college as an art major but switched to writing because she found that writing "was taking on more magical qualities" than painting. She relates, "I could say more when I wrote. Soon it wasn't a choice. Poetry-speaking 'called me' in a sense. And I couldn't say no." She began writing around the age of 22 and says,

Each time I write I am in a different and wild place, and travel toward something I do not know the name of. Each poem is a jumping-off edge and I am not safe, but I take more risks and understand better now how to take them. . . . I could not live without writing and/or thinking about it.

Writing is the medium through which Harjo connects to and recovers her Creek background. For a long time she avoided confronting her Creek heritage because that intersection of self and history would mean the "acknowledgment of destruction." But it is that heritage that gives her poetry its "underlying psychic structure, within which is a wealth of memory." Indeed, she suggests that "the sheer weight of memory coupled with imagery" is what "constructs poems." She says there is an old Creek within her who "participates" in the making of her poetry. And so, she sees it as her responsibility to "keep these stories alive."

Harjo received early encouragement from Leslie Marmon Silko. "I realize more and more how much I owe her in the whole process and business and place of writing poetry," she says. "She was there for me from the beginning." Harjo takes seriously both her art and her teaching; perhaps it is her connection to the oral tradition that does not allow her to see a difference between the two. She tells her literature students that Native American literature is

part of who you are and part of you. This is not some foreign exotic literature, this is not something that is separate from you, but if you are living in this country, or even world, if you were born here, this *is* American literature, this is part of who you are.

Her books include *The Last Song* (1975); *What Moon Drove Me to This* (1980); *She Had Some Horses* (1983); *In Mad Love and War* (1990); *Secrets from the Center of the World* (1989), a book of prose poems with photographs by Stephen Strom; *The Woman Who Fell from the Sky* (1994); and the chapbook *Fishing* (1992).

Harjo lives in Albuquerque, New Mexico, and in addition to her teaching and writing,

she sings and plays saxophone with the band Poetic Justice. (Balassi, Crawford, and Eysturoy 1990; Coltelli 1990; Jaskoski 1989–1990; Swann and Krupat 1987)

See also *She Had Some Horses*; Silko, Leslie Marmon.

Harley

A character in Leslie Marmon Silko's *Ceremony* (1977, 1986), Harley spends most of his time drinking and riding around in beat-up trucks. He has not been able to make an appropriate adjustment after returning from World War II. He still nurses the memories of the times when he was empowered by the uniform of the United States Army. He joins with Leroy, Pinkie, and Emo in their drunken binges.

Though Harley is the best friend of Tayo, the main character, Harley nonetheless betrays him. Harley is dispatched by Emo to bring Tayo to the old uranium mine site for a final confrontation between the two. When Tayo escapes from Harley and Harley can't hand him over to Emo, Emo turns his violence on him. Harley is killed in a slow and ritualistic death that includes mutilations not unlike those forecast in the story of witchery told by Betonie, the Navajo medicine man. (Lincoln 1983; Owens 1992a; Silko 1977, 1986; Wiget 1985)

See also Betonie; *Ceremony*; Emo; Tayo.

Heavy Runner

In James Welch's *Fools Crow* (1986), Heavy Runner is the chief of a band of Blackfeet who are facing the same traumas that the Lone Eaters are encountering. In dealing with the encroaching whites, Heavy Runner takes the position that yielding to the demands of the United States Army is better than trying to avoid them or mounting an attack against them. In negotiations with the army, Heavy Runner capitulates to a number of their requests, even though others present are reluctant to do so. As the negotiations come to a close, Heavy Runner requests a written paper that states his allegiance with the whites in the event of conflict. The paper was "signed by General Alfred

H. Sully and dated 1 January 1870." The paper does little good, however, for it is Heavy Runner's band that is wiped out in the Battle of the Marias. Though he was carrying the piece of paper, Heavy Runner was one of the first killed. (Welch 1986)

See also *Fools Crow*; Rides-at-the-door; Three Bears.

Heavy Shield Woman

Heavy Shield Woman is a character in James Welch's *Fools Crow* (1986). She is the wife of Yellow Kidney and the mother of Red Paint, but she is a fully developed character in her own right. When her husband does not return from the Crow raid, she strengthens her children with her belief that their father will return. Then she makes a sacred vow to the Above Ones that she will yield herself to the arduous role of Sacred Vow Woman in the next Sun Dance ceremony if her husband is returned. Her vow is not one to be taken lightly, for the health of the camp rests on her successful completion of her duties. Three Bears reminds her of the gravity of her request: "If you are successful, the Pikunis will prosper and enjoy favor with the spirit world. If you fail, if you are not strong or virtuous enough, great harm will come to us."

Between the time Heavy Shield Woman makes her vow and the time she must enact the ceremony, Yellow Kidney does return. But he returns pockmarked and mutilated, with all of his former spirit painfully absent. The complexity of Heavy Shield Woman's character emerges, for she is understandably torn in her reaction to his return. On the one hand, she is happy that he is back, but on the other hand, these circumstances are too painful to deal with joyfully. After his return, Yellow Kidney and Heavy Shield Woman have a strained relationship; they no longer live together as man and wife. Heavy Shield Woman is no longer a partner to a respected warrior but becomes a mere caretaker of a broken and dispirited man.

She is equally torn concerning her vow to the Above Ones; as she relates to the council, "I made this vow in a time of great distress. My heart had fallen down, but I told my children

that their father would return to them. I don't know now if I believed it then." Heavy Shield Woman does fulfill her role as Sacred Vow Woman and serves her people well. The experience has taken its toll on her, though; "It's the same as giving birth," she says. "Someday I will appear as I was before, but I will always be different—in here." (Welch 1986)

See also *Fools Crow*; Red Paint; Three Bears; White Man's Dog; Yellow Kidney.

Helen Jean

Helen Jean is a character in Leslie Marmon Silko's *Ceremony* (1977, 1986) who seems to figure only tangentially in the plot but who metonymically represents a whole group of Indian women who get separated from their cultural moorings and are adrift in the world. She most strongly suggests Tayo's mother, Laura, whose story is not fleshed out in the novel. Helen Jean is a Ute Indian who leaves the reservation to make a living and escape the poverty there. In the environment of racial prejudice in Gallup, the only kind of job she can get is as a menial laborer. Living in the city and making ends meet are more difficult than she had imagined, and soon she finds herself in the trap of prostitution. Though she pities the returning Indian veterans who were respected in their uniforms but are once again second-class citizens, she cannot escape the pattern of being abused by them. She is picked up by Harley and Leroy and meets Tayo through them. He is moved by the pathos of her situation and is happy to see her get away from them by slipping off from the bar with another man and his buddies. Tayo realizes, however, that she goes to an uncertain situation in attaching herself to another group of drunken men. The scene reinforces the reader's awareness that Tayo is the appropriate agent of healing for the community.

The technique that Silko uses in interpolating the Helen Jean story into the novel illuminates the way the oral storytelling tradition works in the Laguna community. In the oral tradition, where the part stands for the whole and where a narrative can go straight by going in a circular pattern, the story of Helen Jean tells us about far more than just one character. (Coltelli 1990; Owens 1992a; Silko 1977, 1986)

See also *Ceremony*; Harley; Silko, Leslie Marmon; Tayo.

Henry, Gordon D., Jr.

An enrolled member of the White Earth Chippewa tribe, Gordon Henry was born in 1955 in Philadelphia, Pennsylvania. He earned a bachelor's degree from the University of Wisconsin at Parkside in 1980. His graduate degrees include a master of arts from Michigan State University and a doctoral degree from the University of North Dakota. From 1988 to 1992, Henry was an assistant professor at Ferris State University in Big Rapids, Michigan, and since 1993, he has been teaching at Michigan State University.

He stresses the importance of storytelling in his fiction writing, and his first novel, *The Light People* (1994), certainly validates that claim. The novel, which centers around a bizarre story of a

Gordon Henry, 1998. (Mary Anne Henry)

lost leg and employs multiple genres (essay, poetry, short story, myth, and even transcription of a court case), received positive reviews. Henry has also written other poems besides those in this book. (*Contemporary Authors,* Vol. 146, 1995a)

See also *The Light People.*

Hogan, Linda

Linda Hogan was born in Denver, Colorado, in 1947. Because her father was in the military, the family moved around, but she feels a connection to Oklahoma, where her Chickasaw family roots still exert a pull on her imagination and inform her identity. As a mixed-blood, Hogan has always felt the doubleness endemic to that situation. She says, "When I was a child, two lives lived in me." The split between her two cultures caused "a growing abyss" in Hogan, which she has tried to bridge and heal with her writing.

Hogan's childhood was not bookish; most of her activities as a child were "outdoors and were alone." Though she was not an avid reader, she felt the need for language to express what she was feeling. She explains, "I had a lot of feeling but I did not have the language for putting anything into words. I could not put my feelings or emotions into any kind of words or context." Poetry became the medium that Hogan adopted in her attempt to articulate her feelings and experiences. She affirms that "poetry is a process of uncovering our real knowledge."

Hogan also uses her poetry to define herself in an environment that feels "foreign." She sees her work as "part of the history of our tribe and as part of the history of colonization everywhere." In responding to the still-present and continuing effects of colonization, Hogan has grown "politicized rather than paralyzed by the struggles." She has devoted all of her intellectual energies to learning how to fight the wrongs of classism, racism, oppression, and cruelty. She is particularly sensitive to the wanton destruction of the land and animal life and notes its connection "to the beginning American economy."

For Hogan, "to be spiritually conscious means to undertake a journey that is often a political one, a vision of equality and freedom." Her writing is integral to Hogan's vision: "I just started thinking that being silent was in some way not being honest and that I did not want to be silent about the things that were very important and that our survival is very important." For 20 years, Hogan has been writing her vision. Her volumes of poetry include *Calling Myself Home* (1978); *Daughters, I Love You* (1981); *Eclipse* (1983); *Seeing through the Sun* (1985); *Savings* (1988); *Red Clay: Poems and Stories* (1991); and *The Book of Medicines* (1993). Her first novel, *Mean Spirit* (1990), was a finalist for the Pulitzer Prize and a critical success. Other works include a second novel, *Solar Storms* (1995); a third novel, *Power* (1998); a volume of essays, *Dwellings* (1995); and an edited collection on the relationship between women and nature, *Intimate Nature* (1998). She has won several awards, including the Guggenheim, a National Endowment for the Arts fellowship, and the American Book Award from the Before Columbus Foundation. Hogan teaches in the Creative Writing Program at the University of Colorado. (Hogan 1987a; Hogan 1987b; Hogan 1990; Miller 1990; Witalec 1995)

See also *Mean Spirit*.

Horse, Michael

Michael Horse is a water diviner in Linda Hogan's *Mean Spirit* (1990). He is a "dreamer" with a "sixth sense," who found the oil on Grace Blanket's land. As a spiritual man and the "firekeeper" for the Osage, Horse is greatly respected. The fire he keeps has been handed down to him from his mother and is "descended from the coals of his ancestors. Their lives still burned in the eternal flames."

When Horse's powers go awry and his prediction of two weeks of dry weather is broken almost immediately by a sudden rain, the reader is alerted that something is wrong in Indian Territory. The people start having bad dreams and coming to Horse for help. Horse connects their bad dreams to the oil-drilling industry.

He tells them, "Disturbances of earth made for the disturbances of life and sleep." He cannot help but be aware of the 17 murders in their "small booming corner of Oklahoma" in the last six months.

Horse has an interesting past; during the Boxer Rebellion, he learned Chinese and was a translator in three languages. He still keeps diaries in Chinese of everything that happens in his community and has written what he thinks "is missing" from the pages of the Bible. He has kept pages and pages of writing through the years because he understands that white people "don't believe anything is true unless they see it in writing."

Though Horse is proficient in the ways of the white community, he prefers to live traditionally; he is the "last person in Indian Territory to live in a tepee," and the more the white world intrudes, the farther he moves back into the hills. When the oil wells explode and burn, Horse knows "the words the land spoke were words of breaking, moans of pain." As he moves into the hills, he starts to learn "the languages of owls and bats" as well, though it is not easy to do so. (Hogan 1990)

See also Blanket, Grace; Graycloud, Belle; Graycloud, Moses; *Mean Spirit*; Red Hawk, Stacey.

House Made of Dawn

In 1968, N. Scott Momaday's first novel was published to bewildering success, though critical reception of the book was mixed. But since the 1970s, the novel has come to be seen as a towering work of art. Structurally, the novel consists of a prologue and four sections: "The Longhair," "The Priest of the Sun," "The Night Chanter," and "The Dawn Runner." The first and last words of the book—*Dypaloh* and *Qtsedaba*—are the formulaic words used to open and close a story in the Jemez Pueblo culture. The story is also framed by mirror-image phrases; the book opens with "There was a house made of dawn. It was made of pollen and of rain" and ends with "*House made of pollen, house made of dawn.*" In another enclosing and framing structure, the first and last chapters

N. Scott Momaday uses the Jemez Pueblo, shown here in 1925, to frame his theme in the novel House Made of Dawn. *(Courtesy Museum of New Mexico)*

take place in Walatowa ("Village of the Bear"), the name for their pueblo used by the Jemez people, and the two interior sections are located in Los Angeles. Both the sections and the interior chapters are dated, thus providing some sense of chronological location in this achronological tale.

The prologue introduces the main character, Abel, who is running in a ceremonial race with his arms and shoulders "marked with burnt wood and ashes." The prologue stands apart from the rest of the text and only gathers its meaning and full significance in relation to the whole of the novel, but most especially in relation to the final section of the book, "The Dawn Runner." Momaday says that the race is central to the novel's structure:

> I see [*House Made of Dawn*] as a circle. It ends where it begins and it's informed with a kind of thread that runs through it and holds everything together. The book itself is a race. It focuses upon the race, that's the thing that does hold it all together.

"The Longhair" section opens with a description of the land and of Francisco, Abel's grandfather, who is anxiously awaiting his return from service in World War II. Francisco hears the bus from far off, draws "himself up in the dignity of his age," and waits for Abel to step from the bus. When Abel steps from the bus, "He was drunk, and he fell against his grandfather and did not know him." The contrast presented by the grandfather and grandson signals a major tension of the novel. Francisco is connected to the land by his vocation, by his habits, by his memories. When he comes to "the place called Seytokwa, Francisco remembered the race for good hunting and harvests." He recalls that he won the ceremonial race and had that year killed seven bucks and seven does. Abel returns to the reservation cut off from his past, from the ceremonies and rituals of the Jemez Pueblo, from his relationship to his grandfather, indeed, cut off from himself. He returns drunk and disoriented, unable to recognize his own grandfather.

The first section of the novel presents the major plot and thematic concerns. Abel cannot remember his immediate past but has a series of flashbacks that delineate him as a character. Abel does not know who his father is, and that circumstance has set him apart from the community he lives in; he does not feel fully accepted in the Jemez Pueblo. His brother Vidal and his mother both died when he was a young boy, and by the time he returns from war he is even further estranged from family and community. In another of his flashbacks, we learn that Abel has seen an "awful, holy sight, full of magic and meaning"; he has seen "an eagle overhead with its talons closed upon a snake." The vision foreshadows Abel's encounter with the snakelike albino. Abel is a direct descendant, through Francisco, of the Bahkyush, a group of Tanoan Indians who were raided, tormented, and finally driven from their homeland; only a remnant of this people are left. The Eagle Watchers Society "was the principal ceremonial organization of the Bahkyush," and after Abel sees the eagle and the snake, he is allowed to participate in the annual eagle hunt. He successfully captures a flawless female eagle, but before it can be used in the Bahkyush ceremony, Abel kills it. His action, though ostensibly merciful, is misguided, for it does not achieve either freedom for the bird or any efficacious ceremonial effect.

In the first week that Abel is home, he is inarticulate and unable to reenter the life of the pueblo and of communion with his grandfather:

> He had tried in the days that followed to speak to his grandfather, but he could not say the things he wanted; he had tried to pray, to sing, to enter into the old rhythm of the tongue, but he was no longer attuned to it.

He does take a job splitting wood for a woman who is summering nearby. Angela St. John has come from Los Angeles to take the mineral baths and recover from a depression. She and Abel have a brief affair that is truncated by his encounter with the albino, which ends in murder, a trial, and a prison sentence for Abel.

The second section of the novel, "The Priest of the Sun," takes place in Los Angeles six years after the murder of the albino. Abel is out of prison and is trying to integrate into white society. The Right Reverend John Big Bluff Tosamah is the central mouthpiece of the section; he conducts three services at the pan-Indian mission that reveal the frustrations of the contemporary Indian trying to fit into a society that is alien to his experience. The first service is the sermon on the Gospel of John, the second the peyote service, and the third is the moving and eloquent sermon, "The Way to Rainy Mountain." In the background of the section is Abel, beaten by Martinez, broken in spirit, and lying in a ditch near the sea. Between the three services led by Tosamah, information about Abel is given in sections of memory or flashback. We learn of the deaths of his mother and brother, of fat Josie, of the trial after the murder of the albino, of the runners after evil, of the questionnaires administered by Abel's social worker, Milly, of his relationship with Milly and Ben Benally, and of his war experience; we learn secondhand of Milly's childhood, of her marriage, and of the death of her daughter. The disconcerting movement from memory to memory is achronological and disconnected, but the pattern of memory accurately reflects the brokenness and fragmentation of Abel.

The third section, "The Night Chanter," is narrated by Ben but has passages in italics that are narrated by Abel, though in the second person. From Ben's narration we learn that Abel has made his way back to their apartment after his beating, that he has been hospitalized, and that Angela St. John has come to visit him there. We also learn more of Abel's life in Los Angeles. Most important, we learn that on the night before Abel leaves to return to Jemez Pueblo, he and Ben talk about their plans for the future, and then Ben sings the Navajo Night Chant. The Night Chant is sung over patients who suffer from depression or mental instability, and this song/prayer is the beginning of Abel's spiritual healing.

In his narrative, Abel's memories are of happy times in his childhood with Francisco; of his experience with the girl, Pony, at Cornfields; and of riding a beautiful horse. Already Abel is beginning to show the positive effects of Ben's song. His narration is not fragmented; it is not about brokenness, but about wholeness.

The final section of the novel, "The Dawn Runner," returns to the setting of the first section, Walatowa. Abel has come home to find Francisco dying, and he cares for him in his last days. For six days before he dies, each dawn, Francisco speaks of important times in his life. His last memory is of ceremonial running, and on the seventh dawn, Francisco dies. Abel be-comes the dawn runner of the section title; he goes out and runs and begins singing from the Night Chant, "House made of pollen, house made of dawn." The last section of the book ends where the prologue begins—with Abel running. Momaday's narrative has come full circle. (Evers 1985; Hirsch 1983; Momaday 1968; Oleson 1973; Owens 1992a; Schubnell 1985)

See also Abel; Benally, Ben; Francisco; Martinez; Milly; Momaday, N. Scott; St. John, Angela; Tosamah, John Big Bluff.

I

Iliana

Iliana is the wife of Menardo, entrepreneur and founder of the Universal Insurance Company, in Leslie Marmon Silko's *Almanac of the Dead* (1991). She is a deservedly jealous wife who has endured the countless affairs of her husband. Her patrician background, in contrast to his impoverished one, gives her her only edge of power over her husband, and she uses the network of old money to systematically destroy the women who love Menardo. Before her untimely and accidental death on the stairs of her new mansion, she is able to destroy the career of Menardo's latest lover, Alegria Martinez-Soto. Iliana's inability to carry a child to full term is presumably the reason for Menardo's many affairs and his unquenchable desire to have a son. (Silko 1991)

> **See also** *Almanac of the Dead*; Martinez-Soto, Alegria; Menardo.

Indian Boarding School

The first federally funded boarding school was established in Carlisle, Pennsylvania, in 1879 by Richard Henry Pratt, with his motto, "Kill the Indian and save the man." It was widely hoped that by moving tribal children away from their communities (sometimes across the na-tion), they would more quickly assimilate into white culture and learn a "useful trade." At stake for the Indian children was their language, religion, social and cultural networks, and indeed, their own identity.

By 1899, 20,000 Indian children were placed in 25 boarding schools. The results were often disastrous for the students, many of whom suffered from homesickness and the many diseases that were largely left untreated in the schools. Haskell Institute in Kansas, Carlisle, and other schools had cemeteries to inter the students who died so far away from home.

Though the "model" Carlisle Indian Industrial School closed its doors in 1918, and by the 1930s, John Collier, the Commissioner of Indian Affairs, was pressing for the abandonment of the schools, several persisted through the 1980s. For example, the Chilocco Indian School in Oklahoma was closed in June 1980, and the Phoenix Indian School closed in 1990. However, the Flandreau School in South Dakota (between Sioux Falls and Brookings) is still in operation. And the Chemawa Indian School in Oregon, now with native traditions incorporated into the curriculum, is still open.

The legacy of Indian boarding schools is mixed. To some degree, the government's racist

Students (left to right) Mary Ealy, Frank Cushing, Jennie Hammaker, and Taylor Ealy as they appeared just before entering the Carlisle Indian Industrial School in 1888 . . .

. . . and pictured here as they appeared soon after. (Cumberland County Historical Society)

goal of cultural homogenization was achieved in the schools. However, the schools sometimes became a hotbed of resistance and places where pantribalism began. (Child 1996; Hoxie 1996)

Indian Boyhood

Charles Alexander Eastman's autobiography, *Indian Boyhood* (1902), records the first 15 years of his life as a Santee Sioux, living in the prereservation period. The volume is written for a young audience but has enough interest to hold the attention of a much older audience as well. Eastman dedicates the book to his "little son who came too late to behold for himself the drama of savage existence." Though the book celebrates the way of life that the Sioux enjoyed before they were moved to the reservations, the book is nonetheless imbued with nineteenth-century language that reflects the paradigm of the "noble savage" and "civilization."

The autobiography is chronologically arranged and offers both a personal and tribal story. The young Eastman is named "Hakadah," or "the pitiful last," when his mother dies from childbirth. A medicine man attending Hakadah's mother pronounced, "Another medicine man has come into existence, but the mother must die." The child is lovingly raised by his paternal grandmother, Uncheedah, who accepts the responsibility when she is already 60 years old. Hakadah's father, who took part in what becomes known as the "Minnesota massacre," is believed to be dead, and the young boy's education is watched over by his paternal uncle. For the ten years that Hakadah is separated from his father, he is taught to prepare for the avenging of his father's death as soon as he is able "to go upon the war-path."

In the intervening years, Hakadah is given a new name at a lacrosse game, Ohiyesa, "Winner." Both his uncle and grandmother are highly respected members of their band, and Ohiyesa learns well from them. He becomes proficient at hunting, listening to and telling stories, and gathering herbal medicines with his grandmother.

Indian Boyhood provides an account of the habits and seasonal activities of the Sioux. Eastman tells of the maple sugar camps, of feasts and giveaway ceremonies, of rice gathering, of games and sports, of his first religious offering, of courtship, and much more. Bernd C. Peyer notes that the "harsher realities of Sioux life are occasionally filtered out for the benefit of Anglo readers"; neither does Eastman give anything but the scantiest account of religious ceremonies, making no mention at all of the Sun Dance.

Eastman does tell any number of Siouan legends, including the classic myth of the Stone Boy, a cautionary tale that encourages respect for animals and tribal considerations over individual ones. Eastman also tells the story of a Sioux couple who are away from the larger community on a hunting expedition. One evening as she is rendering fat from the meat her husband has shot, the wife sees the reflection of an enemy in her kettle. An Ojibwa (Anishinabe) scout is peering into their teepee from the smoke hole above. She quietly tells her husband, and he kills the enemy. The story is reminiscent of the famous arrowmaker story told by N. Scott Momaday in *The Way to Rainy Mountain*.

Eastman's autobiography comes to an end when he is 15 years old and his life is irrevocably changed. One day while he is out hunting, his father returns to camp dressed in the clothes of the white man, bearing a white man's name, and fully converted to Christianity. His father was not killed at all but was imprisoned and ultimately pardoned by President Abraham Lincoln. At great personal risk, his father seeks out his son and takes him back to "civilization," where he reads every morning from his Bible and sings a stanza of a hymn. Ohiyesa listens with astonishment to the name "Jesus" and is impressed by the story his father tells him of the Christian savior. Eastman's life story ends rather ambiguously with this notice: "Here my

wild life came to an end, and my school days began." (Eastman 1902, 1971; Peyer 1994a)

See also *The Way to Rainy Mountain*.

Indian Killer

For readers who believe that all injustices toward Indians are historical, Sherman Alexie's novel *Indian Killer* (1996) will inform them with a vengeance. Alexie foregrounds the problems contemporary Indians face: the unauthorized sterilization of Indian women; the unsanitary conditions of Indian Health Service hospitals; the stealing of Indian babies to provide a steady flow of adoptable children to childless white couples; the co-opting of Indian culture, stories, and religion by white wannabes; the claims of authentic Indian experience by nonnatives; the hostilities toward Indians by communities surrounding Indian casinos; and the continuing prejudices that daily confront Native Americans in this country. Alexie's mystery novel lays bare the anger of Indians in the face of active discrimination and residual prejudices. The book is about the pathology of hate, the disintegration of an individual mind, and the growth and disintegration of cultural myths.

A murder novel without the formulaic satisfaction of finding the killer at the end, *Indian Killer* invites the reader into a world of mystery. In Seattle, a white man has been killed and scalped. Immediately, the media dub the killing the work of an "Indian Killer." Already precarious race relations between Indians and whites worsen. The first killing is followed by the disappearance of a white college student on a reservation where he had been gambling in the Indian-owned casino. A third crime involves the kidnapping of a six-year-old white boy, Mark Jones.

At the center of the novel is John Smith, a Native American whose cultural past was erased when he was adopted by a white couple just hours after his birth. Though the reason for his descent into madness and ultimate suicide is never explicitly connected to his adoption and dislocation from his Native American community, Alexie makes a strong case that the mental health of John Smith is not helped by the experience. That he reaches the nadir of his mental health at the time Seattle is experiencing murders and kidnapping by an "Indian Killer" implicates him in the crimes.

John Smith is always a passive character, though; he is the person on whom the other characters act and to whom they react. Marie Polatkin meets John at a campus rally and takes an immediate interest in him. Jack Wilson, retired cop turned mystery writer, sees John as the incarnation of his fictional hero, Aristotle Little Hawk. Reggie Polatkin sees John as a threat to his own Indianness and beats him up. John is also attacked by Aaron Rogers and his friends when they are on an Indian-bashing spree.

Though the novel is filled with physical violence, it is also ripe with intellectual violence. The main perpetrators are Dr. Clarence Mather, the anthropologist wannabe who believes he is more Indian than the Indians he studies and teaches; Jack Wilson, who decided as a school child that he was Indian and who claims authenticity and spokesmanship for Indians through his writing; and Truck Schultz, an inflammatory, right-wing radio talk-show host who reinvigorates the myth of the savage Indian at every opportunity.

Throughout the novel, Alexie maintains a nice balance of mystery and information by using two effective stylistic devices. He inserts chapters that put the reader into the mind of the killer, but he identifies the character only as "the killer." These chapters tantalize the reader by hinting at the identity of the killer but do not provide enough information to make a certain conclusion. Alexie also includes chapters entitled "Testimony," wherein he gives the reader reliable and specific information about the status of the criminal investigations.

Alexie's angry voice is remarkable for its evenness, intensity, and righteousness. That he deals with such volatile subjects with such artistic objectivity is to his credit. The question of this mystery novel is, Who is the Indian Killer? Alexie never shows his hand. It could be any one of several characters—John Smith, Reggie

Polatkin, Marie Polatkin, or perhaps even Jack Wilson. Perhaps the killer is not even a human but a shape-shifting winged creature of mythic dimensions. (Alexie 1996)

See also Alexie, Sherman; Father Duncan; The Indian Killer; Lawrence, Bird; Mather, Dr. Clarence; Polatkin, Marie; Polatkin, Reggie; Rogers, Aaron; Rogers, David; Schultz, Truck; Smith, John; Smith, Olivia and Daniel; Wilson, Jack.

The Indian Killer

In Sherman Alexie's 1996 mystery novel, *Indian Killer*, several brutal crimes are committed by a character identified by Alexie only as "the killer." The community at large quickly names the person the "Indian Killer" and assumes that the killer is both Indian and male, though neither race nor gender is ever established. Driven by a cold and calculating rage, the killer decides to kill a white man. Using a "custom-made bowie," the killer randomly kills Justin Summers, scalps him, plucks his eyes out, eats them, and then leaves two white owl feathers on the body. The killer's satisfaction with the death is short-lived, however. The killer reasons, "Killing a white man, no matter how brutally, was not enough to change the world. But the world would shudder when a white boy was sacrificed. A small, helpless boy." The next move is to kidnap a small boy, Mark Jones. The boy is never physically hurt by the killer, and after some time, Mark is returned to his home alive and safe. Mark's mother is doubly unnerved that the killer has twice entered her home without anyone noticing. When Mark is questioned by the police, he complicates the identity of the killer by saying that it is not a man, and not a woman. He says, "I think it could fly because it had wings."

The killer strikes a third time, with increased brutality. Another white man is killed by repeated stabbings. The killer then "feasted on his heart" and scalped him. Leaving the signature two white owl feathers, the killer felt "depleted but unfulfilled."

The identification of the killer with an owl is strengthened by the final chapter of the novel, when the killer is wearing a "carved wooden mask" at a "cemetery on an Indian reservation" and dances in a way that calls in an audience of owls and other Indians who join in the dance. "The killer gazes skyward and screeches" and "plans on dancing forever." (Alexie 1996)

See also *Indian Killer*; Mather, Dr. Clarence; Polatkin, Marie; Polatkin, Reggie; Smith, John; Wilson, Jack.

The Indian Lawyer

James Welch's 1990 novel, *The Indian Lawyer*, features Sylvester Yellow Calf as the protagonist. Yellow Calf is from the same area as the characters in Welch's previous novels, *Winter in the Blood* (1974, 1986) and *Fools Crow* (1986), and presumably he is a contemporary relative of the old, blind Yellow Calf in *Winter in the Blood*. The Sylvester Yellow Calf we meet in the beginning of the novel has all the outward signs of a fully assimilated Indian. He is a former basketball star at the University of Montana, has made partner at the most prestigious law firm in Helena, Montana, and is being courted by state and national Democratic Party officials to run for Congress. He wears expensive suits, drives a Saab, and has a white girlfriend, Shelley, who is, not inconsequentially, the daughter of a former state senator.

Yellow Calf serves on the Montana State Board of Pardons, and it is his association with this agency that sets in motion the plot concerns of the novel. Yellow Calf and his fellow board members deny pardon to the felon Jack Harwood, and Harwood consequently develops a scheme to blackmail Yellow Calf in the hopes of securing his release. Harwood convinces his wife to seduce Yellow Calf. She does so, and soon Yellow Calf is mired in a situation that endangers his bid for Congress.

Not unlike the protagonist in *Winter in the Blood*, Yellow Calf finds that the way out of his uneasy situation is the way back to the traditional values of his Blackfeet heritage. He has become the token Indian partner in his law firm and the glittering personality of the moment for the Democratic machine, and he realizes that his life will never be his own again. His rela-

tionship with Shelley has suffered an irreparable rupture; he has used and been used by Patti Harwood, the wife of the blackmailing felon; and he feels empty. He withdraws from the congressional race and its altruistic lure of "helping his people" and leaves Helena to work pro bono for the Standing Rock Reservation. After services following the death of his grandfather, he realizes that he had "come a long way home to the simplicity and peace of his birthplace." (Welch 1990)

See also Old Horn, Lena; Welch, James.

The Indian Removal Act of 1830

The Indian Removal Act was ratified by Congress on May 28, 1830, following a bitter debate in Congress and in the public press. The act authorized President Andrew Jackson to divide the land west of the Mississippi River into a "suitable number of districts" in preparation for the removal of Indians from their

This anonymous political cartoon entitled "Andrew Jackson as Great Father" appeared as a satirical comment shortly after the Indian Removal Act was ratified. (Clements Library, University of Michigan)

homes east of the Mississippi. Once divided, the land in the West would be exchanged for the current Indian holdings. In addition, the act guaranteed that the United States would secure those western lands for the Indians and their successors. In the event of Indian extinction or the abandonment of their new territory, the United States would retake its claim to the land. The act further required that the United States appraise the land currently occupied by the Indians and provide compensation for it. Once this payment was made, however, the tribe would forfeit any legal title to the territory. The president also was enabled to grant the tribes aid and assistance "for the first year" following their removal as they emigrated west and to offer them protection in the event of disturbances from other tribes or Indian nations. The president was guaranteed full authority over the tribes removed to the West, unless otherwise stated in an existing treaty. Finally, Congress appropriated $500,000 for the completion of the Indian Removal Act of 1830.

With Jacksonian policy firmly in place by 1830, the process of removal changed from voluntary to forced, and the results grew more tragic. The Removal Act impinged most directly on the Five Civilized Tribes—the Muskogee (Creek), Cherokee, Seminole, Choctaw, and Chickasaw. The tragic Trail of Tears march was a direct result of the Removal Act, as was the Creek War of 1835–1836 and the Second Seminole War of 1835.

The Choctaws were the first to be removed from their native lands to the territory set aside in present-day Oklahoma. The migration on foot during the winter of 1831 caused the death of hundreds, and the name *Trail of Tears* became implanted in the American consciousness. The Muskogee, or Creek Nation, was next to be removed, and when a conservative faction refused to go, the Creek War ensued. Finally, nearly 15,000 Creeks were captured and marched—thousands in chains—to Oklahoma by the U.S. Army under the command of Winfield Scott.

The Seminoles too resisted the forced movement, and the result was the Second Seminole War of 1835. Their removal was finally accomplished by 1859, but again, not without placing many in chains.

The removal of the Cherokees was perhaps the most severe. Though several thousand Cherokees supported the Removal Act and moved between 1835 and 1838, 14,000 Cherokees resisted the directive. Their resistance cost them heavily; by 1839 when the removal was completed, they had suffered the invasion of their homes and lands by the Georgia militia and a roundup by federal troops. They were placed in concentration camps, and with disease rampant, many died or were seriously ill even before the forced march started. One-fourth of the Cherokees died.

Only by comparison can the removal of the Chickasaws be considered less traumatic. Still, over 500 of their tribe died of smallpox alone. (Hoxie 1996; Prucha 1990)

See also The General Allotment Act (Dawes Act) of 1887.

James, Celestine

In Louise Erdrich's novel *The Beet Queen* (1986), Celestine James is the childhood best friend of Sita Kozka until Mary Adare finds her way to Argus, North Dakota, after being abandoned by her mother. Celestine is the half-sister of Russell Kashpaw and the daughter of Dutch James, a character of some importance in Erdrich's *Tracks*. In her adulthood, she works with Mary at the butcher shop. A big-boned, plain woman, Celestine wonders if she will ever feel the pleasures of romance and love. She thinks that perhaps she is too much like men, "too strong or imposing . . . too eager to take control." Celestine is working late one night at the shop when Mary's long-lost brother, Karl Adare, comes looking for her. If Celestine had not been feeling so vulnerable on the night that Karl walked in the shop, doubtless she would never have yielded to his advances. But they end up making love on the floor of the kitchen behind the butcher shop. Karl's behavior immediately afterward is an indication of his character; he tries to sell her knives from his sample case. Karl moves in with Celestine, but after two months, she is bored with him and asks him to leave.

The lasting result of their brief romance is a child. On the night she will give birth, Celestine is trying to make her way to the hospital. In the midst of a blizzard, she gets only to Wallace Pfef's house and, with his assistance, gives birth to her daughter. In gratitude to Pfef, Celestine names the baby Wallacette, but she is soon nicknamed Dot. Soon after the birth of Dot, Celestine marries Karl, but the marriage is nothing more than a formality.

Celestine's love for Dot is so strong that it "hung around her in clear, blowing sheets." Because of Celestine's love and Mary's grasping, jealous love for her niece, Dot grows into an unruly, headstrong child. But by the novel's end, after years of rebellion, Dot recognizes her mother's unfailing love and wants "to lean into her the way wheat leans into the wind." (Erdrich 1986; Owens 1992a; Walsh and Braley 1994)

See also Adare, Karl; Adare, Mary; *The Beet Queen*; James, Dutch; Kashpaw, Russell; Kozka, Sita; Nanapush, Dot Adare; Pfef, Wallace; *Tracks*.

James, Dutch

Dutch James is one of the three men who work for Pete Kozka in his Argus, North Dakota, butcher shop in Louise Erdrich's *Tracks* (1988). Along with Lily Veddar and Tor Grunewald, he attacks and rapes Fleur Pillager because of a dispute over a card game. He is perhaps the unluckiest of the three men, for when Fleur exacts her revenge and the other two die, he lives on with terrible disfigurement and multiple amputations. In his recovery, he marries Regina Puyat Kashpaw and becomes the father of Celestine James and the stepfather of Russell Kashpaw. (Erdrich 1988)

See also James, Celestine; Kashpaw, Russell; Kozka, Pete and Fritzie; Pillager, Fleur; *Tracks*; Veddar, Lily.

Jamey

In Leslie Marmon Silko's *Almanac of the Dead* (1991), Jamey is an undercover cop who works in narcotics and vice for the Tucson police. He is young, beautiful, blue-eyed, and blond, and he becomes the lover of Ferro. Because he has gained the chief of police's favor and because he is believed to be a spy on the others in the narcotics unit, he is killed by his own men in an operation at Tiny's bar, the Stage Coach. Seese is there at the time, trying to sell her kilo of cocaine to Tiny. When Ferro learns of Jamey's death, he car-bombs the police station. (Silko 1991)

See also *Almanac of the Dead*; Ferro; Seese; Tiny.

Johnson, Albertine

Albertine is a primary character in *Love Medicine* (1984, 1993) and a secondary character in *The Bingo Palace* (1994) by Louise Erdrich. She is the daughter of Zelda Kashpaw Johnson and Swede Johnson, a father she knows only by his picture in a military uniform. She is unable to please her critical mother, even though she has gone to nursing school and on to medical school. She is aware of her mother's disapproval that she has not stayed on the reservation and married a Catholic boy.

At 15, Albertine runs away from home to Fargo where, uncertain and scared, she encounters Henry Lamartine, Junior, just back from Vietnam. Though her efforts to help Henry are unsuccessful in the end, she is able to momentarily ease his pain. Albertine's experience with Henry Junior is only the first indication that she possesses healing powers. Her powers are unlike her cousin Lipsha's shamanic powers, but she does have the ability to bridge broken relationships and restore wholeness to people. It is Albertine who fixes the broken pies in the opening chapter of the book, who steps in and ends the fight of King Kashpaw and his wife, and who suggests to Lipsha that knowing his family story could bring him healing.

At the beginning of *Love Medicine*, Albertine returns to the reservation from nursing school when she learns of the death of her aunt June. She feels the strong necessity to properly grieve over her aunt, even though she knows that the visit home will activate the "slow and tedious" abuse between her and her mother, an abuse that requires "long periods of dormancy, living in the blood like hepatitis." Albertine is able to rise above the antagonisms of her mother, and she serves as a connective tissue in the novel, restoring relationships and initiating the restoration of others.

Her life becomes intertwined with the lives of Dot Adare Nanapush and Gerry Nanapush when she works for a short time at a construction site. She befriends Dot and is present at the birth of the couple's baby. She develops a connection with Gerry that alerts her to his desperation later on in *The Bingo Palace*. (Erdrich 1984, 1993; Erdrich 1994; Flavin 1989; Gleason 1987; Hanson 1989; Owens 1992a; Smith 1991)

See also *The Bingo Palace*; Johnson, Zelda Kashpaw; Kashpaw, June Morrissey; Kashpaw, King; Lamartine, Henry Junior; *Love Medicine*; Morrissey, Lipsha; Nanapush, Dot Adare; Nanapush, Gerry.

Johnson, Robert

In Sherman Alexie's novel *Reservation Blues* (1995), the famous blues guitarist Robert Johnson did not die years ago but has been on the run for decades. He explains his appearance on the Spokane reservation: "I sold my soul to the Gentleman so I could play this damn guitar better than anybody ever played guitar. I'm hopin' Big Mom can get it back." Thomas Builds-the-Fire gives him a ride to Big Mom's mountain, and Johnson leaves his guitar in Thomas's van. The guitar eventually finds its way to Victor Joseph and becomes the vehicle for another bargain that "the Gentleman" secures. Johnson knows that by giving the guitar over to other hands, he may be endangering Victor, but he feels "free and guilty at the same time."

Big Mom recognizes the danger that Victor is in and assures him that she can free him of the guitar's charm and call before it is too late; the guitar has no power over Victor that he does not grant it. Free at last from the bargain he made, Robert Johnson decides to stay on the reservation. He shows up at a longhouse feast "wearing a traditional Indian ribbon shirt made of highly traditional silk and polyester." In the final step of the healing process, Big Mom carves a cedar harmonica for Robert Johnson and tells him that he doesn't ever need the guitar or its power again, that he could "play a mean harp" on his own. (Alexie 1995)

> See also Big Mom; Builds-the-Fire, Thomas; Joseph, Victor; Polatkin, Junior; *Reservation Blues*.

Johnson, Zelda Kashpaw

Zelda is a minor character in Louise Erdrich's *Love Medicine* (1984, 1993) and a major character in Erdrich's *The Bingo Palace* (1994). In *Love Medicine*, she "lives just on the very edge of the reservation with her new husband, Bjornson, who owns a solid wheat farm." That mention of Bjornson is the last one, and by the time we see her in *The Bingo Palace*, she is married to no one and still carries a secret passion for the one great love of her life, Xavier Toose. In *Love Medicine*, her major roles are as the young girl who bears an intuitive and premature awareness of her father's flaws and her mother's vulnerabilities and as the nagging mother of Albertine.

As a young girl, she finds the note that her father, Nector, leaves for her mother, Marie, when he decides to leave her and go to Lulu. Though Marie is paralyzed by a mixture of humiliation and her own pride, Zelda finds Nector and leads him home where he belongs. Afterward, she seems to be learning very well from the example of Marie's forgiving spirit. She is a far less attractive character as an adult,

however. She is a harsh and critical mother to Albertine, whose birth "blocked" her "plans for being pure" and "forced her to work for money, keeping books, instead of pursuing tasks that would bring divine glory on her head." In this regard, Zelda is not unlike Leopolda, her maternal grandmother.

In *The Bingo Palace*, Zelda is initially no more of an appealing character; she "is the author of grip-jawed charity on the reservation, the instigator of good works that always get chalked up to her credit." Now she is placing her demands on Shawnee Ray Toose, since Albertine is away in medical school. She has offered to provide housing for Shawnee and her child, Redford, in hopes that she can persuade Shawnee to marry Lyman Lamartine. The constant pressure from Zelda ultimately causes Shawnee to move to her sisters' house, even though neither is a good influence on Redford. However, the price Shawnee pays for her independence from Zelda becomes too great when Zelda interferes mightily. She takes a social worker to Shawnee's sisters' home and has Redford taken from the situation.

Near the end of the novel, Zelda has a heart attack and experiences an epiphany that reverses the course of her life. She has been a woman who "put up a stockade around her own heart since the days when she herself was a girl." Though she loved him, she refused to marry Xavier Toose because he could not offer her the glamorous life she longed for. She was determined to marry a white man who would take her "from the reservation to the Cities" so she might live the life she had planned from "catalogs and magazines." As a result of the heart attack, Zelda realizes that she is "sorrier for the things she had not done than for the things that she had." She acts on her recognition by going to Xavier with the love that she has denied all through the years. (Erdrich 1984, 1993; Erdrich 1994)

> See also *The Bingo Palace*; Johnson, Albertine; Kashpaw, Marie Lazarre; Kashpaw, Nector; Lamartine, Lulu Nanapush; Lamartine, Lyman; *Love Medicine*; Morrissey, Lipsha; Puyat, Pauline; Toose, Shawnee Ray; Toose, Xavier.

Joseph, Victor

In Sherman Alexie's *Reservation Blues* (1995), Victor is the "reservation John Travolta because he still wore clothes from the disco era." In 1979, he won some money in Reno and bought silk shirts and polyester pants, which he has been wearing ever since. His wardrobe makes him "an angry man." His anger contributes to his reputation as the reservation bully and makes him receptive to the seductive guitar brought on the reservation by Robert Johnson. When the guitar plays itself, calling Victor and Junior Polatkin to the house of Thomas Builds-the-Fire to form a band, Victor responds immediately to its alluring whisper.

Victor's past makes him a sympathetic character; his parents are dead, he was sexually abused by a priest when just a young boy, and he has had an early and consistent problem with alcohol. But unlike Thomas, Chess and Checkers Warm Water, and even Junior, Victor does not have the strength of character to move beyond the tragedies of his past and forge a bearable present. He remains a weak and boastful bully, sure of himself only when he is hurting someone else.

When Victor joins Coyote Springs and becomes the lead guitarist, using Robert Johnson's guitar, a struggle for his soul begins. Victor's response to the lure of the guitar provides a major narrative tension in the novel. He accepts the gift of music and hears the guitar speak to him: "Don't play for them. Play for me." Soon Victor is pulled under by his own egotism and goes about shouting such things as "Ladies and gentlemen! Elvis is dead. Long live me!"

Big Mom recognizes the danger that Victor is courting and tries to help him, but he is scornful of her powers. He accuses her of sounding "like a reservation fortune cookie." The whole week that Big Mom instructs Coyote Springs before their audition in New York, Victor resists her. He leaves saying, "I was a great guitar player when I came in here and I'm a great guitar player as I walk out. You taught me a few new tricks. That's it." But it is Victor in his hubris who loses control at the audition and ruins the chances of Coyote Springs. He responds to the disaster with his natural reflexes of violence and alcohol.

When the dispirited band returns to the reservation, the guitar speaks to Victor in a dream: "You have to give up what you love the most. What do you love the most? Who do you love the most?" Ironically, his one affirmation of love is the act that ultimately sacrifices Junior.

After Junior dies, Victor quits drinking. Junior appears to him and tells him to get a job and make something of his life. Victor goes to the tribal chairman and asks for Junior's old job of driving the water truck; David WalksAlong throws him out, ignoring his request for work. Victor crumbles at the first setback. He steals $5 from WalksAlong's secretary's purse and buys beer. "I can do it, too," he says as he pops open the first beer, and "that little explosion of the beer can opening sounded exactly like a smaller, slower version of the explosion that Junior's rifle made on the water tower." (Alexie 1995)

See also Betty and Veronica; Big Mom; Builds-the-Fire, Thomas; Johnson, Robert; *The Lone Ranger and Tonto Fistfight in Heaven*; The-man-who-was-probably-Lakota; Polatkin, Junior; *Reservation Blues*; Warm Water, Chess and Checkers.

K

Kashpaw, Eli

Eli Kashpaw is the son of Margaret (Rushes Bear) Kashpaw and brother of Nector Kashpaw in Louise Erdrich's *Tracks* (1988) and *Love Medicine* (1984, 1993). When the boys were little, Margaret "had let the government put Nector in school, but hidden Eli, the one she couldn't part with, in the root cellar dug beneath her floor. In that way she gained a son on either side of the line." Nector grew up in the world of reading and writing and became a reservation politician, but Eli "knew the woods." He gained his early instruction from Nanapush, the old hunting partner of his late father.

By age 15, Eli is so accustomed to the woods that "he was uncomfortable around humans, especially women." Several years later, when he is lovesick for Fleur Pillager, he is still so awkward he cannot "rub two words together and get a spark." He goes to Nanapush and asks for help in gaining Fleur's love. He is successful and begins a happy life with her that is interrupted when Pauline witches him into an adulterous situation with Sophie Morrissey. Though he finally regains Fleur's love, their relationship is never the same. The book ends with Fleur driven off her land by the lumber company, and Eli going to work for them.

When he appears in *Love Medicine*, he is an old man, leading the life of a bachelor, living far back in the woods. June Morrissey Kashpaw, the child abandoned on the doorstep of Nector and Marie Kashpaw, grows fond of Eli and elects to go live with him in the woods. He raises her as his own, perhaps seeing it as a chance to fulfill the role of father that was taken from him when his daughter Lulu was sent to the government boarding school.

Throughout *Love Medicine*, he is shown in contrast to his brother Nector. Whereas Nector is irresponsible and unreliable, Eli is steady and accountable. On one occasion, when Nector has been untrue to Marie, she and Eli are momentarily tempted. But principled in a way that his brother is not, Eli walks away from the temptation. (Barry and Prescott 1989; Erdrich 1984, 1993; Erdrich 1988; Flavin 1991).

See also Kashpaw, June Morrissey; Kashpaw, Margaret (Rushes Bear); Kashpaw, Marie Lazarre; Kashpaw, Nector; Lamartine, Lulu Nanapush; *Love Medicine*; Morrissey, Sophie; Nanapush; Pillager, Fleur; Puyat, Pauline; *Tracks*.

Kashpaw, Gordie

Gordie Kashpaw is the first child of Nector and Marie Kashpaw in Louise Erdrich's *Love Medicine* (1984, 1993). From the time that June Morrissey Kashpaw comes to live with first Nector and Marie and later Eli Kashpaw, June and Gordie have had a special bond. In spite of being distant cousins, they marry in their impulsive youth. Their married love is alternately hot and cold; though "they knew the good things," they also "knew how to hurt each other, too." They have one son, King, but June nonetheless often leaves Gordie for long spells. It is during a separation that she dies, and after June's death, Gordie is tormented by guilt over the way he often treated her violently. He cannot escape the memory of his hands as they struck June, and a month after she dies, Gordie "took the first drink" and never recovered.

One night, while in a drunken state, Gordie calls out the name of June. He immediately remembers his grandmother's admonition, "Never, never, ever call the dead by their names. . . . They might answer." June does appear at his window, but whether she is the apparition of a drunken dream or a returning spirit is perhaps best left to the reader to decide. At the window, "wild and pale with a bloody mouth," she scratches at the glass. The real or imagined presence of June drives Gordie crazy, and he turns on every possible electrical appliance so that he might drown her out. When he blows the fuses, and June is still present, he leaves the house, gets in the car, and starts driving drunkenly. What happens on his drive moves into either drunken surrealism or a retributive visit from the dead June. Certainly, Ojibwa (Anishinabe) ontology allows for shapeshifting spirits of the dead to return and torment those who have caused them suffering. He accidentally hits a deer and stows it in the backseat, thinking that he might be able to sell it for some wine. When he checks his rearview mirror, he sees that the deer is still alive; he cracks it over the head with a tire iron. When he looks again, he sees June instead of the deer and is certain that it was June and not a deer that he has just killed. He drives to the convent to confess and then wanders off into the surrounding fields. When the tribal police come to collect him, they hear him, Lear-like, "crying like a drowned person, howling in the open fields."

Gordie never recovers from his guilt and alcoholism. When he is at his absolute worst, he goes to his mother's house, and she struggles with him to keep him alive. However, he pours Lysol on a loaf of bread and ingests it. The poison kills him in a frenzied and painful death. (Erdrich 1984, 1993; Ruppert 1995; Vecsey 1983; Whitson 1993)

See also Kashpaw, Eli; Kashpaw, June Morrissey; Kashpaw, King; Kashpaw, Marie Lazarre; Kashpaw, Nector; *Love Medicine*.

Kashpaw, June Morrissey

In Louise Erdrich's *Love Medicine* (1984, 1993), June is a character whose role in the novel is felt more in her absence than in her presence. When the novel opens on the morning before Easter Sunday, she walks "down the clogged main street of oil boomtown Williston, North Dakota, killing time before the noon bus arrived that would take her home." She is going back to the reservation after a time of desperation, poverty, emptiness, and even prostitution. She is a "long-legged Chippewa woman, aged hard in every way except how she moved." Before the end of the first chapter, she commits passive suicide by walking into the teeth of a blizzard.

June's tragic death is prefigured by all of the early shocks of her childhood. Abandoned in the woods by a drunken and irresponsible family, June lives off tree sap and forest foragings until she is delivered to the doorstep of Marie Kashpaw when she is "not older than nine years." She comes to Marie with "black beads on a silver chain" around her neck, looking "as if she really was the child of what the old people called Manitous, invisible ones who live in the woods." Despite Marie's nurturing love for the orphaned child, June cannot grow comfortable in her new home, and she leaves Marie to go live with Eli Kashpaw, who still lives in the old Ojibwa way. Marie allows June to go because she recognizes a sadness in June that she cannot reach: "It was a hurt place, it was deep, it was with her all the time like a broke rib that stabbed when she breathed."

She is raised by her uncle Eli until she runs away to marry her cousin, Gordie Kashpaw. The marriage is disastrous, and June leaves Gordie many times before finally divorcing him. They have one son, King Kashpaw, and in her absences from Gordie, June bears a son to Gerry Nanapush. June does not keep this second son; she abandons him at birth, and Marie and Nector Kashpaw raise Lipsha Morrissey as their own. June "wasn't much as a mother" but "was a good aunt to have—the kind that spoiled you." Albertine Johnson has a special relationship with her aunt June, and June's example of the hard life goes a long way in influencing Albertine to take control of her own life. Albertine watches the gradual decline of June:

> As time went by she broke, little by little, into someone whose shoulders sagged when she thought no one was looking, a woman with long ragged nails and hair always growing from its beauty-parlor cut.

After her death, June enters the novel again when Gordie violates a Chippewa taboo that forbids speaking the names of the dead. June's visit from beyond the dead and his guilt over the abuse she suffered at his hands push Gordie over the edge. Soon after her visit, he dies from alcohol poisoning.

June inhabits the novel throughout at the metonymic level in the agency of the blue Firebird. King buys the car with the insurance money from June's death, and the car accrues significance as the characters come to associate the car with June herself. By the time Lipsha wins the car from King in a poker game, the identities of June and the car have nearly merged in the minds of her sons. The novel ends with an ambiguous pronoun that further connects June and the car; Lipsha is thinking of June when he says, "A good road led on. So there was nothing to do but cross the water, and bring her home."

In *The Bingo Palace*, we learn that June was raped by her mother's boyfriend when she was a little girl. She makes a promise to herself then: "Nobody ever hold me again." The incident offers some explanation for her behaviors as an adult. When she next enters the narrative, it is in connection with the blue Firebird. She visits Lipsha from the dead and leaves him some bingo tickets in exchange for the car. She shows up one more time in the novel; when Gerry and Lipsha are escaping in a stolen car, June pulls up beside them in the Firebird. Even in spirit form, she has the power to lure Gerry, and he joins her in a surrealistic flight across the snowfields.

In *Tales of Burning Love*, Erdrich returns to the scene that opened *Love Medicine*, where June walks into a bar in Williston, North Dakota, while waiting for a bus home. In the first book, the scene is given from June's point of view, but in *Tales*, the scene is retold from Jack Mauser's (know as "Andy" in *Love Medicine*) point of view. This use of June in *Tales* reflects Erdrich's economic use of character and reinforces the inescapable and ghostly presence of June in Erdrich's fictive world. (Erdrich 1984, 1993; Erdrich 1994; Erdrich 1996; Flavin 1989; Hanson 1989; McKenzie 1986; Owens 1992a; Ruppert 1995; Smith 1991)

See also *The Bingo Palace*; Johnson, Albertine; Kashpaw, Eli; Kashpaw, Gordie; Kashpaw, King; Kashpaw, Marie Lazarre; Kashpaw, Nector; *Love Medicine*; Mauser, Jack; Morrissey, Lipsha; Nanapush, Gerry; *Tales of Burning Love*.

Kashpaw, King

King Kashpaw is the son of Gordie Kashpaw and June Morrissey Kashpaw in Louise Erdrich's *Love Medicine* (1984, 1993). He is the character who garners the least sympathy in the novel, for he is a bully to all in his family and is also referred to as an "apple": "That is: red on the outside, white on the inside." His relationship with his wife Lynette is marked by a cycle of physical abuse followed by presumably atoning sex. His own son, King Kashpaw, Jr., distances himself from his father as early as kindergarten, when he asks to be known by his middle name, Howard. Even King notices that Howard "won't claim his dad no more."

As the acknowledged son of June, King spent his childhood tormenting his illegitimate brother, Lipsha, even to the point of taking potshots at him in the woods. King dominates family gatherings by bragging about his nonexistent experience in Vietnam and his cruel treatment of animals. His behavior has landed him in prison at least once, and while serving time with Gerry Nanapush, he "got Gerry's confidence and then betrayed it." Because he is "a squealer, an informer," Gerry comes to King's apartment in the Cities to exact a harmless but fitting revenge the next time he escapes.

King's apartment becomes the locus for one of the novel's most satisfying sequences. When Lipsha is hit on the head by a bottle and receives his vision that Gerry has escaped, he heads to King's place to wait for him. Gerry maneuvers secretly through the bowels of the apartment building and appears both comically and mysteriously at King's kitchen window. Gerry engages Lipsha and King in a poker game in which the stake is the blue Firebird that King bought with the insurance money he collected at June's death. Lipsha crimps the cards in the way that Lulu Lamartine has taught him, and Gerry recognizes that Lipsha is his son. The game is thrown to Lipsha, and he wins the car, a silent acknowledgment that he too is June's son. Gerry and Lipsha both win a satisfying revenge on King for his habits of mistreatment. King is left in a final humiliation when the police knock at the door, looking for Gerry, and Howard rushes to the door, shouting, "King's here! King's here!" (Erdrich 1984, 1993; Flavin 1989; Gleason 1987; Schultz 1991)

>   **See also** Kashpaw, Gordie; Kashpaw, June Morrissey; Lamartine, Lulu Nanapush; *Love Medicine*; Morrissey, Lipsha; Nanapush, Gerry.

Kashpaw, Margaret (Rushes Bear)

Margaret Kashpaw is a character in Louise Erdrich's *Love Medicine* (1984, 1993) and *Tracks* (1988). She is the mother of Eli and Nector Kashpaw, and after the death of her husband, she is the partner of old Nanapush. She witnesses and resists the pressures put on tribal people to assimilate and yield to the new order of white domination. When her sons Nector and Eli are young, she "let the government put Nector in school," but hid Eli "in the root cellar dug beneath her floor. In that way she gained a son on either side of the line."

Margaret does not approve of Eli's relationship with Fleur Pillager, and only the lure of her granddaughter, Lulu, draws her to a reconciliation with the couple. She is a "headlong, bossy" woman, "scared of nobody and full of vinegar," which makes her an equal match to the feisty Nanapush. Their relationship is based on a reluctant but undeniable attraction, a shared granddaughter in Lulu, and on the necessity for survival. Along with Fleur, Margaret and Nanapush are the primary holdouts in the reservation conflict over the leasing of land rights to the timber companies. The position that they take has dangerous consequences, and one day Margaret and Nanapush are captured and tortured by Clarence Morrissey and Boy Lazarre, proponents of the sellout. Nanapush is ridiculed in front of the woman he loves, and Margaret's braids are cut off and her head shaved. What the couple loses in dignity, they gain in shared determination against a common enemy. The growing regard between Margaret and Fleur is cemented when, in an act of solidarity, Fleur shaves her own head and works magic against Clarence Morrissey and Boy Lazarre.

Margaret earned her name, Rushes Bear, at the birth of Lulu. Nanapush was waiting outside the cabin for the birth to occur and had stashed a jug of wine in a rotten stump. A bear got into the wine, and drunkenly charged Nanapush. Margaret flew out of the cabin and charged the bear, only to realize that she had no weapon. She turned and ran back into the cabin, and the bear followed her. When Fleur saw the bear, she raised up and delivered the child.

Though Nanapush and Margaret continue as lifelong companions, their relationship is seriously damaged at one point. Along with Fleur, they work hard to pool enough money to pay their annual allotment fees, and when the money is finally gathered, Margaret and Nector Kashpaw take the money to the agent. Only later do Nanapush and Fleur learn that late fees were assessed, and the Kashpaws had only enough money to pay on one allotment. They paid the Kashpaw fee and Nanapush and Fleur lost their land. After the loss, Nanapush "never believed the best of Margaret again, or loved her quite so much."

When Lulu returns from Indian boarding school to the home of Nanapush and Margaret, she sees Margaret as "a passionate, power-hungry woman" and cannot abide living with her. Their disharmony is, in part, what drives Lulu to the island where Moses Pillager lives.

By the time Margaret comes to live with her daughter-in-law Marie in her old age, "she had withered powerfully, evaporated into the shape of her own opinions." When she lives with Marie, she is so bossy and intrusive that Marie finally asks her to leave. Margaret relents, calms down, and stays. In the process, she forges a relationship with Marie based on their mutual loneliness. Marie senses that "she seemed to have noticed the shape of my loneliness. Maybe she found it was the same as hers." Their relationship grows into an unspoken familial bond that Marie has never felt before. She says, "I never saw her without knowing that she was my own mother, my own blood. What she did went beyond the frailer connections. More than saving my life, she put the shape of it back in place." (Erdrich 1984, 1993; Erdrich 1988; Owens 1992a)

See also Kashpaw, Eli; Kashpaw, Marie Lazarre; Kashpaw, Nector; Lamartine, Lulu Nanapush; *Love Medicine*; Nanapush; Pillager, Fleur; Pillager, Moses; Puyat, Pauline; *Tracks*.

Kashpaw, Marie Lazarre

Marie Kashpaw figures importantly in Louise Erdrich's novel *Love Medicine* (1984, 1993) and is a minor figure in Erdrich's *The Bingo Palace* (1994). She is a character with a fierce energy for anger, revenge, and control, yet she has the unfailing ability to forgive and the unlimited mercy to love. It is as if her impulses to the sins of the heart cannot be acted upon; she is at the core more saintly than even she might imagine.

When she is 14, Marie goes up to Sacred Heart convent so the nuns there would "have a girl from this reservation as a saint they'd have to kneel to." There she enters a complex and seemingly inexplicable relationship with Sister Leopolda that ends in a contest of wills that Marie wins. The deranged Leopolda is certain that she can smell the devil prowling around Marie, and she is determined to burn the evil out of the young girl. She pours a kettle of boiling water on Marie's back as they are working in the kitchen, and Marie retaliates by pushing Leopolda into the bread oven. Leopolda stabs Marie in the hand with a bread fork, whacks her head with a poker, and then claims that Marie has had a "holy vision." The wound on Marie's hand, Leopolda reports, is a stigmata, the miraculous appearance of Christ's nail marks in her hand. The scene has all of the delicious terror and revenge of a fairy tale. The nuns fall down and worship Marie. She attempts to delight in her victory over Leopolda but realizes that there was "no heart in it. No joy when she bent to touch the floor." Not through the trappings of a sham miracle, not through the devotions of a "mail-order Catholic soul you get in a girl raised out in the bush," but through human kindness and untutored goodness, Marie puts on the garb of saintliness. The bizarre dynamics of the relationship between Sister Leopolda and Marie are finally explained when we learn in *Tracks* that Leopolda is Pauline Puyat, Marie's birth mother.

Marie leaves the convent the same day she triumphs over Leopolda and meets Nector Kashpaw on the road. He sees the Sacred Heart pillowcase she has wrapped around her hand, and convinced that she stole it, he wrestles her for it. In the process, he is aware of her body beneath him, and he loses his heart on the road to the convent. In one day, Marie has made the journey from schoolgirl to saint to woman.

Marie and Nector marry and have a large family. Their relationship is strained by Marie's desire to make something of her husband, by their poverty, and by the many homeless children that Marie takes in through the years. It is primarily Marie who holds together the family, and she takes pride in herself for becoming "solid class," for raising well-behaved and educated children, and for helping Nector become tribal chairman. But her pride never overreaches; it is always held in check by her awareness of her own humanness and her ability to forgive. Marie endures and forgives Nector's adultery with Lulu Lamartine and even comes to a redemptive friendship with Lulu after the death of Nector. She goes to visit Sister Leopolda during an illness and is tempted to exact a psychological and emotional revenge, but relents and forgives Leopolda instead. By the time she is a grandmother, Marie has accrued a psychic weight that her granddaughter Albertine Johnson recognizes: "She always seemed the same size to me as the rock cairns commemorating Indian defeats around here."

Of all the children that Marie takes in through the years, none take hold of her heart like June Morrissey Kashpaw, the child of her sister Lucille, and later June's son, Lipsha Morrissey. June is emotionally scarred by her childhood of abuse and neglect, and Marie longs to "hold her against me tighter than any of the others." Marie has the wisdom to let go of June when the child asks to go live with Eli back in the woods. Years later, she is able to channel her love for June to Lipsha, and it is Marie who provides the steady foundation of love for him that enables him to find and accept his identity.

Marie's character, established in *Love Medicine*, continues to grow in *The Bingo Palace*. She ages with grace and power as she becomes more and more traditional; she realizes that many of the new ways that the Ojibwa embraced have ultimately failed her and her children. She starts to speak the old language again and is respected as an elder of the tribe. (Erdrich 1984, 1993; Erdrich 1994; Flavin 1989; Gleason 1987; Owens 1992a; Ruppert 1995; Schultz 1991; Smith 1991)

See also *The Bingo Palace*; Johnson, Albertine; Johnson, Zelda Kashpaw; Kashpaw, Eli; Kashpaw, Gordie; Kashpaw, June Morrissey; Kashpaw, Margaret (Rushes Bear); Kashpaw, Nector; Lamartine, Lulu Nanapush; Lamartine, Lyman; *Love Medicine*; Morrissey, Lipsha; Puyat, Pauline; *Tracks*.

Kashpaw, Nector

In Louise Erdrich's *Tracks* (1988), Nector is teased as "Eli's twin because he so imitated and resembled his older brother." But as Nector grows, he becomes quite different from the outdoorsy Eli. While Eli becomes a quiet man of principle, Nector grows into a selfish and childish man, unwilling to take responsibility for his actions.

Nector is adept at reading and figures from earliest childhood, and Nanapush recognizes when Nector is just nine years old that his calculating mind will make him a "smooth politician." This ability to calculate what's best for him first gives fruit when he takes the fee money for the Kashpaw, Nanapush, and Pillager allotments to the Indian agent for payment. When a late charge is assessed, Nector determines that if only one annual fee can be paid, it will be the Kashpaw family fee. His mother Margaret is complicit in his action. Nanapush and Fleur Pillager lose their allotments as a result of Nector's decision.

After Nector finishes Indian boarding school, he ventures into the larger white world, where the hard lessons he learns are typical for the Native American. He is hired by a talent scout to play the part of an Indian in a western movie but realizes, "they didn't know I was a Kashpaw, because right off I had to die." He discovers that "the only interesting Indian is dead, or dying by falling backwards off a horse." He then meets "this old rich woman" who wants him to pose nude for a painting. He says, "No one had ever told me to take off my clothes just like that. So I pretended not to understand her." Nector is not comfortable in the white world, which interprets the Indian either as a member of an appropriately "vanishing race" or as the noble savage. When he learns "that the greater world was only interested in [his] doom, [he] went home on the back of a train."

Back on the reservation, he becomes "an astute political dealer, people said, horse-trading with the government for bits and shreds. Somehow he'd gotten a school built, a factory too, and he'd kept the land from losing its special Indian status under that policy called termination." For all his ability to succeed in political matters, he does not carry that skill into his personal life. Instead, he transfers his manipulative behaviors into his marriage to Marie Lazarre. While he is married to Marie, he carries on a five-year affair with the girlfriend of his youth, Lulu Lamartine. With her he has a child, Lyman Lamartine, whom he never acknowledges.

All of the major milestones in his life are the result of passivity and acquiescence rather than planned action. As a young man, he is nearly engaged to Lulu when he meets Marie Lazarre on the road from the convent. He stops her, thinking she has stolen something from the nuns, and in the process, he nearly rapes her and then claims, "You made me! You forced me!" In his affair with Lulu many years later, he shows the same degree of surprise at his own actions. When he comes home late after his first tryst with Lulu, Marie questions him. He is speechless and slow to "realize [his] sudden guilt." The same pattern of passivity is evident when, in his job as tribal chairman, he goes to Lulu's house to deliver an eviction notice. He drops the paper, and when his cigarette butt ignites it, he sits quietly by and is dumbfounded that the small blaze grows and grows until it finally burns down her whole house. His only response is, "I swear that I do [sic] nothing to help the fire along."

In his old age, he suffers from loss of memory, though he remembers enough to still be attracted to Lulu Lamartine. Lipsha Morrissey, his adopted grandson, decides to cure Nector of his wandering heart and concocts a Chippewa love medicine. He cannot secure the heart of geese, birds that mate for life, so he substitutes frozen turkey hearts from the grocery store. When Nector is served the heart, he chokes on it and dies. Lipsha is certain that he didn't choke on the heart alone, but that his mistakes in life were choking him as well.

Nector returns from the dead to visit Lipsha and forgive him for his part in the death. He also returns and affirms his love for both Lulu and Marie. Even in death, Nector cannot be faithful to one person. (Barry and Prescott 1989; Erdrich 1984, 1993; Erdrich 1988; Owens 1992a; Ruppert 1995)

> See also Kashpaw, Eli; Kashpaw, Margaret (Rushes Bear); Kashpaw, Marie Lazarre; Lamartine, Lulu Nanapush; Lamartine, Lyman; *Love Medicine*; Morrissey, Lipsha; Nanapush; Pillager, Fleur; *Tracks*.

Kashpaw, Russell

Russell Kashpaw plays a minor role in several of Louise Erdrich's novels. He is a young boy in *Tracks* (1988), working as an errand boy at Pete Kozka's butcher shop. When Fleur Pillager is attacked and raped by the men at the shop, Russell tries to stop them, but he is held down by Pauline Puyat.

In *The Beet Queen* (1986), Russell is a former high school football star and a war hero who has just returned from World War II. He was injured in the war and is given a "bank-clerk job . . . even though he was an Indian." Mary Adare falls impetuously in love with him and makes one embarrassing and failed attempt at winning him.

A dozen years later, he returns to Argus from service in Korea, once again wounded. There is talk of "making him North Dakota's most-decorated hero," but Russell is despondent, "stays in the bars all night, or mopes around the house." Mary gives him a job at the butcher shop, and he begins to improve. Soon after Russell suffers a stroke and is taken to his half-brother Eli's to live. Near the end of his life, he is able only to ride passively in the beet parade as the "Most Decorated Hero." On the parade route, he realizes that he is dying, that he is on "the road that the old-time Chippewa talked about, the four-day road, the road of death." However, as he rides along, he is so amused by the irony of the members of the American Legion "solemnly saluting a dead Indian" that he falls off the road to death and cannot get back on.

Russell lives for many more years and is a character in *The Bingo Palace* (1994), in which he is a tattoo artist who saves Lipsha Morrissey from an embarrassing moment. (Erdrich 1986; Erdrich 1988; Erdrich 1994; Owens 1992a)

See also Adare, Mary; Kashpaw, Eli; Kozka, Pete and Fritzie; Morrissey, Lipsha; Pillager, Fleur; Puyat, Pauline.

Kills-close-to-the-lake

In James Welch's novel *Fools Crow* (1986), Kills-close-to-the-lake is the third wife of Rides-at-the-door, the father of the main character. Rides-at-the-door takes her as his third wife when her father, Mad Wolf, a man of poverty and bad luck, requests that she be taken care of.

Kills-close-to-the-lake lives in the lodge of Rides-at-the-door more in the manner of a child than of a wife. Her husband seldom calls her to the smaller lodge next to the family lodge, and she is treated by the first two wives more as a child than a peer. She is the same age as the sons of Rides-at-the-door, and it is not surprising that her attentions are directed first to White Man's Dog and later Running Fisher. White Man's Dog is aware of her flirtations and steels himself against the temptation of contact with her. When White Man's Dog marries Red Paint, Kills-close-to-the-lake steps away from the potential danger of a relationship with him but offers a wedding gift, a soft-tanned scabbard for his new rifle. Running Fisher does not have the moral courage that White Man's Dog does, however, and when Kills-close-to-the-lake directs her mild attentions toward him, he succumbs and they enter into a dangerous sexual relationship. When Rides-at-the-door offers both of the young lovers a way to leave the band and save face, they both humbly and gratefully accept. Rides-at-the-door releases Kills-close-to-the-lake as his wife:

You are no longer my wife. You will quit this camp in the morning before Sun Chief begins his journey. You may take your riding horse and three others from my herd. Tell your father they are a gift from his friend Rides-at-the-door. But he must never know the real reason for your return. You must vow to the Above Ones that you will tell no one of this.

Kills-close-to-the-lake goes to live with her own band, the Never Laughs. (Barry 1991–1992; Owens 1992a; Welch 1986)

See also *Fools Crow*; Red Paint; Rides-at-the-door; Running Fisher; White Man's Dog.

Ko-sahn

In N. Scott Momaday's *The Way to Rainy Mountain* (1969), Ko-sahn is one of the last living Kiowas who can still remember the Sun Dances. For Momaday, in his quest to recover his Kiowa culture, it was Ko-sahn in whom "the living memory and the verbal tradition which transcends it were brought together." She shares stories of the Kiowa past, and Momaday finds remarkable her confession that "as old as I am, I still have the feeling of play." (Momaday 1969)

See also Momaday, N. Scott; *The Way to Rainy Mountain*.

Kozka, Pete and Fritzie

Pete and Fritzie Kozka are characters in Louise Erdrich's *The Beet Queen* (1986) and *Tracks* (1988). Pete and Fritzie live in Argus, North Dakota, "on the eastern edge of town," and run a butcher shop. In *Tracks*, they hire both Fleur Pillager and Pauline Puyat when they come to town seeking work after their families have been decimated by the consumption of 1912. They are kind people; Fritzie gives Fleur a place to stay that is unknown to the three men who work at the shop. Pete reads the New Testament and carries a good-luck talisman, "the opal-white lens of a cow's eye." Doubtless, had they not taken a vacation during the hot month of August, the terrible events of Fleur's rape and the devastating tornado would not have happened.

Another chapter of their lives in revealed in *The Beet Queen*. They are now the parents of a spoiled child, Sita. Fritzie is the sister of Adelaide Adare, who abandoned her three children, and when Mary Adare shows up at their door, the Kozkas take her in and raise her alongside Sita. Whether from pity, sympathy, or a natural affinity to the strength of Mary's personality, Fritzie seems to like her more than Sita, or at least, that is how Sita feels. In an act of kindness, Pete gives the orphaned Mary his prized cow's lens, and Sita once again feels usurped.

When Mary is 18, Fritzie suffers a physical collapse: "The doctor said that Fritzie's lungs needed dry warmth, a desert climate, and she shouldn't undergo even one more Dakota winter." They turn the butcher shop over to Mary and move to the Southwest. (Erdrich 1986; Erdrich 1988)

See also Adare, Adelaide; Adare, Mary; *The Beet Queen*; James, Dutch; Kashpaw, Russell; Kozka, Sita; Pillager, Fleur; Puyat, Pauline; *Tracks*; Veddar, Lily.

Kozka, Sita

Sita is the cousin of Mary and Karl Adare in Louise Erdrich's *The Beet Queen* (1986), and when Mary comes to Argus, North Dakota, to live with her aunt Fritzie Kozka, Sita has to share a room, her clothes, and even her best friend, Celestine James. She is particularly hurt when her father gives Mary a "cow's diamond," "the hard rounded lens inside a cow's eye that shines when you look through it at the light, almost like an opal." Pete carries it as a lucky piece, and Sita has always wanted it. Pete resists, saying it can be Sita's "inheritance." When he gives it to Mary out of genuine pity, Sita's resentment of Mary grows stronger. Sita is also outraged when Mary goes to the Catholic school and takes tests that place her a year ahead, in Sita's grade. In a final attempt to move Celestine to value her more than she is coming to value Mary, Sita takes her to the graveyard and shows Celestine her breasts, because "they were something that Mary didn't have." Celestine runs away, leaving Sita bare-breasted in the graveyard.

Sita and Mary maintain an uneasy truce in the years that they are roommates, but when Sita moves to Fargo to model clothes for a department store, she takes Mary's blue velvet box that had belonged to Adelaide. In Fargo, Sita leads a sterile life, defined by her need to stay mannequin perfect. She takes "refresher courses at The Dorothy Ludlow Evening School of Charm" and is certain that she has missed her chance in Hollywood.

She has a married lover for years until she realizes that he will not leave his wife; she then dates Jimmy Bohl, refusing to marry him until she determines that she will do no better.

A letter sent to Fritzie by the mother of Jude Miller, Mary's brother who was kidnapped years earlier, is forwarded to Sita. Catherine Miller tells the Kozka family that Jude is being ordained into the priesthood and doesn't know he is "adopted," but she is willing to tell him if the family wants. Uncertain of her motive, Sita goes to Minneapolis to Jude's ordination but doesn't make herself known. While she is in Minneapolis, she goes to a department store and is unnerved to find that back in Fargo, she is not in touch with the latest fashions, the latest looks. She also takes the old pawn ticket from Adelaide's blue velvet box to the pawn shop. She redeems Adelaide's garnet necklace but does not give it to Mary. When she returns to Fargo, she writes to Catherine Miller but neglects to mail her letter. The stamped and addressed letter is found years later by Celestine and mailed.

Her marriage to Jimmy Bohl is endangered by her critical attitude and her constant feeling that she has married beneath herself. She and Jimmy divorce, and she remodels his restaurant, turning it into Chez Sita, Home of the Flambéed Shrimp. During her "Grande Opening," a by-invitation-only affair, her chef and workers all get food poisoning, and Sita must lower herself to ask Mary, Celestine, and Russell to save the day. Louis Tappe, the state health inspector, comes to investigate and soon is visiting unofficially. Two months after he and Sita marry, Karl Adare visits them, and Sita suffers a nervous breakdown. Her mental health is fraying; at one point she refuses to speak for four months, and Louis takes her to the state mental hospital. Sita is placed in a room with a woman who believes she is a cannibal. The woman unnerves Sita, who calls home and announces in her own voice that she is cured.

Through the years, Sita still tries to look young and trim but merely "ends up looking stuffed and preserved." She becomes addicted to prescription drugs, and on the day that

Celestine and Mary go to pick her up for Dot's Beet Queen coronation, they find her dead from an overdose. In one of the novel's scenes of black humor, the dead Sita is stuffed into the House of Meats van and driven to town. The van inadvertently gets included in the parade, and the sight of Sita, looking no more "stuffed and preserved" than usual, does not raise an eyebrow. (Bak 1992; Erdrich 1986; Meisenhelder 1994)

See also Adare, Adelaide; Adare, Karl; Adare, Mary; *The Beet Queen*; James, Celestine; Kashpaw, Russell; Kozka, Pete and Fritzie; Miller, Jude; Nanapush, Dot Adare.

Ku'oosh

In Leslie Marmon Silko's *Ceremony* (1977, 1986), Ku'oosh is the Laguna medicine man who performs the Scalp Ceremony on the veterans returning from World War II. When he visits Tayo, he speaks slowly, using the "old dialect," fully aware of his role as conduit of an age-old ceremony. He reminds Tayo that the world is "fragile" and that the responsibility of being human is to tell the story behind every word. He draws Tayo into the ceremony by telling him that healing is necessary not only for the sick Tayo but also "for this fragile world." However, even the medicine of the respected Ku'oosh is unable to heal Tayo and the other veterans of their shell shock and of the "witchery" brought on by the war. Ku'oosh suggests that Tayo see Betonie, the Navajo medicine man. After Tayo's eventual cure, Ku'oosh invites him into the Laguna kiva to tell the story of his healing, thus completing the ceremony and validating the inclusion of the mixed-blood Tayo into the community. (Herzog 1985; Owens 1992a; Ronnow 1989; Silko 1977, 1986; Swan 1988; Swan 1991–1992)

See also Betonie; *Ceremony*; Silko, Leslie Marmon; Tayo; witchery.

L

La Escapia, Angelita

In Leslie Marmon Silko's *Almanac of the Dead* (1991), Angelita is a Mayan woman, leader of the indigenous peoples who are working to gain back their ancestral lands. She has the rank of colonel in the People's Army of Justice and Redistribution. She is "educated" in Marxism by Bartolomeo de Las Casas and the Cubans, and though she is satisfied that Marx tells the truth about the exploitation of people, she does not fully embrace the political agenda of the Cubans, feeling that they have a different version of history. When Bartolomeo sends out handbills after the capitalist Menardo's death that imply that it was political and not accidental, Angelita orders his arrest and trial.

She attends the International Holistic Healer Convention to gather arms support for the movement. She takes greetings from Tacho and El Feo, two of the central pairs of twins in the story, but fundamentally differs from them in that theirs is a message of peaceful marching and hers is a more violent one. (Silko 1991)

See also *Almanac of the Dead*; Las Casas, Bartolomeo de; El Feo; Tacho.

La Rose, Elise

Elise La Rose is the strong-willed girlfriend of Archilde Leon and granddaughter of Modeste in D'Arcy McNickle's *The Surrounded* (1936,

1978). Her behavior is marked by a rebellious abandon that ultimately serves as the catalyst for the culminating action of the novel. She has always been aggressive in serving her own needs as they are defined by the traditionalism of her grandfather Modeste. She leaves boarding school and its "civilizing" agenda to return to her home, declaring that "the Agent will have to catch me" if she is to be sent back. There is both confidence and challenge in her remark. These qualities set her in contrast to Archilde, who is governed more by passivity than impulsive action.

When Archilde decides to confess the circumstances of the game warden's murder, Elise counsels against it. She "could always smell danger and she had no impulses for heroic action." After the death of Archilde's mother, it is Elise who leads him away into the mountains and guides their flight away from the sheriff and Indian agent. And it is Elise who forces the situation to a climax when she shoots and kills Sheriff Dave Quigley. For all her impulsiveness, Elise is not without reason. She explains to Archilde, "I decided this when we were lying up there on the hill. I said to myself that if Dave Quigley came for you I wouldn't let him take you. I did it and I don't give a damn." (Larson 1978; McNickle 1936, 1978; Owens 1992a; Parker 1997)

See also Agent Parker; Leon, Archilde; Modeste; Quigley, Sheriff Dave.

LaGrinder, Jim

Jim LaGrinder is the mixed-blood suitor of Cogewea in Mourning Dove's 1927 novel *Cogewea, the Half-Blood*. He is a stereotypical Westerner, a rider with no "equal on the range" and "an artist with the rope." He is the 27-year-old foreman of the Horseshoe Bend ranch, "a rough nugget—but with an unconscious dignity peculiar to the Indian." He bears a long-suffering love for Cogewea; when he finally asks her to marry him, she turns him down. He does not abandon his love for her, however, and is always vigilant to guard her against the advances of Alfred Densmore, an Easterner who is intent only on debasing her. The Stemteema, Cogewea's grandmother, recognizes in Jim a man who is worthy of Cogewea, and she places her confidence in him. Jim's patience is rewarded when Cogewea realizes her love for him at the end of the novel. Jim has long identified himself as the "best rider of the Flathead," and Cogewea's remark, "do let up on the 'best rider' stunt," assures the reader of Jim's evolving personality. (Larson 1978; Mourning Dove 1927, 1981; Owens 1992a)

> See also Carter, John and Julia; Cogewea; *Cogewea, the Half-Blood: A Depiction of the Great Montana Cattle Range*; Densmore, Alfred; McDonald, Mary; The Stemteema.

Lakota Woman

Lakota Woman is the first autobiography of the contemporary political activist Mary Crow Dog (born in 1953). Since the 1990 volume, written in collaboration with Richard Erdoes, Mary Crow Dog has retaken her maiden name, Mary Brave Bird, and written a second autobiographical volume.

The book starts off with the author's declaration of who she is: "I am a woman of the Red Nation, a Sioux woman. That is not easy." The theme is repeated throughout the first chapter as Crow Dog sets the stage for a book that is just as full of information and insight as it is full of unbridled anger. She also introduces the theme of assimilation, or "whitemanizing" as she calls it, and the erosion of Indian cultures

that has been its result. The intrusion and influences of white culture have disrupted the "tiyospaye, the extended family group, the basic hunting band" of Siouan culture. She contrasts her background as an *iyeska,* or "breed," with the background of her husband, Leonard Crow Dog, whom she married in 1973. While her family converted to Christianity and intermarried with whites, Crow Dog's family remained traditional "full-bloods—the Sioux of the Sioux."

Crow Dog's early childhood was marked by the absence of her biological father, the drunkenness and abuse of her stepfather, and an ongoing rebellion against her mother. The happiest parts of her childhood were spent with her grandparents, until she was taken away to boarding school. Both her mother and grandmother were acculturated Sioux, having been trained at mission school in Catholicism and having abandoned many traditional Sioux ways. Crow Dog says, "If I wanted to be an Indian I had to go elsewhere to learn how to become one." This quest to understand and reclaim her Indianness becomes a driving force in her life. She sought out older relatives who still maintained traditional ways and language so that she might learn the stories of her culture.

Her education was cut short, however, by the "kidnapping" that took her to boarding school. At boarding school, she experienced many of the cruelties that have marked the institution for generations. Students were forced to speak English, to dress and wear their hair in the fashion of whites, to pray to the Christian God rather than to "Wakan Tanka, the Indian Creator." Crow Dog also learned that "racism breeds racism in reverse," and when she left the school, it was with the burden of a personal racism against whites as well as with a backlog of wrongs committed against her by those with an attitude of cultural superiority.

It is little wonder, then, that Crow Dog left school to enter a cycle of drinking, fighting, joyriding, and shoplifting. In an unarticulated way, Crow Dog felt that her behaviors were at least a weak attempt to redress wrongs. After some while, Crow Dog became aware of her

An unidentified Native American woman is wrapped in an upside-down American flag during the American Indian Affairs takeover of the Bureau of Indian Affairs building in Washington, D.C., in 1972. (UPI/Corbis-Bettmann)

dissatisfaction with herself and her lifestyle. When she was apprehended for theft, she realized that "there were better, more mature ways to fight for my rights." Her "aimlessness ended when [she] encountered AIM."

The American Indian Movement (AIM) "hit our reservation like a tornado," says Crow Dog. When she joined AIM, she quit drinking and found a focus for her anger and a vehicle for her energies. She was with the organization when they occupied the Bureau of Indian Affairs (BIA) building in Washington in 1972, and she participated in the takeover at Wounded Knee, South Dakota, in 1973. In fact, her son Pedro was born during the Wounded Knee occupation. Much of the last portion of the text is given over to a discussion of the political protest at Wounded Knee and a running account of the firefight between AIM and the FBI. Crow Dog's autobiography also sheds light on the civil war that was occurring on the Pine Ridge Reservation in the battle between traditionals and "the half-breed Uncle Tomahawks who did not represent the grass-roots people."

In her association with AIM, Mary Brave Bird met Leonard Crow Dog, and they were later married. With Leonard, Mary found a family of traditional Sioux, and her connection to her tribal background increased. Because of Leonard's position as spiritual and moral leader of the AIM protesters, Mary's involvement escalated, particularly after Leonard was imprisoned for his part in the Wounded Knee occupation. She became a visible focus in the pressure for his ultimate release. The stresses of a marriage to a Lakota holy man took their toll on Mary, but the autobiography ends with Mary's affirmation: "Wherever Native Americans struggle for their rights, Leonard is there. Life goes on."

See also Indian Boarding School; *Ohitika Woman.*

Lamartine, Beverly (Hat)

In Louise Erdrich's *Love Medicine* (1984, 1993), Bev Lamartine is the brother of Henry Lamartine, Senior, who was married to Lulu Lamartine. Bev left the reservation during the time of the government's policies of termination and relocation, policies that proved disastrous to many Indians, including Bev. He believes the promises of the relocation program, however, and convinces himself that in "the Twin Cities there were great relocation opportunities for Indians with a certain amount of natural stick-to-it-iveness and pride." But in the Twin Cities, he marries a blonde woman who won't admit to her family that he is Indian and who refuses to have children. He takes a job selling home workbooks door to door, a job that he realizes later he could never make a living at should he move back to the reservation.

He returns to the reservation for the funeral of his brother, and he and Lulu have a brief but intense affair. Henry Junior is the result of their love, though Lulu never tells Bev that he is indeed the father. Bev returns to the city and creates a fantasy over the years that Henry Junior is his son. He shows pictures of the boy to his customers as a way of moving into his sales pitch, pretending that he is showing them his son. Finally, his dissatisfaction with his life in the city, with his wife, and with his childlessness drives him back to the reservation, where he again begins a relationship with Lulu. In desperation to claim Henry Junior as his son, he marries Lulu. A week later, though, he realizes that he must "retrench" and "forget about Henry Junior." (Erdrich 1984, 1993; Gleason 1987; Schultz 1991)

> See also Lamartine, Henry Junior; Lamartine, Lulu Nanapush; *Love Medicine*; Termination and Relocation.

Lamartine, Henry Junior

A character in Louise Erdrich's *Love Medicine* (1984, 1993), Henry Junior is another whose parentage is unknown or publicly unacknowledged. His mother is Lulu Lamartine, but he was conceived at the funeral of her husband Henry Lamartine, Senior, his supposed father. His actual father is Beverly (Hat) Lamartine, the brother of Henry. Unlike Lyman Lamartine and Lipsha Morrissey, however, the tangle of his heritage does not constitute his personal crisis. Henry Junior's crisis stems from his participation in the Vietnam War.

Before he leaves for his military service, Henry Junior and his brother Lyman buy a red convertible and drive in a big looping circle across the western United States, to Alaska, and then along the Canadian border back home. The trip is marked by a carefree spontaneity that Henry Junior will never again enjoy. Henry's time in the army includes nine months of combat in Vietnam and six months as a prisoner of war of the North Vietnamese. He is released from the army with no real attention given to his posttraumatic stress disorder. He wanders in Fargo, North Dakota, for three weeks before returning to the reservation. While in Fargo, he meets up with Albertine Johnson, a 15-year-old runaway. They recognize each other from the reservation and spend some time together; the connection with Albertine almost allows Henry to reintegrate into society, but in the end, his trauma is too great for him to adjust to civilian life.

He returns to the reservation and sits psychologically paralyzed in front of the TV. His mother sees the stare on his face and recognizes it as the same look on the face of the dead man she found in her childhood playhouse in the woods. Lyman attempts to shake Henry from his depression by giving him a purpose to live. He goes to the red convertible that he has lovingly kept for Henry in his absence, and he takes a hammer to it, pours dirt in the carburetor, and rips the seats. He then waits for Henry to notice it and fix it. Lyman's sacrifice of the car does have a limited success, for Henry begins to recover somewhat. The two brothers drive the car to the river and drink a few beers and talk. But Henry tells Lyman, "It's no use." He dances a frenzied dance and then jumps into the river. His last words are "My boots are filling." (Erdrich 1984, 1993; Flavin 1989; Gleason 1987; Ruppert 1995; Schultz 1991)

> See also Johnson, Albertine; Lamartine, Beverly (Hat); Lamartine, Lulu Nanapush; Lamartine, Lyman; *Love Medicine*; Morrissey, Lipsha.

Lamartine, Lulu Nanapush

Lulu Nanapush Lamartine is a central character in Louise Erdrich's *Love Medicine* (1984, 1993) and *Tracks* (1988) and a minor character in *The Bingo Palace* (1994). She is the daughter of Fleur Pillager and, presumably, of Eli Kashpaw, though her conception is veiled in mystery. Nanapush's narration in *Tracks* is directed to Lulu in an attempt to reconcile her to her mother and to caution her against an ill-advised marriage. Nanapush tells her she was born on "the day we shot the last bear, drunk, on the reservation." When Father Damien looks for help in filling out the birth certificate, Nanapush steps in and gives the child his own name, perhaps deflecting, perhaps stirring up, rumors about her father. He gives her the first name "Lulu" after his own beloved daughter who died in childhood.

Lulu's childhood is marked by her journeys to get help. When Nanapush and Margaret are attacked, Lulu runs off and is spared. When Fleur's second child is coming too early, Lulu is sent to get Margaret to help. This time her feet are badly frozen, and she nearly loses them. It is Nanapush who saves them by keeping them warm and singing healing songs.

Fleur sends Lulu to government school to protect her from being harmed in the allotment battles, which have grown personal. Lulu feels betrayed and believes that Fleur is sending her away to punish her for finding and playing with the dead body of Napoleon, Bernadette Morrissey's brother. Thus begins the rift in their relationship, which Nanapush tries to heal with his stories. When it is safe for Lulu to return to the reservation, Nanapush and Margaret make official efforts to get her back; after five years, she is returned from Indian boarding school, and they are together again.

As a young woman, Lulu's life is marked by reckless love. She is hurt when Nector Kashpaw switches his attentions from her to Marie Lazarre. When they marry, Lulu responds with all the energy of scorned love. She goes to the island of Moses Pillager and wins his love, staying with him until she must leave the island for help in delivering their child. Though for most of her adult life she is married to Henry Lamartine, Senior, none of her eight sons are his. The "three oldest were Nanapushes. The next oldest were Morrisseys who took the name Lamartine, and then there were more assorted younger Lamartines." She carries on a five-year affair with Nector Kashpaw in midlife and bears him a son, Lyman Lamartine. For a week she is married to her dead husband's brother, Beverly Lamartine, who is also the father of her son Henry Lamartine, Junior.

Despite the appearances of blatant promiscuity, Lulu's many loves are not the result of "loving no one" but of being "in love with the whole world and all that lived in its rainy arms." But in embracing all of the good, Lulu gets her share of the bad as well. Her affair with Nector ends painfully when he, as tribal chairman, delivers notice to her door that the land her home is on has never officially belonged to the Lamartines and that she must move. The note is never delivered, though; while waiting for Lulu to return and receive it, Nector allows it to catch fire from a cigarette and eventually burns down the whole house. Lulu returns to the blazing fire just in time to rescue the young Lyman from a closet. She loses her hair in the fire, and it never grows back. Her resulting baldness strengthens her connection to her mother and grandmother, who both had periods of baldness that led to great personal power.

Her sincere marriage to Beverly Lamartine ends just days later when she learns that he already has a wife in the Twin Cities. But her greatest grief comes when her son Henry Junior returns from Vietnam, psychically wounded, unable to readjust, and dies a suicide.

Her later years are marked by personal growth and political involvement. After age 65, she moves into the senior citizens home and becomes friends with her former rival in love, Marie Lazarre Kashpaw. She also becomes friends with Lipsha Morrissey, her grandson who is unaware of their relationship; she reveals to him that Gerry Nanapush is his father, and in doing so enables him to cross the troubled waters of his adolescence into manhood. Lulu returns to the old traditional Ojibwa

(Anishinabe) ways and becomes a political activist for Indian rights; she refuses to allow the U.S. census takers in her door because "every time they counted us they knew the precise number to get rid of." In *The Bingo Palace* she is even able to arrange the prison transfer for her son Gerry Nanapush, which results in his escape. (Barry and Prescott 1989; Bomberry 1994; Erdrich 1984, 1993; Erdrich 1988; Erdrich 1994; Flavin 1991; Owens 1992a; Ruppert 1995)

> See also *The Bingo Palace*; Kashpaw, Marie Lazarre; Kashpaw, Nector; Lamartine, Beverly (Hat); Lamartine, Henry Junior; Lamartine, Lyman; *Love Medicine*; Morrissey, Lipsha; Nanapush; Nanapush, Gerry; Pillager, Fleur; Pillager, Moses; *Tracks*.

Lamartine, Lyman

Lyman is a character in Louise Erdrich's *Love Medicine* (1984, 1993) and *The Bingo Palace* (1994). He is another of her characters who has a complicated family tree; he is the son of Lulu Lamartine and Nector Kashpaw, conceived in the midst of a five-year adultery. He is raised as a Lamartine, but instinctively knows, as does the community, that Kashpaw is his father. He is never acknowledged by Nector, however, and as an adult, he longs for some indication that he was loved by Kashpaw.

Even as a teenager, he realizes that his "one talent" is making money; by 16, he already owns the Joliet Café. Before it is destroyed by a tornado, he has all his relatives and their relatives over to dinner, and he buys, with his brother Henry Junior, a red convertible. He and Henry take the car on a cross-country trip that proves to be the last time of wholeness and normalcy in either of their lives. Henry leaves for Vietnam soon after the trip, and when he returns some years later, he is in deep psychological pain. In an attempt to move Henry toward health, Lyman sacrifices the red convertible; he smashes the car, hoping that Henry will find some purpose and pleasure in life from fixing it back up. The plan is only partially successful, and before long Lyman once again sacrifices the car for his beloved brother. The two go for a

ride and stop at the river to drink a few beers. They talk, almost like old times, and dance; then Henry Junior jumps into the river and drowns. After an unsuccessful rescue, Lyman pushes the car into the river, as if to suggest an accident and not a suicide.

Lyman sinks into a year of guilt and despair over the death of his brother and does not emerge from it until, in an ironic turn that reconstructs his character, he finds his purpose for living in a piece of mail from the IRS saying that he owes money. To the U.S. government, he is alive, existing on paper, and owing money. In a disappointing contradiction to his mother's belief that the government only counted Indians in an effort to know "the precise number to get rid of," Lyman becomes a Bureau of Indian Affairs (BIA) bureaucrat. He quickly rises through the ranks of the BIA, and works in the BIA area office in Aberdeen, South Dakota, until his wily and powerful mother gets him transferred back home to run a tomahawk factory. It is the same factory that was proposed during Nector's time, but now his son is in charge of the factory and is his mother's puppet. Lyman laments, "I was keeping her instinct to control a man alive, giving her strength."

He insists on running the factory according to BIA principles rather than by the advice of his mother, and the decision causes him no end of trouble, until finally the factory explodes in a farcical battle. In the aftermath of the debacle, Lyman asks Marie Kashpaw if Nector ever talked about him. They share a moment of mutual understanding and grief; Marie's hands had been hurt in a birch bark machine during the chaos, and Lyman cradles them in much the same way that Nector had done years before on the path from the convent. Lyman apologizes and realizes that it was the first apology "that ever made [him] feel forgiven too."

When Lyman appears in *The Bingo Palace* (1994), he is the "reservation's biggest cheese" and "has run so many businesses that nobody can keep track." Lyman is "an island of *have* in a sea of *have-nots*." He and Shawnee Ray Toose are "long-term engaged," and there is talk of him "running for elected office, making politician's hay." In view of the ease with which Lyman gains power and money, there is a fitting satisfaction when it is Lipsha, the "biggest waste on the reservation," who is able to challenge his personal and professional plans. Not only is Lipsha in love with Shawnee, but because he is more traditional than political, he realizes that Lyman's plans for a bingo palace on Lake Matchimanito must be stopped.

Though Lyman is "snarled so deeply into the system that [he] can't be pulled without unraveling the bones and guts," and though he cannot value either tradition or people in other than a mercantile manner (he sees only the dollar worth of Nector's ceremonial pipe, and he views Shawnee Ray as an asset in his political career), he does experience some important growth in the novel. He goes on a vision quest under the leadership of Xavier Toose, a respected elder, and experiences a healing vision. He sees Henry Junior, who tells him to put aside his old grass-dancing outfit that Lyman has worn in both honor and guilt. He tells Lyman that it is calm where he is; Lyman need no longer feel responsible for allowing Henry to die "the worst death for a Chippewa to experience," death by drowning.

When Lyman appears in *Tales of Burning Love* (1996), he has "aged carefully, not to wisdom but to power." He uses his power to help rescue Jack Mauser's construction company with the provision that Jack understands Lyman's new role in the deal. "Once you're back," Lyman tells Jack, "you're back for good. You're my man." (Erdrich 1984, 1993; Erdrich 1994; Erdrich 1996; Gleason 1987)

See also *The Bingo Palace*; Johnson, Zelda Kashpaw; Kashpaw, Marie Lazarre; Kashpaw, Nector; Lamartine, Henry Junior; Lamartine, Lulu Nanapush; *Love Medicine*; Mauser, Jack; Morrissey, Lipsha; *Tales of Burning Love*; Toose, Shawnee Ray; Toose, Xavier.

Lame Bull

Lame Bull is the husband of Teresa First Raise and the stepfather of the narrator of James Welch's *Winter in the Blood* (1974, 1986). He is a crude and laughable man but is hardworking,

a good farmer, and apparently a good mate to Teresa. The narrator views him with some suspicion, wondering if he married Teresa's farm rather than her. The arrival of Lame Bull into the life of Teresa significantly alters the life of the narrator; after Teresa marries Lame Bull, eight years her junior, she tells the narrator, "There isn't enough here for you. You would do well to start looking around."

A man who is not wasteful of motion, Lame Bull digs the grave for the nameless narrator's grandmother with just enough room, he imagines, for the coffin. When the coffin is lowered into the grave, it gets stuck halfway down; Lame Bull climbs into the grave and jumps up and down on the coffin until it settles "enough to look respectable." In an act of usurpation, however mild and well intentioned, Lame Bull steps forward to claim the responsibility for delivering the eulogy. He says, "I suppose me being the head of the family, it's up to me to say a few words about our beloved relative and friend."

He delivers a eulogy then that is simultaneously comic and cutting. Teresa moans at the thought of him delivering the eulogy, and his beginning warrants her fear: "Here lies a simple woman . . . who devoted herself to . . . rocking . . . and not a bad word about anybody. . . ." Teresa moans louder as he continues, and the narrator escapes in a daydream. By the time Lame Bull says, "who never gave anybody any crap . . ." Teresa has fallen to her knees on the ground, and the narrator has performed an act of dignity and grace that far exceeds the left-handed praise of Lame Bull—he throws the old grandmother's tobacco pouch into the grave. (Velie 1978; Welch 1974, 1986)

See also First Raise, Teresa; Nameless Narrator; *Winter in the Blood*.

Lame Deer, Seeker of Visions: The Life of a Sioux Medicine Man

John (Fire) Lame Deer teams with Richard Erdoes on this autobiography of a Lakota holy man. *Lame Deer* (1972) is another autobiography in the same vein as *Black Elk Speaks*. Born in 1900, Lame Deer offers a next-generation view of the reservation Lakota holy man. Lame Deer's account lacks the solemnity of *Black Elk Speaks* but offers a very human and engaging account of the foibles and victories of Lame Deer. The narrative is a collaborative work and clearly shows the presence of Erdoes in the text. It is not uncommon for Lame Deer's narrative voice to speak directly to Erdoes, and the effect is one of immediacy to the storytelling act. It is not difficult to sense the physical presence of Erdoes in the scene, and the literal audience does much to engage the reader in a performance situation.

The informality of the text is deceptively simple but cannot belie the underlying structure of the autobiography. The book is arranged in 16 thematic chapters, and each chapter has its own structural integrity. There is a strong sense of a community of listeners, not just Erdoes. At times, Lame Deer calls on another audience member to elaborate on a story or vision. Readers sense that Lame Deer is sitting amid an audience of some size and that the story is truly communal, not singular. There is even a point at which Lame Deer says that he must leave the narrative and go pray; he turns the story over to others in his group. The group is engaged in a sit-in on the top of Mount Rushmore, and Lame Deer says:

> Well, I came up here to pray, to do a ceremony, plant a stick. So I'll crawl into the boulders back there, do a little singing, listen to the voices. In the meantime, you can ask these ladies here, Muriel Waukazoo and Lizzy Fast Horse, why they are up here.

The conversational tone reinforces the reader's impression that Lame Deer's text has not been tampered with to create the kind of literary voice that imbues Black Elk's autobiography, *Black Elk Speaks*.

Lame Deer starts his autobiography not with his entrance into childhood, but with his entrance into manhood, his first vision quest. At age 16, Lame Deer, still bearing his child's name, enters the vision pit, where he will stay for four days and nights, seeking a vision. When it is over, he "would no longer be a boy, but a man." He would have a vision and be "given a man's name." Before he enters the vision pit, he undergoes a ceremonial sweat bath to purify and cleanse himself. Lame Deer enters the pit equipped with a blanket that his grandmother has made for him, a peace pipe left for him by the medicine man, and a gourd rattle in which there were 40 small squares of flesh that his grandmother had cut from her arm. In the pit, Lame Deer hears the voices of "the fowl people, the winged ones, the eagles and the owls." They tell him that it is his gift to become a *wicasa wakan*, a medicine man. He also has a vision of his great-grandfather, Tahca Ushte (Lame Deer), who gives him the gift of his own name. The boy who entered the vision pit with a child's name comes out with a vision, a calling, and a new name—Lame Deer.

In the next chapter, Lame Deer recounts the story of the original Lame Deer, his great-grandfather. This Lame Deer, he says, was killed "by mistake. You could say he was murdered." Lame Deer entered into a treaty with the U.S. government, agreeing to move his people to the newly created reservation near what is now Rapid City, South Dakota. Before moving to the confines of the reservation, Lame Deer gained permission to go on one last buffalo hunt with his people. While they were on this hunt, their peaceful camp was attacked and plundered by Gen. Nelson Appleton Miles and his men. This 1877 battle resulted in the death of Lame Deer. John Lame Deer reports that his great-grandfather's gun now rests in a glass case in the Museum of the American Indian in New York. The moving story of Lame Deer's death is just the first of the many stories that chronicle the efforts of the U.S. government to, at worst, exterminate or, at best, relocate and reinvent the Indian.

The attempts to reeducate the Indian included the enforced use of English at Bureau of Indian (BIA) reservation schools and the shipping of Indian children off to boarding schools. Of his boarding school experience, Lame Deer says:

I wouldn't cooperate in the remaking of myself. I played the dumb Indian. They couldn't make me into an apple—red outside and white inside. . . . I think in the end I got the better of that school. I was more of an Indian when I left them than when I went in.

When John Lame Deer was still a young man, his mother died of tuberculosis, and her last words to him were, "*Onsika, onsika*—pitiful, pitiful." He says, "She wasn't sorry for herself; she was sorry for me." And, indeed, her words are an accurate prediction of the next stage of Lame Deer's life. What followed for him was a period of wandering, poverty, drinking, restlessness, an imprudent marriage and divorce, and finally jail. Along the way, Lame Deer rode the rodeo circuit, was a bronco-buster, and even became a rodeo clown, with a stage persona and name—Alice Jitterbug. He harvested potatoes, herded sheep, and was at various times a tribal policeman, a farmer, and a soldier in World War II. All the while he was drifting from job to job, though, Lame Deer was always seeking out medicine men and learning from them. After a lengthy and circuitous apprenticeship, which included a car-jacking spree and time in a reformatory, Lame Deer settled into his mature years as a medicine man.

John Lame Deer provides much information about Lakota spiritual life in his autobiography. He distinguishes the various types of Lakota medicine men: the *pejuta wicasa*, the man of herbs; the *yuwipi*, "the tied one, the man who uses the power of the rawhide and the stones to find and to cure"; the *wapiya*, the conjurer who can heal or cause illnesses; and the *wicasa wakan*, the medicine man who has had a vision on a *hanblechia* (vision quest). Lame Deer also gives accounts of the Ghost Dance, the Sun Dance, the Native American Church, and other spiritual rituals of the Lakota. Lame Deer lives in a place where "the spiritual and the commonplace are one," and his autobiography reflects that synthesis. (Lame Deer 1972)

See also *Black Elk Speaks*; Native American Autobiography.

Las Casas, Bartolomeo de

In Leslie Marmon Silko's *Almanac of the Dead* (1991), Bartolomeo is the "holy man" who wants to cause a Marxist revolution in Mexico. He is a Cuban communist whose major contribution to the Mexican revolution is in his ability to raise funds worldwide for the cause. He is the "liaison with Cubans and other friends of indigenous people" as well as the sometime lover of both Alegria Martinez-Soto and Angelita La Escapia. When he finally comes to realize that the Indians are not interested in ideological Marxism, that "all they wanted was to retake their land from the white man," Bartolomeo is greatly disturbed. He goes to the mountain headquarters of El Feo and Angelita La Escapia to shake them into compliance but is greeted by a hostile Angelita and her followers. She calls for his arrest in view of his recent unauthorized action of printing handbills with Menardo's dead body and the caption, "This Is How Capitalists Die." His propagandistic action endangers Tacho's life, and Angelita arrests him for that and for "crimes against history," the rewriting and omission of the history of Indian peoples' resistance to the Europeans. He is executed by hanging.

Like his historical antecedent, the sixteenth-century Bartolomé de Las Casas, whose encounters with the Indians of the New World were problematic at best, this contemporary "holy man" does as much harm as good in his social ministry. (Silko 1991)

See also *Almanac of the Dead*; El Feo; La Escapia, Angelita; Martinez-Soto, Alegria; Menardo; Tacho.

Lawrence, Bird

A white man who married a Spokane woman, Bird Lawrence is the father of Reggie Polatkin in Sherman Alexie's *Indian Killer* (1996). Antagonistic toward Indians, he works for the Bureau of Indian Affairs and demands that his mixed-blood son be the "right" kind of Indian. Bird bombards the young Reggie with stories of "hostile" Indians and physically abuses him when Reggie fails to parrot his own hatred of Indians. Until Reggie "earned the right to be a

Lawrence," Bird insists that he "use Polatkin, his Indian surname."

When Bird develops terminal prostate cancer and his wife claims he has changed, Reggie is past caring about his father and refuses to talk with him. (Alexie 1996)

See also *Indian Killer*; Polatkin, Reggie.

Lecha

In Leslie Marmon Silko's *Almanac of the Dead* (1991), Lecha is one of the principal characters who, with her twin sister Zeta, provides a cohesiveness for this sprawling novel. Until their teenage years, the twins were raised in Mexico by their Mexican Indian mother, who disapproved of the influence that her mother, Yoeme, had on them. Their white father is mostly absent from their childhood and reappears in their lives after the death of their mother, but soon after commits suicide. During their childhood in Mexico, the twins were sexually abused by their uncle Federico, and in her adulthood, Lecha travels to Mexico to dig up the bones of her uncle and throw them in the city dump. Having been forced to be near him in life, she refuses to be near him in death in the family graveyard.

Lecha abandoned her son Ferro when he was less than one week old, and he was raised by Zeta. While Lecha found a career as a TV psychic, Zeta remained on the family ranch in Tucson and developed a smuggling business. On her last TV appearance, Lecha has a vision in which she identifies the heads of the U.S. ambassador to Mexico and his chief aide floating in the waters of a river. She realizes that she will become a suspect in the murders because of her knowledge of the crimes. Thus "forced" into retirement, Lecha returns to Tucson and the ranch where her sister and son live.

Lecha arrives at the ranch in a wheelchair and accompanied by Seese, her secretary and "nurse." Lecha's retirement provides the opportunity for her to work on the notebooks that Yoeme had given her and Zeta some 50 years ago. These notebooks are fragments and reconstructions of the almanac containing ancient tribal texts that foretell the future of the Americas. The notebooks "are all in broken Spanish or corrupt Latin" and require months of "research in old grammars" for Lecha to translate. She is aided in this process by Seese.

In addition to typing translations of the almanac, Seese's job is to administer regular doses of drugs, Demerol and Percodan, to Lecha. Lecha accounts for the wheelchair and drugs by claiming she is dying of cancer, but the narrative later reveals that it is the terrible burden of her psychic powers and of the responsibility as a keeper of the almanac that causes her intense physical pain. Historically, many of the keepers of the almanac have gone crazy, and until Lecha is fully absorbed in the translation of the texts, she remains vulnerable. Once she is captured by her task, her need for drugs diminishes; working on the almanac brings both her and Seese to physical and emotional health.

At the end of the novel, Lecha attends the International Holistic Healers Convention and meets up with many of her old psychic friends. Soon after, the Tucson ranch is raided, and Lecha immediately gathers up Seese and Sterling, the compound gardener, and flees in her old white Lincoln. They drop off Sterling near the Laguna Reservation and journey on to South Dakota, where Lecha will join Wilson Weasel Tail and others who are making preparations for the coming war. (Silko 1991)

See also *Almanac of the Dead*; Ferro; Root; Seese; Sterling; Yoeme; Zeta.

Left Handed, Son of Old Man Hat: A Navajo Autobiography

Left Handed, Son of Old Man Hat: A Navajo Autobiography (1938, 1995), recorded by Walter Dyk, is the result of Dyk's trip to the Navajo Reservation in 1934 to "collect material for a study of clan and kinship functions in Navaho [*sic*] society." The wealth of material that Left Handed provided was overwhelming. The present volume accounts for only the first 20 years of his life, taking him to the time of his marriage. After Dyk's death, his wife completed the second volume of Left Handed's life. A

A 1934 photograph of the Navajo Left Handed, the autobiographical subject of Walter Dyk's 1938 publication. (University of Oklahoma Press)

lengthy volume, it is nearly 600 pages in length and covers only the next three years of his life.

Like most mediated autobiographical texts, this one has been arranged and edited by the collector. Dyk says he added "nothing" and left out "only some few minor experiences and repetitious episodes." At times the account is somewhat confusing because, as Dyk points out, kinship terminology is quite different in Navajo culture and white culture: "'mother' refers to a great many other women besides one's real mother."

The volume opens with perhaps the most poetic phrase found in the book: "I was born when the cottonwood leaves were about the size of my thumbnail." In what follows, Left Handed recounts his experiences as a young boy who is just coming to awareness in his world. The narrative voice of Left Handed is quite winning and convincing because it accurately reveals the lack of understanding that a child has of the adult world. For example, Left Handed tells of how his family would move from summer camp to winter camp. The young Left Handed cannot understand why the family must endure the cold and snow when they could simply move back to the summer camp where the weather is always pleasant and warm.

As Left Handed grows older, the major concerns of the text focus around sheepherding, the principal occupation of the agrarian Navajo. He learns that each sheep is precious, that "there's a million in one. . . . you don't want to kill a young ewe . . . for there's a million in one of those." His father also tells him that he must have a song for his sheep, that "if you have only one song for the sheep you'll raise them, nothing will bother them, nothing will happen to them." Caring for sheep requires vigilant care, and Left Handed is being trained by his father to assume the role of a responsible herder.

Left Handed reveals much information, perhaps at the urging of Dyk, about sexual relations in the culture. The narrative also provides considerable information about the chants and ceremonies of the Navajo. Left Handed mentions the Knife Chant, the Night Chant, the Feather Rite, the Enemy Rite, and others. As is true in many mediated autobiographies, the real desire of the collector is to gather information about a *culture*; the *person* interviewed and his or her narrative are secondary to the purpose of the collector. Doubtless the mission of Dyk to gather "the commonplace, the homespun stuff from day to day with which life everywhere is so largely concerned" and "the ordinary, the petty, the humdrum insignificant affairs as well" contributes to the backgrounding of the man Left Handed. (Dyk 1938, 1995; Krupat 1994)

See also Native American Autobiography.

Leon, Archilde

Archilde Leon is the mixed-blood protagonist of D'Arcy McNickle's 1936 novel *The Surrounded*. The essential conflict of the novel is set into motion by the split identity of Archilde's character and by the encroachment of Catholicism onto the "paganism" of the Salish people. When the novel opens, Archilde is just returning to his father's ranch after an absence of nearly a year. He goes first to see his mother, who lives in a small cabin set away from the big house of his father. Their initial encounter highlights the distance in their relationship. Archilde does not value the ways of his mother, who is entrenched in a tribal ethos in spite of her long connection to the Catholic faith. He feels distanced from both the old ways and from Catholicism. And when Archilde goes to the big house to see his father, their relationship is no better. Max Leon is still the demanding, sarcastic, and disapproving father he left a year ago. The old antagonisms immediately surface, and Archilde wonders what is in his father's face "that could so dominate one who was no longer a child."

What Archilde returns to is not so different from what he left, but his changed perspective—that is, his outsider status—causes him to view his home and family in a new way. He wins an unspoken but grudging admiration from his father when he talks back to him in a sudden burst of anger. But as the narrator points out, in Max Leon's family, "There was always this distrust, this warfare."

Archilde has been away in Portland, Oregon, living an acculturated life in the white world, playing the violin for a living. He returns home to say some final good-byes before leaving for good. The novel establishes a series of delays, though, and Archilde's plans do not come to fruition. The first crisis comes when his brother Louis steals some horses. Catharine, Archilde's mother, wants to go into the mountains, ostensibly for a last hunting trip but also to find Louis.

They do meet up with Louis, who has just shot a doe. He is quickly apprehended by Dan Smith, the game warden, and a struggle ensues. Smith shoots Louis, and Archilde's mother kills Smith from behind with a blow to the head with a hatchet. They bury Smith's body on the mountain and take Louis's body home. Archilde is detained in jail by the Indian agent for over a month before he is released.

When he is released, many of Archilde's external situations improve. His relationship with his father moves to one of mutual respect and understanding. Max Leon dies soon after from pneumonia, but he dies holding Archilde's hand and whispering, "Too bad to leave you now. Have to learn many things yourself."

After Max's death, Archilde acts on his behalf to reconcile his parents' broken marriage. He tells his mother of Max's intentions to talk with her and that he "felt bad about the old days." His mother murmurs, "Ah, Max!" and the reconciliation is complete. Through the agency of Archilde, another family problem is solved. His nephew, Mike, returns from school "sick." He is afraid of the dark and is rumored to have been visited by the Evil One. Old Modeste sends for Archilde so that they might plan for Mike's cure. While Archilde is visiting Modeste, he meets Elise La Rose, Modeste's granddaughter, and the two become friends. Though Elise is a wild young woman, she and the quiet Archilde become a couple. Archilde is well aware, however, that his reputation is being changed by his association with Elise. When he and Elise become the subject of rumors, he is angered because "he wasn't inclined to hell-raising . . . These people knew nothing

about him, so their talk came out of spite and dirty thinking."

Within the Salishan community, Archilde gains respect when his mother is ill and dying. When the family thinks she is dead, Archilde sits by her side, and she revives and speaks to him. The extended family thinks, "It was a mysterious thing, this dying and coming to life! There must be a special power in that Archilde!"

But Archilde's power is limited. His mother dies, and he moves into a dazed state during which he cannot reason clearly. When Elise urges him to flee to the mountains, he accompanies her against his better judgment. It is not long before they are found and arrested by the authorities. Elise shoots and kills Sheriff Dave Quigley, and Archilde stands numbly by, holding his hands out for the handcuffs of Agent Parker. In the end, Archilde is truly "the surrounded." (Hoefel 1998; Holton 1997; Larson 1978; McNickle 1936, 1978; Owens 1992a)

See also Agent Parker; Father Grepilloux; La Rose, Elise; Leon, Catharine; Leon, Louis; Leon, Max; Mike and Narcisse; Modeste; Quigley, Sheriff Dave; Smith, Dan; *The Surrounded*.

Leon, Catharine

"Faithful Catharine" is a character in D'Arcy McNickle's *The Surrounded* (1936, 1978). Catharine is the first person in the valley to embrace Christianity, the first to be baptized by the fathers. When she is 14 years old, the "Lady Black Robes" came to "make a school." Catharine, the daughter of Running Wolf, is there to greet the nuns and to attend their school. Though the sisters "taught her many arts," they were unable to help her value the etiquette and homemaking skills of another culture. So when, at 20, she marries the Spaniard Max Leon, she still holds on to the old ways of the Salish. Her marriage to a white man quickly points out cultural differences in their lives. She learns that with a white man she cannot travel to visit her relatives, nor can she welcome them to her home when they travel to see her. She also learns that the white man is controlled by mechanical time. For Catharine, "The clock was a new thing and, small as it was, it was mighty. It made a man march around. A woman marched too."

She grows old raising the children of her Spanish husband, and some of her family never get over the fact that she is *Pu-Soiapi*, married to a white man. Still, she "occupied a place of distinction in the tribe" and "was a woman whose opinions were valued." Her devotion to the Catholic faith inspires many, and she herself never questions her decision to embrace the new faith until the death of her son Louis. She and Archilde go into the mountains for one last hunting trip and to find Louis, who is fleeing authorities because he has stolen some horses. Dan Smith, the game warden, comes upon them and shoots Louis in an argument over an illegal deer kill. In a surge of maternal instinct, Catharine attacks Smith with a hatchet and kills him. She and Archilde bury Smith's body and return to their home with the body of Louis in tow.

After the murder, she goes to confession and starts to "carry out the schedule of penance imposed upon her, and then she stopped." Confession and penance are no longer efficacious. She is drawn away from Catholicism and back to her tribal faith: "She was an old woman now, and it seemed that the older she got the further she went on the trail leading backward." Since the death of Louis and the murder of the game warden, Catharine "had lost something. She was a pagan again. She who had been called Faithful Catharine and who had feared hell for her sons and for herself—her belief and her fear alike had died in her."

Catharine meets with Modeste and a small group of Indians for a secret ceremony, the using of the whip. Before the priests came with the pattern of confession and penance, behaviors that violated the tribal ethic were dealt with by the use of the whip. She says, "In the old days you were whipped and no one spoke of it again. The heart was free." She confesses the murder to the group and tells them of a dream that she had for three straight nights. In the dream she goes to the Christian heaven but is unhappy and out of place. There are no Indians there. She can see from afar the "Indian place" where campfires burned and meat roasted. She longs to join her friends in that

place but is told that she must first reject her Christian baptism. "When I woke up I knew I had to do it," she says. Her story persuades the group to administer the ancient rite, and "Faithful Catharine" finally finds peace.

Not long after Max dies, Catharine too is dangerously ill. At her bedside, Archilde hears her ask for "no priest," but he is so surprised by her request that he imagines her to be out of her head since "everyone knew how faithful his mother had been." Because Archilde does not know of his mother's renunciation of Christianity until after a priest is summoned, her death is attended by Father Jerome. The ministrations are meaningless, though, for Catharine's return to her tribal religion is complete. However, she dies before she can tell the Indian agent that it was she and not Archilde who killed the game warden. (Larson 1978; McNickle 1936, 1978; Owens 1992a; Wiget 1985)

See also Leon, Archilde; Leon, Louis; Leon, Max; Modeste; Smith, Dan; *The Surrounded*.

Leon, Louis

Louis Leon is the son of Max and Catharine Leon in D'Arcy McNickle's *The Surrounded* (1936, 1978). It is the theft of horses by Louis that unwittingly sets into motion the plot that will result in his own death and his brother Archilde's inescapable bad luck. The trouble begins when the fugitive Louis meets up with his mother and brother on their hunting trip. He shoots a deer, and Dan Smith, the game warden, challenges the legality of his kill. In an argument that follows, Smith kills Louis, and his mother kills the warden. The rest of the novel's plot machinations spin out from this event. (Larson 1978; McNickle 1936, 1978; Owens 1992a; Wiget 1985)

See also Leon, Archilde; Leon, Catharine; Leon, Max; Smith, Dan; *The Surrounded*.

Leon, Max

Max Leon is a character in D'Arcy McNickle's *The Surrounded* (1936, 1978) and is the father of the protagonist, Archilde Leon. A Spanish immigrant to the Sniel-emen valley, he has done well as a rancher and has accumulated considerable wealth and regard in the white community. In spite of his success in the ranching and business worlds, he is not a successful husband and father. He has been married to his wife for 40 years and has fathered 11 children with her but knows that she does not trust him. His wife has lived separately from him for many years, and his older sons have all failed to join him in his ranching. He is a rough, surly, unbending, unforgiving man who has alienated his family and has bred years of distrust in them. He commonly curses his seven sons in front of outsiders and counts them as worthless as seven dogs, for all the use they are to him. Only Agnes, the widowed daughter who lives with him and cares for his house, senses any kindness in Max. She says, "Max is a good fellow, if you're good to him. But bite and he bites back."

Spurred by his own sense of failure or perhaps brought to a point of awareness by the changes he sees in his returning son, Archilde, Max begins a period of reflection on the purpose and meaning of his life. Max is a man who cannot "unburden himself readily," and Father Grepilloux is initially his only confidante in the search for meaning. When he talks with Father Grepilloux, he reveals his first impression of the valley: "You stood there and what you saw made you over. You were born again." He went to live with the Indians and took an Indian wife because "he wanted a free life and they had it." However, he quickly tires of "their footloose and improvident existence," but by that time he has taken the daughter of the old and admired Running Wolf as his wife.

In meeting with Father Grepilloux, he learns of the history of the first Christian encounters with the Salish people, and he is considerably impressed by what he learns. It is Grepilloux who tells him, "You have least to complain of. You lose your sons, but these people have lost a way of life, and with it their pride, their dignity, their strength." For the first time, Max is able to see beyond his own self-absorption and deceptive pride.

The gradual softening of Max first yields fruit the day Archilde is packing his bag to leave the valley. Max goes to him and initiates a conversation, shows him genuine respect, and allows himself to ask a favor of Archilde. With the help of Father Grepilloux, Max is able to start seeing Archilde in a new light; he even makes the effort to change his will in favor of Archilde. Still, he is not above playing a trick on his grandsons Mike and Narcisse to send them back to boarding school. His treachery unsettles him, though, and too late he is learning that "nothing was accomplished with the whip" but that friendliness "seemed to work miracles" with his family.

When Father Grepilloux dies, Max is asked to be a pallbearer, and the honor increases his standing in the community. The death of his friend causes him to question more deeply than he ever has before. He is able to ask, "What good had been accomplished? What evil?" by the intrusion of white "civilization" and religion into the lives of the Salish people. Following the funeral, he gets in a heated argument with Moser, the store owner. In Moser he sees a mirror image of his own capitalistic impulses, and he is angry and ashamed of what has happened to the people of the valley at their gain. He says, "People are starving! They're freezing to death in those shacks by the church. They don't know why; they had nothing to do with it. You and me and Father Grepilloux were the ones who brought it on."

Max's realization comes none too early, for he himself is sick and near death. He does have one final heartening talk with Archilde, when his son tells him everything about the hunting trip and Louis's death. Finally, he is able to free his emotions. They embrace and enjoy an ease with each other that both have longed for. They make plans that will never come to fruition, for Max dies soon after from advanced stages of pneumonia. (Larson 1978; McNickle 1936, 1978; Owens 1992a; Wiget 1985)

See also Father Grepilloux; Leon, Archilde; Leon, Catharine; Leon, Louis; McNickle, D'Arcy; Mike and Narcisse; *The Surrounded.*

The Light People

In his novel *The Light People* (1994), Gordon Henry, Jr., calls upon a range of literary genres to tell the story of a young Anishinabe boy's quest for information about his parents. That Henry does so reflects his indebtedness to both the oral and literary traditions.

The story opens with young Oskinaway thinking of his mother, Mary Squandum, and imagining his unknown father. Oskinaway has been raised by his grandparents since his mother "vanished on the powwow trail." On the day that his mother runs away, Oskinaway has an experience that serves as a metaphor for his quest for information. He goes to the river and puts his hand in to reach a smooth stone. When he tries to pull his hand out, the strength of the river holds him, and he is locked in the river's pull until sundown. When Oskinaway initiates the search for his parents, he and the reader are both pulled into the stream of family story and tribal tradition and cannot escape until the river of story provides the release.

Oskinaway's grandfather takes the boy to Jake Seed, a healer, for help. The complex story that follows is actually a group of stories, each living in another story, like so many nested boxes. Seed's helper, Arthur Boozhoo, starts the journey back into the trail of stories, telling how he began practicing the kind of magic seen at children's birthday parties. He asks his grandfather about magic, and the old man dismisses Arthur's magic of "hand and the eye and memory games"; he tells him instead that "there are healers among us, men and women of gifts and visions. Some are relatives of light people. Sometimes their gifts can bring people back." Arthur begins a four-year apprenticeship with Seed and continues learning about magic. One day he returns to the reservation to find Rose Meskwaa Geeshik, Seed's daughter, at the side of the sick healer. The narrative then moves to Rose's story. She tells of the death of her husband in Vietnam, of her career as a visual artist, and of a stone that is thrown through her window. The stone is "different, almost perfectly round and painted," and it brings her a frightening dream, including a vision of one of the little people, not unlike the little man who visited Arthur Boozhoo in one of his dreams. Four days after the stone breaks her window, Rose is visited by a young boy who apologizes for

throwing it. The boy, Oshawa, then tells his story and the narrative continues traveling back in time; the next story is told by Oshawa's uncle, Oshawanung, who reveals more about the special stone. He points out that it is painted on two sides and says: "Each side tells its story. A person can use this stone to remember, or turn it over and use it as a weapon."

Oshawa's uncle gave his nephew the stone and gave him an accompanying gift of a story. The uncle tells Oshawa: "The stone tells me we can't be killed. We can be hurt; we can be changed; we can be consumed by the desires and passions of ourselves and other people; and we can be buried. But as a people we can't be killed." This affirmation of life and endurance leads the uncle to tell the central story of the novel, the story of the leg of Moses Four Bears.

Four Bears's leg has been amputated, and he requests help in burying it. The task falls to Oshawa's uncle; he cannot fulfill the request because of a raging blizzard and the frozen ground. Instead he puts the leg in the top of a tree and tries to find his way back to safety before he freezes. He cannot make the trip home but stops at the library to spend the night in relative safety. There is no wood in the library for the stove, so he burns books and furniture through the night. He also reads a book by Bombarto Rose, *Mixed-Blood Musings in Obscurity*, the story of another young man who is uncertain of his origins. Gordon Henry continues to probe the antecedents of Bombarto Rose's story. We learn of "the prisoner of haiku," an artist who lost his voice as a young boy when he was punished for speaking Ojibwa (Anishinabe) instead of English at school. The "prisoner" becomes "a silent man of hands, a sculptor, then a political artist" whose politics land him in jail. There he communicates only through the writing of haiku. The story ultimately leads to the story of Abetung and reveals that he is the father of Oskinaway.

The impulse of the narrative reverses, and the remainder of the novel brings the reader back from the past and into the present. Henry focuses his attention once again on the leg of Moses Four Bears. Oshawa is now a young man visiting a museum in Minneapolis on a cultural exchange program. He sees there an "authentic leg preserved in dry ice" and labeled "An Ojibwa leg, circa 1880–1940." He remembers the story his uncle told him, and when he returns to the reservation, he goes straight to his uncle's home. His uncle, Oshawanung, calls Four Bears's son, and before long, the family seeks the legal return of their father's leg. In the court scenes that follow, Gordon Henry displays an admirable control of his art. He provides a strong argument against the historical, and regrettably current, practice of housing Native American bones and artifacts in museums. He does so with such grace and humor that it is difficult to imagine how the practice can continue.

After the court scenes, the narrative continues its reverse order back to its origin in Oskinaway. The story telescopes back from Oshawanung to Oshawa to Rose Meskwaa Geeshik to Arthur Boozhoo to Jake Seed and then to Oskinaway. Jake Seed performs a ceremony that yields the information that Oskinaway has been seeking about his parents. Seed tells Oskinaway that while he was on his spiritual journey, he met a man who he believes is Oskinaway's father but that, "When the time is right you, my boy, will have to find the cave on your own."

The end of the novel focuses on Oskinaway, his studies at veterinary college, his experiences with a broken-winged bird he heals, his discoveries of his heritage. In a comic scene with a political edge, Oskinaway buys a language program that promises it can teach his bird to talk and learn the Preamble to the Constitution of the United States. The instructional tapes are defective, though, and the bird never progresses beyond the phrase "we the people" to the next phrase "of the United States." The political barb here reminds the reader that the opening phrases of the Constitution were reputedly borrowed from the language governing the Iroquois Confederacy. The rhetorical elimination of the "United States" underscores the novel's message of native survival. (Henry 1994; Mee 1987)

See also Henry, Gordon D., Jr.

Liria

Liria is a character in Leslie Marmon Silko's *Almanac of the Dead* (1991) and is the lover of Calabazas, a drug smuggler. Her sister, Sarita, is the wife of Calabazas. In their older years, she and her sister join "a Catholic radical group to help smuggle refugees from Mexico and Guatemala to the United States." It is their group that rescues Alegria Martinez-Soto from the desert after she flees Mexico. (Silko 1991)

See also *Almanac of the Dead*; Calabazas; Martinez-Soto, Alegria; Sarita.

Little Big Mouse

See Sun Bear Sun and Little Big Mouse.

The Lone Ranger and Tonto Fistfight in Heaven

This volume of interrelated short stories by Sherman Alexie (1993) was a citation winner for the PEN/Hemingway Award for best first book of fiction, and deservedly so. Alexie brings his startling voice to contemporary fiction after several volumes of poetry. The 22 stories in the volume introduce characters who will emerge in Alexie's later fiction: Victor Joseph, Junior Polatkin, and Thomas Builds-the-Fire.

The first story, "Every Little Hurricane," reveals the tone and propulsive themes of the book. Victor is a nine-year-old who suffers from nightmares. He awakens on New Year's Eve to a metaphoric hurricane that is buffeting his house; the guests at his parents' party are fighting. Onlookers do not interrupt. They are acting out a centuries-old pattern: "For hundreds of years, Indians were witnesses to crimes of an epic scale." Victor learns early that "one Indian killing another did not create a special kind of storm. This little kind of hurricane was generic. It didn't even deserve a name." Victor leaves his bed and finds his parents passed out. He lies down between them and puts a hand on each of them where he feels "enough hunger in both, enough movement, enough geography and history, enough of everything to destroy the reservation and leave only random debris and broken furniture."

The second story, "A Drug Called Tradition," brings the three main characters of the collection together in a quest for the transforming power of tradition. Victor, Thomas, and Junior drive to Benjamin Lake and recapture, through visions and storytelling, events that perhaps would have marked their lives in a more traditional time. Thomas sees Victor stealing a horse, and then the narrative shifts to a first-person account of Victor stealing a horse named Flight. Junior sees Thomas dancing, and in the account that follows Thomas reenacts the Ghost Dance. Victor sees Junior singing, and Junior narrates his story through an honor song for Crazy Horse. The power of "tradition" wears off, and the young men are brought to their present situation in the twentieth century. They cannot disavow their experience, though, and when they return to the Trading Post, they are met by Victor's grandmother, who says, "I know what you saw." She hands Victor an ancient drum small enough to fit in his hand. "That's my pager," she says. "Just give it a tap and I'll be right over." Victor never uses the drum but keeps it always close, with the knowledge that if he played it, "it might fill up the whole world."

The remaining stories are divided between several narrative voices. One-third of them have an omniscient third-person voice, and the rest are in first person. The first-person stories in the first half of the volume generally give voice to Victor; Junior Polatkin's voice is often featured in the narratives of the second half of the book. The character of Thomas Builds-the-Fire is revealed through third-person narratives. All of the stories are charged with a fierce reality that does not gloss over the poverty, alcoholism, and violence on the reservation.

According to Junior Polatkin, "Victor needed more saving than most anybody besides Lester FallsApart." Victor's life is defined, at least for a while, by the alcoholism of his parents, the abandonment by his father, and his own wasted and alcoholic young life. He does move from alcohol to Diet Pepsi as his drink of choice, but his future seems mired in a benign purpose-lessness. In the story "The Only Traffic Signal on the Reservation Doesn't Flash Red Anymore," he and Adrian sit on the porch playing mock Russian roulette with a pellet gun, watching young basketball players go by. They are aware of a certain replaying of their own histories, of a promising life burned out too early. A year later they are still on the same porch, watching the next generation of promising players walk by. In the house lies the drunken star of last year, his life saturated with despair.

Though several stories show Victor's drunken and violent past, the story "This Is What It Means to Say Phoenix, Arizona" shows him in a redemptive light. His long-absent father has died in Phoenix, and Victor needs to go there to make arrangements for the body and to close his estate. He does not have the money to make the trip, but with funds cobbled together by the Tribal Council and Thomas Builds-the-Fire, he is able to go. In the course of the story, Victor's abusive behavior toward Thomas is revealed, as are the childhood kindnesses of Thomas toward Victor. But now they are joined by a common purpose and a common regard for Victor's father. Thomas tells Victor of the time that his father intervened in his life, and Victor is shocked by the respect that his own father has shown Thomas, the reservation misfit. Victor's picture of both is altered. The story does not end without a touching request by Thomas, which Victor promises to honor. This story is the basis of the film *Smoke Signals,* the first directed, produced, and written by Indians.

Thomas is never given a first-person voice in the book, but his voice is heard very strongly in the story "The Trial of Thomas Builds-the-Fire." He is put on trial for unnamed crimes, and in his testimony, he assumes several personae, including the voice of one of 800 ponies captured and slaughtered by the U.S. Cavalry. He is also Qualchan and Wild Coyote, telling stories of murder, extermination, and dispossession.

The voice of Junior Polatkin is foregrounded in the last half of the collection. He is a basketball-playing intellectual with diabetes, the valedictorian of his high school, burdened with the promise of making a life off the reservation. The most revealing story about Junior is "Somebody Kept Saying Powwow." Norma Many Horses, "a cultural lifeguard . . . watching out for those . . . that were close to drowning," befriends Junior and teaches him many things about himself. Because he has been away to college, she asks him what life off the reservation is like. He answers, "It's like a bad dream you never wake up from." When she asks him about the worst thing he ever did, Junior must face a past in which he actively discriminated against a black basketball player. Norma is the trigger to Junior's conscience, and he accepts responsibility for the things he has done.

Easily the most complex narrator in the volume, Junior is probably the first-person voice in the title story, "The Lone Ranger and Tonto Fistfight in Heaven." In the story, a young Indian goes into a 7–11 store late at night, and his race and appearance contribute to an inordinate fear on the part of the white clerk. The young Indian realizes that his cultural difference establishes him in a place of power, and though that power is gained through the ignorance and racism of the clerk, he, rather understandably, pushes his advantage. The result is a satisfying reversal of position and power that calls into question the old Lone Ranger and Tonto paradigm of race relations.

It is true that the stories show the painful social realities of the reservation, but it would take a careless and callous reader indeed to fail to see the celebration, hope, humor, and enduring human spirit of the characters who people Alexie's volume. In "Imagining the Reservation," the narrator says that "Survival = Anger x Imagination." It would be a serious mistake to recoil at Alexie's anger and miss the imagination and survival. (Alexie 1993)

See also Alexie, Sherman; Builds-the-Fire, Thomas; *Indian Killer*; Joseph, Victor; Polatkin, Junior; *Reservation Blues*.

Loney, Ike

Ike Loney is the father of Jim Loney in the James Welch novel *The Death of Jim Loney* (1979,

1987). An irresponsible husband and father, he is the most unsympathetic character in the novel. He left his two children when they were small and was gone for 12 unexplained years. When he returned to Harlem, Montana, where his grown son still lived, Ike went for 14 years without acknowledging him. Both of his children confront him in their adulthood, pressing him for some acknowledgment of their existence and his neglect, but he refuses to take any such responsibility. He explains himself by saying, "I was born to buck and broke to ride."

As the end of Jim Loney's created destiny is coming upon him, he goes to see his father, hoping for information about his mother and Sandra, the woman who cared for him for two years after his father abandoned him. Though Loney accuses his father of destroying his mother, he comes to understand that in Ike Loney's smallness and ignorance, he does indeed dwell in a place of innocence. Ike Loney is almost too inhuman to be held accountable for human failures.

Jim Loney needs one last thing from his father, and in this he will not be disappointed. He is counting on his father to betray him to the police and set into motion the manhunt that will end his life. Loney tells his father that he has killed Myron Pretty Weasel, and he also suggests that it was not an accident. Ike gives him a shotgun and offers some money. Loney leaves his father's dingy green trailer and uses the gun to shoot out the front window. This last action serves two purposes; first, it gives Loney the opportunity to exercise a passionless revenge against his father, and second, it assures him that his father will be sufficiently stirred up to report to the authorities.

His face bleeding from glass shards, Ike is taken to the hospital by Officer Painter Barthelme, where he takes delight in doling out information about the death of Pretty Weasel. Just as Loney knew, "His father was the worst type of dirt—he would squeal and he would enjoy the attention." (Owens 1992a; Sands 1987; Scheckter 1986; Welch 1979, 1987)

See also Barthelme, Painter; *The Death of Jim Loney*; Loney, Jim; Loney, Kate; Pretty Weasel, Myron.

Loney, Jim

Jim Loney is the title character in James Welch's *The Death of Jim Loney* (1979, 1987). Loney is aptly named, for he has trouble feeling connected to others, including his girlfriend Rhea Davis and his own sister, Kate. Both his mother and his father have abandoned him and his sister. His mother is an Indian woman who left the family when he was just a baby, and his father left him and his sister when Jim was 9 or 10 years old. His father was gone for 12 years before returning to the same town to live, but he has never tried to reestablish a relationship with Jim.

Loney suffers from his split heritage in a way that those closest to him cannot understand. Rhea says to him: "Oh, you're so lucky to have two sets of ancestors. Just think, you can be Indian one day and white the next. Whichever suits you." Loney silently disagrees, thinking that being either Indian or white "would be nicer than being a half-breed." As Loney becomes more and more disassociated, he comes to believe that his condition is worse than simply having two sets of ancestors. "In truth," he thinks, "he had none." And although Jim wants to come to an understanding of his past and how his two racial strains combine to create who he is in his present, his sister Kate cannot understand his desire to do so. Kate has made an uneasy pact of survival at the expense of identity and refuses to approach the past because she fears losing it too.

Loney's identity problem is the central focus of the novel. When bad weather slows down his job with a local farmer, Loney falls into a pattern of sitting at his kitchen table, smoking and drinking. Rhea asks what is bothering him, but Loney can only respond that he doesn't know, that "it has something to do with the past." By the end of the novel, Loney has come to realize that "everything had gone dreadfully wrong, and although it had something to do with his family, it had everything to do with himself."

Rhea is alarmed enough by Loney's depression to alert his sister Kate. The two women exchange letters, and Kate plans to visit and perhaps persuade Loney to move to Washington, D.C., with her. Rhea, however, is hoping that she can convince Loney to go with her to Seattle. Rhea knows that she and Kate are "batting him back and forth like a Ping-Pong ball," and she knows that Loney is "scared off easily." The motivations of both women are complicated enough by personal interests that neither is able to reach Loney.

In his own attempt to make some meaning of the scattered images of his past, Loney asks his sister Kate about the woman who took care of him for two years after their father left. Kate reveals that the woman, Sandra, was their father's lover, but that she is now dead. Though the woman has been dead for years, the information strikes Loney deeply. In the course of a few days, his dog, Swipesy, dies; he and Rhea end their relationship; he learns that the only mother figure he ever had is dead; and Kate informs him that she will never again come to Montana to visit him or try to "save" him.

Not long after Kate returns to Washington, Loney goes hunting with Myron Pretty Weasel. Though they were basketball teammates and friends in high school, they haven't maintained a friendship. Loney is a bit puzzled by Pretty Weasel's invitation but goes nonetheless. Pretty Weasel lends Loney a shotgun for the day, and in a horrible irony, Loney accidentally shoots and kills Pretty Weasel. Loney imagines that the shooting is the result of some "quirky and predictable fate" but doesn't yet realize that "he had in that moment devised an end of his own." He leaves Pretty Weasel's body in the woods, and in the days that follow, he earnestly tries to make sense of his life, and the "end" that he has set into motion with the death of Pretty Weasel begins to take shape in his mind. He visits the cemetery, hunting for the grave of Sandra; he calls his sister Kate, only to get her answering service. He even goes to see his father, forcing Ike Loney into acknowledging his existence for the first time in 25 years. He tells Ike that he has shot Pretty Weasel and that he is going to Mission Canyon to think. Just as he had earlier in a dream of Loney's, Ike gives him a shotgun. As Loney leaves his father's trailer, he shoots out a window, thus making sure that his father will perform his unwitting part in Loney's plan by reporting the death of Pretty Weasel to the police.

He spends a few last hours with Rhea and then makes his way to the Little Rockies for the standoff with the tribal police. Loney dies in an exchange of gunfire that he initiates. (Coltelli 1990; McFarland and Browning 1986; Owens 1992a; Sands 1986; Welch 1979, 1987; Westrum 1986)

See also Barthelme, Painter; Davis, Rhea; *The Death of Jim Loney*; Loney, Ike; Loney, Kate; Pretty Weasel, Myron.

Loney, Kate

Kate is the sister of Jim Loney in James Welch's 1979 novel, *The Death of Jim Loney*. She leaves the reservation early in her life and makes a life in Washington, D.C., where she works as an Indian education policymaker. She wants her brother to join her in Washington because she senses that he is not doing well, and that suspicion is confirmed by her brother's girlfriend, Rhea Davis, who writes her a letter. What begins as a shared concern for Jim becomes a kind of competition between the two women for his love.

Kate deals with the absences in her past by declaring that the present and the future are not found in the past. She says of her past, "I gave up on it a long time ago. We have no past. What's the point in thinking about it?" Jim, however, realizes that his present is rooted in the past. Whereas he tries to relocate his past, Kate moves away from hers. Her identity crisis is just as profound as Jim's, but she deals with it differently. Even as a child, she thought of "learning as a kind of salvation, a way to get up and out of being what they were, two half-breed kids caught in the slack water of a minor river."

However, she unknowingly is using her brother to establish a connection with her past that she denies an interest in. When Kate comes to see Jim in a last attempt to "save" him from his life in Montana, all she can think of is "how peaceful his life is."

On the night that Jim dies, Kate is overcome by a feeling of dread, and she knows that she will not see her brother again. She sits rocking back and forth, now truly alone, with no connection to her family or to her home in Montana. (Owens 1992a; Sands 1986; Welch 1979, 1987; Westrum 1986)

See also Davis, Rhea; *The Death of Jim Loney*; Loney, Ike; Loney, Jim; Pretty Weasel, Myron.

Love Medicine

Love Medicine (1984, 1993) is the stunning first novel by Louise Erdrich, the winner of the National Book Critics Circle Award for Best Work of Fiction, and the first volume published in her North Dakota tetralogy. Highly praised for the strength of the writing, *Love Medicine* secured Erdrich's place as a major American writer.

Erdrich uses an achronological structure in the novel, which spans a 50-year period from 1934 to 1984. At the beginning of each chapter, Erdrich has placed the date, a consideration that goes a long way in helping orient the reader. *Love Medicine* opens with an omniscient narrator, but throughout the novel, six first-person narrators intrude upon the story, claiming an immediacy with the reader that heightens the oral qualities of the story. The six first-person narrators are the anchors of the novel and represent the bookend generations of the sprawling story.

Marie Lazarre Kashpaw, Lulu Nanapush Lamartine, and Nector Kashpaw each narrate two sections of the novel, one from their youth and one from their maturity. Marie and Lulu both present a first narration under their maiden names and a second with their married names. Nector's name remains the same. The change in the women's names reflects the change in relationship as well as their dynamic and changing nature. That Nector's name remains the same reflects more than the practice of a male-centered culture that encourages men to keep their names in marriage; it suggests that he is a static character whose essential quality of passivity makes him a person on whom others act.

He is not a character without attractions, however; the two strongest women in the novel are in love with him. Both find in Nector someone on whom they can exercise power and control. Lulu controls him with her vibrant sexuality, and Marie controls him with her maternity and her own need for respect in the community. As Marie tells Sister Leopolda, "He is what he is because I made him."

The three younger first-person narrators are Albertine Johnson, the granddaughter of Nector and Marie; Lipsha Morrissey, the adoptive grandson of Nector and Marie; and Lyman Lamartine, the fruit of Lulu and Nector's five-year love affair. The three younger narrators provide a complicated texture to the story of love and forgiveness, in that they show the results of the devotions and passions of Lulu, Nector, and Marie, but none is as important as Lipsha Morrissey. He is the wild card in this pack of fascinating characters. He does not know who his parents are, and his mono-mythic (Joseph Campbell's term) quest to uncover his heritage is the primary impulse of the narrative. The unacknowledged son of June Morrissey Kashpaw and Gerry Nanapush, Lipsha has shamanic powers from his father's side of the family and the generous and forgiving wisdom of his adoptive grandmother, Marie Kashpaw. The story opens with the death of his mother in the teeth of a snowstorm and ends when he delivers her spirit back home through the agency of her blue Firebird.

The novel introduces a group of characters so interesting and alive that they could not be confined to this novel alone. Many of the characters in *Love Medicine* show up again in Erdrich's subsequent novels. Erdrich herself was so interested in the characters and their behaviors that she could not resist writing a new and expanded version of the book, which was released nine years after the first edition. She added five major stories and made a few editorial changes in order to create or sustain some narrative integrity between this novel and the others in the tetralogy. The additions don't detract from the work, but neither do they significantly improve it. Perhaps the most notable effect of adding the stories is to illustrate the ongoing and ever-changing qualities of the oral tradition, which are present in this work and in so many Native American literary works. Erdrich challenges the borders of the novel and insists that the story is never static, never finished. The additional sections further develop the characters Gordie Kashpaw, June, Lulu, and Lyman. We learn more of the love between June and Gordie and of his tragic death; we learn of the relationship between Lulu and Moses Pillager; and the farcical chapter given to Lyman primarily sets him up for his role in another novel, *The Bingo Palace*. (Catt 1991; Erdrich 1984, 1993; Flavin 1989; Gleason 1987; Hanson 1989; McKenzie 1986; Owens 1992a; Ruppert 1995; Schultz 1991; Smith 1991)

See also *The Beet Queen*; *The Bingo Palace*; Erdrich, Louise; Johnson, Albertine; Johnson, Zelda Kashpaw; Kashpaw, Eli; Kashpaw, Gordie; Kashpaw, June Morrissey; Kashpaw, King; Kashpaw, Margaret (Rushes Bear); Kashpaw, Marie Lazarre; Kashpaw, Nector; Lamartine, Beverly (Hat); Lamartine, Henry Junior; Lamartine, Lulu Nanapush; Lamartine, Lyman; Morrissey, Lipsha; Nanapush, Dot Adare; Nanapush, Gerry; Pillager, Fleur; Pillager, Moses; Puyat, Pauline; *Tales of Burning Love*; *Tracks*.

Lundstrom, Crystal Thunder

In Susan Power's *The Grass Dancer* (1994), Crystal is the "misfit" daughter of Anna (Mercury) Thunder; she is "shunned by tribesmen because [her] mother had too many boyfriends and was rumored to practice Indian medicine." She has an "odd crimson birthmark" on her forehead, "perfectly bowed in the shape of a horseshoe" that her mother claims is the result of her father's abuse while she was still in the womb.

Crystal is thwarted by her mother's jealous powers and is unable to assert herself as she grows up. Anna tells her, "I am your spirit until the day comes when you understand me, and then you should take over." When Crystal rebels by getting pregnant by a white boy, Martin Lundstrom, and leaving the reservation, it is at great cost. Anna demands a "soul for a soul," and takes Crystal's child from her. Though the price is great, Crystal realizes that her spirit is "free and clear, for the first times since [she] grew in the bowl of [her] mother's womb." She tells Martin the child died, and they marry and move to Chicago. Martin's mother soon joins them there, and though she is possessive of her son, Crystal learns to get along with and finally value her.

Meanwhile, her daughter, Charlene, is growing up in the same oppressive atmosphere that Crystal could not abide. When Crystal receives a call from her 17-year-old daughter, she is overjoyed and welcomes Charlene to the stable home she has made with Martin and his mother. (Power 1994)

> See also *The Grass Dancer*; Lundstrom, Martin; McVay, Jeannette; Thunder, Anna (Mercury); Thunder, Charlene.

Lundstrom, Martin

Martin Lundstrom is an odd boy, a classmate of Crystal Thunder's in Susan Power's *The Grass Dancer* (1994). He is a loner with a limp, a student who attracts only negative attention to himself at school. But Crystal is drawn to him because of his artistic abilities and establishes a friendship with him. In spite of his self-effacing habit of speaking indirectly by using third-person pronouns, Crystal finds him attractive. When Crystal ends up pregnant, Martin proposes by saying, "She should marry me."

After high school graduation, Martin buys a black Thunderbird with the money that he has earned illustrating a seed catalog since he was 15 years old. His artistic talents earn him a job in the advertising department of the *Chicago Tribune*, and he and Crystal make a life there, accompanied by his possessive mother.

Because Anna Thunder takes their child away at birth, Crystal allows Martin to believe that the child died. When a 17-year-old Charlene finds her mother, Martin welcomes her without question into the family. (Power 1994)

> See also *The Grass Dancer*; Lundstrom, Crystal Thunder; Thunder, Anna (Mercury); Thunder, Charlene.

M

Malvina

Malvina is a character in James Welch's 1974 novel *Winter in the Blood*. The narrator meets her at a bar in the town of Harlem and gets a ride with her to Havre, so that he might continue looking for Agnes and his gun and razor. Malvina is a woman of about 40 who appears to have had a hard life. She has the initials "JR" tattooed "on the flap of skin between her thumb and index finger." She is jobless; her relationship with JR is a trauma from the past; and she has a young son of five or six who has apparently seen many men such as the narrator wake up with his mother. Her room is full of pictures of herself "alone in various dress," indicating her essential isolation. (Owens 1992a; Ruoff 1978; Welch 1974, 1986)

See also Nameless Narrator; *Winter in the Blood*.

Mammedaty

Mammedaty is the paternal grandfather of N. Scott Momaday, and he figures in Momaday's autobiographical memoirs, *The Names* (1976) and *The Way to Rainy Mountain* (1969). Mammedaty is a Kiowa man whose name means "Walking Above." Though Mammedaty died before Momaday was born, he nonethe-less exerted a tremendous influence on his grandson. (Momaday 1969; Momaday 1976)

See also Momaday, N. Scott; *The Names*; *The Way to Rainy Mountain*.

The-man-who-was-probably-Lakota

The-man-who-was-probably-Lakota is a wonderful comic figure in Sherman Alexie's 1995 novel *Reservation Blues*. He came to the Spokane reservation 30 years ago to play in a basketball tournament and never left. He takes his position every day in front of the Spokane Tribal Trading Post and announces, "The end of the world is near." The repeated phrase punctuates several narrative passages and reinforces their importance. The-man-who-was-probably-Lakota is more than a one-dimensional stock comic character, however. In addition to his doomsaying, he makes the second-best fry bread on the reservation, and he takes a compassionate interest in Thomas Builds-the-Fire. He cautions Thomas to be careful of Robert Johnson's guitar because "music is a dangerous thing." When Victor smashes the guitar and frustrates Thomas to public and humiliating tears, The-man-who-was-probably-Lakota comforts him and suggests, "Maybe things will be better in the morning." In a slice of Alexie's best humor, The-man-who-was-probably-Lakota asks Thomas not to tell anybody, for it "would ruin my reputation." (Alexie 1995)

See also Builds-the-Fire, Thomas; Johnson, Robert; Joseph, Victor; *Reservation Blues*.

Many Wounds, Evelyn

The daughter of Margaret Many Wounds in *The Grass Dancer* (1994) by Susan Power, Evelyn (Evie) is a character caught in a web of bad magic. When she is a young woman, Anna Thunder chooses her as a tool in her scheme of vengeance and thwarted love. Thunder has been rebuffed by Calvin Wind Soldier, Evelyn's brother-in-law, and she puts a spell on Wind Soldier and Evelyn that makes them lovers. The result of the unhappy manipulation is a son, Duane, born to Evelyn and Calvin. Evelyn refuses to accept the child, and her twin sister Lydia steps in and raises the child as her own.

Though Margaret Many Wounds's intent is not malicious like Anna Thunder's, Evelyn's life is shaped just as significantly by an action of her own mother as well. Evie and Lydia are told by their mother that their father was a Canadian Indian who left her. Evie imagines a life and an identity for her father; she dreams that he is the great rodeo star, Sonny Porter, "passionate and adventurous." She constructs her own self-image in the mold of her imaginary father and tells herself, *"I take after him."* She even marries a broken-down rodeo star, Philbert, in an attempt to reify her father.

At her death, Margaret gives Evie a locket in which she finds a picture of Charles Bad Holy MacLeod and Dr. Sei-ichi Sakuma, her own father. (Power 1994)

See also *The Grass Dancer*; Many Wounds, Margaret; Thunder, Anna (Mercury); Wind Soldier, Calvin; Wind Soldier, Lydia.

Many Wounds, Margaret

In Susan Power's *The Grass Dancer* (1994), Margaret Many Wounds is the mother of twins, Evelyn and Lydia. Though she has "spent many years as one of Father Zimmer's faithful," she draws away from him in the weeks near her death. She returns to "an old faith from her youth," and asks her grandson, Harley Wind Soldier, to bury her rosary in the yard.

It is not until her daughters return to her home as she is dying that they learn the secrets of her past life. On her deathbed, she ostensibly tells the stories of her life to those spirits who are gathered around her bed, but Evelyn (Evie) hears the stories and is shocked. Margaret relates: "In seventy-four years I had just two men. One was big passion and one was understanding." Her first husband, Charles Bad Holy MacLeod, was taken from the reservation to Indian boarding school at age four and was not allowed to return until he was 21. Margaret decides to "reclaim" him "for the tribe and for [her]self." They marry, but their delightful happiness is cut short when Charles dies of tuberculosis two years later. Margaret mourns him deeply, imagining that she "wouldn't have left so much of [her]self in his coffin" had they had children.

In 1942, at age 47, Margaret goes to work in Bismarck, North Dakota, as a "nurse" for prisoners of war. There she assists Dr. Sei-ichi Sakuma, "a surgeon from San Francisco," and in their loneliness they become lovers. When she becomes pregnant, she fears the public disapprobation of sleeping with "the Enemy" and leaves the camp without telling her lover. Back on the reservation, she gives out the story that she had married "a Canadian Indian who left me." The lie she tells makes her "a member of the Church" and her daughters "full-blood Indians."

Before she dies, she tends to two important matters. She tells the story of her life to her daughters, saying, "But it's time for the lies to perish, don't you think?" And she gives to her grandson Harley the charge to "liberate" her grandmother's ceremonial dress, which is in the Field Museum in Chicago. She dies just as the first men are walking on the moon, and Harley sees her spirit on the moon with them. (Power 1994)

See also *The Grass Dancer*; Many Wounds, Evelyn; Wind Soldier, Harley; Wind Soldier, Lydia.

Martinez

Martinez is a corrupt policeman in N. Scott Momaday's *House Made of Dawn* (1968). Ben Benally, a friend of the protagonist, Abel, says, "He's always looking for trouble, and if he's got it in for you—if you make him mad—you better look out." He is called *culebra*, the snake, by the people in his neighborhood because he runs roughshod over his Los Angeles beat, extorting money and alcohol from the local bar owners and patrons alike. He uses violence to intimidate people, and once he forced Ben and Abel into an alley where he threatened Ben until he handed over his weekly pay. But when Abel had no money and showed no fear, he cracked Abel's hands with his nightstick. Ben remembers this experience, along with a similar verbal humiliation by Tosamah, as events that push Abel over the edge of control.

When Abel reaches bottom through his alcoholism, the loss of his job, and the loss of his self-respect, he goes in search of Martinez to exact revenge for the earlier beating. That Martinez is known as the *culebra* connects him to the reptilelike albino whom Abel had killed six years earlier. The motivation for Abel's behavior is far more complex than simple revenge for a beating; quite possibly he once again is attempting to confront abstract evil made manifest in a human. However, he is beaten so badly by Martinez that it takes him three days to work his way back home, where Ben gets him to the hospital. The encounter with Martinez ultimately precipitates Abel's return home to the Jemez Reservation. (Evers 1985; Hirsch 1983; Momaday 1968; Schubnell 1985)

See also Abel; The Albino; Benally, Ben; *House Made of Dawn*.

Martinez-Soto, Alegria

Alegria is the "most prized young assistant" in Mexico's top architectural firm, and she lands the account to design the mansion for insurance mogul Menardo and his wife Iliana in Leslie Marmon Silko's *Almanac of the Dead* (1991). During school in Madrid, where she was a top graduate, she flirted with Marxism. Her attraction was not ideological so much as sexual, for she was having an affair with Bartolomeo de Las Casas, a Cuban Marxist leader of the Mexican revolutionaries. Her artistic interest in "the interplay of structure as sculptural form with light" is the genesis of the fatal marble staircase in Menardo's mansion. After the death of Iliana, Alegria—dismissed from her job and suffering deep depression—agrees to marry Menardo. She is not happy with him, is soon bored, and begins an affair with the drug dealer Sonny Blue. She continues to see Bartolomeo from time to time, but his communist associations endanger her in the circle of Menardo's friends. She runs an interior design shop after she can no longer practice architecture. Once Menardo is dead, she realizes that she is in a very vulnerable position; she no longer has the protection of his position to keep away those who would purge all communist influences.

She immediately flees Mexico, taking Menardo's wealth with her. She makes discreet arrangements for crossing the border into the United States with a "deluxe luxury tour" that takes people across the desert without the notice of officials. However, the trip she takes is the payoff trip for the owners of the service. They have been running their business circumspectly for some time, building the trust of the wealthy who are fleeing Central and South America.

On this last trip, they abandon their human cargo in the desert and abscond with all the possessions of their clients. Alegria is determined not to die in the desert, and she carefully conserves her energy and spirits until she is rescued by a group of Catholic political workers. (Silko 1991)

See also *Almanac of the Dead*; Blue, Sonny; Las Casas, Bartolomeo de; Iliana; Menardo.

Mather, Dr. Clarence

Dr. Clarence Mather is a character in Sherman Alexie's 1996 novel *Indian Killer*. An anthropologist at the University of Washington, Mather is a white man who wants to be an

Indian, a "wannabe." Cocooned in his cultural superiority, Mather is certain that he can teach Indians "a thing or two about being Indian if they would listen to him."

Mather enters the story through two characters, Reggie Polatkin and Marie Polatkin. He first befriends his student, Reggie Polatkin, recognizing him as an Indian who is also smart. He decides that Reggie is a fit audience for "two boxes of reel-to-reel tapes filled with the voices of Pacific Northwest Indian elders" that he has found in the bowels of the anthropology building. Recorded "during the summer of 1926, the tapes had just been collecting dust in a storage room when Dr. Mather stumbled upon them." When Reggie hears the tapes, he tells Mather that they are family stories and should not be told out of context. "Burn the tapes. Or I'll burn them for you," he insists. When Reggie asks Mather if he has destroyed the tapes, Mather denies "that the tapes had ever existed." He continues to layer lie after lie on the first; Reggie lodges a formal protest and is brought before the department head. Later Reggie and Mather get in another verbal altercation, and Reggie hits Mather and is expelled from the university.

By denying that the tapes exist, Mather has placed himself in a tight spot, for he can never bring them out as objects of scholarly interest. His resentment over the incident is reactivated some years later when Reggie's cousin, Marie Polatkin, signs up for Mather's class in Native American literature. Mather's hostility finds a temperament of equal strength in Marie, and their relationship is antagonistic from the beginning. By the time the furor over the "Indian Killer" is at its frenzied height, Mather goes to the police and offers testimony that implicates both Marie and Reggie Polatkin in the murders. Furthermore, he writes a book about the Indian Killer, again theorizing that Reggie was the killer, and painting a picture of Marie Polatkin that was "not too flattering." (Alexie 1996)

See also *Indian Killer*; Polatkin, Marie; Polatkin, Reggie; Rogers, David; Smith, John; Wilson, Jack.

Mathews, John Joseph

John Joseph Mathews, the son of a mixed-blood Osage father and a white mother, was born in 1894 and died in 1979. He graduated from high school in 1914 and went on to the University of Oklahoma to earn a degree in geology in 1920. His college years were interrupted by World War I, during which he served in the Signal Corps as a pilot. He was offered a Rhodes scholarship to Oxford but turned it down, preferring to attend Oxford without the benefit of the scholarship. He graduated from Oxford in 1923 and spent several years traveling in Europe and North Africa before growing homesick for Oklahoma and his Osage roots. He returned to Oklahoma and built a cabin, where he lived and wrote for most of the next 50 years.

Mathews is the author of five books, the best known of which is *Sundown* (1934, 1988). *Sundown* is largely autobiographical and is viewed as one of the first novels by a Native American. Though the novel was artistically eclipsed by D'Arcy McNickle's *The Surrounded* two years later, *Sundown* is an important early presentation of the theme of assimilation and the struggles of a mixed-blood protagonist. His *Talking to the Moon* (1945) recalls Thoreau in that it celebrates the natural life of the secluded retreat he called the Blackjacks. *Wah'Kon-Tah: The Osage and the White Man's Road* (1932) is an account of early reservation days and became a Book-of-the-Month Club selection. Mathews also wrote a biography and a volume of history. *Life and Death of an Oilman: The Career of E. W. Marland* (1951) is an objective but little-read account of the life of Marland, an oil entrepreneur and a governor of Oklahoma. Mathews's 1961 volume *The Osages,* a history of the tribe, succeeds as ethnohistory but is less authoritative as history.

During the 1930s, Mathews became involved in tribal politics and was instrumental in the opening of the Osage Tribal Museum in Pawhuska, Oklahoma. (Hunt 1996; Wilson 1994)

See also *Sundown*; *The Surrounded*.

Mauser, Dot

See Nanapush, Dot Adare.

Mauser, Eleanor Schlick

In Louise Erdrich's *Tales of Burning Love* (1996), Eleanor is an academic who carelessly orchestrates her own disgrace when she seduces an undergraduate. She leaves her job at the university and continues "writing on her newest project regarding saintly hungers, those of one particular aged nun named Leopolda." Eleanor goes on an extended retreat at the convent where Leopolda lives so that she can have unlimited access to the nun. In the introspection that comes with retreat, Eleanor is increasingly aware that she still loves her ex-husband, Jack Mauser. When Mauser leaves her a note suggesting a meeting in the convent garden one night,

Eleanor willingly agrees. The meeting is significant for two reasons: Jack and Eleanor witness the death of Sister Leopolda when she is reduced to ash by a bolt of lightning, and their own love is rekindled.

After their passionate reunion, the sisters believe that Eleanor "found God. Eleanor knew she had found Mauser." She makes serious attempts to drive Mauser from her mind by throwing herself into her work, by memorizing information from *The New York Public Library Desk Reference*, and by living on the diet of Saint Theresa—"distilled water and communion wafers"—until she collapses. She is finally taken to the hospital in Argus, North Dakota, and after a short stay there, she calls Jack to come get her. Jack and his new wife Dot Adare Nanapush both show up to collect her. On the trip home, the volatile situation with

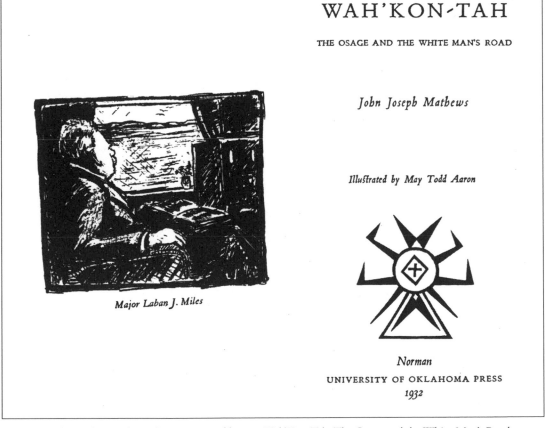

Frontispiece from John Joseph Mathews's 1932 publication Wah'Kon-Tah: The Osage and the White Man's Road. *(Reproduced from Mathews,* Wah'Kon-Tah: The Osage and the White Man's Road, *1932)*

the present and former wives takes an unexpected turn when both women are aligned against Jack rather than each other. Both women are caught off guard by knowledge that Jack has previously kept from them. Dot learns that Jack has four former wives, and Eleanor learns that Jack has fathered a child with his fourth wife, Marlis Cook.

Eleanor describes herself as "precocious in the wrong ways. I learned to read when I was three years old, but I can't even do a cartwheel. No balance." Eleanor is the daughter of a trapeze artist, and though she recognizes the absence of her mother's gift in herself, she hits upon a metaphorical truth. Her early relationship with Mauser is characterized by her lack of balance, as is her behavior as an academic. She lives at the extreme edges of life, even to her physical appearance, which is "overdrawn" and "dramatic."

On the night that Eleanor and the three other surviving wives of Jack Mauser are stranded in a blizzard, she suggests that "no one of us has a quarrel with any woman in this car. No more so than if we'd all had different husbands." The women agree to pretend the "car is a confessional." The long night of confessions yields both catharsis and tensions. When Candice Pantamounty and Marlis reveal their lately acknowledged lesbianism, Eleanor lashes out at them in a burst of condemnation. The next time the women get out of the car to clear the tailpipe of blowing snow, it is Eleanor who spearheads the mission. A gust of wind carries her away from the grasp of Marlis who, after her recent tongue-lashing by Eleanor, is none too eager to risk herself for Eleanor. The wind carries Eleanor along in a surrealistic flight in which she is joined by the presence of Sister Leopolda. Leopolda counsels her, "You want abiding rightness, an assurance of your course. You will *not* find that in a man." Leopolda disappears, and Eleanor is blown right up to the automatic doors of the Fargo airport and survives. Eleanor's flight to the airport, no less, prefigures her new sense of balance. She now can fly through the air as her aerialist mother did. Her newfound balance, along with Jack's

redemptive changes, allow Eleanor to enter a stable relationship with Jack by the end of the story. (Childress 1996; Erdrich 1996)

See also Cook, Marlis; Mauser, Jack; Nanapush, Dot Adare; Pantamounty, Candice; Puyat, Pauline; *Tales of Burning Love*.

Mauser, Jack

In Louise Erdrich's *Tales of Burning Love* (1996), Jack Mauser is the character around whom the story revolves. He has been the husband of five wives, from his first, June Morrissey Kashpaw, who walked into a blizzard and died, to Dot Adare Nanapush, who is simultaneously married to Gerry Nanapush. Far from a deliberate womanizer, Jack is more a man who bumbles into love or, at best, one who always needs a woman to take care of him. Though he is part Ojibwa (Anishinabe) through his mother's side of the family, "the Ojibwa part of him was so buried it didn't know what it saw looking at the dirt or sky or into a human face." A contractor by trade, Jack does "not see land in the old-time Ojibwa sense, as belonging to nobody and nothing but itself. Land was something to use, space for sale." That the Ojibwa part of him is "inaccessible" contributes to Jack's overall instability.

Mauser is "tall, in his early thirties" when he meets June Kashpaw, identifies himself as "Andy," and marries her in a mock ceremony with "beer-can pop-top wedding rings." After the ceremony, they go parking in his truck; their sexual encounter is unsuccessful, and June leaves the truck and walks into a blizzard. Jack is too humiliated to follow her, and his guilt over not saving June follows him into each successive relationship. Thirteen years later, Jack is aware that "he couldn't hold on to a woman ever since he let the first one walk from his arms into Easter snow."

Jack's fifth marriage is one of convenience more than passion. His construction company is suffering serious financial woes, and he marries his bookkeeper, Dot Adare Nanapush, in a gesture of self-protection. If Jack has known true love in any of his marriages, it was with his second wife, Eleanor Schlick Mauser. Now, shortly after marrying Dot, Mauser learns that Eleanor is in town, though at the local convent. He cannot deny his urge to see her and so makes arrangements to meet her in the convent garden at midnight. Their meeting is interrupted by the prayers of Sister Leopolda, 108 years old and supported by a walker. Before she is struck by lightning and reduced to ash before their eyes, Leopolda responds to Eleanor's question about Jack with a prophecy: "I see a picture of the poor soul, bleeding. He will be crushed by a woman. He'll die screaming in a woman's arms. She'll snap his bones like matchsticks and throttle him with her kiss." Leopolda's unlikely prophecy does come true in part.

The adventures of Jack's life are all marked by the extremities of fire and freezing cold. As a young North Dakota State University engineering student and volunteer fireman, he is doused with water from a fire hose and nearly succumbs to hypothermia. His first marriage ends when his wife dies in a blizzard. Years later, when Dot leaves him, he drinks until he is drunk and unable to control the fire that has started in his fireplace. His house is consumed, and he escapes, naked, into a terrible snowstorm. And yet, Mauser survives these tragedies. His ability to survive is amazing, for he also survives the emotional storms of love that are concomitant with five marriages.

After his marriage to June, Mauser marries Eleanor. His past has intersected with Eleanor's in outlandish ways. Eleanor is just a child when Jack nearly freezes to death as a volunteer fireman. It is Eleanor's mother who finds Jack at the fire station and takes him home and saves him. His hypothermia is so advanced that she cannot warm him in a tub of water, so she finally puts him into bed and lays down on top of him to transfer her own body heat. Eleanor's father finds the innocent pair in bed and immediately cuts off his wife and daughter from all affection and support. Eleanor and her mother live for many years in disgrace and poverty until Eleanor spots Jack one day in a department store and forces him to confess to her father that nothing happened. This meeting of Eleanor and

Jack becomes the beginning of their own relationship, which ends in a passionate yet troubled marriage.

Jack's next marriage, to Candice Pantamounty, is his longest, but it ends when he goes on a monthlong spree with Marlis Cook, a troubled young woman hunting for a sugar daddy. His relationship with Marlis is quickly in danger because of its unstable foundation and her immediate pregnancy, which Jack is unwilling to acknowledge. His last marriage, to Dot Adare Nanapush, is likewise the result of a headlong and unwise decision. When she leaves him not too long into the marriage, Jack is overwhelmed by his failures and wonders if his complicity in the death of June Kashpaw is somehow responsible for his present condition. On New Year's Eve, 1994, Jack wallows in self-pity and alcohol, and inadvertently allows his house to burn down. He escapes into the blizzard after putting a piece of his bridgework in a side of beef that is in the basement.

Jack has named his construction company "Mauser and Mauser, Construction. Jack twice. There was no other Mauser, no partner, just himself." Though Jack believes in the myth of his own independence, he is actually a man who cannot be alone. He craves relationships and the approving love of others. The true measure of Jack's growth is revealed after he rescues his son from the car stranded in the storm; he looks at his infant son and thinks, "Mauser and Mauser."

As the story ends, Jack acknowledges his son, he and Eleanor are together in a relationship that is healthier than any he has known before, and he returns to his construction company. He is on-site when the new Italian marble statue is delivered to the convent where he and Eleanor met at the beginning of the novel. In the process of placement, the statue falls on Mauser and nearly crushes him. Though Sister Leopolda's prediction is not fulfilled, Jack does suffer injuries from the accident. He is "the poor soul, bleeding . . . in a woman's arms." Jack's blood is cleaned off the statue, but blood continues to appear on it, and it prompts Father Jude Miller to write to the bishop suggesting that the phenomenon should be investigated.

In the final scene of the novel, Jack reaches the place where he can let go of his guilt over June's death. He knows that her death was a tragic and painful one but realizes too that "it was also hard to bear the pain of coming back to life." (Erdrich 1996)

See also Cook, Marlis; Kashpaw, June Morrissey; Mauser, Eleanor Schlick; Miller, Jude; Nanapush, Dot Adare; Pantamounty, Candice; Puyat, Pauline; *Tales of Burning Love*.

McDonald, Mary

Known as "shy-girl," Mary is the sister of Cogewea in Mourning Dove's *Cogewea, the Half-Blood* (1927, 1981). Though only a secondary character, she is nonetheless fleshed out with some complexity. A "half-blood" like Cogewea, she shows her white background in "eyes of the deepest blue." However, she is more connected to her traditional ways than either Cogewea or her other sister, Julia. Her "Indian coyness and modesty of manner, had not been broken by her convent schooling," and she is often embarrassed by Cogewea's "independence of action and speech."

D'Arcy McNickle, late 1930s. (The Newberry Library)

Though her sister Julia encourages Cogewea's romance with Alfred Densmore, Mary joins Jim LaGrinder, Cogewea's other suitor, and the Stemteema, her grandmother, in their efforts to dissolve the relationship. Mary finds a torn-up letter that Densmore has received from his sweetheart back East; she reassembles it and shows Jim, whereupon both are determined to save Cogewea from Densmore.

Given Mary's identification with her Indianness and her disapproval of the *Shoyahpee* (white man) Densmore, it is somewhat ironic that, in the end, she marries Eugene LaFleur, a French aristocrat. (Mourning Dove, 1927, 1981; Owens 1992a; Wiget 1985)

See also Carter, John and Julia; Cogewea; *Cogewea, the Half-Blood: A Depiction of the Great Montana Cattle Range*; Densmore, Alfred; LaGrinder, Jim; The Stemteema.

McNickle, D'Arcy

Born in 1904 in St. Ignatius, Montana, D'Arcy McNickle lived on the Flathead Indian Reservation with his part Cree mother and white father and was adopted into the Flathead tribe. After attending Indian boarding school, public high school, and the University of Montana, McNickle sold his reservation allotment and used the money to attend Oxford University. As a young man, McNickle rejected his Indian heritage but later returned to it with the desire to improve the condition of the Indian. He worked with the Bureau of Indian Affairs, with the National Congress of American Indians, at the University of Saskatchewan at Regina in the anthropology department, and at the Newberry Library in Chicago, where he helped found the Center for the History of the American Indian.

In his professional life, McNickle wrote several nonfiction books concerning historical and contemporary Indian conditions, the most important being *Native American Tribalism: Indian Survivals and Renewals* (1973). However, he is best known for his work in fiction, especially his 1936 novel, *The Surrounded*. With that novel, McNickle ushered in a new age of Native American literature and set the stage for the swelling current of the Native American Renaissance to come three decades later. *The Surrounded* is the story of a mixed-blood young man who feels estranged from both his white and his Salish cultures. In this way, the protagonist, Archilde Leon, is not unlike the young D'Arcy McNickle, but McNickle's life did not suffer the final tragedy of Archilde's. McNickle died in 1977 after a life of significant contributions to literature and policymaking on Indian affairs. (Bear Don't Walk 1996; Hans 1995; Owens 1992a; Parker 1992; Witalec 1995)

See also *The Surrounded*.

McVay, Jeannette

In Susan Power's *The Grass Dancer* (1994), Jeannette McVay is a skinny white girl who comes to the reservation full of a patronizing naïveté. She leaves the capitalist culture of her parents and their friends to get in touch with core values on the reservation. There she seeks out Herod Small War, an elder, hoping to participate in spiritual rituals. She cannot understand that in Dakota culture, women do not enter the sweat lodge with men and that she cannot be given access to men's rituals; she is certain that "it's a thing against women." She finally quits trying to enter men's rituals and goes to Anna Thunder to learn of women's powers. What happens there changes her life. She learns that Anna's powers are real and not just some "fairy tale." More significant, however, is that Anna Thunder places a spell on McVay when she sprinkles reservation soil in her shoes so that she may not ever leave the reservation. The spell is successful, and McVay stays on the reservation, moving in and out of abusive relationships, earning the scorn of her students, and only after 20 years, finding some measure of happiness.

In her early years, she dyes her hair a "flat black, attempting to match her students' shade," and decides that she can reach her students by teaching them how to be Sioux. Her well-intentioned but culturally offensive actions violate the dignity of her students. Though McVay went to the reservation to "meet humanity rather than just slip it under a microscope or flash slides of it across some institutional-green wall," her attitude constitutes cultural voyeurism nonetheless.

McVay does take the opportunity to perform a deed of inestimable good. In her role as guidance counselor at the reservation high school, McVay is approached by Charlene Thunder when she needs help. McVay tells Charlene who her mother is and helps her get in contact with her. She also counsels Charlene not to return home, where she can once again come under the power and influence of her grandmother, Anna Thunder. She tries to humanize her contact with Charlene by offering the information that she will become a wife and mother soon. Jeannette McVay finally achieves a double victory on the reservation: personal happiness and her original goal of helping people. (Power 1994)

See also *The Grass Dancer*; Lundstrom, Crystal Thunder; Small War, Herod; Thunder, Anna (Mercury); Thunder, Charlene.

Mean Spirit

Linda Hogan's 1990 novel *Mean Spirit* joins James Welch's *Fools Crow* (1986) and Louise Erdrich's *Tracks* (1988) as two of the very few historical novels in the field of Native American literatures. Hogan's *Mean Spirit* takes the reader to the oil fields of Oklahoma in 1922 and 1923, where many recently oil-rich Indians are being swindled and murdered. Hogan says the story "actually took place in Oklahoma in the 1920s in Fairfax and Pawhuska, then called 'Indian Territory.'"

The fictional setting of the novel is called Watona, the Gathering Place, by the Indians, but the white people call the town Talbert. That the town has two names suggests the competing and antithetical value systems that inform the conflict of the novel. When the Indians were moved to Oklahoma, they were placed on land believed to be worthless. But when oil was discovered in Indian Territory, Indians became the target of rapacious whites who would stop at nothing to lay hold of the valuable land. *Mean Spirit* opens with the murder of Grace Blanket,

The Indian in Caricature

Lo, the poor Indian! whose untutored mind
Sees grafters on both sides, before, behind.

Bartholomew in the Minneapolis *Journal*.

This cartoon, illustrating the atmosphere in Linda Hogan's Mean Spirit, *originally appeared in* The Quarterly Journal of the Society of American Indians *on 15 April 1913. (Reproduced from* The Quarterly Journal of the Society of American Indians, *15 April 1913, Vol. 1, No. 1, p. 84)* a beautiful young Indian woman whose allotment yields enough oil to make her the richest Indian in the territory. The murder of Grace makes her daughter and heir, Nola, the next target of foul play.

The Indians in the novel are of two groups, the Hill Indians, an enclave of Indians who left the white world in the 1860s and retreated to the hills where they could restore their life to a simplicity that existed before white encroachment, and the settlement Indians, who adopted some of the white ways and are sitting on pockets of oil that provide them with more money than they need or want.

Lila Blanket is a Hill Indian, a "river prophet," who hears "the river's voice unfolding like its water across the earth." The river tells Lila that "the white world was going to infringe on the peaceful Hill People." Lila insists to her community that some of their children will have to learn white ways in order to "ward off our downfall." The Hill People are loathe to send their children to the town below, so Lila Blanket sends her own daughter, Grace. Grace "hardly seemed like the salvation of the Hill Indians," however; she shows no interest in learning about white laws and returning with her knowledge to the hills, but grows enamored of the town and decides to stay. It is only through her daughter that Grace becomes the vehicle of "salvation."

When Grace comes to the town, she lives with the Graycloud family, Belle and Moses, and their two daughters, Louise and Lettie. The Grayclouds are the spiritual center of the novel. They participate in the old ways and are scornful of the instant wealth that the oil has brought. When oil is discovered on their land, they make every effort to keep the news secret. Not only do they not need the wealth the oil would bring, but they realize that the oil will also bring mortal danger.

Mean Spirit is a mystery novel, a novel of murder and intrigue, but Hogan never sacrifices authentic voice and narrative plausibility for sensationalism. There is a quiet and respectful undertone to the novel that swells and throbs the longer one spends with the book and its characters. Because of the turmoil the community is in, all of the characters are in a state of flux as well. Their predominant response to the crimes around them is bewilderment.

Stacey Red Hawk, a Lakota man who works for the FBI, urges his department to investigate the murders in Watona, and he is on the team that is sent there from Washington. The investigation is confounded on many turns but finally moves forward. The Indian people who survive experience personal growth and return to the truths of their former lives.

In one scene in the book, an Indian evangelist preaches: "And when the spirit touches us, there won't be any more danger here on earth. No mean spirits walking this land, no smallness in people, no heartaches, no sorrow, nor any pain." The novel ends without the fulfillment of this hope, but in returning to the old ways, the Grayclouds and their followers are a step closer. (Hogan 1990; Miller 1990)

See also Benoit; Billy, Joe; Blanket, Grace; Blanket, Nola; Blanket, Sara; Father Dunne; Forrest, Will; Gold, Jess; Graycloud, Belle; Graycloud, Floyd; Graycloud; Lettie; Graycloud, Louise; Graycloud, Moses; Hale, John; Hogan, Linda; Horse, Michael; Red Hawk, Stacey; Stink, John; Tate, John.

Menardo

Menardo is a mixed-blood character in Leslie Marmon Silko's *Almanac of the Dead* (1991). He despises his Indian blood and seeks to erase it by cutting off all relations with his Indian grandfather. He tells people that his nose was broken in a boxing match in order to account for its flatness, a racial feature that he abhors. Menardo uses his ambition and his desire to leave behind his life of poverty and prejudice and to forge Universal Insurance, a company that flourishes in the unstable political climate of Mexico. Menardo makes his millions by insuring against natural disasters and even political disruptions. By the end of his career, he is insuring the government against political unrest and has amassed a considerable arsenal in his private security force. Menardo outfits his security force through the arms dealer Greenlee in Tucson.

No matter how much money Menardo makes, however, he can buy neither respect from his wife's family and others in the ruling class nor a son. He decides to build his wife, Iliana, a mansion, but never having been faithful to her, he begins a disastrous affair with the young female architect at the prestigious firm he hires. Iliana dies in a fall on the marble stairway that is the visual centerpiece of the new home, but not until after she exposes Menardo's affair with Alegria Martinez-Soto and causes the architect to be fired.

Menardo is called "Red Monkey" by Angelita La Escapia and the other revolutionaries who are working to overturn the Mexican government. Menardo becomes their enemy through his activities as an insurer against political unrest.

When Iliana dies, Menardo is compelled to touch her dead body, a fascination with death that only increases until he himself is killed. He is given a bulletproof vest by Tucson drug dealer Sonny Blue and begins to wear it everywhere, even to bed. He obsessively reads the brochure about his vest nightly as he falls to sleep, certain that the vest protects him from his nightmares. He becomes more and more paranoid about his relationships with the power brokers in his Friday golfing and shooting group, El Grupo, and decides that a show of his invincibility is just the thing to remind them of his power. He sets up the test of his vest at the country club where they can all witness his driver, Tacho, shoot him and then marvel as he steps away from the fire unharmed. In the confusion of the moment, Tacho steps closer to make sure his aim is good, and the bullet is not stopped by the vest. Menardo is killed accidentally because of "microscopic imperfections in the fabric's quilting." (Silko 1991)

See also *Almanac of the Dead*; Blue, Sonny; Iliana; La Escapia, Angelita; Martinez-Soto, Alegria; Tacho.

Mik-api

In James Welch's 1986 novel *Fools Crow*, Mik-api is a medicine man who takes a significant role in the education of Fools Crow. He is in-strumental in every important moment of Fools Crow's growth. It is Mik-api who performs a healing ceremony on Fools Crow when he returns from the horse raid and has had a troubling dream. Mik-api helps initiate negotiations for the marriage of Fools Crow and Red Shield. He helps Fools Crow gain his power animal, the skunk bear (wolverine), and helps him establish a relationship with Raven, the Blackfeet trickster. When Fools Crow makes a sacrifice at the annual Sun Dance, it is Mik-api who assists in the ritual and its preparations. Mik-api is the one who trains Fools Crow as a medicine man. (Welch 1986)

See also *Fools Crow*; Rides-at-the-door; White Man's Dog.

Mike and Narcisse

Mike and Narcisse are the nephews of Archilde Leon in D'Arcy McNickle's novel *The Surrounded* (1936, 1978). Their mother is Archilde's older sister Agnes, and their father has died early. They are left largely to their own sources of entertainment, though their grandfather, Max Leon, does exert his tyrannical influence over them when possible. Against their wishes, they are forced back to boarding school. There, they are confronted by the strong-willed priests who wish to put the fear of God and the devil in them. When Mike defies the priests, he is locked in a room that reputedly is visited by the devil, and his spirit is broken as a result. The boys return to the reservation for summer vacation withdrawn, fearful, and dull. Mike, especially, is in need of help, and it is old Modeste who finds the solution to his problem. He realizes that Mike is dislocated from his own Salishan culture by the Christian school and needs to be reconnected to his culture. Modeste decides to give Mike the honor of leading him into the ceremony at the annual Fourth of July celebration. When Mike leads Modeste into the ceremony at the encampment, he is transformed. He is caught up in "the majesty of the dancers," and it seemed, "for a moment, as if they were unconquerable and as if they might move the world were they to set their strength to it." That action is largely responsible for the healing of Mike.

Mike and Narcisse are reoriented into their culture, and they make efforts to regain the old ways when they leave home and camp out in the mountains for the rest of the summer. When Archilde and Elise La Rose flee the authorities after the death of Max's wife Catharine, they find the boys in the mountains and join them. (McNickle 1936, 1978; Owens 1992a; Wiget 1985)

See also La Rose, Elise; Leon, Archilde; Leon, Max; Modeste; *The Surrounded*.

Miller, Jude

In Louise Erdrich's *The Beet Queen* (1986), Jude Miller is the kidnapped orphan brother of Karl and Mary Adare. On the day that their mother flew away in the airplane with The Great Omar, the unnamed infant held in Mary's arms was spotted by a kind but desperate man, Martin Miller. His three-day-old son had just died, and his wife was at home grieving. Miller pressed Karl and Mary to let him help with the baby, and finally, he simply took the child from Mary and walked away. Martin and Catherine Miller "adopted" the boy and named him Jude, "for the patron saint of lost causes, lost hopes, and last-ditch resorts." Catherine found a newspaper article saying that the Kozka family of Argus, North Dakota, was hunting for the child, but not until Jude was being ordained a deacon in the Catholic Church did she write the Kozka family with information about the child.

Sita Kozka, daughter of the couple who takes Mary in, attends Jude's ordination but does not identify herself. Instead she goes home and writes Catherine a note but fails to send it. The note is not sent until years later, when Celestine James finds it and mails it. The note is responsible for bringing Jude to Argus on the day of the Beet Queen parade.

Though Karl Adare meets Jude Miller when he is a young man and recognizes him as his brother, he does not establish a relationship with him. In fact, he tells Jude that he is a "piece of crap." Jude grew up to be "reliable, a

man of good sense, a satisfied priest admired for his tactful sermons and his warmth with the elderly."

Father Jude Miller appears in Erdrich's 1996 novel *Tales of Burning Love* as the local parish priest who suggests to his bishop that the events surrounding the death of Sister Leopolda should be investigated. (Erdrich 1986; Erdrich 1996)

See also Adare, Adelaide; Adare, Karl; Adare, Mary; *The Beet Queen*; James, Celestine; Kozka, Pete and Fritzie; Kozka, Sita; Puyat, Pauline; *Tales of Burning Love*.

Milly

Milly is the social worker in N. Scott Momaday's *House Made of Dawn* (1968) who works with Abel after he is released from prison. She was raised on a hardscrabble farm by a father who loved her but could not provide for her. She left and went to the city, where she got a job and went to school. In her last year of school, she married and had a baby, but her husband left after a number of years, and soon after her baby died. The buffetings of life that Milly has endured and her social isolation cast her as the enabler-victim in a relationship with Abel. Milly has been in Los Angeles for years but does not really know anyone: "No one knew what she thought or felt or who she was." Not long after she is assigned Abel's case, he comes to her one day and "suddenly she realized how lonely they both were, how unspeakably lonely."

Milly "believed in Honor, Industry, the Second Chance, the Brotherhood of Man, the American Dream, and him—Abel." She lavishes her love on Abel, and though he cares for her, he is unable to break the cycle of despair and alcoholism that would help create a mutually sustaining relationship. Abel's friend Ben Benally fears that Milly is too vulnerable to be in a relationship with Abel; he says, "She *trusted* everybody, I guess . . . And she had had a hard time all her life. It would have been pretty easy to hurt her." Though Abel cannot offer Milly a reciprocal commitment, he does care for her, and when he is beaten by Martinez, lying in a ditch nearly dead, he thinks of Milly and gains comfort and strength. (Hylton 1972; McAllister 1974; Momaday 1968; Oleson 1973)

See also Abel; Benally, Ben; *House Made of Dawn*; Martinez.

Misshepeshu

Misshepeshu is a character from Ojibwa (Anishinabe) mythology, the Underwater Manito who is sometimes syncretized with the Christian devil. He figures significantly in Louise Erdrich's *Tracks* (1988) as a protective *manito* to Fleur and Moses Pillager; it is said that, "because of the Old Man's connections," Misshepeshu followed the Pillagers when they were driven to their present home from the east. Generally, he is viewed as a "spirit which they said was neither good nor bad but simply had an appetite." His appetite is inclined especially toward young girls:

> Our mothers warn us that we'll think he's handsome, for he appears with green eyes, copper skin, a mouth tender as a child's. But if you fall into his arms, he sprouts horns, fangs, claws, fins. . . . He holds you under. Then he takes the body of a lion, a fat brown worm, or a familiar man. He's made of gold. He's made of beach moss. He's a thing of dry foam, a thing of death by drowning, the death a Chippewa cannot survive.

Rumors suggest that he has claimed Fleur as his own and that perhaps one or both of her children have been fathered by him.

Pauline Puyat, however, sees him as the Christian devil. When she challenges the old gods with her brand of Christianity, it is Misshepeshu she seeks. She takes a leaky boat out onto the lake and wrestles him until she has killed him. Then she sees that it is the body of her former lover, Napoleon, that she has strangled with her rosary; nonetheless, she is certain that Misshepeshu has merely masked himself in Napoleon's body. (Erdrich 1988; Sergi 1992; Vecsey 1983)

See also Kashpaw, Eli; Napoleon; Pillager, Fleur; Pillager, Moses; Puyat, Pauline; *Tracks*.

Modeste

Modeste is a blind chief in D'Arcy McNickle's novel *The Surrounded* (1936, 1978). He is the uncle of Catharine Leon and the grandfather of Elise La Rose. Like Catharine, he too embraced Catholicism in his youth but has slowly been falling away, back to the traditionalism of the Salish. He is instrumental in helping others retrieve traditional values. When Catharine's grandson Mike comes back from boarding school traumatized by the priests and their threats of the devil's designs on him, it is Modeste who involves Mike in a traditional ceremony that restores him to soundness. Modeste is also the person to whom Catharine goes when she decides that she must obey the ceremony of the whip in her renunciation of her Christian baptism. He, in turn, tells Archilde of Catharine's decision.

Modeste is also a storyteller. He tells the story of how the Salish came to welcome the Black Robes to their lands. In the old days, the traditional enemies of the Salish respected their hunting grounds, until the Blackfeet were given guns by the whites. The intrusion of the new technology changed more than the way game was hunted. The ethos that governed war and revenge killings was no longer relevant:

> In the old days of our wars a few men would be killed and fighting was a thing you could enjoy, like hunting. But now it became a bitter thing. Old scores of blood revenge could never be settled because too many were killed.

The Salish got guns too, in an attempt to level the playing field, but the old social structures were forever obliterated, and nothing was gained. Then the Salish heard of the power of the *Somesh*, the crucifix of the black-robe fathers, and they sent for it. Modeste explains, "We thought they would bring back the power we had lost—but today we have less." (McNickle 1936, 1978; Owens 1992a; Wiget 1985)

See also La Rose, Elise; Leon, Archilde; Leon, Catharine; Mike and Narcisse; *The Surrounded*.

Momaday, N. Scott

Navarre Scott Momaday was born on February 27, 1934, at the Kiowa and Comanche Indian Hospital in Lawton, Oklahoma, "near the old stone corral at Fort Sill, where [his] ancestors were imprisoned in 1873 for having fled to the last buffalo range in the Staked Plains." In August 1934, Momaday was given his Kiowa name, Tsoai-talee (Rock-Tree Boy) by Pohdlohk, his step-great-grandfather. Tsoai, a sacred place to the Kiowas, is "the great black igneous monolith that rises out of the Black Hills of Wyoming to a height of 1,200 feet above the Belle Fourche River."

Born to a Kiowa father and part-Cherokee mother, Momaday was raised on Navajo and Jemez Pueblo reservations because his parents taught at Indian schools in those communities. The time Momaday spent on the Navajo reservation during his formative years accounts for the profound affinity he has for the Navajo. He says, "I feel very close to the Navajo because they were like family to me when I was little. Even now, when I go among them, I feel at home." It is not surprising, therefore, that both of his novels (*House Made of Dawn* and *The Ancient Child*) feature Navajo characters and mythic associations. The title of the first novel is taken from the Navajo Night Chant, and the reader is ill-equipped to understand Momaday's work without some awareness of Navajo culture.

Following their tenure at the Navajo school, Momaday's parents took positions at the Indian school in the Jemez Pueblo. Momaday lived there from the time he was 12 until he "ventured out to seek [his] fortune in the world." His experience in the Jemez community also leaves its mark in Momaday's work. Abel, the protagonist of *House Made of Dawn*, is a mixed-blood Jemez man, and the latter part of Momaday's memoir, *The Names* (1976), is given over to a recollection of significant events during his years in the Jemez Pueblo.

After studying at the mission school in the pueblo, he attended high school in Bernalillo and Albuquerque. His last year of high school was spent at Augustus Military Academy in Fort

N. Scott Momaday, 1969. (UPI/Corbis-Bettmann)

Defiance, Virginia. He then attended the University of New Mexico, where he received his bachelor's degree in political science in 1958. He won the Wallace Stegner Creative Scholarship to study creative writing at Stanford University, and he finished a master's degree there in 1960. He went on to complete a doctoral degree in American literature at Stanford in 1963, studying under the renowned poet and professor, Yvor Winters.

Momaday's first book was a revision of his dissertation on Frederick Goddard Tuckerman's poetry and was published in 1965. *The Journey of Tai-Me*, a collection of Kiowa oral tales, was privately published in 1967. Momaday's first novel, *House Made of Dawn*, was awarded the Pulitzer Prize in 1969, the first novel by a Native American to be so honored. The novel focuses on Abel, a mixed-blood Jemez man who returns from World War II in a state of psychic disorder. He must enter into a healing ritual that will reunite him with his tribal and cultural life.

In 1969, Momaday followed with an autobiographical reminiscence fused with Kiowa oral and recorded history, *The Way to Rainy Mountain*. The book is a further evolution of his earlier work, *The Journey of Tai-Me*. The volume features three distinctive narrative voices, "the mythical, the historical, and the immediate," and it is, as the title suggests, a journey. The narrative is Momaday's journey into the "racial memory" of the Kiowa people.

Momaday's next work is his memoir, *The Names* (1976). It is not unlike *The Way to Rainy Mountain* in its densely poetic and reflective tone. Therein, Momaday chronicles the genealogy of both sides of his family, back to the fourth generation. In the long space between the appearance of *The Names* and his next book, *The Ancient Child* (1989), Momaday spent most of his creative energies on his painting.

Momaday has also written three volumes of poetry: *Angle of Geese* (1974), *The Gourd Dancer* (1976), and *In the Presence of the Sun: Stories and Poems* (1992). His 1997 volume, *The Man Made of Words,* is a collection of essays and stories.

A core myth of the Kiowa people is the story of the young boy who turns into a bear. In the story, a young boy and his seven sisters are playing chase, when suddenly the boy starts to take on the physical characteristics of a bear. He chases his sisters, and they climb the rock tower tree, which lifts them to safety in the heavens. There they are reconfigured as the stars of the Big Dipper. From that time forward, the Kiowa always had kinspeople in the sky. The myth appears in most of Momaday's work, and in fact, the mythic power of the bear has been an important talismanic force in the life of Momaday himself. He thinks of the bear as another kind of self who watches over him. He tells the story of his early days in school:

When I think back on my early education—those schools on the Reservation where I was sometimes the only kid who could speak English—I shudder; and I ask myself: How did I survive that? How did I come through that experience with my tongue in one piece? It was of course medicine. The bear was watching close by. The bear is always there.

Though he is accomplished in several literary genres, Momaday thinks of himself primarily as a poet. He says, "Fiction is kind of a spinoff from my poetry. I started writing poetry first, and so I think virtually everything I write is lyrical."

Momaday sees himself as an artist, and he eschews the political. He says:

I don't think of [my writing] as political at all. That's not my disposition somehow. I'm not a political person. A lot of people I know will read my work as a political statement, and it can be read that way I suppose, but so can anything.

Momaday joins many Native American writers in the idea that he does not wish to be categorized as an "Indian writer":

I don't see myself as an Indian writer. I don't know what that means. I am an Indian, and I am a writer, but I don't just want to say "Indian writer" or to talk about Indian literature. I don't know what that means, exactly, and I don't identify with it at all.

He does agree that the body of recent literature by Native Americans has done much to change the popular stereotype of the Indian. He notes:

There was at one time a real danger [of the] Indian simply being frozen as an image in the American mind. But I think we have largely dislodged that image and he becomes something also more vital and infinitely more adaptable than the figure on the screen who is being chased by John Wayne.

Momaday lives in Tucson, Arizona, where he continues to write and paint. He is a professor of English at the University of Arizona. (Coltelli 1990; Givens 1985; King 1983; Momaday 1976; Owens 1992a; Ruoff 1990; Schubnell 1985; Weiler 1988; Woodard 1989)

See also *The Ancient Child*; *House Made of Dawn*; *The Names*; *The Way to Rainy Mountain*.

Montaño, Ts'eh

Ts'eh is a character of mythic and sacred proportions in Leslie Marmon Silko's *Ceremony* (1977, 1986). Tayo meets Ts'eh when he travels north looking for the spotted cattle on the mountain. When she introduces herself, saying, "I'm a Moñtano . . . You can call me Ts'eh. That's my nickname because my Indian name is so long," she also introduces her connection with both Thought Woman, "Ts'its'tsi'nako," and the mountain itself, "Tse-pi'na, the woman veiled in clouds." As Kenneth Lincoln points out, "Ts'i" is Keresan (a Pueblo language) for water, and "Montaño" is the Spanish word for mountain. She is, in effect, Water Mountain, embodying both the generative element water and the sacredness of the mountain.

When Betonie, the medicine man, sends Tayo on his curative journey, his enactment of the ceremony, he tells Tayo to "remember these stars . . . I've seen them and I've seen the spotted cattle; I've seen a mountain and I've seen a woman." All four of the elements of Betonie's dream come together when Tayo meets Ts'eh. She directs Tayo to look at the sky, and he sees Betonie's stars. The sight is confirmation that he is in the right place at the right time. Tayo's healing can begin, and Ts'eh effects that cure on several levels. Tayo experiences love through Ts'eh; her association with water signals the end of the drought of both Tayo's spirit and the whole Laguna land; and she instructs Tayo in the gathering and uses of healing herbs.

Tayo does not forget the meaning of his encounter with Ts'eh. When he completes the ceremony by refusing to respond to Emo's violence at the uranium mine, he is again aware of Ts'eh's love for him: "She had always loved him,

she had never left him; she had always been there." The realization of this sustaining love enables him to forgive himself for his cousin Rocky's death and to claim his connection with his own mother, Laura. (Allen 1979; Herzog 1985; Lincoln 1983; Mitchell 1979; Owens 1992a; Silko 19774, 1986; Swan 1992)

See also Betonie; *Ceremony*; Emo; Night Swan; Rocky; Tayo.

Monte

Monte is the son of Seese and David in Leslie Marmon Silko's 1991 book, *Almanac of the Dead*. Since before his birth, he has been a pawn in the hands of Beaufrey, David, Eric, and even his own mother, Seese. Seese, the secretary of the woman who is reconstructing the almanac of the title, is the only character truly able to love him and feel concern for his welfare. Though she is a careless and inadequate mother, she desires to do what is best for him.

Monte is kidnapped twice in his infancy. When he is only six months old, David and Beaufrey kidnap him and leave San Diego for Colombia in an effort to eliminate Seese from their lives. Later, when Beaufrey tires of David, he arranges to kidnap Monte a second time. What happens next is truly horrific; Monte becomes another innocent victim in Beaufrey's pornographic snuff film industry. (Silko 1991)

See also *Almanac of the Dead*; Beaufrey; David; Eric; Lecha; Seese.

Moon, Caryl

In Louise Erdrich's *Tales of Burning Love* (1996), Caryl Moon works for Jack Mauser only because Mauser owes Moon's father a favor. His father is Mauser's attorney at a time when Mauser and Mauser Construction is in financial difficulties. Because of his strategic advantage over Mauser, Moon is a slacker in his work, and he keeps Jack's patience at the boiling point. Moon is a "laid-back good-time boy with a stupid sentimental streak, self-consciously flowery bullshit lines, high school basketball trophies collecting dust on the TV, and girlfriends, lots of those, besides his wife." He tries his charm on Dot Adare Nanapush, Jack's record keeper at the construction company, and Dot changes the records in the office to make it appear as if Moon is pulling his weight. When Jack finds Moon making a pass at Dot, and when he later finds Dot's altered accounts, he fires her.

The firing becomes the fulcrum for a shift in the relationships between the three. In one scene, Caryl is returning to the construction site with a Mack truck full of gravel, and Dot decides to play chicken with him. With her compact car and her characteristic willfulness, she forces Moon into the ditch. The scene is further complicated when Mauser comes along and parks his red Cadillac near the truck. Soon the wheels of the truck sink and the off-balance load empties before the truck topples over and crushes Jack's car. Dot and Jack leave Moon trapped in the overturned truck, and their complicity in the abandonment triggers a new relationship—their "first real date." The episode also cements the hostility between Moon and Mauser.

Moon exacts his revenge on Mauser later, when Jack escapes his burning house and is running naked in a snowstorm. It is Caryl Moon who finds him and refuses to help. They begin to fight, and Moon kicks Jack senseless, saying, "That's for us little guys." Moon's advantage over Mauser is greater than the satisfaction he receives from beating Jack. Because Moon sees Jack alive after his house burns, the widely held theory of Jack's death in the fire is exploded. Moon makes it impossible for Jack to conveniently disappear and create a new life elsewhere. When the adventure of Jack's "death" and "resurrection" is finally over, and Jack is back at work in his construction company, Maynard Moon—Caryl's father and Jack's lawyer—has enough leverage to ensure Caryl's life-time employment with Mauser. Thus it is Caryl Moon who plays a part in the partial fulfillment of Sister Leopolda's prophecy about Mauser. Moon operates the crane that lifts the new stone virgin in place at the convent, and it is Moon who lets the statue fall into the arms of Jack Mauser. (Erdrich 1996)

See also Mauser, Jack; Nanapush, Dot Adare; Puyat, Pauline; *Tales of Burning Love*.

Morrissey, Bernadette

Bernadette Morrissey is a character in Louise Erdrich's *Tracks* (1988). A widow, she lives with her children and her brother Napoleon on one of the reservation's most productive farms. The Morrisseys were "well-off people, mixed-bloods who profited from acquiring allotments that many old Chippewa did not know how to keep." Bernadette also is the person in the community who helps lay out the dead. When Pauline Puyat comes to Bernadette looking for work, she finds working with the dead and dying so comfortable that she wonders if she is not related to Bernadette. (Erdrich 1988)

See also Morrissey, Sophie; Napoleon; Puyat, Pauline; *Tracks*.

Morrissey, June

See Kashpaw, June Morrissey.

Morrissey, Lipsha

Lipsha Morrissey figures prominently in two of the volumes in Louise Erdrich's North Dakota tetralogy, *Love Medicine* (1984, 1993) and *The Bingo Palace* (1994). He is a young innocent in *Love Medicine,* who comes by his wisdom in the difficult process of determining his identity and heritage. In *The Bingo Palace,* he has moved past his longing for a mother, and his growth allows him to fall in love with Shawnee Ray Toose.

His Grandma Kashpaw has called him "the biggest waste on the reservation," but her love for Lipsha anchors him and prepares him for his role as healer and linchpin between the Lamartine and Kashpaw families.

Lipsha is a half-brother to King Kashpaw, born to June Morrissey Kashpaw "in one of those years she left Gordie." The only knowledge he has of his mother, however, is that she abandoned him in a slough at birth. The major impulse that propels the narrative in *Love Medicine* and that provides cohesion in the loosely jointed novel is Lipsha's quest for a literal identity and a moral vision to provide a foundation for his unsettled life.

Albertine Johnson sees her cousin Lipsha as "more a listener than a talker, a shy one with a wide, sweet, intelligent face." She is amazed that he knows "surprising things" but at other times does not "make even the simplest sense." Lipsha himself realizes that he does not have "the cold hard potatoes it takes to understand everything," but he does know that he has "the touch." As the great-grandson of Fleur Pillager and the grandson of Moses Pillager, the two most prominent and powerful tribal medicine people, Lipsha has powers that even he does not yet understand. He knows that he has "secrets in [his] hands that nobody ever knew to ask," but when the novel opens, he is primarily using his power to heal sick stomachs and tired legs knotted with blue veins.

Unlike his half-brother King, Lipsha feels a strong connection to his traditional Ojibwa background. He is aware of the shortcomings of Christianity and its agenda of assimilation into white culture for Indian converts. He notes: "Since the Old Testament, God's been deafening up on us," and though the Chippewa Gods aren't perfect, "at least they come around." When he tries to heal his Grandpa Nector Kashpaw's adulterous ways, he turns to his traditional power of "the touch," but he overlays it with the trappings of his residual Catholicism. The most telling measure of Lipsha's immaturity as a healer emerges when he realizes he should go to Fleur Pillager for help in planning the ceremony, but his fear stops him. He instead goes hunting to shoot a pair of geese, birds that mate for life. His plan is to have both Nector and Marie eat the heart of a goose so that their own love relationship might be restored. But when his hunting is unsuccessful, he resorts to buying frozen turkey hearts at the grocery store. Unable to trust fully in his touch, he takes the hearts to the church to have them blessed. Again, his plan fails when he cannot persuade Sister Mary Martin to bless them. He touches the hearts himself with holy water as he leaves the church. His healing ceremony meets its final obstruction when Nector chokes on his turkey heart and dies. Lipsha has cured Nector's adultery only in the most macabre sense.

The death of Nector provides Lipsha with a new perspective; he realizes the fragility of life, the strength of grief, and the necessity for forgiveness. He decides that if he ever sees King again, he will forgive him for all the years of mistreatment. In dealing with his own grief, he realizes: "Forgiving somebody else made the whole thing easier to bear." Though he is humbled by his failure with the love medicine, Lipsha believes that Nector "wasn't choking on the heart alone." He tells Marie that Nector did love her "over time and distance"; Marie is touched by Lipsha's love and offers him the next best thing to the knowledge of his parentage—June's talismanic beads that she wore as she came out of the bush and into Marie's household so many years before.

Lipsha's next great adventure has a much happier outcome, and it begins when Lulu Lamartine decides it is time to tell him the truth about his parents. Lulu gambles that she will gain Lipsha as a grandson when she tells him that June is his mother and that his father is her son, Gerry Nanapush. Lipsha's initial reaction is anger, and with money he takes from Marie, he leaves the reservation and joins the army before coming to his senses. Lipsha has a vision, perhaps sent by Nector, when in a comic twist he is hit on the head with an empty Old Grand Dad bottle. His vision tells him that his father, Gerry Nanapush, is ready to make a break from prison. Lipsha hastens to the Cities, where he waits at King's apartment for Gerry to appear.

Soon he is joined by Gerry, and they immediately recognize their relatedness and join in a plan to secure for Lipsha June's legacy, the blue Firebird. In a card game thrown Lipsha's way, he wins the car and uses it to safely deliver his prison-breaking father to the Canadian border, but not before Gerry tells him he has nothing to fear from the irrational decision to join the army. Lipsha, he says, will not pass the physical because all Nanapush men have "this odd thing" with their hearts. Lipsha drives the car toward the reservation but first stops at the boundary river and offers tobacco to the water, thinks of June, forgives her, and then crosses the water and brings her home.

In *Love Medicine*, Lipsha notices the profound love between his grandparents that abides even in spite of difficulties. It makes him want "to go out and find a woman" to love until one of them "died or went crazy." *The Bingo Palace* is chiefly concerned with Lipsha's journey into the deep waters of love. Shawnee Ray Toose, the object of his early infatuations and maturing love, has a hot and cold relationship with Lyman Lamartine, and the conflict of the novel centers around these two suitors. Lyman has a serious advantage over Lipsha in that he is the father of her child. Shawnee has repeatedly postponed marriage to Lyman in spite of the extreme pressure placed on both of them by Zelda Kashpaw Johnson, with whom Shawnee and her son live.

Lipsha is in an adversarial relationship with Lyman not only over Shawnee. Lyman is making plans to build a bingo palace on tribal lands at Lake Matchimanito, land that has historically belonged to the fierce Pillager clan. Because of his familial connection with the Pillagers and because of his deeper connection with traditional tribal ways, Lipsha realizes that Lyman should not build in an area that is sacred to the water monster, Misshepeshu. Lipsha's awareness is reinforced when he and Lyman go on a vision quest, and he is visited by a skunk. In a comic scene befitting the hapless Lipsha, the skunk delivers a message, "This ain't real estate," and then sprays him. After a second visit from the skunk, the message sinks in, and Lipsha is able to block Lyman's plans.

The novel also reconnects Lipsha to his parents, June Morrissey Kashpaw and Gerry Nanapush. One night while he is working at Lyman's bar, Lipsha is spared no details about the way he was abandoned by June. Zelda tells him that June put him in the slough in a bag of rocks and that he was underwater far too long to have survived. He is so disturbed by the story that he can't sleep that night, and in his restlessness, June's spirit visits him. He wants to ask her about the incident, but she is quick and brusque. She takes her blue Firebird back, leaves Lipsha some bingo tickets, and tells him to start playing bingo. Lipsha senses that his luck is changing.

Soon afterward, Lipsha's life intersects with Gerry's. Lulu Lamartine has used her considerable political power to get her son moved from one prison to another, and in the transfer, Gerry escapes. He calls Lipsha and speaks to him in the old language, which Lipsha has trouble understanding, and consequently he is not sure where to meet his father so that he might usher him to safety. When they finally find one another, Lipsha's battery is dead, so they decide to steal a car. They wait in a drugstore, timing their move to hop in a running car, and Lipsha inexplicably shoplifts a stuffed toucan, drawing attention to himself and his escaped convict father. They flee the drugstore and find a running car at the train station, which they take, only to discover later that there is a baby in the backseat. Gerry and Lipsha drive off into another surrealistic twist of the plot as June's ghostly blue Firebird pulls up beside the stolen car and then takes off. Gerry, who has endured his prison time by dreaming of June, takes off after her. He leaves the road and gets stuck in a field of snow, where he vaults from the car and leaves in the Firebird with June. Lipsha is left in the blizzard with the baby, and as he cares for it until their rescue, he comes to understand the parent-child relationship in a way that reinforces his love for his parents and instructs him on Shawnee's love for her son.

As the central character in *The Bingo Palace*, Lipsha is the one for whom Fleur Pillager waits, "a successor, someone to carry on her knowledge." He has grown past his fear of Fleur and goes to see her for advice; he wins the love of Shawnee; he saves Matchimanito from the vulgarity of a bingo palace; and he gains a deeper understanding of family. Early in his narration, he says, "I have this sudden knowledge that no matter what I do with my life, no matter how far away I go, or change, or grow and gain, I will never get away from here." But Lipsha's ties to the reservation are not constraining; they give him the freedom to become the rightful heir to the Pillager powers. (Catt 1991; Erdrich 1984, 1993; Erdrich 1994; Flavin 1989; Gleason 1987; Hanson 1989; McKenzie 1986; Owens 1992a; Ruppert 1995; Schultz 1991; Smith 1991)

See also *The Bingo Palace*; Johnson, Albertine; Johnson, Zelda Kashpaw; Kashpaw, June Morrissey; Kashpaw, King; Kashpaw, Marie Lazarre; Kashpaw, Nector; Lamartine, Lulu Nanapush; Lamartine, Lyman; *Love Medicine*; Nanapush, Gerry; Pillager, Fleur; Pillager, Moses; *Tales of Burning Love*; Toose, Shawnee Ray.

Morrissey, Sophie

A character in Louise Erdrich's *Tracks* (1988), Sophie is the daughter of Bernadette Morrissey, the widow who has taken in Pauline Puyat. It is young Sophie, ripened prematurely with sexuality and doomed by her childlike innocence, who is used as a pawn in a treacherous game of love spun by Pauline. When Bernadette learns of Sophie's behavior, she immediately makes plans to send her daughter away to Grand Forks, North Dakota, "where a strict aunt lived, devout and childless, next door to a church." Sophie bolts from the wagon that is taking her away and runs to Fleur Pillager's home, where she sits stone still for days, refusing all food, drink, and encouragement to leave her silent vigil. Though Sophie is undone by the whole experience, Pauline justifies the way she has manipulated the young girl by saying that in Sophie, the "devil found an empty vessel, lazy, crammed with greed for little pleasures." (Erdrich 1988)

See also Kashpaw, Eli; Morrissey, Bernadette; Pillager, Fleur; Puyat, Pauline; *Tracks*.

Mosca (Carlos)

Mosca is a character in Leslie Marmon Silko's *Almanac of the Dead* (1991). He works for Calabazas, who has nicknamed him Mosca, or "the Fly," because of his constant activity. Though he works for Calabazas, he runs a business on the side selling cocaine. He is friends with the minor character Root and is fascinated by Root's accident. He regularly tries to encourage Root to remember the accident that has changed his life. Mosca has the ability to see witches and wizards on the street, and he spins a theory that witchcraft is responsible for Root's accident, that perhaps Root's own mother hired a witch to bring misfortune on her son. In the course of the novel, his spiritual powers do grow, and ideas and theories fill his head.

He has a "spirit" in his shoulder that tells him to kill Sonny and Bingo Blue and their cousin, Angelo. He attempts to shoot Sonny but instead kills a bystander, a British poet, at the Yaqui Easter Dance. He quickly takes the case of money that Sonny was getting in exchange for the cocaine in his broken deal and escapes to safety in the crowd, where he watches Sonny and Bingo get beaten by the Tucson police. After the International Holistic Healers Convention, he quits working for Calabazas and goes to work with the Barefoot Hopi, whom he once knew in prison. (Silko 1991)

See also *Almanac of the Dead*; The Barefoot Hopi; Blue, Bingo; Blue, Sonny; Calabazas; Root.

Mose

Mose is the brother of the nameless narrator in James Welch's *Winter in the Blood* (1974, 1986). When Mose was 14 years old and the narrator 12, Mose was killed as the brothers were driving cattle across a road. The event has marked the narrator for life; he feels responsible for the death and cannot move past it. The novel is largely about the narrator's journey from guilt over the death of Mose to health produced by the proper memory of the accident. By remembering the whole story, the narrator is absolved of the guilt and comes to his own sense of identity. (Owens 1992a; Sands 1978; Welch 1974, 1986)

See also Amos; Bird; Nameless Narrator; *Winter in the Blood*.

Mourning Dove (Christine Quintasket)

Mourning Dove, also know as Humishuma, Christine Quintasket, Christal McLeod, and Christine Galler, was born sometime between

April 1882 and 1888 in a canoe as her mother was crossing the Kootenai River near Bonner's Ferry, Idaho. Her birth holds metaphoric as well as literal truth, for, born on neither shore, Mourning Dove lived a life that was caught between the boundaries of her Okanogan culture and of the intruding white world and between the oral tradition and the literate tradition.

Her education was incomplete and not without considerable personal cost. She grew very ill during her first stay at the Goodwin Catholic Mission near Kettle Falls, Washington, but she persisted in her quest. Another attempt at schooling was interrupted by the death of her mother and the need for Mourning Dove to return home and assume household responsibilities. From ages 17 to 21, she sporadically attended government Indian schools, even serving as matron for the younger girls. The position earned her no salary but did enable her to continue her own studies. Her final formal education came in the winter of 1912–1913, when she studied English and typing at a Calgary, British Columbia, business college.

Mourning Dove is best known for her novel *Cogewea, the Half-Blood* (1927, 1981), thought to be the first novel by a Native American woman. It is clear that in her writing, she wanted to achieve both cultural and personal goals. On the one hand, Mourning Dove longed to serve her culture by revealing "the true Indian character." On the other hand, she was anxious to gain proficiency in English and to gain acknowledgment of her literary gift. Still, Mourning Dove never quite felt competent in English, as a 1930 letter to her friend and mentor, Lucullus Virgil McWhorter, reveals: "I am still studying hard nearly every day, so I can learn to place my words for my writing and recasting of my new novel of the Okanogans."

She also tirelessly recorded tales of the Okanogans and collected them in the volume *Coyote Stories*, published in 1933. The effort strengthened her determination to preserve the traditions of her people; with the encouragement of McWhorter she even gave several public lectures on her culture. Her final volume, one that is gaining considerable scholarly at-

tention, was her autobiography. *Mourning Dove: A Salishan Autobiography* was not published until 1990, 54 years after her death in 1936.

Mourning Dove's achievement is remarkable. She suffered from poverty, broken health, and two tumultuous marriages. She gained a rudimentary education against tremendous odds; she wrote in the most inhospitable of conditions. As a migrant worker for most of her adult life, she hammered out her stories on an old typewriter at the end of a day of picking and culling apples, often while living in a tent as she followed the harvest. Yet she produced a novel, a collection of Okanogan tales, and an autobiography before she died at age 49. (Brown 1994; Fisher 1980; Fisher 1985; J. Miller 1990a; J. Miller 1990b)

See also *Cogewea, the Half-Blood: A Depiction of the Great Montana Cattle Range*; *Coyote Stories*; *Mourning Dove: A Salishan Autobiography*.

Mourning Dove: A Salishan Autobiography

Mourning Dove: A Salishan Autobiography is a posthumous book published in 1990 and edited by Jay Miller. Mourning Dove's autobiography suffers from the same editorial intrusion, though to a lesser degree, as *Cogewea, the Half-Blood* and *Coyote Stories*. She wrote the draft without collaboration, but afterward the manuscript came under the influence of others. She first gave the completed draft to Lucullus Virgil McWhorter in the early 1930s but later passed the draft on to Heister Dean Guie, a Yakima newspaperman. Guie put the pages away and at some point rewrote Chapter Five on "Baby Care." From Guie the draft passed to Erna Gunther, "a legend in Northwest scholarship," who returned the drafts to Guie after some revisions. In 1981, the manuscript, with typed copies and some revisions, found its way to Miller, who finally edited it for publication. Miller found the text to be "the most sustained discussion of Interior Salish life by an insider" that he had ever seen. He declared the text "full of historical and ethnographic gems, but badly disjointed and ungrammatical."

Mourning Dove in full dress, 1916. (Washington State University)

Though the surviving text does record some particulars of Mourning Dove's personal life, it is largely an ethnographic and historical autobiography. Miller divides the text into three sections, "A Woman's World," "Seasonal Activities," and "Okanogan History."

In the first—and largest—section, Chapter One begins, "There are two things I am most grateful for in my life. The first is that I was born a descendant of the genuine Americans, the Indians; the second, that my birth happened in the year 1888." By 1888, the Salishan people were "well into the cycle of history involving their readjustment in living conditions," and Mourning Dove is grateful to "have known people who lived in the ancient way before everything started to change." The chapter tells of Mourning Dove's family and of Teequalt, the old woman who came to live with them and tutor her in the traditional ways of her tribe. Mourning Dove's childhood was devoted to "living in the old way," but as she grew up, she had to "adapt to the modern world and the sacred teachings of the Catholic church." The

time she spends away at the mission school further disrupts Mourning Dove's happy childhood. Her rudimentary schooling does awaken in Mourning Dove the desire to learn English well so that she might write.

Chapter Two, "Spiritual Training," relates puberty rites and the manner in which Salishan children are encouraged to find their spiritual powers. With the help of Teequalt, Mourning Dove is coached to "hunt for the spiritual blessings of a medicine woman." Her quest creates some family tensions, however, as her father presses for the adoption of white ways and her mother encourages her in the traditional ways. Chapter Three moves into matters of courtship and marriage. Mourning Dove tells the story of a marriage contract that was established for her as a baby and of an unwelcome proposal from an old man. Her mother's traditionalism, though welcomed by Mourning Dove in other situations, was not welcomed in matters of marriage.

In Chapters Four and Five, Mourning Dove provides information about the roles of the Salishan wife and mother. A young wife was oftentimes enslaved to the will of her mother-in-law. Once she became pregnant, her activities were dictated by the strict observance of taboos. Though the life of women seems difficult, Mourning Dove suggests that they were sustained by "the knowledge that everything on the earth has a purpose, every disease an herb to cure it, and every person a mission."

Chapter Six tells the story of how Mourning Dove's grandmother tried to "bequeath" to her the "carefully guarded lore of charms." Mourning Dove is not interested and ignores her grandmother's instruction. She realizes her mistake only after her grandmother is dead; she then goes to a medicine woman in the tribe and pays dearly for the valuable knowledge. Mourning Dove learns the secrets of love charms but misuses a charm and loses it.

The first section of the autobiography ends with a chapter on "Widowhood" and relates the story of a particular neighbor's experience. The behaviors of Ka-at-qhu after the death of her husband reflect traditional and "ancient ideas."

The next section of the book gives detailed information concerning hunting and fishing practices and comments on several spiritual rituals, including winter dancing, seancing, and the purifying ritual of the sweat lodge. The final section of the book is primarily historical, focusing on the transition to reservation and agrarian life. Mourning Dove does include the painful story of her family's struggle to survive the poverty and starvation that accompanied their drastic change in lifestyle.

Part of Mourning Dove's motivation in writing the autobiography was to represent her culture to the Euroamerican culture and to correct Euroamerican attitudes about Indians. In his introduction to the text, Miller quotes Mourning Dove from a newspaper article she wrote: "It is all wrong, this saying that Indians do not feel as deeply as whites. We do feel, and by and by some of us are going to be able to make our feelings appreciated, and then will the true Indian character be revealed." Her autobiography is an important step in the movement toward understanding. (Brown 1994; J. Miller 1990; Mourning Dove 1990b)

> See also *Cogewea, the Half-Blood: A Depiction of the Great Montana Cattle Range*; *Coyote Stories*; Mourning Dove (Christine Quintasket).

My Indian Boyhood

Luther Standing Bear's 1931 autobiography, *My Indian Boyhood,* is dedicated to "the boys and girls of America." A prefatory note follows: "I write this book with the hope that the hearts of the white boys and girls who read these pages will be made kinder toward the little Indian boys and girls." The volume is largely given to general accounts of the daily customs of the Sioux before the reservation system changed their lives forever. In particular, Standing Bear relates his own adventures as a young boy when he was still called Ota K'te, or "Plenty Kill." He tells of making and using bows and arrows, of hunting and fishing, of childhood games, of the useful arts of tanning and designing hides, and of gathering and using herbs. The book is filled with so much detailed information about the

ways of the prereservation Sioux that it could easily serve as a handbook of rudimentary survival skills.

But the book also bears study beyond its presentation as a child's book on the customs of the Sioux. It is interesting because of the bifurcated rhetorical posture of Standing Bear as he writes. On the one hand, he is presenting the glories of the Sioux before the intrusion of the white culture in a childlike simplicity; on the other hand, he is striking a political note that takes the book far beyond children's fare. For example, early in the book he begins a history of great Sioux men. He notes:

> Now, in the naming of these great men you will notice that I have not mentioned the names you usually see mentioned in books written by white men. The white men who have written histories of the Indian could not, of course, know of inner tribal matters nor of the attitudes of the people in general.

Even in his gentle tone, Standing Bear's message is sharp. In other places, his criticism of white life is indirect but present. He says that the Indian tries "to fit in with Nature and to understand, not to conquer and to rule." By oblique comparison, he shows the inferiority of white ways. Even his direct comparisons are rhetorically nonconfrontational: "The white man seems to look upon all animal life as enemies, while we looked upon them as friends and benefactors." In other examples, he comments on the health of the Indians. Their teeth are strong and white, whereas the dentist is much in demand in the white society. The Indian is strong and lean, eating only healthy foods, but the white man is often obese and weak. Seeing white men brand animals fills him "with disgust" and elicits this observation: "We had no humane societies in my time, but I know that we were humane and many times were puzzled at the things that the white man did and said."

He draws comparisons between the two cultures when he praises the way Indians break their horses without ever cursing or abusing the animals. He makes the same observations about the child-rearing practices of Indians: "In all the days spent with my mother and father, never did I feel the sting and humiliation of a blow from their hands." Standing Bear drives the comparison home with his ironic remark, "Though they were full-blooded Indians, they were good and wise and worthy of my tenderest thoughts."

My Indian Boyhood gives Standing Bear's life story only until the time he is 11 when he is sent to the Indian boarding school in Carlisle, Pennsylvania. He readily agrees to attending the school because by that time, "there were no more wars for the Indian, so I did not have a chance to earn my name as did my father." To go away from his family and way of life "meant death" to him and was his only remaining way to prove his bravery as a young Sioux warrior. (Standing Bear 1931, 1988)

See also Indian Boarding School; Standing Bear, Luther.

N

Nameless Narrator

In James Welch's first novel, *Winter in the Blood* (1974, 1986), the protagonist is nameless. Much has been made of the omission, including the suggestions that the narrator suffers from a profound identity crisis, that he has been denied the opportunity to earn a name in the manner of his historical culture, and that he becomes a universal everyman. Welch rather coyly explains:

> The narrator in *Winter in the Blood* was nameless because for the first thirty pages, I really had no reason to name him. The book is written in first person, so the narrator is the one doing all the acting. . . . But for a while there, I didn't see any reason for anybody to address him by a particular name. You have to remember that was my first novel. I was feeling my way around.

Welch's explanation notwithstanding, the narrator of the novel suffers from a tremendous sense of separation from all that is around him, including himself. He says, "I was distant from myself as a hawk from the moon. And that was why I had no particular feelings toward my mother and grandmother. Or the girl who had come to live with me."

Through the course of the novel, the narrator comes to understand his relationship both to his immediate family and to his past. He has had an incomplete understanding of his parents and of his grandmother and grandfather. His harsh attitude toward his mother begins to soften when he realizes that it was she and not his father who had to kill Amos the duck for Christmas dinner because his father was seldom around. He also learns that Yellow Calf, the wise tribal elder, is his own grandfather.

The narrator's memory is scarred by the death of his brother Mose, and he must reconcile his own part in the accident before he can move toward wholeness. When he finally realizes that he was not responsible for the death, he is freed from the "winter in his blood."

The last act of the novel shows that indeed the narrator has come to an understanding of his culture and his own place in it. His grandmother has died, and in a gesture of respect, he throws her tobacco pouch into her grave. (Barnett 1978; Owens 1992a; Velie 1994; Welch 1974, 1986)

See also The Airplane Man; Amos; Bird; First Raise, John; First Raise, Teresa; Lame Bull; Malvina; Mose; Welch, James; *Winter in the Blood*; Yellow Calf.

The Names

N. Scott Momaday has said that "in the Native American worldview," there is "the idea that naming is coincidental with creation; that, when you bestow a name upon someone or something you at the same time invest it with being." His autobiography, *The Names* (1976), is both an act of self-creation and an account of several generations of his family.

The Names is a highly poetic narrative, rich with Momaday's signature lyrical and penetrating prose. There is an underlying chronology in the volume; Momaday starts with an account of the Kiowa emergence myth, the coming out of the Kiowa people from a hollow log. A significant element of that story is that the first act of the emerging people was the naming of themselves, "Kwuda, *coming out.*" He moves to an introduction of the land and the weather that shapes and defines it. Only after acknowledging the creation of his people and their relationship to the land does he start the four-generation account of his ancestors. Momaday devotes nearly half of his autobiography to the accounts of his ancestors, indicative of his strong sense of connection to the past, to his family and culture. In these early sections of the book, Momaday blends pictures and stories of his ancestors with his own imaginative account of events. For example, when he relates the story of his own naming ceremony performed by his step-great-grandfather Pohd-lohk, he moves the reader into a moment-by-moment account of Pohd-lohk's day. The passage reaches a historical and cultural peak when Momaday imagines Pohd-lohk "reading" the pictorial history of the Kiowa people that he has been compiling for some time. This blending of fact and imagination is part of Momaday's plan. He says in the preface,

> In general, my narrative is an autobiographical account. Specifically it is an act of the imagination. When I turn my mind to my early life, it is the imaginative part of it that comes first and irresistibly into reach, and of that part I take hold. This is one way to tell a story.

The midsection of the book reveals the young Momaday's process of coming to awareness. He reminds us:

> Notions of the past and future are essentially notions of the present. In the same way an idea of one's ancestry and posterity is really an idea of the self. About this time I was formulating an idea of myself.

That idea of himself is dominated by an awareness of language. Momaday has said elsewhere that "we don't really begin . . . to exist until we convert ourselves into language." What follows is a lengthy stream-of-consciousness section where the reader is transported into the mind of Momaday. The section is framed by a passage revealing Momaday's fascination with language, "Miss Johnson said Mayre not Mary." An early reviewer of the text noticed Momaday's similarities to James Joyce and called the book "a portrait of the artist as a young Indian." The description certainly is not without merit, for Momaday's autobiography shares much in common, both in content and in style, with Joyce's *Portrait of the Artist as a Young Man.*

The next section of the book recounts Momaday's many experiences at Jemez Pueblo, where he and his parents lived. His parents taught at the Jemez Day School for over a quarter of a century, and the landscape and people there became indelibly etched on Momaday's consciousness. The section also records a significant stage in Momaday's growth as a Kiowa. When he was 13, he was given a horse by his parents, and his world enlarged. Of that experience he writes:

> On the back of my horse I had a different view of the world. I could see more of it, how it reached way beyond all the horizons I had ever seen; and yet it was more concentrated in its appearance, too, and more accessible to my mind, my imagination.

The gift of the horse secured Momaday's place in his cultural history. The Kiowas were known as "the horse culture" and the "centaur culture," and they held "an old, sacred notion of the horse." Momaday says that at some point in his "racial life," this sacred notion "must needs be expressed in order that [he] may be true to [his] nature. The rest of the narrative is the account of Momaday's excursions on his horse and his further awareness of the world around him. The story ends with a near-fatal accident while Momaday was rock climbing at Jemez. Of the experience Momaday says, "I should never again see the world as I saw it on the other side of that moment, in the bright reflection of time lost. There are such reflections, and for some of them I have the names."

In the epilogue, Momaday shares a final experience: he is traveling to Rainy Mountain, and when he arrives at the cemetery there, he visits with the spirits of the "old people." He writes, "They called me by my Indian name. And to each one, face to face, weeping, I spoke his name: *Mammedaty, Aho, Pohd-lohk, Keahdinekeah, Kau-au-ointy.*" He continues his journey until he arrives at Tsoai, the rock-tree (Devil's Tower), and then continues on to the place of the very origin of the Kiowa, "the hollow log there in the thin crust of the ice." Momaday's personal narrative is inextricably woven into the Kiowa narrative. The autobiography both begins and ends with the hollow log of the Kiowa origin tale.

Momaday says that when his great-grandfather Pohd-lohk told a story, "he began by being quiet." The quality of this volume would indicate that Momaday has followed Pohd-lohk's example, for the book is ripe with the wisdom of reflection. (McAllister 1978; Momaday 1976; Schubnell 1985)

See also Aho; Mammedaty; Momaday, N. Scott; *The Way to Rainy Mountain.*

Nanapush

Nanapush is a main character and one of two primary narrators in Louise Erdrich's *Tracks* (1988). The character is clearly modeled on the Ojibwa (Anishinabe) trickster and culture hero, Nanabozho. Erdrich's Nanapush lives up to his mythological name, for he is both culture hero and scatological trickster. As guardian of a threatened culture, Nanapush resists the impinging imperialism of allotment and refuses to sign the settlement papers that would disperse Ojibwa lands. Even though he eventually loses his land, Nanapush's resistance is important; he provides a cultural touchstone that gives encouragement to those who seek to maintain their tribal integrity, and he pricks the conscience of those who are willing to abandon the ancient ways out of desperation or the lure of government money.

In his behavior toward the sick and the dead, Nanapush also exemplifies the traits of a culture hero. He properly buries the Pillager dead when others are afraid to, and he rescues Fleur Pillager and nurses her back to health after the consumption epidemic. Years later, he saves Lulu Lamartine's feet from amputation after they are frozen in her desperate run for help during Fleur's difficult labor. The significant aspect of his healing is that Nanapush is aided in the process by singing the old songs. The life and history, even the health, of the tribal community are buried in the stories and songs, and by invoking them, Nanapush calls upon and receives the power and strength of his entire culture. Nanapush is the repository of cultural memory, and by voicing the songs and stories, he strengthens tribal health.

For all his benevolent and humane qualities, Nanapush is also the scatological trickster. Nanapush, like Nanabozho, is too pleased with his own sexual powers, is sexually frank with others—usually in an attempt only to embarrass—and delights in what he calls "the lower functions." He boasts that he has satisfied three wives, and he brags to Margaret Kashpaw about his sexual capabilities. He tries to shock Father Damien by whispering in church, "I'm having relations with Margaret already." When Father Damien directs him to make a confession, Nanapush slides into the confessional and provides a detailed accounting that the priest cuts short.

Nanapush uses his trickster ways with Pauline Puyat in an attempt to show her the follies of her obsession with Catholicism. Nanapush notices that Pauline, in an effort to mortify the flesh, uses the outhouse only at dawn and at dusk each day. He brews some sweet sassafras tea and plies her with it and with stories of floods until she miserably breaks her vow of restraint. The lesson is lost on Pauline, though, and she does not turn back to traditional culture.

Through his own wiliness, Nanapush manages to claim he is the father of Lulu; he gives his name and powers to her, and through her, to Gerry Nanapush and ultimately to Lipsha Morrissey, both characters in Erdrich's *Love Medicine*. (Erdrich 1988; Flavin 1991; Owens 1992a; Sergi 1992; Stripes 1991; Walker 1991)

See also Father Damien; Kashpaw, Margaret (Rushes Bear); Lamartine, Lulu Nanapush; *Love Medicine*; Pillager, Fleur; Puyat, Pauline.

Nanapush, Dot Adare

Dot Adare Nanapush figures prominently in two of Louise Erdrich's novels—*The Beet Queen* (1986) and *Tales of Burning Love* (1996)—and marginally in another, *Love Medicine* (1984, 1993). She is the child of Celestine James and Karl Adare, the result of a fierce but brief and selfish passion. On the night of her birth, a blizzard is raging, and Celestine cannot make it to the hospital. She is taken in by Wallace Pfef, and he delivers the child in his house. Out of gratitude, Celestine names the baby Wallacette. Mary Adare, the baby's aunt, is scornful of the name and immediately nicknames her "Dot." Though Dot's parents marry, Karl does not stay with the family, and Dot is raised by Celestine and Mary, with the help of Wallace Pfef as surrogate father. The complicated personal relationships of her parents, both biological and surrogate, create an environment ripe for the development of a willful child. Dot does not disappoint in this respect: "She became a bully, a demanding child, impossible to satisfy. . . . whose first clear word was MORE." Mary is aggressive in competing for Dot's affection, and Dot is quick to exploit the situation. Wallace recognizes that Mary and Celestine "loved Dot

too much, and for that sin she made them miserable."

During Dot's painful adolescence, she turns more and more to Wallace Pfef for an escape from the smothering household of her mother and aunt. But Pfef also falls victim to the impulse to do too much for Dot. He orchestrates a festival to honor the sugar beet that has brought prosperity to the community, but he makes a mistake when he rigs the contest for Beet Queen in Dot's favor. In her humiliation at having had the title bought for her, Dot leaves the coronation ceremony and gets in the plane that is waiting to spell the queen's name in the sky. The scene is eerily reminiscent of the opening scene of *The Beet Queen*, when her own grandmother, Adelaide Adare, gets into a plane at a fair and flies off, abandoning her children. Dot's flight, however, ends on a much happier note. She helps the pilot seed the clouds for a much-needed rain, but the flight is significant beyond her accidental contribution to the bringing of the rains. The act is a cutting of apron strings, a movement out of the nest, a fledgling motion toward independence. When Dot returns to the ground, it is not to the grasping neediness of all those who would smother her and hold her close. Only her mother is left waiting in the stands, and in her eyes, Dot sees "the force of her love. It is bulky and hard to carry, like a package that keeps untying."

In Erdrich's *Love Medicine* (1984, 1993), Dot Adare Nanapush appears as a young woman married to Gerry Nanapush, the son of Lulu Lamartine, best known for his Ojibwa activism and his inability to stay out of jail. Dot and Gerry do manage to conceive a child while she is visiting him in prison, and their child, Shawn, is "a powerful distillation" of the two strong parents. During her pregnancy, Dot works in the weighing shack of a construction site and, with her usual fierceness, knits suits for her unborn child, "transforming that gentle task into something perverse."

When we next encounter Dot Adare Nanapush, in *Tales of Burning Love* (1996), 13 years have passed; her daughter is a tomboyish adolescent, and her husband has been in jail for most of their marriage. In a moment of weakness, she consents to marry Jack Mauser, a local contractor; the marriage is both bigamous and, in view of Jack's history of unstable relationships, ill advised. Soon after their "marriage," Jack reestablishes a relationship with one of his former wives, and Dot finds her memories of Gerry Nanapush growing more and more active. Though Dot and Jack's relationship grows more platonic as time goes on, Dot is nonetheless outraged at Jack's infidelities and secrets from the past. Their relationship is rocky at best, and on December 31, 1994, Dot leaves Mauser for a fourth and final time. On that night, Jack drinks until he senselessly allows the house to catch on fire and burn. Evidence indicates that he has died in the fire, and Dot is left as the most recent of the four remaining widows of Jack Mauser.

After Mauser's funeral, Dot puts his ashes in a Valentine candy box that she had thought was a last-minute peace offering from Jack. At the funeral, she learns that the candy was meant for Marlis, one of his ex-wives. The candy was Jack's traditional way of thanking Marlis after each time they were together. Dot immediately sees that her grief for Jack would be misplaced; she feels absolved of any responsibility to mourn and throws the ashes into the air.

Wearing the dust of Jack's ashes, the four widows get in Dot's car to go home. Along the way, they pick up a hitchhiker who crawls into the back of the Ford Explorer and falls asleep. They get stuck in a snowstorm and spend the night telling stories about their "tales of burning love." Toward morning, when the other women are asleep, the hitchhiker reveals himself as Gerry Nanapush, recently escaped from prison, and he and Dot repeat their extraordinary feat of coupling in awkward places. Though Dot's love for Gerry is reconfirmed, she knows "having a man by my side a few hours every few years is about as much as I can stand of a marriage."

Back on her own, no longer working for or married to Jack Mauser, and once again separated from a husband on the run from the law, Dot decides to open a gas station at the loca-

tion of her aunt Mary's butcher shop. (Erdrich 1984, 1993; Erdrich 1986; Erdrich 1996)

See also Adare, Adelaide; Adare, Karl; Adare, Mary; *The Beet Queen*; Cook, Marlis; James, Celestine; *Love Medicine*; Mauser, Jack; Nanapush, Gerry; Nanapush, Shawn; Pfef, Wallace; *Tales of Burning Love*.

Nanapush, Gerry

In Louise Erdrich's *Love Medicine* (1984, 1993) and *The Bingo Palace* (1994), Gerry Nanapush is the contemporary manifestation of the Ojibwa (Anishinabe) trickster and culture hero Nanabozho. He shares characteristics of the traditional character, including voracious gastronomical and sexual appetites. He fathers a child in the visiting room of a prison; he can make "stacks of pork chops, whole fryers, thick steaks" disappear overnight. He has the shape-shifting abilities of the trickster, and he uses them to escape from prison, to squeeze through the frame of a hospital window when the police are chasing him, to break into King Kashpaw's apartment unnoticed, to ease 6 feet, 4 inches and 320 pounds into the tiny trunk of a Firebird. His son Lipsha Morrissey claims that Gerry "could strip and flee and change into shapes of swift release. Owls and bees, two-toned Ramblers, buzzards, cottontails, and motes of dust."

In addition to the comic attributes of the trickster, Gerry has the characteristics of the culture hero. As "the famous Chippewa who had songs wrote for him, whose face was on protest buttons, whose fate was argued over in courts of law, who sent press releases to the world," he has a political power that keeps the unjust treatment of Native Americans in the public eye. He is the "charismatic member of the American Indian Movement," and at age 35, Gerry has been in prison or on the run from prison "for almost half of those years." Initially given a prison term for his part in a fight with a cowboy, Gerry's subsequent stays were mainly for breaking out since he "believed in justice, not laws." It is not until Gerry's arrest on the Pine Ridge Reservation, though (in a situation that may have its genesis in the real-life case of

Leonard Peltier), that he moves into the national spotlight.

In his younger years, Gerry falls in love with June Morrissey Kashpaw, and they have a son. Gerry's life in prison and on the run has ill equipped him for fatherhood, and June herself abandons the child, who is eventually raised by Nector and Marie Kashpaw. It is not until the end of *Love Medicine* that Gerry meets and acknowledges Lipsha as his son and begins a relationship that brings healing to both. Lipsha safely delivers Gerry across the border to Canada, where he hopes to have some kind of normal life with his wife, Dot Adare Nanapush, and their new baby, Shawn.

When Erdrich introduces Gerry Nanapush into the narrative of *The Bingo Palace*, he is again in prison and again escapes, continuing his life on the run. In a surrealistic scene, Gerry sees the ghostly June and chases her off into the distance.

The scene from *The Bingo Palace* is further developed in *Tales of Burning Love* (1996). After the plane that is transferring Gerry from one prison to another goes down in a blizzard, Gerry escapes. In *The Bingo Palace*, we learn that he has a reunion with his son Lipsha. In *Tales of Burning Love*, he also meets his wife Dot Adare Nanapush; he shows up in the B&B casino disguised as "a massive Indian woman." She later picks him up as the mysterious hitchhiker while she and the other former wives of Jack Mauser are driving through the storm. Toward morning, after Eleanor Mauser has been lost to high winds and while Candice and Marlis are suffering from mild carbon monoxide poisoning, Gerry and Dot have an intimate visit in the front seat while they are waiting to be rescued. The scene is reminiscent of the time in *Love Medicine* when their daughter Shawn is conceived in a prison visiting room. Afterward, Dot gives Gerry a key to her apartment so that he can have a quick visit with Shawn before fleeing the police. (Erdrich 1984, 1993; Erdrich 1994; Erdrich 1996)

> See also *The Bingo Palace*; Kashpaw, June Morrissey; Kashpaw, King; Lamartine, Lulu Nanapush; *Love Medicine*; Morrissey, Lipsha; Nanapush, Dot Adare; Nanapush, Shawn; *Tales of Burning Love*.

Nanapush, Shawn

Shawn Nanapush is the child of Gerry Nanapush and Dot Adare Nanapush. Her birth is recorded in Louise Erdrich's *Love Medicine* (1984, 1993), and she appears as a 13-year-old tomboyish girl in Erdrich's *Tales of Burning Love* (1996). When her parents have a surreptitious meeting in the Ford Explorer, her mother hands Gerry Nanapush a key to her apartment so that he can visit his daughter. Their visit is marked by tenderness, and when the authorities smash in the apartment door looking for Gerry, Shawn convincingly decoys them from her father's trail. Her last look at the officers reveals her grin, "like a wolf pup," evidence that Shawn carries the characteristics of her Pillager and Nanapush ancestors. (Erdrich 1996)

> See also *Love Medicine*; Nanapush, Dot Adare; Nanapush, Gerry; Pillager, Fleur; *Tales of Burning Love*.

Napoleon

The old, grizzled bachelor brother of Bernadette Morrissey in Louise Erdrich's *Tracks* (1988), Napoleon pays inappropriate sexual attention to Pauline Puyat, the young girl who works in their home. Pauline responds to him once her sexual curiosity is aroused by the intimacy she witnesses between Eli Kashpaw and Fleur Pillager. The loveless sexual union between Pauline and Napoleon is as much the result of Pauline's using Napoleon as of his using her. By him, Pauline is pregnant with a child that she abandons to Bernadette. After the birth, Pauline goes to the convent, where her already unstable personality grows even more so in her twisted attempts to mortify herself into sainthood. When she reaches the peak of her erratic behavior, she launches out onto Lake Matchimanito to challenge the devil. Napoleon goes out to rescue her, but she mistakes him for the devil and strangles him with her rosary. She hides his dead body in the bush and returns to the convent.

In the novel *Love Medicine* (1984, 1993), Lulu Lamartine tells the story of finding the body of a dead man in the woods behind her house. The body she finds is Napoleon. (Erdrich 1984, 1993; Erdrich 1988)

See also Kashpaw, Eli; Lamartine, Lulu Nanapush; *Love Medicine*; Misshepeshu; Morrissey, Bernadette; Pillager, Fleur; Puyat, Pauline; *Tracks*.

Native American Autobiography

The term *Native American autobiography* is one of complexity and imprecision, not unlike the oxymoronic phrase "oral literature." With the latter phrase, the problem results from the absence of cognitive categories in the Western mind. For those raised in a literate culture, it is difficult to imagine "literature" in cultures without writing. Likewise, it is difficult to imagine the *self-life-writing* of autobiography in those cultures that have not historically had writing *or* an individuated sense of self. Certainly it is true, as David Brumble notes, that "conceptions of the self and identity differ from one culture to another." Hertha Wong suggests:

A native American concept of self differs from a Western (or Euro-American) idea of self in that it is more inclusive. Generally, native people tend to see themselves first as family, clan, and tribal *members*, and second as discrete individuals.

It follows, then, as Andrew Wiget notes, that without "a culturally sanctioned concentration on the individual self or person" and in the absence of "the technology of alphabetic writing," "autobiography, as it is generally understood in the West, did not traditionally exist as a genre of discourse among the indigenous peoples of the present-day United States."

However, after five centuries of colonization, "civilization," and "Christianizing," there developed the inevitable syncretism of differing worldviews, and Native Americans began producing autobiographies, of a sort. Arnold Krupat has shown that the first Native American autobiographies were collaborative efforts written in the interest of history. That is, Native Americans (with a collector, editor, or interpreter) were writing their versions of what happened in the moments of historical genocide and conquest. The first example of such

texts is J. B. Patterson's edition of *The Life of Ma-ka-tai-me-she-kia-kiak, or Black Hawk* (1833). Other autobiographies in this vein are by Wooden Leg, "a warrior who fought Custer," and Joseph White Bull, "the warrior who killed Custer."

As Krupat suggests, "If the first Indian autobiographies came out of a certain concern on the part of Indians and Euroamericans to set the historical record straight, the next group of these texts came from a concern to set the cultural record straight." Under the direction of Franz Boas, one of the twentieth century's most noted anthropologists, a cadre of graduate students at Columbia University flooded the pockets of Native American culture, gathering linguistic and folkloric information. This rush of field collection, often termed "salvage anthropology," was a result of the fear that these cultures were vanishing. In his 1925 annual report to the Bureau of American Ethnology, J. Walter Fewkes writes:

It is evident that aboriginal manners and customs are rapidly disappearing, but notwithstanding that disappearance much remains unknown, and there has come a more urgent necessity to preserve for posterity by adequate record the many survivals before they disappear forever.

Of course, this passage expresses a painful irony. Native American cultures are recognized as important and worthy of saving just when they are on the brink of extinction. Nonetheless, life stories of many native peoples were recorded, no longer with the intention to set a historical record straight, but rather to capture a whole culture as it was embedded in one life. Informants were chosen, not on the basis of their historical importance or their acts of heroism, as was true with the selection of subjects for the historical Indian autobiographies, but rather for their lack of importance, for their *representativeness*.

We recognize today that within every culture, no matter how rigid and codified the group behavior, there is a degree of diversity that

Frontispiece from the 1856 edition of Black Hawk's autobiography, The Great Indian Chief of the West: or, Life and Adventures of Black Hawk. *(Reproduced from* The Great Indian Chief of the West: or, Life and Adventures of Black Hawk, *1856)*

disallows understanding of the whole by a summary nod at the part. This metonymic shorthand of these researchers, however ethnocentric it may have been, did leave a collection of mediated autobiographies, some of which are just now receiving analytic and interpretative attention.

Though the historical and cultural Native American autobiographies were collected for different purposes, they share in common a methodology of collaboration. The field worker/collector would solicit, sometimes for pay, stories from a Native American informant who would often be spoken to through an interpreter other than the collector and whose story would be recorded by perhaps yet another person. The possibilities for confusion, misunderstanding, mishearing, misinterpretation, or

unabashed editorial intrusion were numerous. The resulting historical and anthropological documents, however "objective" and careful the collectors, are undeniably subject to taintings of all kinds. David Brumble grants that all autobiographies are "fictions" in some sense but that "self-written autobiography is at least the subject's *own* fiction, the subject's own conception of the self, and so it must always be authentic in this sense at least. With the as-told-to autobiographies of the nonliterate Indians, on the other hand, it is the Anglo editor, who decides, finally, what is to be the shape of his subject's 'autobiography.'"

Arnold Krupat calls these "as-told-to" autobiographies "Indian autobiographies" and distinguishes them from "autobiographies by Indians," using the criterion of the number of contributing voices. Whereas Indian autobiographies "are not actually self-written, but are, rather, texts marked by the principle of original, bicultural composite composition," autobiographies by Indians are "individually composed texts . . . written by those whose lives they chronicle." The "as-told-to" autobiographies have a layering of voices that contributes to the final production. With a subject, a collector, possibly a translator, and even a transcriber, the possibilities for editorial intrusion abound in such a system.

As Native Americans became literate in English, many produced their own autobiographies without the mediating collector/editor. The more highly educated the writers were, generally, the less chance of collaborative and editorial intrusion into the text. Luther Standing Bear, Charles Alexander Eastman, and Zitkala-Ša produced autobiographies in the late nineteenth and early twentieth centuries that demonstrate greater control over their texts than previous Native American autobiographies had.

The autobiography, as genre, continues to flourish in the late twentieth century. There are examples of both the "as-told-to," or "Indian autobiographies," as well as "autobiographies by Indians." John (Fire) Lame Deer and Mary Crow Dog have both written "Indian autobiographies" with the same collaborative writer, Richard Erdoes. N. Scott Momaday and Leslie Marmon Silko have taken the "autobiographies by Indians" to a new level with their literary autobiographies, *The Names* and *Storyteller*. Furthermore, Arnold Krupat and Brian Swann have edited a volume of autobiographical essays by Native American *writers*. Clearly, Indian writers have provided life stories reflecting all gradients on the range from orality to literacy. Doubtless, the genre will remain a fertile one for Native American writers for some time to come. (Brumble 1988; Fewkes 1925; Krupat 1994; Wiget 1994; Wong 1992)

See also *Lakota Woman; Lame Deer, Seeker of Visions: The Life of a Sioux Medicine Man; Left Handed, Son of Old Man Hat: A Navajo Autobiography; The Names;* Standing Bear, Luther; *Storyteller;* Zitkala-Ša.

Nickles, Dayton

In Michael Dorris's *A Yellow Raft in Blue Water* (1987), Dayton Nickles is Lee George's "friend from high school, a mixed-blood living on lease land close to Aunt Ida's." His relationship with Lee is so close that many suspect they are homosexual. Lee's sister Christine Taylor accuses him of as much when she makes a pass at him and he resists her.

When Lee and Dayton reach the age where they must register for the draft, they are unwilling to yield to the mandates of the U.S. government. They have become involved with the American Indian Movement (AIM), and Dayton says, "I'm an enrolled member of this Indian nation. A sovereign citizen. My tribe has not declared war." Dayton claims his 4-F classification, and as a "sole surviving son" cannot be drafted. He encourages Lee to resist the draft as well and becomes embroiled in a tug-of-war with Christine over Lee's allegiance. Christine "wins" the battle for Lee, who enlists only to be killed in Vietnam. At his funeral, Dayton extends forgiveness to Christine, who is struggling with her guilt about forcing Lee to enlist. Christine rebuffs Dayton's overture.

Dayton makes a life for himself, goes to college, and becomes a "teacher of science and a basketball coach." His career is interrupted, however, when he is charged with "improper conduct." Though he claims innocence, he is convicted and is sentenced to five years in the state penitentiary. Dayton is released early on good behavior just eight months before Christine returns to the reservation and shows up at his house. The boy who accused him is "currently on trial himself for manslaughter." While he was in prison, Dayton studied accounting and now has a "job working on the tribe's books and helping them balance their budget and write proposals."

When Christine arrives at Dayton's house, he tells her, "It's funny. Yesterday I decided to move, to get the hell off this reservation." Now he has a purpose: Christine needs care and moves into his guest room. Christine thinks, "Dayton needed some mess in his life, and I had plenty to spare." She realizes that in all the time that they have been living together, "I don't think we had touched each other once." As they care for each other, theirs becomes a relationship of mutual need and emotional fulfillment.

When Christine's daughter Rayona Taylor returns to the reservation after the Fourth of July rodeo, it is clear that Dayton will step in to parent her once her ailing mother dies. (Dorris 1987)

> See also Cree, Kennedy (Foxy); George, Ida; George, Lee; Taylor, Christine; Taylor, Rayona; *A Yellow Raft in Blue Water*.

Night Swan

A character in Leslie Marmon Silko's *Ceremony* (1977, 1986), Night Swan is a Mexican mixed-blood with hazel eyes. Associated with the color blue and with rain, she is an admixture of myth and reality and is rightfully associated with other universal feminine creative characters in the novel —Thought-Woman, Ts'eh, and Descheeny's wife—as they embody the qualities of the mythic Yellow Woman figure in Laguna cosmology. She has been a flamenco dancer in the small towns of the Southwest for years and says, "I remember every time I have danced." She comes from Socorro to Cubero to retire so that she might be in proximity to Tse-pi'na, "the woman veiled in clouds" (Mt. Taylor). There she develops a relationship with Josiah and later Tayo, the main character of the novel. It is she who tells Tayo's uncle Josiah of the hardy, drought-enduring spotted cattle and who first empowers Tayo by recognizing his Mexican eyes and prophesying his connection to the healing ceremony. She says to Tayo, "You don't have to understand what is happening. But remember this day. You will recognize it later. You are part of it now." It is with her that Tayo first hears the refrain *Y volvere* ("And I will return"), which has increased significance once he encounters Ts'eh. (Allen 1986; Nelson 1988; Owens 1992a; Silko 1977, 1986; Swan 1988)

> See also *Ceremony*; Descheeny's Wife; Montano, Ts'eh, Silko, Leslie Marmon; Tayo.

Occom, Samson

Samson Occom was born in 1723 in a traditional Mohegan family in New London, Connecticut. By this time, the Mohegans were already exposed to Christian missionaries, and when he was 16 or 17 years old, Occom converted to Christianity. After his conversion, Occom wanted to learn to read and write so that he might study the scriptures. His mother helped gain his acceptance at Moor's Indian Charity School, founded by Eleazar Wheelock. There he studied the Bible, English, Greek, and Latin. His goal was to attend college, but he suffered from failing eyesight and poor health.

Called the "Pious Mohegan," Occom became a schoolteacher for the Montauk Indians on Long Island for two years. For the next 11 years, he served the Montauks as a Christian missionary. He was licensed to preach and was ordained by the Long Island Presbytery. In 1751, he married Mary Fowler, a Montauk, but always had trouble supporting their growing family. Occom was well aware that he was paid only half the salary that his white missionary counterparts earned, and he had to supplement his income from preaching by working various other jobs. In 1761, while Occom was with the Montauk, he wrote an ethnographic study, *An Account of the Montauk Indians on Long Island,* which was published posthumously in 1809 by the Massachusetts Historical Society.

In December 1765, Occom was sent to England on a fund-raising tour for Wheelock and the Indian Charity School (later to become Dartmouth College). Occom preached over 300 sermons, and the two-year tour earned well over 11,000 pounds, including a generous contribution from the second Earl of Dartmouth. When Occom returned in 1768, he was greatly disturbed to learn that the school that had begun as an institution for the education of Indians now enrolled only three Indian students. Furthermore, the school had been moved from New London, Connecticut, to Hanover, New Hampshire, and by 1769 was called Dartmouth College. In 1771, Occom wrote a testy letter reminding Wheelock of the school's purpose.

During the American Revolutionary War, Occom counseled Indians to remain neutral and not involve themselves in the "Quarrils among the White People." He became more involved in local Indian affairs, trying to help settle land claims of several groups of Indians. But Occom achieved his greatest recognition by preaching a funeral sermon for Moses Paul, a Christian Mohegan who, in a drunken rage, killed Moses Cook, a respected white citizen of Waterbury, Connecticut. The public execution drew a great

A broadside taken from Samson Occom's "Address to His Indian Brethren," which he had delivered as a sermon at the funeral of Moses Paul, a Christian Wampanoag. (American Antiquarian Society)

crowd, and Occom's sermon was soon published. It gained great acclaim as a temperance tract and went through at least 19 editions. The published sermon grants Occom the distinction of being the first Native American writer in English.

Rhetorically, the sermon is interesting because it is given by an Indian to a largely white audience at the execution of an Indian man. That Occom is preaching against the evils of alcohol, which was introduced to the Indians by the whites, creates further ironies. Most remarkable for the liminal position from which Occom writes—as a Christianized Indian—the work is in the genre of the execution sermon, a popular genre in the eighteenth century.

Occom published *A Choice Collection of Hymns and Spiritual Songs*, some of which were original to him, two years after his famous ser-

mon. He died in 1792 of natural causes, at the age of 69. (Elliot 1994; Peyer 1994; Ruoff 1992; Strong 1996)

Ohitika Woman

Ohitika Woman (1993) is Mary Brave Bird's (formerly Mary Crow Dog) second volume of autobiography, again told with the help of Richard Erdoes. Brave Bird picks up where her first, *Lakota Woman* (1990), left off. A loosely organized and rambling volume, without the compelling narrative focus of the Wounded Knee episode, *Ohitika Woman* nonetheless captures the reader's attention with its story of one woman's struggle for survival in a hostile world. However, Brave Bird refuses to allow a sympathetic reader to see her as a flawless leader in a heroic battle for racial and gender equity. Brave Bird's narrative is enriched, but complicated, by her unapologetic truthfulness and blunt revelations. Her world is often hostile to an Indian and a woman, but just as fast as Brave Bird lets fly accusations, she also accepts personal responsibility for her actions. This mixture makes it impossible to dismiss Brave Bird's story as a mere rant and makes it just as impossible to turn her into an icon of political struggle.

After the struggle at Wounded Knee in 1973, Mary and Leonard Crow Dog were married in the Indian way, and she moved to his home, called Crow Dog's Paradise. There, with their growing family and Leonard's prominent role in American Indian Movement (AIM) politics and Lakota spiritual life, Mary began to feel a personal erasure. For Mary, Crow Dog's Paradise was not always a paradise; it was "sometimes hell." Finally, she says, "the life at Paradise simply wore me out."

Ohitika Woman opens 18 years later with Mary now separated from Leonard and struggling with alcoholism and depression. Her life descends into drinking, partying, and a recklessness that endangers her and her family. It took a serious car wreck in which she nearly lost her life to turn Brave Bird around. Now she is happily married and is growing strong in "Indian religion," which "made [her] survive."

She proclaims, "I will endure. I will fight to the end of my days—for everything that lives."

Ohitika Woman not only gives an emotional account of Brave Bird's life but also provides information about the continuing political struggles of Indian peoples and the traditional ways of the Lakota. Brave Bird reveals the problems of land disputes, poverty, housing problems, alcohol, and joblessness on the reservation. In discussing Lakota traditions, she never claims to be someone she is not. For instance, when she shares information about the Sun Dance, she says, "I don't want to talk here about the innermost meanings and details of rituals of the sun dance. That should be for a respected medicine man to do (or not to do)." The book is rich with information about the history of the Native American Church; the history of gender relations among the Sioux; and about the sweat bath, Sun Dance, *yuwipi*, and other ceremonies of the Lakota. Brave Bird even gives a history of tattooing among indigenous peoples.

In his foreword, Erdoes says that the stories of Indian men were being told, but "the Indian women, whose strength kept the movement going, were being ignored." With *Lakota Woman*, and now *Ohitika Woman*, that trend is being reversed. (Brave Bird with Erdoes 1993)

See also *Lakota Woman*; Native American Autobiography.

Old Horn, Lena

In James Welch's 1990 novel, *The Indian Lawyer*, Lena Old Horn is the high school counselor who recognizes the potential in her student, Sylvester Yellow Calf. Her interest in him is both genuine and self-serving. She wants to go to law school and finds some satisfaction in knowing that Sylvester is following that dream for both of them. Furthermore, as a young teacher not much older than Sylvester, Old Horn feels an attraction for him that neither dares act on. Sylvester "had been her friend in a way no one else had. He would never know it but he had made her feel confident, bright, a young woman of sex and substance." Though they maintain only the most minimal contact in the years that follow, when Sylvester needs advice about his decision to run for Congress, it is to Lena that he goes.

Lena and Sylvester are similar in two respects. Both are outsiders in their communities; Lena is a Crow woman in a Blackfeet community, and Sylvester is a Blackfeet man in a white community. By the end of the book, both decide to leave the communities that they have been a part of for so long and seek the dictates of their hearts. Their similar lives offer a parallel construction to the text that serves to reinforce the soundness of Sylvester's decision to leave his lucrative practice in Helena and go to Native American communities that need his legal counsel. (Welch 1990)

See also *The Indian Lawyer*.

Ortiz, Simon

Simon Ortiz was born on May 27, 1941, at Acoma Pueblo near Albuquerque, New Mexico. He is deeply connected to his Acoma roots, and their presence is never far from his writing.

Simon Ortiz, 1991. (John Fago)

Primarily a poet, Ortiz also writes some short stories, essays, and children's books. As a poet, Ortiz writes on the rituals of everyday life, on environmental and political issues, and about the goals and effects of colonization.

Ortiz spent his childhood at Acoma Pueblo, where he recognized the differences in the education he received from his family and community and the one he received at school. His tribal education was "experiential." He says, "You live it, breathe it, talk it. You touch it. You are involved with the motion of it." In contrast, his formal schooling taught him "about" things: "You learn about life. You read about it, you study it, you solve problems. But it's not an experienced learning; rather, you acquire it."

Ortiz's formal schooling started in the Bureau of Indian Affairs day school in McCarty's, New Mexico; after elementary school, he moved to St. Catherine's and the Albuquerque Indian boarding schools. He attended Fort Lewis College, the University of New Mexico, and the University of Iowa. Ortiz has taught at several institutions—San Diego State, the Institute of American Indian Arts, Navajo Community College, and Sinte Gleska College, among them—to support his career in writing. He also served some time in the United States Army after high school.

"I don't remember a world without language," Ortiz says, and his desire to become a "user of language as a writer, singer, and storyteller" was an early one. Though he resented the punishment for speaking the Acoma language in Catholic school and Indian boarding school, Ortiz realized that in learning English he had another medium for his art. Furthermore, as a social activist, Ortiz has learned that to fight back against a colonizing system, he had to learn that system. Ortiz came of age during the 1950s, when "there were the beginnings of a bolder and more vocalized resistance against the current U.S. public policies of repression, racism, and cultural ethnocide." For decades now, Ortiz has used the language of the colonizers to fight against oppression.

Ortiz's poetry includes *Going for the Rain* (1976), *A Good Journey* (1977), and *Fight Back:* *For the Sake of the People, for the Sake of the Land* (1980), which were collected and published in 1992 as *Woven Stone*. Other volumes are *From Sand Creek: Rising in This Heart Which Is Our America* (1981) and *After and Before the Lightning* (1994). (Nelson 1994; Ortiz 1987a; Ortiz 1987b; Ortiz 1992)

See also *Woven Stone*.

Oskison, John Milton

Before 1968, when N. Scott Momaday's *House Made of Dawn* set off what is now called the Native American Renaissance, only nine novels had been published by Native Americans. Three of those nine were by John Milton Oskison. If for no other reason than his early contribution to the body of literary works by Native Americans, Oskison is an important figure.

One-eighth Cherokee, Oskison was born at Vinita, Cherokee Nation, on September 1, 1874. His formal education included attending Willie Halsell College, receiving a bachelor's degree from Stanford in 1898, and pursuing graduate work in literature at Harvard. Oskison's interest in writing and journalism began at Stanford, and his early promise showed fruit when, in 1898, he won the *Century Magazine*'s prize for college graduates for his

John M. Oskison. (Oklahoma Historical Society #5828.1)

story called "Only the Master Shall Praise." For the next two and a half decades, Oskison wrote stories that found publication in major periodicals. He pursued a career in journalism, working for the *New York Evening Post* and for *Collier's* as an editor and writer. During World War I, he served in the army as a lieutenant and correspondent.

Though he first gained a reputation as a short story writer, by the 1920s, Oskison began writing novels. In quick succession *Wild Harvest* (1925) and *Black Jack Davy* (1926) were published, and after that apprenticeship in the novel, he wrote his strongest—and most autobiographical—work, *Brothers Three* (1933). In *Brothers Three*, Oskison demonstrates greater control over character development and plot than in his earlier novels.

The Oklahoma Territory is the setting for most of Oskison's work, and because of the rich diversity of characters that peopled the territory in the decades just before and after the turn of the century, the setting was ripe for a regional writer such as Oskison. Oskison's early work does not feature Indians as main characters, nor does his work center around Indian concerns, but in *Brothers Three*, he does include major characters who are part Indian. Oskison is praised for his close observation of the range of characters who peopled the territory and came to inhabit his fiction. His portraits of characters are marked by his careful use of dialect. Oskison died in 1947, but half a century later, his work is receiving more critical attention than it did when he wrote it. (Littlefield and Parins 1982; Owens 1992a; Ronnow 1994; Ruoff 1983)

See also *Wild Harvest.*

Louis Owens, 1997. (Jay Cox)

Owens, Louis

Born in 1948 in Lompoc, California, Owens is a novelist, critic, and educator. Owens holds bachelor's and master's of arts degrees from University of California at Santa Barbara and a doctoral degree from the University of California at Davis. He is professor of Native American literature and creative writing at the University of New Mexico. Owens has distinguished himself as a critic of Native American literatures; his 1992 book, *Other Destinies: Understanding the American Indian Novel,* was well received and is a useful tool for the study of the Native American novel. Owens is a fine novelist in his own right; his books *Wolfsong* (1991), *The Sharpest Sight* (1992), and *Bone Game* (1994) are moving him toward a recognized place in Native American literatures.

Owens says he writes to explore his "identity as a mixed-blood American of Choctaw, Cherokee, and Irish-American heritage" and to "explore the dilemmas of all mixed-bloods in America." (*Contemporary Authors* 1992b, vol. 137; Furman 1994; Krupat 1993; Witalec 1995)

See also *Bone Game; The Sharpest Sight.*

Owl Child

In James Welch's *Fools Crow* (1986), Owl Child is the renegade Pikuni who believes that the only way to deal with white encroachment on Blackfeet hunting grounds is through guerrilla warfare. He attracts a crowd of impatient young warriors to his band, and they lawlessly scourge the whites in the area. Even before Owl Child started his guerrilla warfare, he was looked upon with disapproval by many of the Pikuni because "he had killed Bear Head, a great warrior, the previous summer in an argument over a Cutthroat scalp." He is "feared and hated by many bands of his own people," but Fast Horse "looked upon him with awe, for of all the Pikunis, Owl Child had made the Napikwans [white men] cry the most."

Owl Child does seem to have an understanding of the situation that the Pikuni face with the invading whites. He, even more than many of the chiefs, understands that there will be no stopping the whites and their advances. He does not believe that treaties and the gradual signing away of territory will satisfy the whites. He warns, "If they have their way they will push us into the Backbone [Rocky Mountains] and take all the ground and the blackhorns [buffalo] for themselves."

On one occasion, when Owl Child has been refused hospitality in the camp of the Lone Eaters, Three Bears tries to reason with him. He tells Owl Child that whatever victories he and his band may achieve, their actions bring serious repercussions to the whole of the Pikuni people. Owl Child counters with a prophecy:

Someday, old man, a Napikwan [white] will be standing right where you are and all around him will be grazing thousands of the whitehorns [cattle]. You will be only a part of the dust they kick up. If I have my way I will kill that white man and all his whitehorns before this happens. It is the young who will lead the Pikunis to drive these devils from our land.

(Barry 1991–1992; Owens 1992a; Welch 1986)

See also Fast Horse; *Fools Crow*; Three Bears; White Man's Dog.

P

Pantamounty, Candice

In Louise Erdrich's *Tales of Burning Love* (1996), Candice is Jack Mauser's former high school sweetheart and third wife. In the years between their high school relationship and their marriage, Candice was "fitted with a Dalkon shield in the midseventies," which caused severe problems: a "perforated uterus, quick infection, hysterectomy." She went to college and on to dental school and, with a settlement from A. H. Robins, "put a down payment on a house, an office space" for her dental practice. She thinks of her life as "before the shield, BS, and after the shield. AS."

One day she takes some bags of leaves to the dump and finds Jack Mauser there, just ready to kill his dog. A fanatic dog lover, Candice intervenes and offers Jack free dental services in exchange for the dog. The extent of Jack's dental neglect places him and Candice together enough that they soon develop a romantic involvement. In his characteristic offhanded manner, Jack proposes, "I have made an enemy of everyone I've ever touched, except you. Let's get engaged or something, Candy." Against her better judgment, they marry, but the marriage "was a triangle from the first" between Candice, Jack, and Pepperboy, the dog that she rescued from Jack. That Jack leaves their wedding reception without her is a first hint to Candice

that there might be troubles with the marriage, but not until a year later, when Jack viciously kicks Pepperboy, does Candice lose all respect for Jack. Their marriage struggles along until Candice agrees to go hunting with Jack in an attempt to restore their former love. The outing holds great promise for them at first, but when Jack carelessly leaves Pepperboy tied to the back of the truck and inadvertently drags him to his death, the end of the marriage is sealed. Candice looks into the eyes of her dying dog and sees "farther than my marriage, straight to its end, into the heart of helpless things." Years later, in the stranded Ford Explorer, Candice puts the marriage into perspective: "It was a dog that drove us together, though, and a dog that drove us apart."

As their relationship crumbles, Jack leaves Candice for a monthlong spree with Marlis Cook, a young girl who is soon pregnant with Jack's child. When Jack will not acknowledge the child and ends his reckless relationship with Marlis, Candice sees an opportunity to have the child that she has always wanted but could never have. She goes to Marlis and suggests that Marlis bear the child so that Candice might adopt and raise it. The surprising result of a complicated and hostile bartering for the child is a relationship between the two women. They become lovers and raise Jack's child together.

Candice's self-assessment is accurate when she says, "I don't get beaten, I keep going. I have never stopped, not for loss or tragedy or sickness or embarrassment, not for Jack, not for anyone." (Erdrich 1996)

See also Cook, Marlis; Mauser, Eleanor Schlick; Mauser, Jack; Nanapush, Dot Adare; *Tales of Burning Love.*

Parasimo, Bishop Omax

Another of the characters from the cathedral who joins Proude Cedarfair's pilgrim band in Gerald Vizenor's *Bearheart: The Heirship Chronicles* (1978, 1990), Bishop Parasimo is one of Inawa Biwide's "religious masters." In a time when "tribal people were banished to reservations," the Bishop is "obsessed with the romantic and spiritual power of tribal people," and he goes out looking for tribal people to lead to "secure underground shelter." He wears "metamasks" of different characters in his rescue operations. His metamasks include the likenesses of Scintilla Shruggles, Princess Gallroad from Fortuna, and "the beautiful face of Sister Eternal Flame."

When the pilgrims reach the dangerous Antelope Hills, where lightning strikes "seventeen times a minute," the Bishop gives the masks to Pio Wissakodewinini so that he will carry them through the lightning. The bishop does not make it through the lightning fields, however; he who had a "triune word habit in speech" is struck by lightning three times and burned to dust. (Velie 1982; Vizenor 1978, 1990)

See also *Bearheart: The Heirship Chronicles*; Biwide, Inawa; Wissakodewinini, Pio.

Paulie

Paulie is the lover of Ferro in Leslie Marmon Silko's *Almanac of the Dead* (1991). He is the keeper of the Dobermans at the ranch, and he is able to relate to the dogs far better than he can to people. When one of the dogs is ready to give birth to a litter of puppies, Paulie is aware that she will have too many to safely deliver or adequately take care of. In a moving scene at the birth of the puppies, we see a human and tender side of Paulie that does not emerge otherwise. The 12 dogs that he cares for have names such as Cyanide, Nitroglycerin, Magnum, and Stray Bullet. (Silko 1991)

See also *Almanac of the Dead*; Ferro; Zeta.

Penn, William S.

William Penn was born in 1949 in Los Angeles, California, to an ethnically mixed family. The Native American ancestry of his father (Nez Perce and Osage) contributes to Penn's fascination with stories and his use of the mythic in his fiction. His first novel, *The Absence of Angels* (1994), is a coming-of-age story of the young mixed-blood Alley Hummingbird. It garnered positive critical attention, and *All My Sins Are Relatives* (1995), a volume of essays about three generations of the author's family, was the winner of the 1994 North American Indian Prose Award.

Penn holds degrees from the University of California at Davis (A.B.) and from Syracuse University (D.A.). A member of the National

William Penn, 1998. (Jennifer S. Penn)

Advisory Caucus on Native American Writing and a coordinator for Wordcraft Circle of Native American Writers, he teaches at Michigan State University. (*Contemporary Authors* 1995, vol. 145)

See also *The Absence of Angels*.

Pfef, Wallace

In Louise Erdrich's *The Beet Queen* (1986), Pfef introduces himself in a segment of his first-person narration: "Wallace Pfef. Chamber of commerce, Sugar Beet Promoters, Optimists, Knights of Columbus, park board, and other organizations too numerous to mention." Pfef keeps a woman's picture that he bought at an auction in his living room; people in the community call her "Pfef's poor dead sweetheart," and she becomes the reason he never has to marry. A "slim man with a lot of thick blond hair, wide gray eyes," Pfef meets Karl Adare at a convention in Minneapolis, and they have a sexual liaison. This is the first homosexual experience for Pfef, and he returns to Argus, North Dakota, a bit stunned by what has happened. He pulls into a dirt side road, the local Lover's Lane, and stares at the sky and thinks. In trying to keep his mind off his recent experience with Karl, he gets a vision of what the sugar beet could do for the local economy. He feverishly begins making plans and soon introduces a booming sugar beet industry to Argus.

Soon after, Karl Adare stops in Argus and looks Pfef up. They stay together for two weeks before Karl meets Celestine James and begins an affair with her. Following his instinct one night, Pfef discovers the two and allows Karl to know that he knows. Karl stays with neither Pfef nor Celestine, even though she becomes pregnant with his child.

In the following years, Pfef becomes a surrogate father to Dot, the child of Karl and Celestine. His love for her balloons out of control, becoming as obsessive as the love of Celestine and Karl's sister Mary. In an attempt to bolster Dot's adolescent self-esteem, Pfef arranges a Beet Festival with a Beet Queen. He throws the election so that Dot wins, but she

learns of his intervention and is humiliated and angry. She finds an appropriate moment to express her rage when Pfef is the target at a dunking pool. She throws with such accuracy and power that Pfef is knocked out when he reaches the water. Karl, back in Argus for the Beet Festival, senses Pfef's danger and runs to his rescue, his effort serving as their reconciliation. (Erdrich 1986)

See also Adare, Karl; Adare, Mary; *The Beet Queen*; James, Celestine; Nanapush, Dot Adare.

Pillager, Fleur

Fleur Pillager is a primary character in Louise Erdrich's *Tracks* (1988) and figures in minor roles in *The Beet Queen* (1986) and *The Bingo Palace* (1994). From childhood, it is obvious that Fleur also has a connection with "Misshepeshu, the water man, the monster, [who] wanted her for himself." She has survived two drownings, and after each, the people who save her mysteriously die; for the surrounding community, the events confirm her powers and contribute to their fear of her.

Along with her distant cousin Moses Pillager, Fleur is the last of "the Pillagers, who knew the secret ways to cure or kill." The rest of the Pillager clan died in the 1912 outbreak of consumption. Near death herself and surrounded by all her family members who have died, she is rescued by Nanapush and is brought back to health with food and healing songs. Of the bear clan, the Pillagers have always had strong powers, and Fleur too has the totemic powers of the bear. She is a shape-shifter, assuming the shape of the bear when she hunts at night.

When she is fully recovered, she leaves Matchimanito, goes to Argus, North Dakota, and gets a job at Kozka Meats so that she might make the money needed to pay the annual fees on her Pillager allotments. In the evenings she plays cards with the three men who work at the butcher shop, and each night she wins exactly one dollar. Her patient and exact ways infuriate the men, and they raise the ante in an attempt to make her lose or at least win more than one dollar. She does win, and when she leaves the game with all the money, they attack and rape her. The tornado that kills two of the men and severely maims the third the next day bears the mark of Fleur's revenge.

She returns to Matchimanito and concerns herself with survival until Eli Kashpaw enters the picture. His fierce desire and his quiet, steady love for Fleur bring her once again into the fold of family and community. When Fleur gives birth to Lulu some time after, Eli assumes the role of father, and their happiness is complete until Pauline Puyat disrupts their lives. Pauline is so jealous of their love that she concocts a love medicine and sets a trap of adultery that ensnares Eli and young Sophie Morrissey. The result is the estrangement of Fleur and Eli. Fleur spends many evenings in Lake Matchimanito, and when she becomes pregnant with a second child, Eli reveals that Fleur has denied him relations and that the child must belong to Misshepeshu.

The pregnancy ends in a painful miscarriage, however, and the blow to Fleur is profound. She loses her confidence and her powers, and Nanapush recognizes that he must enact a cure for her. Again, Pauline Puyat is the source of disruption; in the middle of Nanapush's ceremony, she intrudes and challenges him with the powers of her Christian god. In spite of the interruption, Fleur does improve, though Nanapush does not know whether to attribute her healing to the cure or to the fee money that they have once again raised to secure their allotments.

Fleur's peace is short, however. Though Nector Kashpaw was sent to pay the fee on all Pillager, Nanapush, and Kashpaw allotments, the Indian agent assessed a late charge, and Nector was able to pay only the Kashpaw fee. Fleur loses her allotments, and the Turcot Company comes to Matchimanito to cut the timber from the ancestral Pillager home. The skein of Fleur's life unravels quickly: Eli goes to work for the lumber company to make a living; Lulu is sent to the government Indian school; and, pushed off her homeland, Fleur loads her few possessions on a cart and leaves Matchimanito. Before she leaves, though, Fleur gives a threatening sign to the lumber company. She saws the trees surrounding her home nearly in two, leaving only enough wood to provide the thinnest support. When the men from the lumber company arrive to take possession of her home, a wind—at Fleur's command—topples the trees and pins the men beneath branches, smashed wagons, and equipment.

Although Fleur's story occupies center stage only in *Tracks*, she does make an appearance as a minor character in *The Beet Queen*, in which she is the woman who finds and heals Karl Adare after he jumps from a moving train. She also appears in *The Bingo Palace*, in which she is sought out for advice by Lipsha Morrissey, her great-grandson. He becomes Fleur's "successor, someone to carry on her knowledge," and it is certain that Fleur's powers will continue. (Bird 1992; Erdrich 1986; Erdrich 1988; Erdrich 1994; Flavin 1991; Owens 1992a; Sergi 1992; Stripes 1991)

See also Adare, Karl; *The Beet Queen*; *The Bingo Palace*; James, Dutch; Kashpaw, Eli; Kashpaw, Margaret (Rushes Bear); Kashpaw, Nector; Kozka, Pete and Fritzie; Lamartine, Lulu Nanapush; Misshepeshu; Morrissey, Lipsha; Nanapush; Pillager, Moses; Puyat, Pauline; *Tracks*; Veddar, Lily.

Pillager, Moses

Moses Pillager is a character in Louise Erdrich's *Love Medicine* (1984, 1993) and *Tracks* (1988). As a member of the spiritually powerful Pillager clan, Moses is viewed with some trepidation and suspicion. He is further estranged from the Chippewa (Ojibwa) community as a result of his eccentricities. He was just a "nursing boy" when the "first sickness came and thinned" out the tribal community. His mother "decided to fool the spirits by pretending that Moses was already dead." His name was never spoken, and he was never acknowledged; he "lived invisible, and he survived." Though "the sickness spared Moses, the cure bent his mind." He lives in isolation on an island, surrounded by cats, wearing his clothes backward.

When Pauline Puyat needs a love medicine to work a spell on Eli Kashpaw, she goes to

Moses Pillager. Nanapush also goes to him when he needs help with a cure for Fleur, who is suffering from depression and a loss of her powers after the death of her second child.

When Lulu Nanapush (Lamartine) returns from government boarding school and finds in her home with Nanapush the inescapable presence of Margaret (Rushes Bear) Kashpaw, she leaves home to go live with Moses on his island in Lake Matchimanito. She takes 12 nickels, a sack of potatoes, and a small block of lard. She and Moses becomes lovers, and "touch by touch," she takes down the metaphoric mausoleum that had been built over him as a child. She speaks his name, but only once, "so he would know he was alive." Together they have a child. (Erdrich 1984, 1993; Erdrich 1988)

> See also Kashpaw, Eli; Kashpaw, Margaret (Rushes Bear); Lamartine, Lulu Nanapush; *Love Medicine*; Nanapush; Pillager, Fleur; Puyat, Pauline; *Tracks*.

Polatkin, Junior

Junior is a character in Sherman Alexie's *Reservation Blues* (1995). He is the best friend of Victor Joseph, "but nobody could figure out why, since Junior was supposed to be smart." Junior works for the Bureau of Indian Affairs as the driver of the reservation water truck. Victor tags along with him each day, bumming food and money from Junior. Together, they are "two of the most accomplished bullies of recent Native American history," and Thomas Builds-the-Fire has always been their main target.

Junior's parents die in a car wreck on the way home from a New Year's Eve party at Thomas's parents' house. Junior is the oldest of his siblings but is still quite young himself, and he is unable to keep the family intact.

Tall, good-looking, and with hair so beautiful he could be "president of the Native American Hair Club," Junior attends a semester or two of college before dropping out and returning to the reservation. In college, Junior falls in love with a white woman, and when she gets pregnant, he wants to marry her. She refuses, saying, "I can't marry you. You're Indian." She

aborts the child, and once more, Junior is cut off from the hope of love and family.

Junior is the drummer in the Indian band, Coyote Springs, though he spends most of the time drunk with Victor or carousing with Betty and Veronica, two white women who hear about the band and show up on the reservation. Not a traditional, and "as contemporary as cable television," Junior is still willing to respect Big Mom and learn from her. When Coyote Springs leaves Big Mom's mountain, Junior leaves a letter with her explaining why he puts up with Victor because Victor has been there in the past for him: "He can be a jerk but he's a good guy, too. He's always taken care of me." The burden of responsibility in the friendship has always rested more completely with Junior, however. On the night that the band blows their audition in New York City and Victor goes on a drunken rampage, Junior doesn't drink but instead watches out for his friend. Chess notes, "You know, Junior, you're always saving Victor from something." That realization only increases the poignancy and irony of Junior's death. When Victor trades the one thing he loves most for the gift of the guitar, it is Junior's name that he whispers.

A week after Coyote Springs gets back from New York, Junior climbs the water tower on the reservation and shoots himself. Junior appears to the grieving Victor, who asks Junior why he killed himself. Junior finally answers, "Because when I closed my eyes like Thomas, I didn't see a damn thing. Nothing. Zilch. No stories, no songs. Nothing." (Alexie 1995)

> See also Betty and Veronica; Big Mom; Builds-the-Fire, Thomas; Joseph, Victor; *The Lone Ranger and Tonto Fistfight in Heaven*; The-man-who-was-probably-Lakota; *Reservation Blues*; Warm Water, Chess and Checkers.

Polatkin, Marie

Marie Polatkin is a character in Sherman Alexie's *Indian Killer* (1996). She is a Spokane Indian woman who is an aggressive activist for Indian rights and for the rights of the homeless. Marie's parents taught at the tribal school on the reservation, and they would not let their precocious child learn to speak Spokane, certain that doing so would negate her success "in the larger world." For that reason, and because "she did not dance or sing traditionally," Marie "was often thought of as being less than Indian."

At the University of Washington, Marie takes Dr. Clarence Mather's Native American literature class and recognizes on the first day that the class is given over to a study of literature that is only marginally Indian. She remembers that her cousin Reggie had been befriended by Mather until there was some dramatic break in their relationship. Because she and Reggie are not close, though, she doesn't know the nature of their quarrel.

Another student in the class, David Rogers, makes attempts at friendship with Marie, but she is largely uninterested. Her increasing antagonism toward Dr. Mather and the course syllabus is exacerbated by the fear that is running rampant through the college community and the city over the "Indian killings." When attention for the murders is focused on an Indian suspect, Marie's anger increases. She is fueled by "hateful, powerful thoughts" and wants "every white man to disappear." She wants "to burn them all down to ash and feast on their smoke."

Marie is not a one-dimensional character, delineated only by her hatred, however. She is the Sandwich Lady who daily delivers sandwiches to the homeless of Seattle. Her acts of kindness are her anchor to sanity; she knows that if she were to ignore a homeless person, "something would crumble inside of her." Her sympathy is born of the recognition that the individual disenfranchisement of the homeless is not unlike the disenfranchisement of Indian people generally.

Marie meets John Smith, an Indian man raised by a white couple, several times throughout the novel, and each time, neither is able to quite push through the distance that separates them from each other and from themselves. Marie and her sandwich delivery team do rescue John when he is being beaten by David's brother Aaron and his friends, though, and John

is with her on the night she protests Jack Wilson's reading at the Elliott Bay Book Company. They follow Wilson home and have a confrontation that ends with Wilson believing that John is the essence of his fictional character, Aristotle Little Hawk.

Meanwhile, Marie's relationship with Dr. Mather is not improving, and in an outburst in class, she insists that an "Indian man" is not responsible for the killings. She challenges Mather, "Who's to say I'm not the Indian Killer: Who's to say you're not the Indian Killer?" Her questions complicate the issue of the identity of the killer and confirm her position that John Smith is *not* the Indian killer. Finally, Mather cannot control his class with Marie in it and calls for a meeting with the head of the department. Marie suggests there that the Indian killer is perhaps a manifestation of the Ghost Dance working its power in contemporary times. Mather counters that the Ghost Dance is about "peace and beauty," but Marie reminds him that if the Ghost Dance had come true, all white people would be killed. She predicts, "Indians are dancing now, and I don't think they're going to stop." (Alexie 1996)

See also *Indian Killer*; Mather, Dr. Clarence; Polatkin, Reggie; Rogers, David; Smith, John.

Polatkin, Reggie

Reggie Polatkin is the mixed-blood cousin of Marie Polatkin in Sherman Alexie's *Indian Killer* (1996). He is another of the characters for whom identity is a complex and debilitating issue. A "handsome man, with a strong nose, clear brown skin, and startling blue eyes that instantly revealed his half-breed status," Reggie grew up in Seattle with his Spokane mother and white father, Bird Lawrence. Reggie suffered through childhood with his abusive and racist father, and from his mother's side of the family, he was burdened with "the collective dreams of the family." He was the one who was to "make a difference." In response to his father's abuse, he came to believe that his Indian blood was bad and that any of his successes were the result of his white blood. By young adulthood, he had "buried his Indian identity so successfully that he'd become invisible." With the outward indications of "success," he graduated from high school with honors and went to the University of Washington to major in history. There he met Dr. Clarence Mather, his "mirror opposite." Mather longs to be validated by the Indian community, and Reggie wants to "be completely white" or at least "earn the respect of white men." Together, the two form an alliance; Reggie supplies the authenticity, and Mather supplies the respect for Native cultures. Working with Mather and his group of "sad and lonely white men," Reggie plays "the part of shaman," and for the first time, feels a sense of pride in being Indian.

The breaking point in their relationship comes when Mather shows Reggie a collection of tapes recording the voices of Pacific Northwest Indian elders, gathered in 1926 by a forgotten anthropologist. When Reggie hears the Spokane stories, he tells Mather that the tapes should be erased because the story is a "family story." Reggie's reaction baffles Mather, but he realizes that his research project is endangered by Reggie's tribal sensitivities. The situation ends badly, with Mather lying to the dean about the tapes and Reggie ultimately getting kicked out of the university.

When the news of the "Indian Killer" becomes the talk of Seattle, Reggie goes out on a rampage in a parallel fashion to Aaron Rogers, hunting for and beating white people. In one particularly painful incident, he beats a young man senseless and then plucks his eyes out. He forces the young man to endure a lesson in Indian history, to bear the collective guilt of an entire race. In an ironic twist, Reggie tape records the event and later asks, in a deliberate reflection on the Mather tapes, "Who can say which story is more traditional than any other?"

Reggie's violence is not limited to token white people; he picks a fight with John Smith one night at Big Heart's Soda and Juice Bar and beats him unmercifully. By this time, his accomplices, Ty and Harley, refuse to join him in any more adventures. As the case of the Indian Killer heats up, Reggie leaves Seattle, hitchhik-ing in any direction, knowing that wherever he goes, "every city was a city of white men." (Alexie 1996)

See also *Indian Killer*; Lawrence, Bird; Mather, Dr. Clarence; Polatkin, Marie; Rogers, Aaron; Smith, John.

Pretty Dog, Willard

In Michael Dorris's *A Yellow Raft in Blue Water* (1987), Ida George says Willard Pretty Dog is "the one all the girls wanted, the one whose golden life we dreamed to touch." He is a handsome and vain man who joins an "all-Indian regiment" and is sent to Italy where he is injured by a land mine. He returns to the reservation with extensive wounds and must have multiple plastic surgeries. Pretty Dog is vain about his looks and refuses to be seen, even to the extent of having the windows of his mother's car painted so that he will remain unseen as he travels to and from the hospital.

Father Hurlburt arranges for Ida George, one of the main characters, to meet with Pretty Dog, and they have dinner one evening. They meet each other from their points of pain and begin a relationship that brings both of them a measure of healing. In her attempts to guard Pretty Dog's vulnerabilities, however, Ida feigns an inferior intellect and lets him feel smart.

After his reconstructive surgeries, Pretty Dog's mother is certain that he can do better than Ida since he has "a Silver Star and a letter from Truman. An honorable discharge and veterans' benefits for life." Though Ida is carrying their child, she refuses to accept his love that is driven merely by loyalty and pity. When she ends their relationship, he marries "one of the nurses who cared for him at the hospital" and has a family of his own. (Dorris 1987)

See also Father Hurlburt; George, Ida; George, Lee; *A Yellow Raft in Blue Water*.

Pretty Weasel, Myron

Myron Pretty Weasel is a character in James Welch's 1979 novel, *The Death of Jim Loney*. Pretty Weasel is the high school friend and teammate of Jim Loney, though they have fallen out of touch since their high school days. Pretty Weasel went to college in Wyoming on a basketball scholarship but left in his junior year, refusing to be the token Indian any longer. He goes back to the family farm and turns it into the most prosperous ranch around. One night he sees Loney coming out of the liquor store; when he sees him a second night, he invites him hunting the next day. Loney accepts but is not certain that he wants to go at all. Pretty Weasel thinks of Loney as "the last friend he'd had" and is aware of the irony that he has become the "solid citizen" and that "Loney was the derelict." As he watches Loney, he silently asks, "What happened?"

The next day, in the hunt, Loney imagines that he is seeing a bear and takes a shot. The "bear" is Pretty Weasel, and he is killed by Loney's shot. Loney leaves his body in the woods and returns home without telling anyone that he has accidentally killed his friend. (Owens 1992a; Welch 1979, 1987; Westrum 1986)

See also *The Death of Jim Loney*; Loney, Jim.

Pumpkin

In Susan Power's *The Grass Dancer* (1994), Pumpkin is a character who figures briefly but significantly. She is the 18-year-old daughter of a "full-blood Menominee mother" and a "half-Irish" father, and her name is the result of her bright red hair and freckles. She is a prepossessing and intelligent young woman who is traveling the powwow highway during the summer before she reports to Stanford for college. She has always been out of place among her peers because "her world was constantly expanding, until she could no longer fit herself into the culture that was most important to her."

Pumpkin is a prize-winning grass dancer in a category usually reserved only for men. She meets the popular young Harley Wind Soldier at the powwow and senses his deep pain. With Pumpkin, Harley is able to share things he never has before. She reaches out to him by giving a part of her soul to him. After the powwow, Pumpkin and her friends go to the next pow-

wow on Fort Berthold Reservation. They drive into a terrible rainstorm, and the driver loses control of the car. Pumpkin is killed; she melts "into the sky, and so she never came down."

Charlene Thunder believes that her grandmother has caused Pumpkin's death on her behalf, and she is troubled by nightmares for a year. Charlene is released from her self-imposed guilt when Pumpkin visits her in a dream and absolves her: "It wasn't your fault. These things happen. There was nothing you could do." (Power 1994)

See also *The Grass Dancer*; Thunder, Anna (Mercury); Thunder, Charlene; Wind Soldier, Harley.

Puyat, Pauline

In Louise Erdrich's *Tracks* (1988), Pauline is another character who has lost most of her relatives in the 1912 consumption epidemic. After the death of her mother and sisters, she begs her father for permission to go south to the town to learn "the lace-making trade from nuns." Her father warns her that she will "fade out" there, will no longer be an Indian once she returns. But determined to assimilate into the white world and lose her Indianness, Pauline welcomes the idea. From her childhood on, she believes "that to hang back was to perish. I saw through the eyes of the world outside of us. I would not speak our language." In her attempt to distance herself from all things Ojibwa (Anishinabe), she grows into Catholicism, albeit a twisted and perverse version of the faith.

At 15, she leaves her father and goes to Argus, North Dakota, but ends up in the butcher shop running errands rather than making lace. There she works with Fleur Pillager and begins a jealous attraction to her that only intensifies as the years go by. Pauline is "so poor-looking" that she is "invisible to most customers and to the men in the shop." She envies Fleur's good looks and strong sense of self; she is torn among viewing Fleur as role model, maternal figure, or rival. Her complicated feelings toward Fleur are responsible for her behavior when Fleur is being raped by the three men who work at the butcher shop. Not only does she not help Fleur, but she stops Russell Kashpaw from alerting Fleur. The next day, when Fleur brings down a vengeful tornado, Pauline watches the three men seek shelter in the meat locker, and she locks them in from the outside. She is slow in revealing the information in her first-person narrative, though; she first reports, "It was Russell, I am sure, who first put his arms on the bar, thick iron that was made to slide along the wall and fall across the hasp and lock." This narrative equivocation is yet another sign of the divided mind of Pauline.

Just as Fleur leaves Argus and returns to the reservation after the tornado, so too does Pauline. She finds work with Bernadette Morrissey, doing housework and helping prepare the dead for burial, but she continues to be haunted by dreams of the events in Argus. She finally finds relief from the dreams in two ways: she tells the story of Argus to Margaret Kashpaw and feels lighter once the burden of private knowledge is gone, and she watches a young girl, Mary Pepewas, die. As Mary dies, Pauline experiences "death as a form of grace." She becomes comfortable with death and the sights and smells that surround it.

When Pauline is present at the birth of Fleur's child, Lulu, Nanapush recognizes that she is "good at easing souls into death but bad at breathing them to life, afraid of life in fact, afraid of birth, and afraid of Fleur Pillager." In spite of her fear of Fleur, Pauline continues her jealous fascination with Fleur's new family of Eli and Lulu. Pauline is especially drawn to and repelled by the sexual intimacy shared by Fleur and Eli. Realizing that her only sexual access to Eli is vicarious, she uses a love medicine to lure Eli into adultery with Bernadette's daughter Sophie. The event that she orchestrates contributes to the bad blood between the two existing factions on the reservation. Whereas the Morrisseys favor selling lease rights to the lumber company, the Kashpaws, the Pillagers, and Nanapush are against it. As usual, Pauline remains blissfully unaware of the disruption she causes to the fragile web of community relationships.

Unable to contain her sexual curiosity any longer, Pauline begins sleeping with the grizzled old bachelor, Napoleon, the brother of Bernadette Morrissey. When she becomes pregnant, she tries to abort the baby, but Bernadette intervenes and promises to take the child after birth. By the time of the birth, however, Pauline refuses to deliver the child so as to spare it the blight of original sin. Bernadette extracts the child from Pauline with a hastily made set of forceps, two iron spoons wired together at the handles.

When she recovers from the delivery, Pauline enters the convent and reinvents herself. The nuns will accept no Indians, and Pauline convinces them that she is white, continuing the fiction begun by her own racial self-hatred. She also hears a "call" to save the Indians, and once again begins visiting Fleur, Nanapush, and the Kashpaws, hoping to win them to Christ. She is present at Matchimanito when Fleur's second child comes early. Pauline is all thumbs and makes the situation worse. When Fleur loses the baby, Pauline can only think of it as a soul to be baptized.

Meanwhile, Pauline is growing more and more fanatical in her twisted spirituality. She decides that Christ is an ineffective savior in the New World, that "new devils require new gods," and that she will become Christ's "champion, His savior too." In an attempt to parallel Christ's 40 days in the desert, Pauline launches a leaky boat on Lake Matchimanito to meet her devil, Misshepeshu. The scene becomes a tragic parody that ends with Pauline strangling Napoleon with her rosary and hiding his body in the woods. She then returns to the convent, and at the appropriate time, takes her vows, a new name—Sister Leopolda—and her first assignment, teaching arithmetic at St. Catherine's School in Argus. (Bird 1992; Erdrich 1988; Owens 1992a; Sergi 1992; Stripes 1991; Walker 1991)

See also Kashpaw, Eli; Kashpaw, Marie Lazarre; Kashpaw, Margaret (Rushes Bear); Lamartine, Lulu Nanapush; *Love Medicine*; Misshepeshu; Morrissey, Bernadette; Morrissey, Sophie; Nanapush; Napoleon; Pillager, Fleur; Puyat, Pauline; *Tales of Burning Love*; *Tracks*.

Q

Quigley, Sheriff Dave

In D'Arcy McNickle's *The Surrounded* (1936, 1978), the name of Quigley itself "could frighten most Indians, for the Sheriff had a reputation." Quigley is the Indian-hating sheriff who has fashioned himself into the stereotypical "hard-riding, quick-shooting dispenser of peace" that he had heard about in stories of the Old West. When Archilde Leon and his mother are hunting in the mountains, Quigley comes upon them and questions them on the whereabouts of Louis Leon, who is wanted for horse theft, taking care to intimidate them unnecessarily.

Quigley continues to intimidate Archilde in the coming months, hoping to trap him into an admission of guilt concerning the death of the game warden, Dan Smith. The cat-and-mouse game comes to a dramatic close when Quigley follows Archilde once more into the mountains. It is after the death of Archilde's mother, Catharine, and Archilde, his nephews, and Elise La Rose are camping in the mountains until they can plan an escape from the area by train. Quigley enters their camp and announces his intention to take all four back in to the Indian agent. Though Archilde is resigned, Elise is defiant; she throws a cup of hot coffee in Quigley's face and then shoots and kills him. Though the futures of Elise and Archilde are uncertain, Quigley's brutal demise gives the satisfaction that the death of a stock villain usually provides in such a narrative. (McNickle 1936, 1978)

See also Agent Parker; La Rose, Elise; Leon, Archilde; Leon, Catharine; Leon, Louis; Mike and Narcisse; Smith, Dan; *The Surrounded*.

Quintasket, Christine

See Mourning Dove (Christine Quintasket).

R

Rambo (Roy)

Rambo is a Vietnam veteran in Leslie Marmon Silko's *Almanac of the Dead* (1991) who works for Eddie Trigg "recruiting" blood donors and as a night watchman at Trigg's plasma storage center. He also works with the homeless men around the river's edge in Tucson, recruiting them for his "ragged army against the government." He scouts through wealthy neighborhoods looking for houses that are abandoned for months at a time. He keeps a list of these homes and marks them on his map as "Locations of Resources: Army of the Homeless." Going through the mail at one empty home, he found an ATM card and PIN number that gave him access to $30,000, which he used to outfit his army and pay for their expenses.

From searching through Trigg's files and from Peaches, another worker at the plasma center, Rambo learns that Trigg's business is not so innocent as only gathering blood and plasma, but that Trigg also harvests skin and internal organs in thoroughly unethical ways. He plans to "mobilize and rally his army of homeless to accuse the blood and biomaterials industry of mass murder." His partner in the plans for the homeless army and in the murder of Trigg is Clinton, another veteran. By the end of the novel, Rambo meets the Barefoot Hopi, and

their intentions to realign power structures merge. (Silko 1991)

> See also *Almanac of the Dead*; The Barefoot Hopi; Clinton; Trigg, Eddie.

Red Dress

In Susan Power's *The Grass Dancer* (1994), Red Dress is the sister of Anna Thunder's grandmother. She enters the present-day story through repeated legend and the dreams of the main characters. She also has her own narration of the events that occurred in 1864. She tells of her totemic connection with rattlesnakes and how she is earmarked by Father La Frambois as a possible convert to Christianity. He works with her steadily, teaching her to read and write English, hoping to convert her. Her own value system is too firmly entrenched, though, for her to succumb to the entreaties of the priest. She resists his efforts, and finally, in a dream, comes to understand her mission on behalf of her people.

At age 18, she leaves her family and travels, according to the dictates of her dream, to Fort Laramie. There she becomes the personal secretary to Reverend Pyke, a half-deranged chaplain. As Red Dress's dream continues to inform her, she casts spells on three soldiers and they hang themselves. Pyke suspects her involvement in the rash of hangings and goes to her lodge one night and kills her. Her spirit follows him and causes his own suicide.

Her brother, Long Chase, takes her body back to the family, and Ghost Horse, a young man who has been in love with Red Dress, asks to marry her spirit. He does so and mourns her "as a devoted husband would grieve." One year later at her "spirit release ceremony," Ghost Horse is unable to set her free. His "heart was a stone room without doors," and Red Dress is forever "hitched to the living, still moved by their concerns." Her spirit "never abandons the Dakota people, though sometimes all it can do is watch." Sometimes, however, she speaks to her people in their sleep, telling them, "*I am memory.*" (Power 1994)

See also Father La Frambois; *The Grass Dancer*; Reverend Pyke; Thunder, Anna (Mercury); Thunder, Charlene; Wind Soldier, Calvin; Wind Soldier, Harley; Wind Soldier, Lydia.

Red Hawk, Stacey

Stacey (Stace) Red Hawk is a Lakota Sioux from South Dakota who comes to Oklahoma to help solve the spate of murders there in Linda Hogan's *Mean Spirit* (1990). He is "a keeper of tradition, and a carrier of the sacred pipe of his people," but works in Washington for the Federal Bureau of Investigation because he believes "he could do more for his people" there. Red Hawk's investigation is stalled because he can only "move on federal land," and "not one of the murders took place on Indian land." He believes that the guilty parties are smart enough to be aware of the restrictions on federal agents and that they may even work for the government.

His friend, Lionel Tall, "one of the strongest of the Lakota medicine people in South Dakota," comes to Oklahoma to help Stace out with the investigation. Stace finally grows thoroughly disenchanted with the corruption that surrounds the investigation and strikes out on his own. Spiritually and emotionally depleted,

he tells Belle Graycloud, "I need hope." He goes to the river and offers tobacco and prays all night until he feels the aliveness of the world around him. He returns from the river looking "stronger, like a man who knew who he was and where he was going." When the Graycloud family's home is bombed and they flee to the settlement of the Hill Indians, Red Hawk goes with them. (Hogan 1990)

See also Father Dunne; Graycloud, Belle; Graycloud, Lettie; Graycloud, Moses; Horse, Michael; *Mean Spirit*.

Red Paint

In James Welch's *Fools Crow* (1986), Red Paint is the wife of the title character, Fools Crow. Red Paint is the daughter of Yellow Kidney and Heavy Shield Woman and is particularly suited to a life with Fools Crow by her strong rootedness in Pikuni culture. Unlike Kills-close-to-the-lake, Red Paint understands her role in the Pikuni society and does not move beyond the bounds of behavior prescribed by her family and tribal group. In the first year of their marriage, Red Paint becomes pregnant with their child, Sleep-bringer (also called Butterfly), who represents the hope of the Lone Eaters band in the face of certain decimation by the impinging settlers and the U.S. government. With the characteristic fears of a young mother living in apocalyptic times, Red Paint wonders, "Would he live to be born? Would it be better to be born and killed or killed inside of her?"

By the end of the novel, Red Paint's father has been killed by a settler, her brother has died of smallpox, and her mother is a worn shadow of the woman she once was. In spite of these tragedies, Red Paint is able to enter into the ritual dance of thanksgiving and continuance, with her child on her back and her husband at her side. (Welch 1986)

See also *Fools Crow*; Heavy Shield Woman; Kills-close-to-the-lake; White Man's Dog; Yellow Kidney.

Relocation

See Termination and Relocation.

Reservation Blues

Reservation Blues (1995) is the first novel by Spokane/Coeur d'Alene writer Sherman Alexie. The main characters, Thomas Builds-the-Fire, Junior Polatkin, and Victor Joseph, were also the main characters in his volume of short stories, *The Lone Ranger and Tonto Fistfight in Heaven.*

The novel opens when Robert Johnson, the black blues musician, finds his way to the crossroads on the Spokane reservation. He is drawn to the reservation by Big Mom, a mythic woman who has nurtured many great musicians through the years. According to Alexie's account, Johnson did not really die years ago, but all these years has been running from The Gentleman, to whom he traded his soul. He traded his freedom for his ability to play guitar, and every time he tries to be rid of his guitar, it finds its way back to him. When he catches a ride with Thomas from the crossroads to Big Mom's mountain, he leaves the guitar in the blue van.

The guitar finds its way to Victor Joseph, who will be transformed by it into a great player. Soon Victor, Junior, and Thomas are jamming in an abandoned building, gathering crowds with their music. Thomas is the lead singer and bass player, Victor plays lead guitar, and Junior is the drummer. They form a band named Coyote Springs and are asked to perform off the reservation. Their first gig is in Arlee, Montana, on the Flathead reservation. There they meet Chess and Checkers Warm Water, two sisters who join them on stage and soon become backup singers for the band. Thomas and Chess fall in love, and Checkers falls in love with the local parish priest on the Spokane reservation, Father Arnold. Victor and Junior take as lovers two white women, Betty and Veronica, New Age groupies who also want to sing backup with the band.

The mixture of love and jealousy provides much of the energy of this comic novel. But Alexie mines a darker vein of the plot as he follows the effect of Robert Johnson's guitar on Victor Joseph. The magical guitar, the vehicle of The Gentleman, insinuates its way into Victor's consciousness and leads to the final tragedy of the novel. Along the way, Victor accepts the gift of the guitar's power without acknowledging its source or considering its final cost.

Coyote Springs wins a battle of the bands in Seattle but comes home to division on the reservation. An old woman warns Thomas, "The Christians don't like your devil's music. The traditionals don't like your white man's music. The Tribal Council don't like you're more famous than they are. Nobody likes those white women with you." On the heels of their first step to success, Coyote Springs starts to fall apart. Victor and Junior spend their prize money on drinking; they get into a fight with Michael White Hawk, the antagonist nephew of the antagonistic Tribal Council Chairman, David WalksAlong. All three, and even Betty and Veronica, are hurt in the fight. Betty and Veronica decide to leave the Spokane reservation and go back home, where they start their own musical duo. WalksAlong calls an emergency meeting of the Tribal Council and moves to "excommunicate" Coyote Springs from the tribe. The band members are kept in only by the narrowest of margins.

At the band's darkest hour and in a multi-leveled set of ironies, Alexie sends in the cavalry. Phil Sheridan and George Wright from Cavalry Records in New York City drive onto the reservation looking for Coyote Springs to offer them an audition and possible recording contract. In surrealistic fashion, Alexie moves Sheridan and Wright back and forth through time, merging their characters with their historical antecedents. These modern cavalry officers are no more scrupulous than their nineteenth-century counterparts and are willing to exploit Coyote Springs. In a memo to the home office, they write, "We can really dress this group up, give them war paint, feathers, etc., and really play up the Indian angle. I think this band could prove to be very lucrative for Cavalry Records."

In the time before Coyote Springs must fly to New York to audition, they spend a week with Big Mom at her invitation. Though Victor resists her help, the others gain a measure of confidence and preparation. The audition is a disaster, however; Victor cannot control his ego or his guitar, and his mistakes spread like wildfire through the band. After tearing up the recording studio, Victor storms out into the city. Junior follows him through the night, keeping Victor safe while he binges on alcohol and his own anger.

The band returns to the reservation, aware that they have blown their only opportunity. Their return triggers a series of decisions that culminate in tragedy. Father Arnold determines that he must leave the priesthood because the presence of Checkers Warm Waters is calling him to carnality. Big Mom carves a harmonica of cedar and presents it to Robert Johnson, telling him that he has been saved from the call of his guitar. Chess and Thomas decide to leave the reservation for good. Victor Joseph hears the call of the guitar: "You can have me back. You can take me and you can be anybody you want to be. You can have anything you want to have. But you have to trade me for it." The guitar continues, "You have to give up what you love the most. What do you love the most? Who do you love the most?" Victor whispers Junior's name. Junior climbs the empty water tower on the reservation and shoots himself.

Big Mom and Father Arnold conduct Junior's graveside service, and Father Arnold returns to the ministry. Victor turns his attention to drinking himself to death. Checkers decides to join Thomas and Chess in Spokane. As they leave the reservation, Big Mom invites them to a longhouse feast for a final meal. She takes a collection for the three and sends them on their way. When they drive across the reservation border, "nothing happened. No locks clicked shut behind them." Shadow horses run beside the blue van, and the three sing with the shadow horses, "we are alive, we'll keep living." The novel is darkly comic and reveals the painful realities of reservation life in such an offhand manner that their weight and impact are increased rather than diminished. (Alexie 1995)

See also Alexie, Sherman; Betty and Veronica; Big Mom; Builds-the-Fire, Thomas; Father Arnold; Johnson, Robert; Joseph, Victor; *The Lone Ranger and Tonto Fistfight in Heaven*; The-man-who-was-probably-Lakota; Polatkin, Junior; Warm Water, Chess and Checkers.

Revard, Carter

Carter Revard was born in Pawhuska, Oklahoma, in 1931 and grew up on the Osage reservation with his mixed-blood Osage family and Ponca relatives. He earned a bachelor's degree from the University of Tulsa, a master's degree from Oxford as a Rhodes scholar, and a doctoral degree from Yale. He has taught medieval literature at Washington University in St. Louis since 1961.

Revard's own poetry is richly informed by his family and childhood experiences. Volumes include *My Right Hand Don't Leave Me No More* (1970); *Ponca War Dancers* (1980); *Cowboys and Indians, Christmas Shopping* (1992); and *An Eagle Nation* (1993). (Ballinger 1994; Revard 1987; Witalec 1995)

Carter Revard, 1993. (Washington University, St. Louis)

Reverend Pyke

Reverend Pyke is the chaplain at Fort Laramie in Susan Power's *The Grass Dancer* (1994). He is a half-deranged fanatic whose vision of America is "a place where animals were bred for food behind neat fences, mountains were leveled, valleys filled, rivers straightened, and grass trained with a ruler." He says that "there was nothing natural about the natural world; it was an evil disorder requiring the cleansing hand of God."

Red Dress becomes his personal secretary by passing herself off as "the Christian whom Father La Frambois had tried so long to create." Pyke keeps a close eye on her, however, convinced that "the Sioux will never be real Christians." He suspects that Red Dress's powers are behind the hangings that occur at the fort and follows her one night to her tepee, claiming the power of the Lord as he kills her. The spirit of Red Dress follows Pyke and causes him to turn his gun on himself. (Power 1994)

See also *The Grass Dancer*; Red Dress.

Rides-at-the-door

In James Welch's *Fools Crow* (1986), Rides-at-the-door is the father of White Man's Dog, the main character of the novel. A man of wealth and position, he "had many horses and three wives," and he is "the man Three Bears depended on most."

Rides-at-the-door is a man of sound judgment, which earns him the respect of the Pikunis. When White Man's Dog comes to him fearful that he has caused some of Yellow Kidney's troubles by not telling of his dream about the lodge filled with white girls, his father responds:

Men, even experienced warriors, do not always listen to reason when they are close to their prize. It is like a fever. The closer to the prize, the more the fever obscures the judgment. The world is thrown out of balance.

Rides-at-the-door recognizes that the world is out of balance in many regards. The Pikunis are being threatened on all sides by the encroaching white men, and Rides-at-the-door presses for negotiations with them. He cautions the council, "We are up against a force we cannot fight. It is our children and their children we must think of now." Later, as conditions with the United States Army worsen, Rides-at-the-door grants that more concessions will have to be made, even to the point of handing over the renegade Owl Child. Despite all attempts at compromise, Rides-at-the-door finally realizes that there will be no equitable agreement: "We will lose our grandchildren, Three Bears," he says. "They will be wiped out or they will turn into Napikwans."

Rides-at-the-door is a man moved more by reason than by passion; he takes his second wife at the urgings of his first wife, Double Strike Woman. Striped Face is her sister, "a wild girl" whose parents feared "she would be too much for any young man to handle." Rides-at-the-door takes his third wife in much the same manner of responsibility. Kills-close-to-the-lake is the daughter of a poor man who is "neither a good hunter nor a warrior"; he has no dowry to offer, "so it was unlikely that a young man would take her as wife." Out of friendship for the young girl's father, Rides-at-the-door agrees to bring her into the protection of his lodge as third wife.

When Kills-close-to-the-lake and Running Fisher fall into adultery, Rides-at-the-door admits his error in taking Kills-close-to-the-lake as his wife and then neglecting her. He says, "I have allowed my other wives to treat you badly. And now I caused you to commit this bad thing with my young son. I ask you to forgive me. . . ." He continues, "My son has wronged you. There is not much honor in him, I fear, and for that I also take the blame." He sends Running Fisher away to the north to live for a while with the people of his mother. He suggests that if Running Fisher comes back with dignity, he will assist him in dancing at the Sun Dance in the next year.

The prudence and wisdom of Rides-at-the-door are recognized and honored by the members of his band. Three Bears says that Rides-at-the-door has "the blood of a warrior flowing through a peace-talker's body," and when Three Bears is dying from smallpox, in one of his last lucid moments, he hands his red-stone pipe to Rides-at-the-door, thus signifying the transfer of power. (Owens 1992a; Welch 1986)

See also *Fools Crow*; Kills-close-to-the-lake; Owl Child; Running Fisher; Three Bears; White Man's Dog; Yellow Kidney.

Rocky

Rocky is a character in Leslie Marmon Silko's *Ceremony* (1977, 1986) who dies in the Philippine jungle during World War II. He is the full-blood cousin of Tayo and grows up with him on the Laguna reservation. Rocky is not at all interested in the old Laguna ways and is willing to abandon them completely in the attempt to assimilate and find success in the white world. A natural athlete, he wins a scholarship to play college football but is recruited by the army before he can fulfill his and his mother's dream. His mother holds Tayo responsible for his death. (Lincoln 1983; Owens 1992; Silko 1977, 1986; Swan 1991–1992a)

See also *Ceremony*; Silko, Leslie Marmon; Tayo.

Rogers, Aaron

In Sherman Alexie's *Indian Killer* (1996), Aaron Rogers is the vengeful brother of David Rogers, who disappeared after winning at the reservation casino. An Indian hater all his life, Aaron now sees revenge as his responsibility and, indeed, as a pleasurable vent for his hatred. Accompanied by his two roommates and wearing a ski mask, he takes a baseball bat and goes on a rampage, brutally beating any Indians he finds. He is encouraged in his actions by Truck Schultz, who calls him personally to tell him that David's body has been found.

His father persuades him to quit beating Indians because "they're not worth anything" and because he doesn't want to lose a second son. When, in a moment of remorseful reflection, Aaron confesses to his father that he was aiming at an Indian on the long-ago night they tried to scare an Indian family off their camas fields by shooting over their heads, his father dismisses his confession as nonsense. (Alexie 1996)

See also *Indian Killer*; Polatkin, Marie; Polatkin, Reggie; Rogers, David; Schultz, Truck; Smith, John.

Rogers, David

In Sherman Alexie's *Indian Killer* (1996), David Rogers is a student at the University of Washington. He takes a class in Native American literature, which both sparks his interest in native cultures and activates a significant childhood memory. On land unused by David's father grows camas root, a traditional food of the Spokane Indians. Though the elder Rogers refuses permission for the Indians to dig, they sneak in under cover of darkness to gather the roots. One night Rogers takes his sons to shoot at the Indians as they are digging, and the experience becomes a signal moment for both David and his brother Aaron. Even though he is told to shoot above the Indians only to scare them, David is horrified at the activity his father is directing. He is further horrified to see that his brother is aiming his AK-47 not above the head of an Indian man, but *at* it. When the incident is over and no one is hurt, David sneaks to the field and retrieves the root-digging stick left behind by one of the frightened Indians. He "buried it where his brother and father would never find it."

David's enrollment in the Native American literature class and his new acquaintance with Marie Polatkin continue to spur his interest in things Native American. One night he decides to go to the reservation gambling casino and wins $2,000. As he is taking the wad of small bills to his truck, he is cracked over the head. His disappearance heightens the fear of the "Indian Killer" spreading through the Seattle community. Truck Schultz, the local right-wing talk-show host, connects David's disappearance with the murders even though there is no evidence to confirm his claims. When David's brother, Aaron, calls in to the show, Schultz feeds his hatred of Indians.

The discovery of David's body with "a single bullet hole between his eyes" some time later is anticlimactic for those who fueled the fires of racism by claiming David's death was connected to the scalpings in Seattle. The narrator reveals that David was killed by two white men, Spud and Lyle, who stole his money and gambled it away and were killed themselves that same night. (Alexie 1996)

See also *Indian Killer*; Polatkin, Marie; Rogers, Aaron; Schultz, Truck.

Root

In Leslie Marmon Silko's *Almanac of the Dead* (1991), Root is the biker boyfriend of Lecha, who keeps the almanac of the title, and is a regular at Tiny's Stage Coach. Root was in a serious accident as a young man, and the results of it change his life. He feels a complete estrangement from his family and finds a surrogate family in the underworld of Tucson. He becomes a contact for drug sales on the local college campus. Though he has residual paralysis and speech impediments, he has come to accept the results of his accident as a kind of blessing, one that allows him to see the world in a different way.

Calabazas employs Root in his drug-smuggling business because he senses that he is a "throwback"—that though his great-grandfather, Gorgon, made a fortune off the Apache wars with the United States, Root identifies with the small amount of Indian blood that he has and that his mother and grandmother would just as soon forget. Calabazas also feels a sense of obligation to Root because his grandfather first employed Calabazas.

Root keeps his mangled motorcycle in his front yard wherever he lives to remind him "where he'd been and where he'd come back from." Root's house in Tucson is the place where two major narrative strains of the novel cross, for it is there that Lecha goes when she is fleeing suspicious authorities, and it is there that Seese finds Lecha when she starts searching for her son, Monte. (Silko 1991)

See also *Almanac of the Dead*; Calabazas; Lecha; Mosca (Carlos); Seese; Tiny.

Rose, Wendy

Wendy Rose is a Hopi/Miwok Indian born in 1948 in Oakland, California, as Bronwen Elizabeth Edwards. Rose received her bachelor's and master's degrees from the University of California at Berkeley, and has done doctoral work in anthropology at Berkeley. Her mixed-blood, urban, "pan-Indian" experience informs her best-known work, *The Halfbreed Chronicles and Other Poems* (1985). Rose says a mixed-blood is "a condition of history, a condition of context, a condition of circumstance." She further comments that being a mixed-blood means not having insight enough into either group.

Her studies as an anthropologist have been an attempt to "neutralize the very weapons that are being used against Indians, by mastering those weapons and then in a sense breaking them from within." Rose has devoted time to protecting Indian burial grounds and sees her role in the world of anthropology as a "spy."

Rose has taught Native American studies at California State University at Fresno, and has served as an editor of the *American Indian Quarterly*. In addition to being a poet, she is a gifted visual artist and illustrated Duane Niatum's *Carriers of the Dream Wheel* (1975). Her 1980 volume of poetry, *Lost Copper,* was nominated for the Pulitzer Prize. (Rose 1987; Rose 1990; Wilson 1994).

Running Fisher

Running Fisher is the younger brother of White Man's Dog in James Welch's *Fools Crow* (1986). Running Fisher shares more in common with the reckless Fast Horse than he does with his own brother, though, for he is inordinately proud and is willing to violate community values in order to please himself. Though the younger brother, Running Fisher early on shows great promise, even beyond that of White Man's Dog, but once White Man's Dog steps quietly into his maturity, Running Fisher feels diminished by the success of his brother. Resentment begins to fester in him, and he is forced to learn some unflattering truths about himself. He is allowed to participate in the attack on the Crows in revenge for the mutilation of Yellow Kidney. But when he gets to the edge of the Crow camp, he becomes fearful and remains at the perimeter, shooting his gun ineffectively into the air. When the first wave of Lone Eaters leaves the camp in victory, Running Fisher falls in with them and feigns the exultation of victory. Humiliated by his own failure but too proud to confess to his father, Rides-at-the-door, Running Fisher grows sullen and distant. He leaves the lodge of his parents and moves off by himself, which opens the possibility for further disaster.

His father's young third wife shows attention to Running Fisher, and he reciprocates. Soon the two are intimately involved, and they risk bringing shame to the entire family. Rides-at-the-door learns of his son's violation of taboo and confronts both Running Fisher and his third wife, Kills-close-to-the-lake. It is at this point that Running Fisher shows his first step into growth and maturity. He acknowledges his mistake, takes responsibility for it, and willingly accepts the temporary exile that his father offers him as a way of saving face. (Barry 1991–1992; Owens 1992a; Welch 1986)

See also Fast Horse; *Fools Crow*; Kills-close-to-the-lake; Rides-at-the-door; White Man's Dog.

S

Sáanii Dahataał:
The Women Are Singing

Luci Tapahonso is a Navajo poet and educator who teaches in the English department at the University of Kansas. The distance between Kansas and her roots in Shiprock, New Mexico, is very much a part of her 1993 volume of stories and poems, *Sáanii Dahataał: The Women Are Singing*. The volume opens with the story of Tapahonso and her daughter making the long trip back to New Mexico. They are greeted by family, eat mutton stew, and fall asleep to the sounds of the Yeis, "the grandfathers of the holy people," as they are dancing and singing in the distance. From the opening piece, Tapahonso invites the reader into the circle of family and language that envelops her work.

For Tapahonso, the land and the stories cannot be separated. The poem "The Weekend Is Over" shows the sorrow of leaving "home country—Dinetah" to return to Kansas. The journey is more than geographic; it is a journey away from the family and tribal stories that provide identity and a sense of one's own place in a larger community. In "Just Past Shiprock," Tapahonso gives a historical account of a family whose baby daughter dies on a trip. The baby was buried along the way, and later when the family would pass the spot, they would wipe their tears and remember the baby. This story is framed by a contemporary narrator who adds this lesson: "This land that may seem arid and forlorn to the newcomer is full of stories which hold the spirits of the people, those who live here today and those who lived centuries and other worlds ago."

Tapahonso uses the framing technique again in the poem "In 1864," but this time the technique is doubled: she tells a story within a story within a story. The nested stories reinforce rather than detract from her point. Each story of separation from home grows a shade darker and more tragic, so that they resonate off each other and become "a steady hum." In the first frame, Tapahonso and her daughters are again traveling from Dinetah to Kansas, and she tells the story of another Navajo who was away from home working on an electrical crew. His story moves into the story of the Long March, the relocation of 8,354 Navajos in 1864 by Kit Carson from Dinetah to Bosque Redondo. The poem ends by returning to the present and notes those things of the whites that the Navajos assimilated and converted to their own uses.

Tapahonso reinforces tradition through her work. In "It Has Always Been This Way," she reminds the reader of the traditions surrounding the birth of a Navajo child that have "worked well for centuries." "Shaa Ako Dahjinileh: Remember the Things They Told Us"

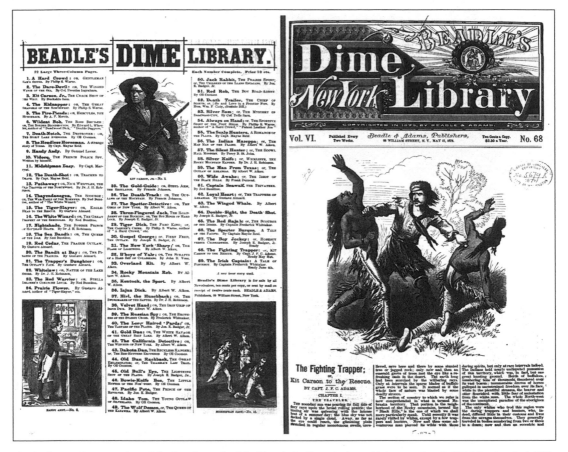

An Anglo-centric accounting of the forced march of the Navajo Indians during which more than 2,500 Navajos died. This is typical of the sort of stereotype that inflamed racist feeling and strengthened the notion of "manifest destiny." (Library of Congress)

is another poem reinforcing tradition. Tapahonso lists six admonishments, and even though some are now separated from their original purpose, the warnings are still in place. She adds to the final one, "It's not clear why this rule exists, but so far no one is willing to become the example of what happens to someone who doesn't abide by it."

The volume includes love poems too. A particular gem is "Leda and the Cowboy," a wonderful reversal of William Butler Yeats's poem "Leda and the Swan." Whereas the Leda of Yeats's poem is raped by Zeus, Tapahonso's Leda reverses the conquest paradigm, though without the violence. "Raisin Eyes" is a lighthearted poem about a woman who cannot help but fall for "Navajo cowboys with raisin eyes / and pointed boots."

Tapahonso ends the volume with several prose pieces. "The Snakeman" is the story of a group of Indian girls in boarding school longing for home and their mothers. Their fears are of ghosts; the "snakeman," a man in the attic; and dorm mothers who whip them. One little girl risks punishment every night by climbing down the fire escape to visit the graves of her parents. She talks each evening with her mother and returns to the buzz of the dormitory to fall asleep. The other girls have an imperfect understanding of her loss and fear instead the "man in the attic or the sandman," traditional childhood bogeymen.

The final story, "What I Am," is a story of a young Navajo girl who goes to Paris and realizes what it is like to be separated from family and home. She knows that she could not know who she is were it not for the generations of women who established the home. She remembers the story of her great-grandmother, who always said, "Having a mother is everything. Your mother is your home." The young girl stands at the top of the Eiffel Tower and says, "I understood that who I am is my mother, her mother, and my great-grandmother." Even from Paris, the pull of family and land and story comprise the bedrock of Tapahonso's world. (Tapahonso 1993)

See also Tapahonso, Luci.

Saint Plumero, Benito

In Gerald Vizenor's *Bearheart: The Heirship Chronicles* (1978, 1990), Benito Saint Plumero is a trickster figure whose appetite for sex is equaled only by the prodigiousness of his penis, which is named "president jackson." Proude and Rosina Cedarfair meet him at the "scapehouse of weirds and sensitives," where his inexhaustible powers are appreciated by the 13 women poets who live there. Saint Plumero is also known as "Bigfoot," a name given to him "in prison where he was sentenced for stealing a bronze statue from a park." Saint Plumero is a "short mixed-blood with huge feet" and thus feels an affinity for his beloved statue, a "woman with big metal feet."

Saint Plumero found his statue woman in "Rice Park" downtown and "saved her from her terrible isolation in the park." His obsession with the statue is so great that he has killed a man to save the statue "from sexual abuse and loneliness."

Saint Plumero leaves the house of the women poets and becomes a pilgrim with Proude and Rosina. Along the way, Saint Plumero is made a saint by the Pilgrim Pope of the Wheel of Dreams Parish. Henceforth he is known as Saint Benito Saint Plumero, or "Double Saint." When he forces himself sexually on Rosina, however, Pio Wissakodewinini, in his Sister Eternal Flame metamask, comes upon him and kills him. (Vizenor 1978, 1990)

See also *Bearheart: The Heirship Chronicles*; Cedarfair, Proude; Wissakodewinini, Pio.

Sandridge, Bent

Sandridge, a character in N. Scott Momaday's novel *The Ancient Child* (1989), is the adoptive father of the main character, Locke Setman. A retired philosopher and academic, Sandridge adopts Set from the Peter and Paul Home for orphans and provides him with stability and opportunity. Momaday's list of characters at the beginning of the novel describes him as "humane and wise."

Sandridge has an intuitive knowledge of Set and recognizes that Set's "presumption and arrogance" are "pronounced and dangerous." He warns Set that these characteristics will lead to "the Sin of Despair, thence to death and nothingness." Sandridge's maturity and wisdom provide for Set the emotional and moral touchstone that was lost when his parents died young and tragically. It is with Bent Sandridge that Set has imaginary conversations when he is troubled, and it is for Bent that Set calls when he is in a crisis. Bent has told Set that he must come to grips with his "demon" and that that is the "most ancient exorcism of all." But he also cautions Set, "Never take yourself too damned seriously."

It is the death of Bent Sandridge that precipitates the final stage of Set's journey toward self-knowledge. As a result of Sandridge's death, Set must face and exorcise his personal "demon"; the journey leads him through alcohol, depression, a six-week hospital stay, and ultimately, back to Oklahoma, where he is brought back to health through a ceremony by Grey. (Momaday 1989)

See also *The Ancient Child*; Grey; Setman, Locke.

Sarita

Sarita is a character in Leslie Marmon Silko's *Almanac of the Dead* (1991), the wife of Calabazas and the lover of the parish priest. As eldest sister, she is forced by her father to marry Calabazas even though her sister Liria is in love with him. The marriage becomes a convenient guise for her long-standing affair with first the monsignor and later the radical young priests in the parish. When her father suffers a sudden attack and dies, Calabazas rushes to the church where she is supposedly ironing altar cloths and finds her with the monsignor. Sarita and her sister cooperate through the years of her marriage to Calabazas to create a satisfactory arrangement for all. In their later years, the sisters join "a Catholic radical group to help smuggle refugees from Mexico and Guatemala to the United States." (Silko 1991)

See also *Almanac of the Dead*; Calabazas; Liria; Martinez-Soto, Alegria.

Schultz, Truck

Despite all the characters involved in physical violence in Sherman Alexie's *Indian Killer* (1996), the author reserves the greatest disgust for the dispenser of intellectual violence, Truck Schultz. Schultz affronts the Seattle talk-radio community with the violence of ignorance and inflammatory rhetoric in the service of racial hatred. A Rush Limbaugh wannabe, Schultz fuels public fear and distrust with his "news" about the Indian Killer.

Schultz has an insider at the state police office, "Johnny Law," who provides him with information. When Johnny Law calls Truck with the news that David Rogers's body has been found and that the connection to the Indian Killer is doubtful, Truck immediately goes on the air and reports: "The Seattle Police Department believes that a serial killer, known only as the Indian Killer, is responsible for David Rogers' murder, as well as the murder of Justin Summers, the bartender whose bloody body was found in Fremont." He also reports that David's body had been scalped, even though there was no suggestion that it was. He then launches into a diatribe against Indians, claiming, "We should have terminated Indian tribes from the very beginning." In another instance, he proposes that "we sterilize any girl whose I.Q. is below one hundred" so that "Indian women will not give birth to Indian killers."

In a lovely turn of poetic justice, Schultz goes out of his radio studio one night to smoke a cigar and gets locked out of the building. The community hysteria that he has worked so hard to produce has created an unnatural fear in him, and soon he imagines that he is being stalked by the Indian Killer in the alley. The police can find no evidence that anyone was in the alley with him, and Schultz loses face. As the situation with the Indian Killer reaches its frenzied peak, a Seattle police officer physically goes to Schultz's studio and shuts down his program. (Alexie 1996)

See also *Indian Killer*; Rogers, Aaron; Rogers, David.

Seese

Seese is a character in Leslie Marmon Silko's *Almanac of the Dead* (1991). She is from a military family, and after her father was killed over the South China Sea, she left home at age 16. Until she meets Lecha, the keeper of the almanac, her life is governed by personal excesses and bad decisions. She is a nude dancer at Tiny's club, the Stage Coach. She becomes involved with David, a photographer who draws her into his web of twisted relationships. Her first pregnancy with David is quickly terminated by David and his lover, Beaufrey. When she gets pregnant a second time, she is determined to keep the child, and in spite of her alcohol and cocaine habits, she delivers a healthy baby. Together David and Beaufrey kidnap the infant, Monte, in an attempt to remove Seese from their lives. Driven by total desperation to find Monte, Seese finds the now retired TV psychic, Lecha. Because her psychic gift is only to find the dead, Lecha refuses to take Seese's case but does hire her as a secretary and personal "nurse."

Beaufrey leaves Seese with a kilo of cocaine, certain that in her grief and addictive behaviors she will overdose and rid him cleanly of her presence. Once she gets connected with Lecha and the job of transcribing the almanac, though, Seese leaves behind her cocaine addiction and grows in her determination to find Monte. Another measure of her increasing health is the friendship with Sterling, the gardener at Zeta's ranch. She realizes that they both have come to the ranch as an act of final desperation, their own lives having grown complicated beyond their abilities to unravel.

Over time, Seese cannot escape the pressing intuition that Monte is dead. The weight of the knowledge drives her temporarily back to alcohol and cocaine. To save herself, she takes the cocaine into Tucson to sell it. Her initial attempts are unsuccessful, but Tiny arranges a meeting for her. Unknown to Seese, the arrangement is a setup by the Tucson police, and in the bust, Tiny is killed. The corrupt police have orchestrated the setup to kill one of their own undercover cops, Jamey, who has gotten out of control. They keep Seese tied to a chair, covered with the splattered blood and fat of Tiny, until she is coerced into giving a statement that will absolve them of Jamey's death. She barely escapes with her life and places a call to Lecha, who comes to her rescue.

When Lecha's nephew Ferro retaliates against the Tucson police for the death of Jamey, the ranch is raided. Seese flees with Lecha and Sterling and continues on to South Dakota with Lecha. (Silko 1991)

See also *Almanac of the Dead*; Beaufrey; David; Eric; Ferro; Jamey; Lecha; Monte; Sterling; Tiny; Zeta.

Setman, Locke

One of the two main characters in N. Scott Momaday's *The Ancient Child* (1989), Locke Setman must come to a revised sense of identity. Set, as he is called, is an artist working in San Francisco. He is dislocated from his past as a result of having been orphaned by age seven. His mother died in childbirth, and his father was killed in a car accident. Set is totemically connected to the bear; in fact, his name "Set" comes from the Kiowa word for "bear." The journey that Set must make is from a lack of awareness about his Kiowa identity to a realization of his self and his powers as a medicine man in his own right.

At 44, Set is a successful artist who realizes that his commercial success has been at the expense of his artistic integrity. "More and more often he was asked to compromise his art or himself in one way or another, and more often than not he did so." Though Set has "a commitment to be his own man," he is fundamentally "passive and naive." This combination creates a sense of conflict in him that he is unable to resolve. It is not until he receives a cryptic telegram requesting his presence at the deathbed of his paternal grandmother that he is able to even begin the stage of his growth that will lead him out of his moral lethargy. The trip to Oklahoma sets into action the events that will lead to his healing. In Oklahoma he meets Grey, his future wife and the young woman who will aid him in his recovery of identity and health. (Momaday 1989; Owens 1992a; Velie 1994)

See also *The Ancient Child*; Bourne, Lola; Grey; Sandridge, Bent.

The Sharpest Sight

The Sharpest Sight (1992) is the second novel by Louis Owens, a Choctaw/Cherokee/Irish-American writer. It is a murder mystery, certainly, but the novel's genre is secondary to the quest for cultural identification by the main characters. Owens does a fine job of maintaining the intrigue of the plot while focusing on the development of the characters, Cole McCurtain, his father Hoey McCurtain, and Mundo Morales.

The story takes place during the Vietnam War after Morales and his best friend, Attis McCurtain, return from the war. Morales and Attis were high school basketball stars and best friends who went into the Marines under the buddy system. They both return but have varying degrees of difficulty reintegrating into society. Recently the janitor at the high school, Mundo is now a deputy sheriff for the county. Attis suffers from posttraumatic stress disorder and is in a hospital for the criminally insane, having been accused of murdering his girlfriend, Jenna Nemi.

The novel opens on the night that Attis escapes from the hospital; Mundo is making his rounds through the county and stops at the river. From the bridge he looks down and sees the dead body of Attis drifting past him, lifting a hand, "as if in casual farewell." At every turn, Mundo's investigation is blocked by important men in the county who clearly have something to hide. The FBI is even called in to investigate the disappearance of Attis, but they too are unwilling to believe that Morales has seen the dead body. They insist that Attis has been spotted on his journey to Mississippi, where his Choctaw relatives could hide him in the swamps of their homeland.

The FBI is also looking for Attis's younger brother, Cole McCurtain, who is not responding to his draft notice. Hoey McCurtain tells Cole that the family has given enough: "You don't owe this sonafabitchin government nothing." Cole is surreptitiously sent to Mississippi to stay with Hoey's uncle Luther, an old-time Choctaw. The trip achieves more than saving Cole from the draft. He is searching for his identity; he feels the pull of his Choctaw blood but looks far more Anglo than either his brother or father. That he does not look Indian and that he and his family have lived in California since he was eight contribute to his feeling of dislocation from his Choctaw culture. Cole's time in Mississippi with his uncle Luther Cole and Onatima, called Old Lady Blue Wood, the friend and companion of Luther, establishes Cole's identity. His father has told him once, "You are what you think you are," and now Cole is able to claim his Choctaw heritage.

Hoey has a stronger connection to the culture than his son does, but even for him, the strength of that culture is diminishing the longer he is in California. However, he does have a dream in which he sees the killing of Attis, and he feels compelled to avenge the murder, according to traditional Choctaw values. Hoey's vow of vengeance complicates Mundo Morales's investigation; not only must he convince the FBI that Attis has been murdered, but also he must prevent his friend Hoey from killing the murderer.

The case grows more complicated for Morales as Diana Nemi enters the picture. She is the sister of the murdered Jenna, and it is obvious that she is a troubled and troubling character. She seduces Cole McCurtain and tries to seduce Mundo Morales. The spirit of Morales's grandfather watches over him and talks to him from beyond death, telling him, "This bruja Nemi is a dangerous one." The grandfather's spirit also goes to Diana and urges her to break the cycle of evil. Diana cannot quit flirting with evil, however, and she falls into the web of Jessard Deal, a local bar owner who is on the fringes of insanity. Deal recognizes that Diana too practices evil, and he kidnaps and rapes her. He claims that he wants a "sacred communion of kindred souls" and that he knows her secret. Diana's secret is that she, not Attis, killed her sister. Diana's jealousy over the relationship between her sister and Attis and her own dysfunctional past (the narrative hints that she has been sexually abused by her father) presumably trigger the murder.

When Cole is in Mississippi, he learns from his uncle Luther and Onatima that the Choctaws believe in soul dualism, that each person has an inside and an outside soul. The outside soul cannot join the first soul or attain rest until it is united with its bones. They give Cole the responsibility of finding Attis's bones and returning them to Mississippi. When the FBI agents come to Luther's house hunting for the escaped Attis, they find the draft-evading Cole. Cole returns with them but fails his physical for the army and is free to follow the charge he has been given to find Attis's bones and keep Hoey from killing the murderer.

Cole is able to fulfill his responsibility, and Mundo Morales solves the mystery of the murders of Jenna Nemi and Attis McCurtain. In the process, both Cole and Mundo come to a fuller understanding of who they are and where they belong in relation to their culture and family. After the mysteries unravel, Hoey and Cole McCurtain leave California and return to Mississippi. They leave Attis's gun, dog, and '57 Chevy with Mundo Morales. (Krupat 1996; Owens 1992a)

See also *Bone Game*; Owens, Louis.

She Had Some Horses

Joy Harjo's book of poetry, *She Had Some Horses* (1983), is divided into four sections: "Survivors," "What I Should Have Said," "She Had Some Horses," and "I Give You Back." The first section opens with "Call It Fear," a poem about the "edge where shadow / and bones of some of us walk / backwards." The edge of fear pulls at the persona, who resists by talking and hearing "any other voice to stay alive with." The poems here are about resisting the fear and staying alive, telling stories in order to survive. In "Anchorage," Harjo asks, "Because who would believe / the fantastic and terrible story of all of our survival / those who were never meant / to survive?"

"The Woman Hanging from the Thirteenth Floor Window" is a powerful poem about being on the edge and fear and survival. The woman hanging is "crying for / the lost beauty of her own life." The poem ends ambiguously. The woman "thinks she remembers listening to her own life / break loose, as she falls from the 13th floor / window on the east side of Chicago, or as she / climbs back up to claim herself again."

Many of the poems speak of the liminal hours between the end of night and the beginning of morning. In "Heartbeat," Noni Daylight is afraid and "waits through traffic lights at intersections / that at four a.m. are desolate oceans of concrete." In "Connection," a character speeds "in a Ford truck and it's five / in the morning, the sun and dogs / only ones up."

The poems chronicle the hard and perilous lives of people living on the edge, people who need saving. In "The Friday before the Long Weekend," the persona cries out, "I can't do anything / but talk to the wind, / to the moon / but cry out goddamn goddamn / to stones / and to other deathless voices / that I hope will carry / us all through." But for all the pain exposed in the volume, it is not a book about despair. The people who were never meant to survive will survive through remembering. "Remember" is a prayer, a hope, a lesson. "Remember," the poet says, that "the plants, trees, animal life" are "alive poems." "Remember that all is in motion, is growing, is you. / Remember that language comes from this. / Remember the dance that language is, that life is. / Remember."

The second section of the volume focuses on poems of loss, separation, and distance. In "What I Should Have Said," the persona says, "I feel like a traitor / telling someone else things I can't tell / to you. What is it that keeps us together?" She and her lover are "caught between / clouds and wet earth / and there is no motion / either way / no life / to speak of."

In "Your Phone Call at 8 AM," the lover's voice comes across the phone lines and could have been a "deadly rope." In the course of the poem, the persona shifts from scorned lover to self-affirming survivor: "But that's alright because / this poem isn't for you / but for me / after all."

Harjo says that she sees horses as "very sensitive and finely tuned spirits of the psyche. There's this strength running through them." The third section of the volume illustrates this notion. The poems center around the metaphoric and literal powers of horses—their danger, their strength, and their beauty.

The final section of the book is the single poem, "I Give You Back." The poem brings the poetic journey to a satisfying and triumphant close. The edge of fear from the first poem, "Call It Fear," is defeated. The persona releases the "beautiful and terrible" fear and recognizes that "I am alive and you are so afraid / of dying." (Harjo 1983; Harjo 1987)

See also Harjo, Joy.

Silko, Leslie Marmon

Leslie Marmon Silko was born in Albuquerque in 1948 and grew up at the Laguna Pueblo, where she absorbed the stories and culture of the Laguna people. Of mixed-blood ancestry—Laguna, Mexican, and white—Silko says that at the core of her writing "is the attempt to identify what it is to be a half-breed, or mixed-blooded person; what it is to grow up neither white nor fully traditional Indian." In the 1880s Silko's great-grandfather, Robert Gunn Marmon, and his brother Walter left Ohio and went to New Mexico Territory, where they both married Laguna women and became somewhat important figures in the Laguna Pueblo. Robert was even elected to a term as governor of the pueblo.

Leslie Marmon Silko, 1991. (Courtesy of Leslie Marmon Silko)

Of her childhood, Silko says, "My earliest memories are of being outside, under the sky." Indeed, her childhood seems to have been most influenced by the Laguna landscape and by the stories told by her great-grandmother, Grandma A'mooh. She spent a great deal of time with her horse, Joey, in the sandhills around Laguna, lost in her "thoughts and imagination." By age seven, her father taught her how to shoot a .22 rifle, and at age 13, she had killed her first mule deer buck. Because her mother worked out of the home, Silko spent many of her childhood hours next door with her Grandma A'mooh, helping with the chores and listening to the *"hummah-hah* stories, about an earlier time when animals and humans shared a common language." The Laguna of her childhood was a community that had no telephones and still had a town crier who called out announcements at dawn and dusk each day. It was a community that valued and participated in storytelling and the oral tradition.

Silko attended the Bureau of Indian Affairs day school in Laguna from kindergarten until fifth grade, when she and her sisters became commuters to the Indian boarding school in Albuquerque. Her parents made the 100-mile-a-day round-trip to save their children the horrors still found in Indian boarding schools in the 1950s and 1960s. As a sophomore in high school, Silko decided on a career in law. After taking a degree in English at the University of New Mexico in 1969, she completed three semesters in the American Indian Law School Fellowship Program at the University of New Mexico before she "realized that injustice is built into the Anglo-American legal system." Wanting "nothing to do with such a barbaric legal system," Silko decided "the only way to seek justice was through the power of the stories." She left law school to pursue a career in writing.

Silko remembers that her first story was written in fifth grade when the teacher asked her to create a narrative using her list of weekly spelling words. In college she wrote a short story, "A Man to Send Rain Clouds," based on an actual happening at Laguna. On the strength of that work, which was published in 1969, Silko was awarded a National Endowment for the Humanities Discovery Grant. In 1974, her volume of poetry, *Laguna Woman*, was published, and in 1977, her first novel, *Ceremony*, was published to stunning critical success. With *Ceremony*, Silko was firmly established at the forefront of the Native American Renaissance, along with N. Scott Momaday and James Welch. In 1981, Silko's *Storyteller* was published. In that same year, she was awarded a MacArthur Prize Fellowship that allowed her to work on *Almanac of the Dead* (1991), a novel that was ten years in the making.

Silko has always been interested in the visual arts as well. In 1980, she made the movie *Estoymuut and the Gunnadeyah* (Arrowboy and the Witches), "an experiment with storytelling on film." Photography plays an important role in the life of Silko. Her father is a professional photographer, and she grew up around the taking and developing of pictures. Her grandmother Lily "kept a tall Hopi basket full of old family snapshots," and Silko learned early the connection of the image and the story. She says in *Storyteller*, "The photographs are here because they are part of many of the stories / and because many of the stories can be traced in the photographs." *Storyteller* incorporates photos into the text, not merely in an illustrative way, but as part of the fabric of the story. In 1993, Silko self-published an autobiography, *Sacred Water*, which is a melding of text and image. Silko says, "I am interested in the effect that a photograph or other visual image has on our reading of a text. *Sacred Water* is my experiment." Silko's latest volume is yet another departure from previous forms, a collection of essays, *Yellow Woman and a Beauty of the Spirit* (1996).

Silko has taught at several schools through the years, including the University of New Mexico and the University of Arizona. She has two sons, Robert, born in 1966, and Cazimir, born in 1972, and she presently lives in Tucson, Arizona. (Coltelli 1990; Fisher 1980; Jahner 1981; Ruoff 1990; Silko 1996)

See also *Almanac of the Dead*; *Ceremony*; *Storyteller*.

Sister Leopolda

See Puyat, Pauline.

Small War, Herod

Herod Small War is a "*Yuwipi* man" who prays to "Wakan Tanka rather than Jesus Christ" in Susan Power's *The Grass Dancer* (1994). He serves as mentor, best man, and spiritual protector to Calvin Wind Soldier. When Anna Thunder tries to seduce Calvin, Small War makes him a snakeskin belt to counteract her evil. He is the grandfather of Frank Pipe, the best friend of Harley Wind Soldier, and acts as a surrogate grandparent to Harley.

In the days of Jeannette McVay's misguided enthusiasms, he will not allow her to enter a men's sweat lodge. Many years later, though, when Jeannette gives birth to a mixed-blood child, Herod encourages her to tell the child both sides of her heritage, saying, "Otherwise she'll stand off-balance and walk funny and talk

out of one side of her mouth. Tell her *two* stories." (Power 1994)

See also *The Grass Dancer*; McVay, Jeannette; Thunder, Anna (Mercury); Wind Soldier, Calvin; Wind Soldier, Harley.

Smith, Dan

In D'Arcy McNickle's *The Surrounded* (1936, 1978), Dan Smith is the game warden who kills Louis Leon in a botched inspection. After shooting Louis, Smith bends over his body to examine him, and from behind, Catharine Leon splits his head with a hatchet. Archilde and his mother hurriedly bury Smith's body in a shallow grave and then take Louis's body home. (McNickle 1936, 1978)

See also Leon, Archilde; Leon, Catharine; Leon, Louis; *The Surrounded*.

Smith, John

A main character in Sherman Alexie's novel *Indian Killer* (1996), John Smith was born in the late 1960s on an unnamed reservation to a 14-year-old mother. The lack of specific information surrounding his birth gives root to one of the main concerns of the novel—identity politics. The question of who is and who is not an Indian begins with John Smith. Even his name suggests that his connection to Indianness is just as tenuous as the historical John Smith's.

Immediately after birth, John is whisked away by helicopter to his adoptive parents. Upon hearing the helicopter, a bystander "wonders if there is a war beginning." There is a prophetic quality to the question, for the adult John Smith becomes the epicenter around which a race war will brew. Until that time, though, John is raised by his well-meaning white parents, who make every attempt to connect him to an Indian background. He is given lots of books on Indians by his mother, but he never knows his tribal affiliation, and the books are about generic Indians, Indians as artifacts. When his father takes him to an Indian basketball game, "John felt like crying. He did not recognize these Indians. They were nothing like the Indians he had read about. John felt betrayed."

What his parents cannot do for John is tell him his own tribal identity, and this lack of information becomes the single most important definer of John's individual identity. He is set adrift from his Indian background and can find no way to rest easily in white culture.

His parents have John baptized by Father Duncan, "a Spokane Indian Jesuit, a strange man." He is taken under the priest's wing, but Father Duncan has so many eccentricities that it is easy to wonder if his own mental instability does not also contribute to John's. By the time John enters high school at St. Francis Catholic School, he is viewed as "a trailblazer, a nice trophy for St. Francis, a successfully integrated Indian boy." But his appearance of normalcy is at great cost; each day he goes to the bathroom and bites his tongue and lips in an attempt to hold in his anger. Though he dates many white girls, their fathers always step in and suggest that they might date someone more "appropriate."

After graduation from high school in 1987, John refuses to go to college. Instead he takes a job with a construction company working on high-rise buildings in downtown Seattle. His mental health continues to deteriorate. When he is 20 years old, he imagines that he is pregnant and forces "himself to throw up every morning to prove it." At age 27, John is "six feet, six inches tall and heavily muscled, a young construction worker perfect for all of the heavy lifting." Though he is a "good worker, quiet and efficient," he continues to hear voices in his head, and he often hears Father Duncan's "leather sandals brush[ing] against the sand on his long walk through the desert." As his anger escalates, John decides that he needs to kill a white man. He thinks hard about which white man to kill—the richest? the poorest? He asks himself, "Which white man had done the most harm to Indians?" He is determined to "see fear in every pair of blue eyes."

At the same time that John's mental health is at its most serious point of disintegration, he meets up with several other Indians who are on a parallel course of racial anger. He meets Marie Polatkin, an Indian rights activist and self-appointed social worker to the homeless of Seattle, and her cousin, Reggie Polatkin, a sympathetic but dangerous character spoiling for a fight. Congregating with Marie and Reggie and their Indian friends is not easy for John, because the first question he is asked on every occasion concerns his tribal identity. His identity is even more precarious with Indians than it is with whites, for he fears that he will be found out, that they will see beyond the mask that is his face. Though essentially nonviolent himself, John is caught up in a series of violent episodes. Reggie and his two friends beat up John for dancing with a Crow woman that Reggie has been trying to date for years; Aaron Rogers and his roommates beat up John on one of their rampages of revenge. Marie and her workers in the sandwich truck come to John's rescue, and for a moment, he feels as if he might be able to talk with them, to tell his story, but "there was no language in which he could express himself."

John continues to hear voices, now telling him that his friends and acquaintances are the devil. He cannot escape the voices and even wonders if the voice belongs to Father Duncan. The last act of John's unhappy life is when he kidnaps Jack Wilson and takes him to an unfinished fortieth floor of a downtown skyscraper and ties him to the wall. There John cuts Wilson with a knife and tells him, "Let us have our own pain." Wilson, the Indian wannabe, survives, but John walks off the edge of the building to his death. As his soul separates from his body, he goes in search of his Indian parents. (Alexie 1996)

See also Father Duncan; *Indian Killer*; Polatkin, Marie; Polatkin, Reggie; Rogers, Aaron; Smith, Olivia and Daniel; Wilson, Jack.

Smith, Olivia and Daniel

Characters in Sherman Alexie's novel *Indian Killer* (1996), the Smiths are a well-to-do childless couple. Daniel, an architect, and Olivia, who has a degree in art history, have lived the model life except for producing a child. Their decision to adopt an Indian baby is validated when the adoption agent tells them, "This child will be saved a lot of pain by growing up in a white family. It's the best thing, really." The baby is delivered to them in Seattle straight from his birth in an unidentified Indian Health Service Hospital. The Smiths are well-meaning parents who make every attempt to introduce their son to all things Indian, never realizing that a generic Indian identity is not a suitable substitute for a connection to a particular tribal group.

As their son, John, grows older, Olivia becomes aware of his problems and thinks of him in relation to the eccentric and possibly mentally ill pianist Glenn Gould. She wonders if John "would ever be able to create anything of value."

On separate occasions, both Daniel and Olivia go into the city searching for John when the frenzy surrounding the "Indian Killer" is at its height. Olivia is alone at John's apartment when Jack Wilson visits there, and she briefly entertains him. Her concerns about John convince Wilson that John is the Indian Killer. (Alexie 1996)

See also *Indian Killer*; Smith, John; Wilson, Jack.

So-at-sa-ki
See Feather Woman.

The Soul of the Indian: An Interpretation

Charles Alexander Eastman's *The Soul of the Indian* (1911) is an essay in the genre of religious apologetic literature. Eastman wrote the essay after returning from a trip to northern Minnesota and southern Ontario, where he spent some time in 1910 attempting to reestablish his childhood roots. In his foreword, Eastman suggests that he is trying to capture the heart of Indian religious life as it was before the influence of the Euroamerican. It is necessary to do so, Eastman says, because it has never "been seriously, adequately, or sincerely done." *The Soul of the Indian* presents a generalized but primarily Siouan, Indian spiritual paradigm.

Although Eastman is generally sympathetic toward Christianity, he nonetheless notes:

> The first missionaries, good men imbued with the narrowness of their age, branded us as pagans and devil-worshipers, and demanded of us that we abjure our false gods before bowing the knee at their sacred altar. They even told us that we were eternally lost, unless we adopted a tangible symbol and professed a particular form of their hydra-headed faith.

He continues, "We of the twentieth century know better!" Eastman then explains the Indian conception of "the Great Mystery" and the way the Indian recognizes sacredness in all manifestations of life. He admits that there is "much in primitive Christianity to appeal" to the Indian but that the Christian religion that is preached and lived out by its missionaries is "extremely repellent." He suggests that in its abstractions, the "spirit of Christianity" and the

Charles Eastman, 1915. (Reproduced from The Quarterly Journal of the Society of American Indians, *Vol. 3, No. 1, Jan.–March, 1915)*

ancient Indian religion are "essentially the same."

In the second chapter of *The Soul of the Indian*, Eastman describes the familial and clan responsibilities in nurturing the spiritual growth of Indian children. The chapter provides a wealth of information about kinship responsibilities in the culture. Eastman again emphasizes, "In the life of the Indian there was only one inevitable duty,—the duty of prayer —the daily recognition of the Unseen and Eternal."

Chapter Three, "Ceremonial and Symbolic Worship," covers the religious rites of the Sun Dance, the Grand Medicine Lodge, the sweat lodge, and the ceremonial pipe. In Chapter Four, "Barbarism and the Moral Codes," Eastman testifies to the faith he had in God long before he "ever heard of Christ, or saw a white man." He learned the "essence of morality" from his elders and says, "Civilization has not taught me anything better!" He goes on to suggest that in his "civilized" life, he has even unlearned the graces of his youth.

In Chapter Five, "The Unwritten Scriptures," Eastman acknowledges, "Every religion has its Holy Book, and ours was a mingling of history, poetry, and prophecy, of precept and folk-lore." He relates some stories of the Siouan trickster, "Unk-to-mee, the Spider, the original trouble-maker," of the Little Boy Man, and of Star Boy.

The final chapter discusses death and burial customs and beliefs. Eastman says, "Certainly the Indian never doubted the immortal nature of the spirit or soul of man, but neither did he care to speculate upon its probable state or condition in a future life." The spiritual powers of Indians were great and included prophecy as well as healing. Eastman suggests that the Indian's "nearness to nature . . . keeps the spirit sensitive to impressions not commonly felt, and in touch with the unseen powers."

In *The Soul of the Indian*, Eastman makes a strong case for the religion of the Indian and boldly censures the failures of Christianity. (Eastman 1911; Miller 1996; Peyer 1994a)

See also *Indian Boyhood*.

St. John, Angela

Angela St. John is a character in N. Scott Momaday's *House Made of Dawn* (1968). She comes to the Jemez Pueblo from Los Angeles and rents a house so that she might rest and take the mineral baths. She is the wife of a Los Angeles doctor, Martin St. John, and though she is pregnant with his child, she does not feel a connection to him or to his child growing within her. The time she spends in the Jemez Pueblo becomes a time of identity formation and healing for her, particularly as she interacts with Abel, the main character of the novel.

Angela meets Abel when he comes to split some firewood for her. As she watches Abel cut wood, she is reminded of "a badger or a bear" she had once seen. She fantasizes for a moment about the bear and longs "to hold for a moment the hot blowing of the bear's life." Later, when Abel returns to finish cutting wood and they sleep together, she sees him "dark and massive above her, poised and tinged with pale blue light. And in that split second she thought again of the badger at the water, and the great bear, blue-black and blowing."

When Angela first comes to the pueblo, she is in a state of self-hatred and depression: "she could think of nothing more vile and obscene than the raw flesh and blood of her body, the raveled veins and the gore upon her bones." Her experience with Abel brings her some measure of healing, and soon "all the mean and myriad fears that had laid hold of her in the past" are gone.

Ben Benally, a friend of Abel's from Los Angeles, calls Angela to the hospital six years later when Abel is beaten nearly to death by the evil cop Martinez. She tells Abel about her son Peter, the child she was carrying when she first met him. She says that Peter always asks about Indians and that she tells him the story of a "young Indian brave . . . born of a bear and a maiden." She always thinks of Abel when she tells the story. Ben notices that the story is "kind of secret and important to her." (Evers 1985; McAllister 1974; Momaday 1968; Owens 1992a)

See also Abel; Benally, Ben; Father Olguin; *House Made of Dawn*; Martinez.

Standing Bear, Luther

Luther Standing Bear, known as Ota K'te (Plenty Kill) in his boyhood, was in the last generation of Sioux raised in prereservation days. All of his childhood training prepared him for a life that ceased to exist by the time he was ready to enter manhood. Ota K'te was a student in the first class at the Carlisle Indian Industrial School, the boarding school of Richard Henry Pratt, which was designed to "kill the Indian and save the man." At Carlisle, Ota K'te was enrolled as Luther Standing Bear; the Anglicizing of his name was only the first of many assimilationist changes forced upon him. When his hair was cut short, the 11-year-old could not keep back his tears.

After his education at Carlisle was completed in 1884, Standing Bear returned to the Rosebud Reservation and discovered that his vocational training in tinsmithing was not very useful on the reservation. With a letter of recommendation from Captain Pratt, Standing Bear was hired as an assistant at the government school on the reservation. In 1891 he took charge of the day school on Pine Ridge Reservation and worked part-time as a rancher. In 1902, he auditioned for and won a role in Buffalo Bill's Wild West Show; he spent 11 months in England with the show before he was severely injured in a train accident in 1903.

In 1905, after the death of his father, Standing Bear was chosen as the chief of his *tiospaye* (extended family group) but was frustrated by the limitations of the position in helping his people. By 1912, he sold his allotted land and moved to California. There he worked in the film industry and noticed the racial inequity in casting. Not only were white and Japanese actors filling the Indian roles, but the portrayals of Indians were inaccurate. Standing Bear drew attention to the problems but received no encouragement from directors, stage managers, and playwrights that they were willing to address the problem.

Standing Bear was elected to the American Indian Progressive Association and served for two years in that capacity, trying to help the causes of Indian people. He was a strong advocate for citizenship, which was finally achieved in 1924. In the last decade of his life, Standing Bear devoted his attentions to writing, producing *My People, the Sioux* (1928, 1975); *My Indian Boyhood* (1931, 1988); *Land of the Spotted Eagle* (1933); and *Stories of the Sioux* (1934). Luther Standing Bear died in 1939. (Brumble and Krupat 1994; Markowitz 1996; Ruoff 1990; Standing Bear 1928, 1975)

See also *My Indian Boyhood*.

Staples, Sir Cecil

Sir Cecil Staples is the Evil Gambler in Gerald Vizenor's *Bearheart: The Heirship Chronicles* (1978, 1990). In a time when fossil fuels are depleted, Sir Cecil is the "monarch of unleaded gasoline." He runs an "evil business" where travelers can gamble with their lives for 5 gallons of gasoline. Suggestive of the gambler in many tribal myths, Sir Cecil features both "new traps and old tortures."

Sir Cecil's childhood offers some explanation for his evil business. He was kidnapped by a woman who had given birth to three children who were subsequently taken from her by the welfare agency. To have the family she has always wanted, she rustles children "from shopping centers across the country," each from a different state. The children ride in the back of her truck as the "mother" drives around the country. Sir Cecil was four years old when he was stolen by the truck-driving mother and was kept until he was 26. Then he was dropped off in Iowa, where he still stays at his trailer park, which memorializes his mother. Sir Cecil's mother was repulsed by insects and sprayed the truck for them constantly. The years of exposure to insect poison leave him without hair and teeth.

According to her custom, each child was given an honorific name; thus, Sir Cecil. The children are educated by hitchhikers whom the mother picks up along the way. A large part of their education is the introduction to violence. By the time he was 13, Sir Cecil had committed his first murder. His mother "stopped the truck right on the interstate to celebrate the

Luther Standing Bear around the turn of the century. (Nebraska State Historical Society)

event." He quit counting his victims when he reached 100 deaths, over 15 years ago.

Sir Cecil is attracted to traps, tortures, and poisons, "secrets and surprises on the road to death." So when Staples loses his gambling game to Proude Cedarfair, he is placed in one of his tortures, a "mechanical neckband death instrument." The neckband is locked into place on his neck, and the pilgrims leave. Benito Saint Plumero throws Staples the key, but Staples is choked to death before he can reach it. (Owens 1992a; Velie 1982; Vizenor 1978, 1990)

See also *Bearheart: The Heirship Chronicles*; Cedarfair, Proude; Farrier, Lilith Mae; Saint Plumero, Benito.

The Stemteema

The Stemteema is the grandmother of Cogewea in Mourning Dove's 1927 novel, *Cogewea, the Half-Blood*. As a revered elder, "the Stemteema knew many interesting tales of the past; legends finer than the myths of the Old World; but few of them known to the reading public and none of them understood."

She was responsible for parenting Cogewea and her two sisters after the death of their mother and abandonment by their father. She is generally suspicious of the *Shoyahpee* (white man) and is particularly distrustful of Alfred Densmore and his advances toward Cogewea. She warns Cogewea against Densmore and tells her two stories of Indian women who went with white men and met only tragedy in the end. The story of Green Blanket Feet, who lost her husband and her two children and became a slave for a while, has a short-term impact on Cogewea. Some time later, the Stemteema reinforces her message by telling of a similar experience that happened to her aunt. Neither story ultimately saves Cogewea from her headstrong impulses. However, Jim LaGrinder comes to value the wisdom of the Stemteema and forms a relationship with her that validates his suitability as a future mate for Cogewea. (Mourning Dove 1927, 1981)

See also Carter, John and Julia; Cogewea, *Cogewea, the Half-Blood: A Depiction of the Great Montana Cattle Range*; Densmore, Alfred; LaGrinder, Jim; McDonald, Mary.

Sterling

In Leslie Marmon Silko's *Almanac of the Dead* (1991), Sterling is a character who retires to Laguna Pueblo at age 59 after working off-reservation for many years on the railroad line, repairing tracks. One of the only characters in the novel who is free of greed and the motivations of evil, he returns to live with and take final care of his Auntie Marie. As a result of his inadvertent involvement in the violation of a cultural icon, however, he is exiled from his Laguna community. A great stone snake has appeared near the mouth of the uranium mine on the Laguna Pueblo reservation, and though Sterling has been charged by the tribal council to keep a visiting film crew from Hollywood from seeing it, he allows them to see and film it. For this breach, Sterling is exiled. When Sterling is accused by the council, Auntie Marie wills herself to die to shame them for their scheme against Sterling. The action only proves to the council that Sterling has grieved his aunt to death.

After the action of the tribal council and the death of his aunt, Sterling is alone with his subscriptions to *Police Gazette*, *True Detective*, and *Reader's Digest*. From the detective magazines, he learns that "injustice has been going on for a long time," and from the *Reader's Digest* he learns to focus on the positive, to combat depression with activity and a positive attitude. He has become a sort of armchair psychologist, his own doctor.

Through a series of blunders, he comes to be the gardener at Zeta's ranch. He ends up in Tucson because he fell asleep on his bus and forgot to get off in Phoenix. He wanders into a bar, and just as accidentally, he is hired by Ferro, Zeta's nephew, and his lover Paulie to become the new gardener. He prides himself on the fact that although somewhere his "life has taken a wrong turn," he has never been reduced to selling his own blood, an observation filled with metaphoric as well as literal truth.

At the Tucson ranch, Sterling befriends Seese and seeks to understand his own life. When the ranch is raided and he and Lecha and Seese make their escape, Sterling asks to be dropped off on the interstate near the Laguna reservation. Lecha gives him a bundle of money as they separate, but even before he goes to buy food, Sterling makes his way to the stone snake, and he realizes that the snake is looking south in anticipation of the coming of the twins and their army of people from the south. (Silko 1991)

See also *Almanac of the Dead*; El Feo; Ferro; Lecha; Paulie; Seese; Tacho; Zeta.

Stink, John

John Stink is a comic character in Linda Hogan's *Mean Spirit* (1990). He is an old Osage hermit, greatly loved by the older people but left alone by the younger ones. A childhood disease renders him mute, and he no "longer tried to communicate with anyone he didn't already know." His eccentric behaviors—he wears a red babushka on his head and is followed by a pack of mongrel dogs—make him something of a community character. One day Stink is found collapsed and surrounded by his dogs. He is pronounced dead and buried. Only his dogs realize that he has been buried alive, and they dig him out of his grave. He wanders about in his winding sheet and is mistaken for a ghost by the Indians. Out of their politeness to spirits, no one approaches him, and the mute John Stink wanders about for a year before the Indians realize that he is alive. After many sightings of the "ghost," both the traditional people and the members of the Indian Baptist Church hold meetings for the soul of John Stink, but their prayers cannot put his "spirit" to rest.

The white people in the community believe that Stink is oil-rich, and the rancher John Hale arranges for his mistress, China, to woo and marry John Stink. She is successful in her plot, but when the two go to the courthouse to marry, Stink's death certificate disallows the ceremony. Hale is foiled in his attempt to gain Stink's money through his scam of marriage and murder.

It is only when Belle Graycloud is shot that people realize that Stink is not dead. When the bullet is deflected by Belle's meteorite, she believes for a moment that she is dead. She sees the "ghost" of John Stink coming toward her and protests that she is not ready to cross over. Stink, who all this time has believed that he did die and has been wandering the "world of death's limbo," is eager to welcome another soul into the "middle ground between the worlds." Belle's family rushes to her and finds that Stink is "solid" and alive. Meanwhile, Hale is so angry that he has failed in his attempt to get Stink's money that he goes to the courthouse and files a lien on Stink's money. (Hogan 1990)

See also Graycloud, Belle; Graycloud, Lettie; Graycloud, Moses; Hale, John; *Mean Spirit*.

Stokes, Harvey

Harvey Stokes is a character in John Milton Oskison's *Wild Harvest* (1925). A hardworking young farmer, he wins a promise of marriage from Nan Forest. He is the first to suspect Jack Hayes's involvement in a bank robbery, and through amateur detective work, he is able to locate the cache of money Hayes and his accomplices stole.

Stokes recognizes the positive qualities of Nan when he is hired to complete a haying job on her father's leaseholding. He admires her hard work and practicality. What he does not recognize, however, is her free spirit and independent streak. After they are engaged, he grows increasingly jealous of her and of any association she has with anyone other than himself, but the main focus of his intense jealousy is Tom Winger, Nan's former beau.

After Harvey is instrumental in the capture of Jack Hayes, Jack's brother Buster vows to get revenge on him. Though Harvey is warned by Nan and others to be on the watch for Buster, Stokes chooses to ignore the danger. He puts himself in a vulnerable position, and it is only thanks to Tom Winger that Harvey is not killed by Buster. In the brief skirmish, Tom is hit in the arm by a bullet and spends the first days of his convalescence in Stokes's home. Rather than express gratitude toward Winger, Harvey grows more and more agitated with him.

A final showdown occurs at Christmas, when Harvey interrupts the program at the school where Nan is teaching. In the scuffle, Harvey shoots Nan, vowing that if he can't marry her, no one will. Tom flies to the scene and in a wrestling match for the gun, Harvey is killed. (Oskison 1925)

See also Forest, Nancy; *Wild Harvest*; Winger, Tom.

Storyteller

Storyteller (1981) is Leslie Marmon Silko's mixed-genre autobiography. In it she uses photographs, stories, poems, and Laguna cultural tales to create a tapestry of her own life. The opening selection in the text is a poem that recounts the story of the Hopi basket that holds family photographs taken since the "1890s around Laguna." Silko notes the relatedness of the photos to the stories that she includes in the volume. She says, "The photographs are here because they are part of many of the stories / and because many of the stories can be traced in the photographs." Indeed, the first photo in the volume tells the story of a biracial family, of the forward-looking flinty determination of Walter K. Marmon and of his Laguna wife, Susie. Although it appears that Walter is looking forward, is seems as if Susie is looking backward with a sad and secret knowledge. A beautiful baby rests on her lap, in the same posture as Walter. It is as if Susie is simultaneously embracing the future and looking back to the past. Silko says that Susie was of the "last generation here at Laguna, / that passed down an entire culture / by word of mouth." Silko's early poems in the volume adumbrate the central focus of her text. It is in the telling of the stories that an entire culture is passed down, but the act is not an individual one; the act of remembering belongs to the whole community. "I only remember a small part," she says, "but this is what I remember."

With this introduction, Silko tells a Laguna tale as she remembers hearing it from her great-aunt Susie. A young Laguna girl, Waithea, asks her mother for some *yashtoah* to eat. Her mother sends her out to gather wood so that she might cook the *yashtoah*. The girl finds the wood but returns to her mother and discovers that the pieces of wood have turned to snakes in her basket. The little girl is so embarrassed by her mistake that upon returning the snakes, she decides to run away and drown herself. She does drown herself, and the grieving mother scatters

A 1925 Edward Curtis photograph of the Laguna Pueblo, which so strongly shaped Leslie Marmon Silko's experience and writing. (Courtesy Museum of New Mexico)

her daughter's clothing off the edge of the high mesa, where they turn into butterflies. At the end of the tale, Silko relates how Aunt Susie would say each part of the story, the tone of her voice, the intensity of her feeling. The inclusion of this performance element reflects the oral tradition that Silko is trying to reproduce for the reader.

The first short story of the volume is the previously published "Storyteller," written when Silko was living in Alaska. With its tundra setting, the story is a departure from Silko's other work, which is characteristically set in her native Laguna homeland. Silko captures the importance of place and context as skillfully here as she does in her other work. The story operates on two levels. It is essentially the story of a young girl who plans and seeks revenge for the deaths of her parents, but the plot is corollary and complementary to another narrative strain. The other thread of the story is the story of a bear hunt told by the old man with whom the young girl lives. By the end of the story, the two plotlines converge so skillfully that the reader is left with a resonant hum of meaning.

The anchor story of the collection is "Yellow Woman," in which Silko tells the Laguna myth of Yellow Woman. In this story, a woman goes to the river to get water and is seduced by a *ka'tsina,* or mountain spirit. The woman in the story is confused by the blurring of her life and the Yellow Woman myth. "I will see someone . . . and I will be sure that I am not Yellow Woman," she thinks. She tries to convince herself, "I don't believe it. Those stories couldn't happen now." The narrator is seduced by a man named Silva, who claims to be a *ka'tsina.* She is skeptical yet intrigued by the mystery surrounding the man. The conflation of myth and reality traps the woman in a state that does not allow her to separate herself from Silva. When they are on a trip to Mexico, though, they are stopped by a rancher who accuses Silva of cattle theft. Only when Silva warns the woman to go back to the mountain is she free from his spell. When she takes a final look at Silva, she is aware of something "ancient and dark" in his eyes. She returns to her family, is awed by the ordi-

nariness of their routine, and feels a certainty that the *ka'tsina* spirit will one day return for her. The story leaves the reader in that vaguely familiar place between dream and waking, between myth and reality.

The Yellow Woman story of seduction, kidnapping, and return (and its variations) threads its way into several of the selections in the volume, including "Cottonwood Part Two: Buffalo Story," "Storytelling," and "Estoy-eh-muut and the Kunideeyahs." Silko weaves Laguna myths into the volume as well; the stories of *Ck'o'yo* magic and witchery will be familiar to those who have read *Ceremony.*

"Tony's Story" is a tragic tale based on an actual event that happened in Grants, New Mexico, in 1952. In the story, a state cop harasses Leon and his friend Tony. In the belief that he is confronting the essence of evil, Tony kills the cop. The story reveals cultural differences about the nature of evil. "The Man to Send Rain Clouds" also shows cultures in conflict; old Teofilo dies, and the parish priest is tricked into sprinkling holy water on the grave so that Teofilo's spirit will send rainfall. Another noteworthy story is "Lullaby," a moving story of memory and loss. As her husband is dying, an old Navajo woman remembers the way her children were taken from her to go to boarding school and the way her son Jimmie was killed in the war. All of Silko's stories have the sharp edge of insight, and though they are located in the places of most profound feeling, they never give way to mere sentiment. (Hirsch 1988; Ruoff 1978; Silko 1981)

See also *Ceremony*; Silko, Leslie Marmon.

Sun Bear Sun and Little Big Mouse

In Gerald Vizenor's *Bearheart: The Heirship Chronicles* (1978, 1990), Sun Bear Sun and Little Big Mouse are an unlikely couple who join the pilgrim band on their way from Minnesota to New Mexico. He is a "three hundred pound seven foot son of the utopian tribal organizer Sun Bear," and Little Big Mouse is "a small whitewoman with fresh water blue eyes" who has forgotten her birth name. Sun Bear

Sun carries her most of the time with her feet in holsters attached to his waist.

When the pilgrims encounter the group of cripples, Little Big Mouse ministers to them by telling them stories and dancing. Her dancing moves them to a lustful aggression, and the "cripples gnawed and pulled at her until nothing remained of Little Big Mouse." Only the constellation quilt that another pilgrim, Lilith Mae Farrier, had given Little Big Mouse remained.

Sun Bear Sun continues on the journey; at one point he tells the pilgrims the lessons he has learned from his father, that "a nation grows when we take the earth back into our hearts and walk in balance and natural harmonies." When the pilgrims are detained and subjected to inquisition by New Governor Circle Back Wallace and New Governor Hart Camp Pile, Sun Bear Sun is left in the halls of inquisition, "answering unanswerable questions." (Owens 1992a; Vizenor 1978, 1990)

See also *Bearheart: The Heirship Chronicles*; Farrier, Lilith Mae.

Sundown

John Joseph Mathews's 1934 novel is significant for its anticipation of themes that will dominate the Native American novel for the rest of the century—the struggle of the mixed-blood to find his or her place in two worlds, neither of which welcomes or understands the other. The book focuses on the development of character over plot considerations, which is both its credit and its flaw. The lack of plot machinations creates a very flat story. The linear story is motivated only by the chronological progression of the main character, Challenge (Chal) Windzer. The problem he recognizes as a young boy, the dislocation that he feels as a mixed-blood, reflects a precociousness that is not developed. He is still feeling the same dislocation at 15 and 21 and 30, and he doesn't move beyond it. Mathews's novel loses momentum not because he focuses on character, but because the character remains static. The novel ends on a note of paralysis, with Chal sleeping under the shade of a post oak at his mother's house.

Chal is born late in life to a full-blood Osage mother and mixed-blood father. His four sisters are grown and gone from the home, and Chal is raised essentially as an only child. As the mixed-blood son of a mixed-blood father, Chal has some of the same problems as his father. In naming his long-awaited son, John Windzer says, "I live as a challenge," but it is not clear to him what he challenges, nor has it ever been definite. It is not surprising, then, that Chal is equally unable to define what he is challenging. His given name is a directive that Chal never fulfills. There is a time when he is alone in a field and feels compelled to dance an Osage dance. After the dance, "he wanted to challenge something," but he cannot name the "something."

Chal Windzer is growing up in Indian Territory at the time when oil is discovered on Osage land and when the holdings of the Osage Nation are being divided by allotment. The economic and political situation is highly charged, as many unscrupulous people come to the territory to seek a fortune. John Windzer is a member of the Osage Council and urges the acceptance of allotment. The full-blood, traditional Osage were against the move, realizing that tribal customs and their communal life would disappear as a result. All the while Chal is growing up, he sees the black oil derricks moving across the landscape. All registered Osage Indians received a percentage of the price of every barrel of oil taken from under their lands; however, the rapid acquisition of great wealth not only dangerously accelerated cultural assimilation for the Indians but also made individual Indians targets of outsiders determined to gain a share of the riches in any way they could. Indian Territory became a hotbed of extortion and murder, and Mathews's *Sundown* accurately reflects the historical situation.

The narrative traces Chal's development from his birth and childhood through college and service in the army. During his childhood, Chal shows an affinity to nature and often imagines himself as a coyote or hawk or panther. He is able to engage in an imaginative world that would have served him well in the traditional culture of the Osage, but the times are moving him quickly toward an entropic assimilation.

When he graduates from high school, he and the other Osage young men are heavily recruited by representatives of the university football team and fraternity. Chal attends the university along with his childhood friends, Running Elk and Sun-on-His-Wings. Although Chal is willing to suffer the humiliations of pledging the fraternity, his two full-blood friends will not. They are viewed as "stupid and unresponsive" and are derogatorily called "Blanket Indians." Chal is torn between defending his friends and separating himself from them and their all-too-Indian ways. Though he feels intensely "out of step," he decides "to be like other people"; he does not rise to the moral challenge of supporting Running Elk and Sun-on-His-Wings. Thus begins Chal's incremental denial of his Indian heritage.

By the time Chal leaves school to fly in the Signal Corps during World War I, he completely denies his Indian heritage and claims he is Spanish. When Chal returns from the war, it is to an explosive situation. Laws have been enacted to declare many of the Osage incompetent to run their financial affairs, and court-appointed guardians are draining wealth from their wards. Chal's father has been killed in a suspicious accident, and many other Indians are being lured into a volatile mixture of drugs and alcohol. Chal himself falls into dissolution, drinking, and running with an outlaw crowd.

Back home, Chal does feel some faint pull to reintegrate himself into his Osage culture, but all of his efforts prove ineffective. When his mother challenges him to move in a positive direction, he emptily boasts that he will go to Harvard Law School and become "a great orator." Though the novel ends ambiguously, there is hope that perhaps Chal will regain his childhood curiosity about language and use it in his journey back to his culture. (Hunter 1982a; Hunter 1982b; Larson 1978; Mathews 1934, 1988; Owens 1992a; Wiget 1985)

See also Mathews, John Joseph; Windzer, Challenge; Windzer, John.

The Surrounded

Publication of D'Arcy McNickle's first novel, *The Surrounded* (1936, 1978), was an event that many critics now view as the precursor to the Native American Renaissance beginning in 1968. McNickle tells the story of Archilde Leon, the mixed-blood protagonist who is torn between both sides of his heritage. In the novel's beginning, he is returning to the reservation from an assimilated life in Portland, where he lives more as a white man than as a traditional Indian. Back home, his Salish mother still lives the traditional life and, indeed, is growing more and more traditional all the time. She does not understand her son's attraction to the life in the city. When Archilde comes back, he intends to stay only long enough to greet his family; however, he is pulled into the web of family troubles that keep him from leaving as soon as he had intended. He first finds that his brother Louis has stolen some horses and is hiding in the mountains with a reward on his head. His nephews Mike and Narcisse are running wild and without direction. His father Max is growing old, coming into a time of his life when he finally begins to reflect on the mistakes he has made.

Max Leon has always been a stern and unyielding father to his children and has alienated them from his affections. He has trouble especially with his sons, "seven sons—damn them to hell!" he thinks. "Seven sons, they might have been seven dogs." But when Archilde, his youngest son, returns from Portland, Max begins to soften and seek an understanding with him. He goes to Father Grepilloux, his old friend, to ask advice in reaching Archilde.

Archilde's hostility toward his father begins to erode with the change in Max's attitude; at the same time, he begins to accept his mother's Salishan ways with more tolerance than he previously did. As his relationship with each of his parents improves, Archilde is desirous to see his father and mother mend their long-term separation. Max finally tells his story to Archilde and is ready to reconcile with his wife; before he can do so, though, he dies. Meanwhile his mother has requested that Archilde accompany her on one last hunting trip to the mountains. They go, but the trip triggers a chain of consequences that alter Archilde's life forever.

Archilde and his mother are surprised one day by the appearance of Sheriff Dave Quigley, a sinister and punishing agent of the law. Quigley is in the mountains hunting for Louis and does not miss the opportunity to implicitly threaten Archilde and his mother. Not long after Quigley's visit, Louis comes upon them. The next day he and Archilde go hunting game, and though Archilde cannot bring himself to kill a deer, Louis kills a doe. His shot brings the local game warden, Dan Smith, to their camp, and he promptly arrests them all. Louis retaliates in anger, reaching for his gun, but the warden shoots and kills him. When Smith bends over Louis's body, Catharine Leon kills the warden with a hatchet. Archilde digs a shallow grave, and they bury Smith before returning home with Louis's body.

Archilde is not officially arrested but is held in jail for a month because the Indian agent is uneasy about the case. Not long after Archilde is released from jail, Max dies.

A wave of events continues to sweep Archilde to disaster. He meets Elise La Rose, the granddaughter of the tribal elder, Modeste, and they become friends and lovers. In all the ways that Archilde is guarded and passive, Elise is wild and impetuous. When Archilde's mother dies, and there is no longer a witness to confirm that Archilde did not murder the game warden, should his body be found, Elise's is the voice that urges Archilde to run to the mountains. Archilde is dazed as they go, not even completely aware of the implications of his flight.

It is not long before their camp is disrupted by the appearance of Sheriff Quigley, who attempts to take them back to the custody of the Indian agent. Elise distracts the sheriff by throwing coffee in his face, and then she shoots him. The Indian agent steps into camp with a deputy and arrests both Archilde and Elise, saying, "You had everything, every chance, and this is the best you could do with it! A man gets pretty tired of you and all your kind." In silence, Archilde "extended his hands to be shackled."

McNickle achieves a structural sophistication in his novel by interpolating myth, legend, and history into the text. He uses the occasion of the tribal feast when Archilde returns to the area to introduce three stories—the story of Flint, the story of the axe, and the story of the gun. Each story tells of a technological change that comes to the Salish. The first story explains how Coyote fought with Flint and broke him all to pieces. Coyote then took the pieces to his people so that they might put them on the ends of arrows and improve their hunting.

The second story tells how an old man dreams that "something is coming that will make life easy." The dream comes true when the old man comes to the people with an axe and is able to cut down trees faster than ever before. When he demonstrates his axe, though, the tree that is chopped falls on and kills some old people.

The third story is of the coming of the gun to the Salish. Modeste says that the first two stories "make the heart light" but that the third story is different. Before the gun was introduced to the Salish, they were a "mighty race and their land went from the plains east of the mountains to the Snpoilshi River." But the introduction of the gun had far-reaching and devastating consequences for the culture. The first guns the Salish got from the white men created an appetite for more guns. Relations with the whites had to be maintained in order to keep the supply of guns coming. The gun changed intertribal warfare. Modeste says:

> In the old days of our wars a few men would be killed and fighting was a thing you could enjoy, like hunting. But now it became a bitter thing. Old scores of blood revenge could never be settled because too many were killed.

The gun changed hunting practices as well. According to Modeste, "We thought guns would save our hunting grounds and make the old times return. But that was a mistake."

Modeste's stories about three technologies that came to the Salish suggest that technologies that emerge from within a culture are far less harmful to the social fabric than those that come to the culture from the outside.

The changes in Salishan life caused by the appearance of the gun led to further disruptions of the culture. With so many having been killed by the gun, the Salishan "wise ones" went off alone on "praying-fasts," hoping to understand why their powers no longer protected them. At about this time, some Iroquois Indians came to their hunting grounds to trap, and they told the Salish of the black-robe fathers who carried a powerful *Somesh,* the cross. The Salish were ready to hear of spiritual powers since they were feeling disconnected from their own powers.

Not surprisingly, Father Grepilloux tells a different version of the coming of Christianity to the Salish. In his version, the Salish "stood ready to be Christianized, and even sought out the priests." Although it is true that the Salish sought the priests, hoping to reestablish their connection to spiritual powers, that they were ready to be "Christianized"—with all the necessary accompanying forfeitures of their own culture, language, and lifeways—is doubtful. Father Grepilloux is completely unaware of the connection of the Salishan spiritual quest to the cultural devastation wrought by the introduction of the gun to their society.

Although Father Grepilloux's story as recorded in his journal is filled with ethnocentric misunderstandings, the stories that Modeste shares from the oral tradition of the Salishan peoples embed a truth that resonates for Archilde when he hears them. McNickle's use of these stories adds texture to his theme of split identity and cultural dislocation. (Larson 1978; McNickle 1936, 1978; Owens 1992a; Parker 1997; Wiget 1985)

See also Agent Parker; Father Grepilloux; La Rose, Elise; Leon, Archilde; Leon, Catharine; Leon, Max; McNickle, D'Arcy; Mike and Narcisse; Modeste; Quigley, Sheriff Dave; Smith, Dan.

T

Tacho

Tacho is Menardo's Indian chauffeur in Leslie Marmon Silko's *Almanac of the Dead* (1991). Tacho and his twin brother, El Feo, are from a village near the Guatemalan border, and both are working to restore the land to its aboriginal owners. Tacho has been called to this mission by the sacred macaws. They speak to him, give him power, and even share their name, *wacah*, with him. The macaws reveal to him that "the battle would be won or lost in the realm of dreams, not with airplanes or weapons." The macaws are speaking to him because they know that it is "a time of great change and danger."

One day, Tacho is directed by a voice to pick up a nearby package. In the package is an opal "the size of a macaw egg" dressed in ceremonial clothing and surrounded by 12 coca leaves. Tacho senses that the stone is very powerful and looks at it for the first time only when El Feo is with him; they both realize that the stone has the power to reveal information. El Feo looks in the stone and sees a vision of his lover, Angelita La Escapia, with another man. Tacho would like to see a vision about his life but instead sees the Americas in a state of destruction, with Mexico City burning. Tacho's personal life is absorbed by his duty to the sacred macaws and their messages.

After Tacho accidentally kills Menardo, he immediately leaves the city and goes to the Mexican mountains with his macaws before the incident is investigated. All the while Tacho has been in Menardo's employ, he has been spying on the activities of Menardo and funneling that information to El Feo and Angelita in the mountains. Tacho tells the people that as long as the macaws speak through him and the people stay with him, they will not want for food. Though surrounded by Angelita La Escapia and others who would take the revolution to violent extremes, Tacho is committed to the warning of the macaws that "they must not shed blood or the destruction would continue to accompany them." (Silko 1991)

See also *Almanac of the Dead*; El Feo; La Escapia, Angelita; Menardo.

Tales of Burning Love

Louise Erdrich toyed with the phrase and the accompanying images of "tales of burning love" for some time before the idea took full flesh and became her fifth novel in 1996. In *The Beet Queen* (1986), Celestine James becomes pregnant after a reckless passion with Karl Adare, and she is fully aware that in "the love books a baby never comes of it all. . . . The tales of burning love never mention how I lie awake, alone in the heat of an August night, and panic." In Erdrich's 1994 novel, *The Bingo Palace*, the phrase recurs when Zelda Kashpaw Johnson tells Lipsha Morrissey the story of her first love: "'It's what you might call,' she says . . . 'a tale of burning love.'" She relates how Xavier Toose sat on her doorstep in a snowstorm, burning matches to keep warm while he waited for her to give in and marry him. Toose lost his fingers to the cold that night, wasted "to the stubs like candles, one by one."

In *Tales of Burning Love*, Erdrich folds the intense passions of ordinary people into the constraints of the drugstore paperback novel, and though the outcome is uneven, Erdrich's achievement is nonetheless significant. The potential for narrative cliché is offset by the strength of her prose and the profundities of the loves she records. The characters in the novel are excessive, flawed, but startlingly real.

In a characteristic Erdrichian motion, the novel opens with the same scene that opens *Love Medicine*; June Morrissey Kashpaw is in Williston, North Dakota, waiting for a bus that will take her home. She walks into a bar and takes an egg from the hand of a man identified as Andy in *Love Medicine*, but here Erdrich calls him "Jack Mauser" and spins the web of concealed identity to account for the difference. Mauser becomes a main character in the novel, and June is now identified as his first wife, the first of five. June's presence hovers over this novel as it does over *Love Medicine*. As in the previous novel, June walks into the face of a blizzard and freezes to death, but only after a mock marriage ceremony with Mauser. Mauser feels committed enough to June to mourn her for years, but not committed enough to follow her into the blizzard and keep her from death by freezing. As is true for many of Erdrich's characters, one signal event shapes the rest of a character's life; the death of June is such an event for Mauser.

Thirteen years later, Jack Mauser arrives in Argus, North Dakota, with his latest and fifth wife, Dot Adare Nanapush Mauser. Both have entered the marriage with secrets; Mauser has failed to mention his former wives, and Dot has not told Mauser of her present husband, the imprisoned Gerry Nanapush. Nonetheless, Dot is stricken to learn that Jack has kept his history of failed marriages a secret. The secret is only the first of Dot's worries; Jack's second wife, Eleanor Schlick Mauser, the one who truly loves him, has entered his life again. Eleanor is on extended retreat in the Our Lady of the Wheat convent in Argus, recovering from charges of sexual harassment against her by a student in her undergraduate class. She has clearly violated the professor-student relationship, and her public humiliation contributes to her desire to continue hiding out in the convent. Furthermore, she has taken on the scholarly project of studying the life and potential sainthood of Sister Leopolda, a 108-year-old nun at the convent, the same crazed nun who appears in *Love Medicine* and *Tracks*. The possible rivalry between Dot and Eleanor soon becomes a moot point when Jack is reported dead after a devastating fire in his house. His dental work is found, and his ashes are boxed for the funeral by Eleanor's father, the mortician, Lawrence Schlick. Three of Jack's wives gather at the funeral home and try to determine what to do with his ashes. They agree to go to Marlis Cook, the other remaining widow, to make the decision. Marlis is dealing blackjack at the B&B casino, and the three widows join her there until she is off work. Then the four get into Jack's Ford Explorer, driven by Dot, and try to get home in a fast-brewing snowstorm. In the blinding snow, their car happens upon a nearly frozen hitchhiker, to whom they give shelter in the cargo compartment of the utility vehicle. They continue on in the storm until they can go no more, and then their immediate concern becomes survival. The four women who have little more in common than their choice of a husband are trapped in a life-threatening situation, a North Dakota blizzard in the heart of the winter. They determine to keep awake by the Chaucerian ploy of telling stories. Each is to tell a story within these requirements: "Rule one . . . No shutting up until dawn. Rule two. Tell a true story. Rule three.

The story has to be something about you. Something you've never told another soul, a story that would scorch paper, heat up air." The stories are to be "tales of burning love."

The four women who survived marriage to Jack Mauser are Eleanor, his second wife, a burned-out academic; Candice Pantamounty, a high school classmate who has gone on to become a successful dentist; Marlis, a very young woman who came to love Jack only after scamming him for a huge sum of money; and Dot, who was perhaps lured into marriage by Jack so that she could not be called to testify against him in a court of law. While the four women are trying to survive the night, the hitchhiker sleeps behind them, and across town, Jack Mauser is trying to kidnap his infant son. Mauser has not died in the house fire but crawled out of the house and made it to safety in one of his equipment sheds, where he sleeps for several days. The narrative takes on a Huck Finn quality as Mauser reads the news of his death in the newspaper. Mauser's financial condition is so disastrous that it would be to his advantage to be believed dead, but his suspicious banker, Hegelstead, finds him in the shed, and the two cook up a deal that will allow Mauser to return to his contracting business in the northern part of the state in the hopes of recouping his losses.

Jack fares better than he expects or deserves, but his attempt to visit with his son dissolves into complete disaster. Failing to convince the nanny that he only wants to see the child, Jack resorts to tying her up and kidnapping his son; when he realizes that his own flight will be complicated by the presence of the child, he decides to abandon the car and the child at the train station, in the hopes that the child will be returned to safety. The car is hijacked, though, and Mauser watches his son disappear into the frozen night with two desperate men. This scene is another reworking of a section from a previous novel; in *The Bingo Palace*, the recently escaped Gerry Nanapush and his son Lipsha are running from the police, and they do not realize until they are in midflight that the car they have stolen has an infant in the backseat.

The complications of the novel resolve: all of the characters survive the fierce snowstorm; two former Mauser wives, Candice and Marlis, become lovers and raise Jack's son; Jack and Eleanor reestablish a relationship with a comfortable measure of both commitment and distance; Dot and Gerry Nanapush have a rushed but passionate meeting before he must go back on the run; and Jack is given another chance to run his contracting business, though he is a junior partner to Lyman Lamartine.

Though the novel is filled with improbabilities and narrative contortions, its merit lies in the strength of the stories that the women tell in the storm. Erdrich skillfully captures the voices of four different women, each with different habits of love and its accompanying violences. These are truly tales of fierce and passionate love, "burning love," but they are also tales about the women who are *burning* love—purging their lives of a destructive love. (Erdrich 1984, 1993; Erdrich 1994; Erdrich 1996)

See also Adare, Karl; *The Beet Queen*; *The Bingo Palace*; Cook, Marlis; James, Celestine; Johnson, Zelda Kashpaw; Kashpaw, June Morrissey; Lamartine, Lyman; *Love Medicine*; Mauser, Eleanor Schlick; Mauser, Jack; Morrissey, Lipsha; Nanapush, Dot Adare; Nanapush, Gerry; Pantamounty, Candice; Puyat, Pauline; Toose, Xavier.

TallMountain, Mary

Mary TallMountain's life is an odyssey of separation, loss, and return. She was born in 1918 in the interior of Alaska to Mary Joe Demoski, her Athabascan-Russian mother and Clem Stroupe, her Scotch-Irish father. Her parents were together for ten years and had two children—Mary and her brother Billy—but marriage was prohibited to them by both the United States Army and the Catholic Church. When Mary Joe contracted tuberculosis, the white doctor and his wife, Dr. and Mrs. Randle, urged the family to allow them to adopt the children. The village was against the dissolution of the family but finally agreed that Mary could go with the Randles but Billy would stay with his uncle. Thus at age six, Mary was separated from her beloved mother. The Randles moved to Oregon for a while and back to Alaska later, but Mary's mother died when the child was only eight, and Billy succumbed to tuberculosis when he was just 17.

TallMountain's young life was one of cultural adjustment and difficulties. When she was 18, Dr. Randle died; by 1945, Mary had survived two failed marriages and the suicide of her adoptive mother. The toll of Mary's uprooted life was heavy; she gave way to alcoholism, depression, and lost jobs before finding the help she needed. However, the "resentment, frustration, anger hidden for years exploded first in one radical cancer and ten years later in a second." In the mid-1960s, TallMountain began her first explorations with writing. She came under the tutelage of Paula Gunn Allen, who nurtured her talent. Her writing and her return to her natal village, 50 years after her adoption, helped TallMountain come to terms with her difficult life.

Much of TallMountain's poetry concerns the Athabascan culture she was taken from and returned to. For instance, in her poem, "There Is No Word for Goodbye," her aunt explains that there is no word for goodbye in Athabascan by asking, "When does your mouth / say goodbye to your heart?" Family cannot be cut off from each other any more than the mouth can be separated from the heart.

TallMountain says, and her poetry confirms, "Alaska is my talisman, my strength, my spirit's home. Despite loss and disillusion, I count myself rich, fertile, and magical. I tell you now. You *can* go home again." Her works include *Nine Poems* (1977), *There Is No Word for Goodbye* (1982), *Continuum* (1988), and *A Light on the Tent Wall: A Bridging*. She died in 1994. (Niatum 1988; TallMountain 1987)

See also Allen, Paula Gunn.

Tapahonso, Luci

Luci Tapahonso, a Navajo poet and short story writer, was born in 1953 in Shiprock, New Mexico. One of 11 children, Tapahonso's poetry richly reflects the importance of family and of place. She says, "I know that I cannot divide myself or separate myself from that place—my home, my land, and my people. And that realization is my security and my mainstay in my life away from there." Much of her writing has its genesis in personal and family memories. The mother of two daughters, Tapahonso says, "I always begin my work, no matter what I'm doing, with something for my children. I think it's a good thing to do because I feel good about my children. They're not a hindrance to me."

Tapahonso attended Navajo Methodist Mission school and graduated from Shiprock High School in 1971. From an early age, she was "fascinated with words and stories, books." She began studying journalism in 1976 at the University of New Mexico but switched her major to English after studying with Leslie Marmon Silko. Tapahonso credits Silko with nurturing her career as a writer: "She helped me. . . . I would not have done much probably if I had not met her. I didn't take what I was doing to be something important to the general community."

Tapahonso holds a master of arts degree from the University of New Mexico and is an associate professor of English at the University of Kansas in Lawrence, Kansas. During the summer of 1995, she was the poet-in-residence at the prestigious Robert Frost Place in Franconia, New Hampshire. In 1996, the Center for Southwest Research announced the opening of the Luci Tapahonso Papers at the University of New Mexico General Library. Her works include four volumes of poetry: *One More Shiprock Night* (1981), *Seasonal Woman* (1982), *A Breeze Swept Through* (1987), and *Sáanii Dahataał: The Women Are Singing* (1993); a children's book, *Bah's Baby Brother Is Born*, published by the National Organization on Fetal Alcohol Syndrome; and a Navajo alphabet book, *Navajo ABC: A Dine Alphabet Book*, published by Simon and Schuster. A work in progress is an autobiography, to be published by W. W. Norton. (Bruchac 1987; Witalec 1995)

See also *Sáanii Dahataał: The Women Are Singing.*

Tate, John

John Tate is the white husband of Ruth Graycloud Tate in Linda Hogan's *Mean Spirit* (1990). He is a "small, fussy man with only one eye" and "nothing warm, nothing human" about him. He marries Ruth, the sister of Moses Graycloud, so that he might cause the accident of her death and inherit her money. He is a photographer who is always present, recording events with his camera. He is generally regarded as a suspicious man, and those suspicions are borne out when he kills his wife. Moses Graycloud kills Tate and then flees to the settlement of the Hill Indians. (Hogan 1990)

See also Graycloud, Moses; *Mean Spirit*; Tate, Ruth.

Tate, Ruth

Ruth Tate is "the strong and beautiful twin sister of Moses Graycloud" in Linda Hogan's *Mean Spirit* (1990). She married John Tate late in life, and though her former loneliness is gone, she now has a "sadness about her." Her sister-in-law Belle Graycloud notices that Tate "loved to capture Ruth on film, through the camera, but he didn't seem to love her living presence, in public at least." Belle's worries are unfortunately confirmed when John Tate kills his wife for her wealth. (Hogan 1990)

See also Graycloud, Belle; Graycloud, Moses; *Mean Spirit*; Tate, John.

Taylor, Christine

Christine Taylor is a main character in Michael Dorris's novel, *A Yellow Raft in Blue Water* (1987). She is an irresponsible mother who nonetheless loves her daughter, Rayona. She has abused her body with hard living and alcohol and is slowly dying as the novel opens. With the irrationality of a well-meaning but dysfunctional parent, she tells her daughter,

I figure I've worn out my welcome in this world and the only thing I've got that's worth anything is the insurance on this fucking car. So it's going to have a little accident and you're going to win the lottery. Kiss me goodbye.

Rayona convinces her not to drive off a cliff, and the two drive instead to Christine's home on a Montana reservation.

When Christine arrives at Aunt Ida's home, their old antagonisms rise to the surface, and within minutes Christine leaves in anger and rejection. She makes her way to the home of Dayton Nickles, the best friend of her brother Lee.

During their teenage years, Christine's relationship with Dayton is marked by two experiences. The first is her embarrassing attempt to gain Dayton's romantic attentions. Dayton and Lee are such close friends that Christine is certain Dayton is trying to find ways to be near her. When she provides him with an opportunity for a physical relationship, Dayton turns her down. The rejection ruptures their relationship and exacerbates their rivalry for Lee. The break causes the two of them to "pull Lee in two directions, to force him to choose between" them. Christine holds Dayton responsible for her drifting relationship with Lee.

When Dayton and Lee begin questioning the necessity of the draft and the Vietnam conflict, Christine shifts the grounds of argument from the ideological to the personal. She tells Lee that if he does not join the military, he's not her brother, that he will be a disgrace to the reservation. The pressure she puts on Lee finally forces him to join the military, and when he is counted missing in action (MIA), Christine feels responsible. Meanwhile, she has gone to work part-time at the Tribal Council office after graduation, and spends most of her time running around with men. Aunt Ida accuses her of turning into a "slut," so when the opportunity to work in Seattle arises, Christine jumps at the chance.

On the day that Christine hears that Lee is MIA, she goes to a bar and there meets Elgin Taylor. He is kind to her, and they begin a relationship that quickly moves to the conception of their child and then marriage. By the time Rayona is born, the marriage is clearly headed for disaster. Just as she is about to enter labor, Christine receives a letter from Dayton telling her that Lee's status has changed from MIA to dead. She shows the letter to Elgin, certain that he can offer an alternative reading to the letter, that he can unmake the death of her brother. When he cannot offer any hope, Christine feels let down. After that experience, she says, "I never let down my guard, never believed him the way I used to."

Nearly two years later, when Lee's body is finally returned, Christine and the toddler Rayona go to the reservation alone for his funeral. On the trip, they spin out in a snowstorm, and Christine sees "a flight of golden stairsteps, and halfway up Lee was waiting, holding out his hand" to her. Because of her responsibility to Rayona, Christine cannot accept Lee's waiting hand, and they make their way through the storm to the funeral. At Lee's funeral, Christine imagines that one of the men there was probably her and Lee's father, "but that was an old question that would never be answered." Also at the funeral, Dayton tells her that it was not her fault that Lee was killed, but she abruptly dismisses his kindness.

From the time of Lee's death until Christine returns to the reservation herself to die, her life is marked by excesses and irresponsible behaviors. On two occasions, Rayona is removed from her home and put in foster care, and by the time Rayona is 15 years old, Christine has only six months to live. She has worn out her liver and pancreas, and the onset of diabetes is near. She recognizes, "I was going downhill with my brakes out, always barely avoiding a crash."

In the way that she has learned to rationalize, Christine is certain Rayona will be fine with Aunt Ida. She has always felt superfluous in their relationship, certain that Rayona "rarely needed me for more than my size and strength." Before they leave Seattle, Christine does make a sincere but outwardly trivial gesture of love toward Rayona. She joins a video club to establish a kind of inheritance for Rayona. She tells her daughter, "And this way, if the worst happens to me, you can still rent tapes at the members' rate. It's like something I'd leave you."

As Christine's certain death draws closer, she and Aunt Ida have a moment of reconciliation. As they express their mutual concern when

Rayona disappears early in the summer, they are able to soften toward one another too. Finally, they are both able to give and receive love. The action prepares Christine for the necessary reconciliation with Rayona when she returns to the reservation on the night of the Fourth of July. By this time, Christine has also mended her relationship with Dayton and feels comfortable knowing that she will leave Rayona in his care and in the care of her mother. (Dorris 1987; Owens 1992a)

See also George, Ida; George, Lee; Nickles, Dayton; Taylor, Elgin; Taylor, Rayona; *A Yellow Raft in Blue Water*.

Taylor, Elgin

Elgin Taylor is the off-again-on-again husband and father in Michael Dorris's *A Yellow Raft in Blue Water* (1987). After 15 years of unfaithful marriage to Christine, Elgin announces that he wants to marry another woman. The timing of his announcement, when she is hospitalized with a serious illness, provides the trigger for the plot of the novel. Christine sneaks out of the hospital in anger and is determined to go kill herself. Instead, she and her daughter Rayona Taylor go to Aunt Ida's home in Montana, and the narrative is set on its course.

Elgin is just two weeks out of the service when he meets Christine in a bar, sorrowing over the news that her brother is missing in action. He comforts her and offers her an understanding and emotional safety that she has never had before. When Christine becomes pregnant, he insists that they marry. He settles down and takes a job as a postal carrier, but his devotion to married life is tenuous. By the time of Rayona's birth, Elgin is already staying out late and is often absent altogether. He arrives at the birth of Rayona late but assures Christine, "It's all going to change. Starting today, all new. Give me a chance."

Despite his promise, Elgin does not change, and though he and Christine stay married through the years, theirs is an estranged and part-time relationship at best. (Dorris 1987)

See also George, Lee; Taylor, Christine; Taylor, Rayona; *A Yellow Raft in Blue Water*.

Taylor, Rayona

In Michael Dorris's *A Yellow Raft in Blue Water* (1987), Rayona Taylor, the biracial daughter of a African-American father and an Indian mother, is the first of three narrators. She is a 15-year-old who is mature beyond her years and the possessor of a wry charm. She once found in a hardware store her family's "exact shades on a paint mix-tone chart. Mom was Almond Joy, Dad was Burnt Clay, and I was Maple Walnut." Rayona suffers from their inconsistent parenting and recognizes that "being married never stops either one of them from doing what they want. It doesn't interfere."

In the reversal of parent-child roles, it is left to Rayona to convince her mother Christine not to commit suicide but to try life again. They pack their belongings in garbage bags and drive to Aunt Ida's house on the reservation in Montana. Two of the bags they label "Christine," one "Ray," and one "Junk." Within minutes after arriving at Aunt Ida's, Christine leaves in a fit of anger, and Rayona is left in an unfamiliar setting with a grandmother she barely knows. Rayona tries to drag her unwieldy garbage bags to the house, but she drops everything. The action is a metaphoric representation of Rayona's new life. In order to move beyond the pain of her childhood, she must let go of the "garbage" of her past and begin again.

Father Tom Novak introduces Rayona to her cousin, Kennedy (Foxy) Cree, and another member of the God Squad, Annabelle Stiffarm. Rayona senses immediately that she will not be accepted by the other teenagers on the reservation. She unwillingly becomes Father Tom's "project" and is the only one who goes to the "Teens for Christ Jamboree" with him. On the way to the meeting, Father Tom displays inappropriate sexual behavior toward Rayona and leaves her at Bearpaw Lake State Park to catch a bus back to Seattle. Instead, Rayona reads and obeys a sign meant for lost hikers: "Attention hikers! If lost, stay where you are. Don't panic. You will be found." The sign holds prophetic promise for Rayona in that she stays at the park for the summer, finds a job, makes friends, and grows to the point where she confronts her mother with the gift of forgiveness and the request for love.

Rayona meets Sky Dial at his filling station when she decides to stay at the park rather than return to Seattle. He and his wife, Evelyn, are instrumental in helping Rayona grow. They allow her to stay with them, and Evelyn gets Rayona a job with the cleanup crew at the park. They believe her stories of an ideal family that loves her, yet when they learn the truth of her situation, they simply take her to find her mother. When Rayona asks Evelyn why she is being so kind, Evelyn replies, "Because somebody should have done it for me." They go to Havre, Montana, to the Fourth of July rodeo, where Rayona suspects she might see her mother. Christine is not there, but Rayona meets a drunken Foxy Cree who coerces her to ride a bareback bronco in his place lest he be disqualified from the entire rodeo circuit for drunkenness. Rayona tucks her hair under a hat, puts on Foxy's jacket and number, and enters the stall. She is immediately thrown off the horse but gets back on two more times. She wins the rodeo's "hard-luck buckle, for the amazing feat of being bucked off the same horse three times in less than a minute." She also wins a measure of self-confidence; she recognizes that the "ride on Babe is a boundary I can't recross, and I'm struck on this side for better or worse."

It happens that the bronco belongs to Dayton Nickles, the friend with whom Christine is staying, and he takes Rayona home to see her mother. After an initial confrontation, Rayona and Christine come to an understanding that serves as truce in the war that is their love. (Dorris 1987; Owens 1992a; Rayson 1991)

See also Cree, Kennedy (Foxy); Dial, Evelyn and Sky; Father Tom Novak; George, Ida; Nickles, Dayton; Taylor, Christine; *A Yellow Raft in Blue Water*.

Tayo

Tayo is the protagonist of Leslie Marmon Silko's *Ceremony* (1977). He returns to the Laguna Reservation from a six-year experience that includes service in the army during World War II, internment in a Japanese prisoner-of-war camp, and an extended stay in a mental hospital in Los Angeles. Tayo does not return home well, though. He is nearly catatonic, and his most characteristic impulse is to vomit. The impulse to void his stomach is metaphoric as well as literal. While away in the war, Tayo was exposed to the lies of violence and war, and he struggles against swallowing them. The urge to vomit reflects his attempt not to give in to the "witchery" of violence.

Tayo has several experiences while he is in the Philippine jungle that cause him to feel responsible for the deaths of his Uncle Josiah and his cousin Rocky and for the drought that has settled over Laguna land. When Tayo is commanded to shoot a group of Japanese soldiers lined up in front of a cave, he freezes and is unable to pull the trigger. He sees the face of his uncle Josiah in the face of one of the Japanese soldiers. As others fire at the Japanese, Tayo cannot rid himself of Josiah's image, and he becomes hysterical. Even Rocky cannot comfort him or dissuade him of his notion about Josiah.

When Tayo and Rocky sign up for the army, Tayo is charged with the responsibility of bringing Rocky home safely. In the jungle, though, Rocky is hit by a grenade, and the heavy rains make a passage for medical attention impossible. Tayo prays for dry air, "air to dry out the oozing wounds of Rocky's leg, to let the torn flesh and broken bones breathe, to clear the sweat that filled Rocky's eyes." No reprieve from the rain comes, and Tayo finally damns the rain and prays against it. Rocky does not survive, and Tayo cannot forgive himself for the death of his cousin. When Tayo finally returns to Laguna and finds that the countryside is caught in a six-year drought, he feels responsible for it because of his damning prayers against the rain. Tayo's feeling of responsibility is not simply hypersensitivity but rather is a measure of his awareness of the connection of all things in the world. This attribute is what fits him for the role of protagonist and key figure in the healing ceremony.

Tayo's illness is parallel to the illness of the land and of a society that wages war on a world-wide scale. His quest for personal wholeness and health is directly connected to the need for wholeness and health in the Laguna nation, the United States, and indeed, in the world. His connection to the healing ceremony that informs the structure and content of the novel thus has a significance far greater than his own personal healing.

In completing the ceremony, Tayo is assisted by a series of helpers: Night Swan, Ku'oosh, Betonie, Ts'eh Montaño, and the Mountain Lion Man. Even before Tayo joins the army, Night Swan realizes that he is going to be a central figure in the healing ceremony. When she first meets him, she says, "I have been watching you for a long time." And after an experience of sexual initiation, she tells him, "You are a part of [the ceremony] now."

When Tayo finally returns to Laguna after his six-year absence, he still feels "invisible," like "white smoke" with "no consciousness of [him]self." His grandmother decides that the white doctors have not been able to help him and that Ku'oosh, the medicine man, needs to be brought in. Ku'oosh's medicine cannot cure Tayo, however, so he recommends the Navajo medicine man, Betonie. It is through the agency of Betonie that Tayo finally comes to some measure of health. But like all heroes in the monomythic culture hero pattern, Tayo must accomplish some good deed on behalf of the community. He goes in quest of Josiah's spotted cattle and is aided in the search by Ts'eh, an embodiment of the mythic Yellow Woman character, and her companion, Mountain Lion Man. With the quest successfully completed, Tayo must meet a final test; he must resist becoming a part of the "witchery," which manifests itself as the temptation to kill Emo at the old uranium mine site. His ability to resist reflects his growth as a character. He is no longer the Tayo who tries to combat evil with evil, as he did earlier when he plunged a broken beer bottle in the stomach of Emo in an honest, but ineffective, attempt to purge Emo of the lies that he had swallowed. (Allen 1986; Jahner 1979; Lincoln 1983; Owens 1992a; Ruppert

1988; Scarberry 1979; Swan 1988; Swan 1991–1992; Wiget 1985)

See also Betonie; *Ceremony*; Emo; Harley; Helen Jean; Ku'oosh; Montaño; Ts'eh; Night Swan; Rocky; Silko, Leslie Marmon; Witchery.

Termination and Relocation

The termination policy of the U.S. government was an attempt in the 1950s to end all federal ties with tribal governments. According to Frederick E. Hoxie, the bill "called for the preparation of a final roll of tribal members, the distribution of tribal assets to members, and the removal of Indian lands from federally protected trust status." The bill was passed as House Concurrent Resolution no. 108 in 1953, and its effect was the undermining of tribal authority and a further disruption of tribal values.

A program with similar disruptive qualities was the relocation program that began after World War II and was expanded in the 1950s. This program encouraged Indians to move from the reservations and seek jobs in major urban areas. The program was renamed the Employment Assistance Program in 1962 and continued to place Indians far from their reservation origins. The culture shock of urban life was too traumatic for the program to have lasting effect, however, and it is estimated that anywhere from 30 to 75 percent of the Indians participating in the program returned to the reservation.

Both of these federal programs were driven by an assimilationist ideology that ultimately was viewed as flawed and even hostile to Indian self-determination. (Hoxie 1996; Janke 1994)

Three Bears

Three Bears is the respected chief of the Lone Eaters band of the Pikuni tribe in James Welch's *Fools Crow* (1986). When the Lone Eaters are contemplating how to react to the encroaching whites, Three Bears takes a middle ground and

As part of the Employment Assistance Program, these two Navajos are being taught carpentry in this Arizona school, 1963. (UPI/Corbis-Bettmann)

counsels his people to join neither Heavy Runner in his accommodationist position nor Mountain Chief in his more militant stand. As Three Bears comes to the end of his life, he passes his red-stone pipe and the leadership of the Lone Eaters to Rides-at-the-door, the father of the protagonist in the book. (Welch 1986)

See also *Fools Crow*; Heavy Runner; Rides-at-the-door.

Thunder, Anna (Mercury)

Anna Thunder is a compelling character in Susan Power's 1994 novel, *The Grass Dancer*. She christens herself "Mercury" after her granddaughter comes home with the following information about elements from the periodic table: "An element is a substance that can't be split into simpler substances." She tells her granddaughter, "That's my story," and in choosing the poisonous element of mercury, she is not far from wrong. Mercury Thunder is the "reservation witch" and practices "selfish magic."

The "selfish magic" that Anna works draws young men half her age to her bed and pushes away her daughter and the larger community. What motivates Anna to practice bad medicine is a need to avenge past hurts and the need to correct wrongheaded notions of what constitutes Indianness.

Anna Thunder did not always practice bad magic, but the death of her first husband and young son pushed her over the edge. She was happily married for seven years to a white man, Emery Bauer. Then Bauer contracted consumption, but before the disease could take him, he was thrown from a horse and killed. Anna's gratitude that he didn't linger is offset when she learns that their young son, Chaske, also has consumption. As Chaske's condition worsens, she sends her cousin to get the doctor. Her cousin goes to a dance instead, and Chaske dies. In a heated act of vengeance, Anna beads a pair of red moccasins and gives them to her cousin's daughter, Bernadine. She dresses Bernadine in ceremonial dress and wills her to dance. Under Anna's spell, the young girl dances in the cold until she freezes to death.

Anna's second marriage ends in tragedy as well. Her husband, Clive Broken Rope, fights in World War II and returns with memories that "chewed his mind away." He abuses Anna by kicking her in the stomach while she is pregnant with Crystal. Anna later tells Crystal, "So he kicked you as well. The toe of his boot left that mark on your face." The only other information she offers Crystal about her father is that he died a week before she was born. The lack of further information creates an aura of suspicion around his death.

Anna's descent into bad medicine continues and culminates in her orchestration of the adultery between Calvin Wind Soldier and his sister-in-law, Evelyn Many Wounds. Wind Soldier is the descendant of Ghost Horse, the man who loved Anna's ancestor, Red Dress. Anna decides that she is "going to right a wrong of history" and come together with Wind Soldier to "close the unhappy circle, change the ending of that story." When Anna comes for Calvin Wind Soldier, he resists her magic and thus angers her. She retaliates by putting a spell on his bed and the bed of Evelyn Many Wounds. Her actions result in the birth of a child and much pain for all involved. Anna Thunder's response to the situation indicates how deeply she is addicted to the use of bad medicine: "The only thing I knew for sure was that I had filled these young people with hurtful desires, changed the course of their destinies, because, after all, I could do it." Anna is clearly a character in conflict, however, for at other times she denies that she uses her powers for ill. She says, "I didn't practice good medicine or bad medicine, or a weak magic summoned by poems; I simply had potent blood inherited from my grandmother's sister, Red Dress."

On another level, it could be argued that Anna uses her power to a good purpose, though the end hardly justifies the means. She is trying to teach Jeannette McVay, a young, white anthropology student, that Dakota culture is not dead. She tells Jeannette, "I am not a bedtime story; I am not a dream." Anna's point counters the brand of anthropology that turns native legends into children's stories and reduces religion to superstition, but she overreaches. In grasping powers from the past, she abuses them and violates the culture herself. She forces McVay to recognize that her powers are nightmarishly real. She punctuates her lesson by sprinkling reservation soil inside McVay's loafers so that she can never leave the reservation, no matter how she might try. Over 20 years later, McVay is still on the reservation because Anna has "willed it" and because she is determined to not be a simple "fairy tale."

Anna's assertion of power is at a cost to herself that she does not acknowledge, however; she drives both her daughter and granddaughter away from their home on the reservation. (Power 1994)

> See also *The Grass Dancer*; Lundstrom, Crystal Thunder; Many Wounds, Evelyn; McVay, Jeannette; Red Dress; Small War, Herod; Thunder, Charlene; Wind Soldier, Calvin; Wind Soldier, Lydia.

Thunder, Charlene

Charlene is the granddaughter of Anna (Mercury) Thunder in Susan Power's novel, *The Grass Dancer* (1994). Because her grandmother practices bad medicine, Charlene identifies with "Darrin from the television show *Bewitched*." She tries to keep the witchcraft out of her house, but her grandmother answers to no one. Charlene no longer enters powwow dance contests because her grandmother arranges for her to win, even if it is at the expense of bodily harm to other contestants. When Charlene hears that the winning dancer, Pumpkin, has been killed in a car wreck, she wonders if her grandmother caused the accident.

From her birth, Charlene has been controlled by her grandmother. When Charlene's mother Crystal rebelled against the unnatural control of her mother, Anna Thunder demanded "a soul for a soul." She snatched Charlene away from Crystal and raised her as her own, not even telling Charlene who her mother is. Charlene is trapped by her grandmother's reputation and behaviors. Because of her relationship to Anna, Charlene bears the reproaches of the community and is almost driven to suicide as a result.

She determines to live and try some magic of her own. She creates a love spell by baking her eyelashes into some cupcakes and giving them to six boys in her homeroom. They do become attracted to her but take her to the deserted house of Clara Miller and finally rape her. Charlene awakens the next morning to find the spirits of two women hovering over her, Clara Miller and Red Dress. Red Dress tells her,

> You misused the medicine because you have a bad example. If you are selfish with it, someday it will be selfish with you. We do not own the power, we aren't supposed to direct it ourselves. Give it up if you don't understand my meaning. Put the medicine behind you. Will you do that for yourself and for your people?

Charlene answers "yes" and goes to visit the guidance counselor, Jeannette McVay, at school the next morning.

Jeannette McVay helps Charlene move to another homeroom, but more importantly, tells her who and where her mother is. She helps Charlene establish connection with Crystal, tells her not to go home, and gives her bus fare to her mother's house in Chicago. On the bus ride, Charlene dreams of Pumpkin who tells her, "It wasn't your fault. These things happen. There was nothing you could do." Forgiven by Pumpkin and by her own self, Charlene leaves the reservation and her grandmother's powers behind. (Power 1994)

> See also *The Grass Dancer*; Lundstrom, Crystal Thunder; Lundstrom, Martin; McVay, Jeannette; Pumpkin; Red Dress; Thunder, Anna (Mercury).

Thunder, Crystal
See Lundstrom, Crystal Thunder.

Tiny
A character in Leslie Marmon Silko's *Almanac of the Dead* (1991), Tiny is a large man who runs the Stage Coach, a topless dancing club in Tucson. Lecha's secretary Seese worked for Tiny

four or five years before she met David and, later, Lecha, the keeper of the almanac. Lecha warns Seese to stay away from Tiny, but in a desperate moment she returns to Tiny, trying to sell the kilo of cocaine that Beaufrey has left with her. In the final stage of their negotiations, Tiny is killed in a police raid at the Stage Coach.

See also *Almanac of the Dead*; Jamey; Lecha; Seese.

Toose, Shawnee Ray

A character in Louise Erdrich's *The Bingo Palace* (1994), Shawnee is the focus of the attentions of both Lyman Lamartine and Lipsha Morrissey. Lamartine is the father of Shawnee's son, Redford, and takes a casual interest in the child. She realizes that if she stays with Lyman, she will only be an accessory to him as he becomes the consummate businessman and politician of his dreams. Lipsha is madly in love with Shawnee, Miss Little Shell, famous jingle dancer, but she withholds her love from him until he matures enough to value her priorities as a mother as well as a lover.

As the novel opens, Shawnee lives with Zelda Kashpaw Johnson, "the author of grit-jawed charity on the reservation," and feels the strengthening grip of Zelda on all aspects of her life. She decides to take her son and return to the home of her two sisters. Zelda finds her sisters to be too rough-cut and pulls official strings to have Redford temporarily taken from the home by a social worker.

Shawnee is determined to go to college, to pursue her interests in textiles and fashion, and to make a life for her son. She has strong connections to her traditional Chippewa (Ojibwa) heritage. She "talks to spirits in the sweat lodge in such a sweet way, in such an old-time way, respectful, that they can't help but answer." As the "best of our past, our present, our hope of a future," Shawnee knows that Lyman should not be thinking of building a bingo palace on the Pillager land.

Zelda continues to pressure Shawnee to marry Lyman, but Shawnee is aware of her growing love for Lipsha. She takes charge of her life by moving away to go to school and

by making her own decisions of the heart. (Erdrich 1994)

See also *The Bingo Palace*; Johnson, Zelda Kashpaw; Lamartine, Lyman; Morrissey, Lipsha.

Toose, Xavier

Xavier Toose is a character in Louise Erdrich's *The Bingo Palace* (1994). He is the uncle of Shawnee Ray Toose, the tribal elder who guides Lyman Lamartine and Lipsha Morrissey in their vision quests, and the man who loved Zelda Kashpaw Johnson with a dangerous devotion. The "lookingest man around" and "a smart one too," Xavier falls in love with Zelda, and though she loves him too, she refuses to marry him. Both have an astonishing power to wait. She waits fruitlessly all her life for the white man who will give her the life she reads about in magazines, and Xavier waits through a frozen night on her doorstep. On the night that Zelda refuses his wedding band, Xavier sits on her doorstep and by morning has lost the fingers on the hand he held over his heart. In spite of his losses, Xavier "never believed or allowed himself to be treated like a man with something missing." He learns the lesson that Zelda takes many more years to learn: "He had simplified his heart." When Zelda realizes that she still loves Xavier, she goes to him, and they begin a life together. (Erdrich 1994)

See also *The Bingo Palace*; Johnson, Zelda Kashpaw; Lamartine, Lyman; Morrissey, Lipsha; Toose, Shawnee Ray.

Tosamah, John Big Bluff

Tosamah, the Priest of the Sun, is the character in N. Scott Momaday's *House Made of Dawn* (1968) who runs the Holiness Pan-Indian Rescue Mission in Los Angeles, assisted by his disciple Cruz. He is "big, lithe as a cat, narrow-eyed." In the second section of the book, Tosamah performs three services. The first is the Saturday night sermon on the Gospel of John, the second is the peyote ceremony, and the third is "The Way to Rainy Mountain" sermon.

The first sermon is about the supremacy of the Word. Tosamah affirms the truth spoken by the apostle, "In the beginning was the Word," but goes on to say that John got carried away and spoke too much. "Right then and there he should have stopped. There was nothing more to say, but he went on," Tosamah claims. The danger in talking too much about the word is that it becomes diluted and glib, emptied of meaning and devoid of truth. Tosamah contrasts the way of the apostle John, "a white man," with the attitude toward language held by his Kiowa grandmother, a storyteller. She taught Tosamah that "in words and in language, and there only, she could have whole and consummate being." For his grandmother, Tosamah says, "words were medicine; they were magic and invisible." Embedded in Tosamah's sermon is his grandmother's story of the Sun Dance culture of the Kiowas and the coming of Tai-me, their representation of the Sun Dance culture. The latter part of Tosamah's sermon appears in a slightly altered version in Section Ten of Momaday's *The Way to Rainy Mountain* (1969). Tosamah ends his sermon with the irreverent "Good night and gets yours." The narrator describes the attitude of Tosamah as a movement between "Conviction, caricature, callousness."

In a prefatory note before the peyote service and before the second sermon, the text identifies Tosamah as "orator, physician, Priest of the Sun, son of Hummingbird." The list of descriptors reveals the several identities of Tosamah. In the first sermon, Tosamah is all "Big Bluff" and bluster; the sermon is a showcase of Tosamah's oratorical gifts, which are great. In the peyote ceremony, Tosamah becomes the spiritual physician. He describes the peyote in scientific language: "It contains nine narcotic alkaloids of the isoquinoline series, some of them strychnine-like in physiological action, the rest morphine-like."

The third service is the sermon "The Way to Rainy Mountain," during which the tone and narrative voice are intelligent, sensitive, and sincere. Here Tosamah is the Priest of the Sun as he delivers the account of the Kiowa people, a sun-worshipping people, from their cultural origins to their tragic end. The sermon is the same story that Momaday tells in his introduction to *The Way to Rainy Mountain*.

In the third section of *House Made of Dawn*, "The Night Chanter," we see Tosamah out of the church setting. He is a friend of Ben Benally's and warns Ben that Abel is a loose cannon. Tosamah says that Abel must learn to change, learn not to be a "longhair." He says, "You know, you have to change. That's the only way you can live in a place like this. You have to forget about the way it was, how you grew up and all."

Tosamah is not a careful pastor to his flock. One night at a party, he baits Abel about his disinterest in assimilating into the urban Los Angeles culture until Abel lunges at him. The men are too drunk to fight, but Tosamah humiliates Abel by laughing at him. The psychic blow starts Abel on his downward spiral. (Evers 1985; Hirsch 1983; Oleson 1973; Raymond 1983)

See also Abel; Benally, Ben; *House Made of Dawn*; *The Way to Rainy Mountain*.

Tracks

Louise Erdrich's *Tracks* (1988) is the chronological origin of her North Dakota tetralogy. The novel is told in the voices of two narrators, Nanapush and Pauline Puyat, and much attention has been given to the reliability of the sometimes contradictory voices. Nanapush narrates the beginning and ending chapters and thus gains the privilege of first and last words; Pauline gives voice to four of the interior chapters. Nanapush narrates directly to his now-grown granddaughter Lulu, who is ready to marry a Morrissey. Nanapush concentrates his narrative efforts on dissuading her from the marriage and attempting to heal the rift between her and her mother, Fleur Pillager. Pauline's narrative is directed to no one in particular but carries the fanatic intensity of a martyr justifying moral choices.

The tracks of the novel's title are any of several things: the tracks of Fleur Pillager, the focal point of both narrators; the tracks of orality in a literary text; and the tracks of newsprint, legalese, and map boundaries as they divide the Anishinabe (Ojibwa or Chippewa in Euroamerican terminology) clans and lands.

The novel spans a 12-year period, from 1912 to 1924. The years of the text wrap around one of the most traumatic historical events of the Western world, World War I, and yet the novel barely mentions it. What is at stake in the lives of these few Ojibwa Indians is just as cataclysmic as the Great War; their own nation is being destroyed, first by disease and then by the "progress" of the young democratic nation that surrounds them. Allotment, the governmental policy set in place to fragment the reservations, is fragmenting social bonds as well. The larger conflict of the novel centers around those Ojibwa who are willing to sell their allotments to a lumber company and those who hold out, refusing to parcel off their ancestral lands for a pittance, more tracks on paper issued by a government that does not have their interests at heart. Towering in the center of the novel is Fleur Pillager, the character who fascinates those around her and who is revealed by alternating fond and resentful narrators. Fleur is 17 when consumption takes her family, leaving only her and a distant cousin, Moses, as the remnants of the powerful Pillager clan. She is found by Nanapush, who restores her to health and becomes her ally in a community that has always feared Pillagers.

In order to pay the annual fees on the Pillager allotments, Fleur goes to the small town of Argus, North Dakota, to find work. She takes a job at Pete Kozka's butcher shop, where Pauline Puyat also works. In the evenings, she joins the card games of the three men who work at the shop, and her small but steady winnings provoke them to violence against her. They attack and rape her; all the while Pauline looks on with fascination, refusing to intervene. Fleur leaves Argus and returns to her allotment at Lake Matchimanito, but not before marshaling the forces of a tornado to wreak a terrible revenge on the men who attacked her.

Back at Matchimanito, she again becomes the center of interest and much speculation. Eli Kashpaw sets his desire on her, and with the help of Nanapush, wins her love. Soon afterward, it is obvious that she is pregnant, but there is much narrative equivocation about the father of the child. The possibilities range from Eli to one of the men who raped her to the agency of Misshepeshu, the water monster who controls Lake Matchimanito and who has had a reputed connection to Fleur since her early childhood. Nanapush muddies the waters for the curious community by telling Father Damien that the child is named Lulu Nanapush. With this action he protects both Fleur and the child and extends his own line.

After the tornado in Argus, Pauline also returns to the reservation and finds work with Bernadette Morrissey on the farm she runs with her brother Napoleon. She becomes involved once again in the life of Fleur, feeding a jealous interest in Fleur's relationship with Eli and the baby Lulu. All of Pauline's interferences promote disorder in the community. With a potent love medicine, she entices Eli to couple with young Sophie Morrissey and disrupts the home of Eli and Fleur. She clumsily contributes to the premature birth and death of Fleur's second child.

Furthermore, Pauline becomes pregnant with Napoleon's child and tries to abort it until she is caught by Bernadette, who intervenes. After giving birth, Pauline abandons the child and joins the convent, where her twisted nature finds an outlet in the extremes of denial and martyrdom. She is determined to save the Indians and, indeed, save Christ himself by a confrontation with the devil on Lake Matchimanito. She reconfigures Misshepeshu into the devil and herself into a savior and launches out on the lake in a leaky boat. She rebuffs the efforts of all who try to reason with her and save her. When Napoleon makes his way to her boat, she wrestles him with the certainty that he is Misshepeshu and strangles him with her rosary. Her warped spiritual contest ends in murder, and she hides the body and retreats to the convent. The murder is unsolved but community consensus lays the blame on Fleur.

The descent of Pauline into fanaticism and the confrontations she forces between traditional Ojibwa belief and her brand of twisted Catholicism all take place within the larger context of the land wars on the reservation. The final scenes of the novel are set into place by the struggles between those Ojibwas who have sold off their allotments to the lumber company and the holdouts, Fleur, Nanapush, and the Kashpaws. The results of the conflicts are largely tragic, but the novel ends in a moment of reconciliation when Lulu returns from Indian boarding school to the welcoming arms of Nanapush and Margaret Kashpaw. (Erdrich 1988)

See also Father Damien; James, Dutch; Kashpaw, Eli; Kashpaw, Margaret (Rushes Bear); Kashpaw, Nector; Kashpaw, Russell; Kozka, Pete and Fritzie; Lamartine, Lulu Nanapush; Misshepeshu; Morrissey, Bernadette; Morrissey, Sophie; Nanapush; Napoleon; Pillager, Fleur; Pillager, Moses; Puyat, Pauline; Veddar, Lily.

Trickster

The trickster character is found in Native American cultures and oral and written literatures. The figure varies from culture to culture, taking the form of raven, coyote, rabbit, or any number of other forms. The character is neither good nor bad, nor even amoral; trickster simply is. Trickster can shift shape and even gender; he/she simultaneously embodies the "sacred and the scatological" and is both the "culture hero and the fool." Trickster is known for the attributes of a voracious appetite, seeking both food and sex. As a rule breaker, Trickster "throws into sharp relief the relationships, categories, and patterns of his culture." (Babcock and Cox 1994)

Trigg, Eddie

In Leslie Marmon Silko's *Almanac of the Dead* (1991), Trigg is a character who deals in both real estate and biomaterials. Early in his career, he grasped a connection between the two dissimilar businesses when he realized that he could drive down the prices in an area by opening a blood bank. With that one step, he could rapidly change the demographics of a neighborhood in ways that were to his financial advantage. When it was time to "upgrade" the neighborhood again, he would move his blood bank.

His interest in biomaterials is personal as well as financial; he became a paraplegic after a drunken driving accident when he was a young man, and he lives with the expectation that technology and science will soon make his complete recovery possible. In the meantime, he is expanding his biomaterials business from blood and blood plasma to skin and organs, which he keeps viable in a highly secret solution developed by the Japanese. He is unscrupulous about harvesting the body parts needed to keep his stock up. He buys skin and organs from bodies killed because of revolution and crime. Perhaps worst of all is his practice of picking up hitchhikers and offering to pay them for a pint of blood. He puts them in the back of his van, and while he distracts them with sexual favors, he drains their blood until they die. He then harvests their bodies for usable organs.

He is fascinated with his own life and keeps extensive diaries of all his activities. He shares his closet full of diaries with his lover, Leah Blue, and she uses them to glean information that may be useful in building her own real estate empire. Trigg does not live to see his pet real estate projects—a sex mall and a detoxification and addiction health care complex—come to fruition. He is murdered by Clinton, a Vietnam veteran, and Rambo, also a veteran and Trigg's night watchman, and is found in a freezer compartment in the basement of his biomaterials headquarters. (Silko 1991)

See also *Almanac of the Dead*; Blue, Leah.

V

Veddar, Lily

In Louise Erdrich's *Tracks* (1988), Lily is one of the men who works for Pete Kozka's butcher shop. He is "fat, with a snake's pale eyes and precious skin, smooth and lily-white, which is how he got his name," and has a "dog, a stumpy mean little bull of a thing with a belly drum-tight from eating pork rinds." It is Lily who is primarily responsible for the attack on Fleur, including the rape, and the possibility exists that Lulu is his child.

When the tornado strikes the day after the attack on Fleur, the three men seek shelter in the meat locker. Pauline Puyat closes the locker from the outside; Lily and Tor Grunewald freeze to death, but Dutch James recovers. (Erdrich 1988)

See also James, Dutch; Kashpaw, Russell; Kozka, Pete and Fritzie; Lamartine, Lulu Nanapush; Pillager, Fleur; Puyat, Pauline; *Tracks*.

Vizenor, Gerald

Gerald Vizenor was born in 1934 in Minneapolis, Minnesota. His mixed-blood Anishinaabe (Chippewa or Ojibwa in Euroamerican terminology) father was murdered when Gerald was only 20 months old. The violence of his father's death and the subsequent dismissal of the police investigation wound the springs of Vizenor's literary imagination. The tragedy had a more immediate negative effect on Vizenor's childhood, however. He sometimes stayed at the White Earth Reservation home of his grandmother and was sometimes sent to foster homes. He joined the army in his teens and traveled to Japan, where he recognized familiar tribal aesthetics in the haiku art form, and consequently he has written haiku throughout his literary career.

Gerald Vizenor, 1996. (Courtesy of Gerald Vizenor)

When he returned from the army, Vizenor attended college at New York University and then the University of Minnesota, where he earned a bachelor's degree. After several years of graduate school, he worked as a journalist; for the Minnesota Department of Corrections; and as a university professor at Lake Forest University, Bemidji State College, the University of Minnesota, the University of California at Berkeley, and the University of California at Santa Cruz.

Since the early 1970s, Vizenor has been one of the most prolific writers in American letters. He writes in many genres and often blurs the distinction between genres. Vizenor's work is marked by his wordplay and inventiveness with language. For all his playfulness, Vizenor is quite serious about language, however. He avoids using the word "Indian," noting that it is "a problem word. . . . It doesn't mean anything, it is a historical blunder, and has negative associations." His coinage, "wordarrows," "is an obvious metaphor for the cultural and racial tensions between tribal and European cultures and it's a verbal device."

The mythic trickster (Nanabozho in Vizenor's Chippewa tradition) is a literal and metaphorical presence in nearly all of Vizenor's works. For Vizenor, the trickster is a compassionate and comic survivor in spite of the darkness that is present in all lives.

Vizenor's many works include *Darkness in Saint Louis Bearheart* (1978; reissued in 1990 as *Bearheart: The Heirship Chronicles*); *Griever: An American Monkey King in China* (1987); *The Heirs of Columbus* (1992); *Dead Voices: Natural Agonies in the New World* (1992); *Wordarrows: Indians and Whites in the New Fur Trade* (1978); *The People Named the Chippewa: Narrative Histories* (1984); and *Shadow Distance: A Gerald Vizenor Reader* (1994). Vizenor is a literary critic and has edited the volume *Narrative Chance: Postmodern Discourse on Native American Literatures*. (Owens 1992a; Velie 1994; Vizenor 1987; Vizenor 1990)

See also *Bearheart: The Heirship Chronicles.*

Walters, Anna Lee

A Pawnee/Otooe-Missouria writer and publisher, Anna Lee Walters was born in Pawnee, Oklahoma, in 1941 and educated at the Institute of American Indian Arts in Santa Fe, New Mexico. Her books include a very well received collection of short stories, *The Sun Is Not Merciful* (1985); the novel *Ghost Singer* (1988); a mixed-genre collection, *Talking Indian: Reflections on Survival and Writing* (1992); and a children's book, *The Two-Legged Creature: An Otoe Story* (1993).

Walters says of her writing: "I write about things I know, people I know. I write because of my need to write. It is my 'true' love." (*Contemporary Authors* 1995a, vol. 146; Scholer 1986; Witalec 1995)

Warm Water, Chess and Checkers

Chess and Checkers Warm Water are two beautiful Flathead Indian sisters who become backup singers for Coyote Springs in Sherman Alexie's novel *Reservation Blues* (1995). The women meet the members of the band when Coyote Springs performs their first off-reservation gig in Arlee, Montana, on the Flathead reservation where the sisters live. Chess immediately falls in love with Thomas, and when the sisters follow the band to the Spokane reservation,

Checkers falls for the reservation priest, Father Arnold. She temporarily leaves the band to sing at the Catholic church.

As Chess and Thomas become emotionally intimate, she tells the story of their parents and their younger brother, Backgammon, who died as a child. Chess finds that her personal tragedies are only a variation of the pain and loss that Thomas has suffered. In their growing friendship and mutual respect, the two become the anchors of Coyote Springs.

During the summer, the sisters fight fires for the Bureau of Indian Affairs (BIA) and live off the money during the winter. Coyote Springs finds that their fire-fighting experience is useful when, in the more surrealistic moments of the narrative, Victor's guitar playing starts fires. The two women are disgusted with Victor and Junior because of their irresponsible drinking and their relationships with Betty and Veronica. Chess "hated Indian men who chased after white women; she hated white women who chased after Indian men." The difficulties of their lives as Indian women makes Chess say, "You ain't really Indian unless there was some point in your life that you didn't want to be."

Because of the early death of their mother, the sisters have not previously had the kind of role model that they find in Big Mom when they meet her. Big Mom calls them by their real names, Eunice and Gladys, tells them they are "special women," and invites them to join her in the sweat lodge. Checkers is awed by Big Mom's wisdom, though she is still confused by her feelings for Father Arnold. She writes in her journal, "I looked at Big Mom and thought that God must be made up mostly of Indian and woman pieces. Then I looked at Father Arnold and thought that God must be made up of white and man pieces. I don't know what's true."

When Coyote Springs comes back from New York, having failed their audition, the sisters realize it is time to leave the reservation. Chess presses Thomas to join them. He consents, and she answers an ad to work for the telephone company in Spokane. The sisters and Thomas leave the reservation for Spokane, where Chess and Thomas will marry. Chess tells Thomas, "Let's have lots of brown babies. I want my babies to look up and see two brown faces. That's the best thing we can give them, enit?"

See also Betty and Veronica; Big Mom; Builds-the-Fire, Thomas; Father Arnold; Joseph, Victor; Polatkin, Junior; *Reservation Blues*.

Waterlily

Though Ella Cara Deloria's *Waterlily* was written by 1948, it was not published until 1988, 40 years later. Deloria had been working with anthropologists Franz Boas and Ruth Benedict at Columbia University in New York since 1928 and was encouraged by them to write a novel that would represent the position of a woman in Siouan culture before the onset of changes that were the result of contact with Euroamerican culture. The 1942 death of Boas and Benedict's death in 1948 left Deloria without the professional help she needed to get the volume published. Her own attempts proved fruitless, but the posthumous publication of *Waterlily* has certainly found a more hospitable welcome than it would have had in 1948.

The plot of *Waterlily* is clearly dependent on the ethnographic information that Deloria wants to highlight. For instance, in order to illustrate the several ways in which a Siouan woman can be married, both Waterlily and her mother marry twice. And in Waterlily's first marriage, in which she is "bought," narrative pressure is put on her to accept the marriage proposal with its gift of two horses because, quite conveniently, just the night before, the two horses her father was honor bound to give in a ghost-keeping ceremony were found dead. In another instance, in order to describe the *hunka* ceremony in which a child is "elevated to a high station in the tribe," Deloria must create a reason for Waterlily to become the subject of this special ceremony. The explanation Deloria provides is thin, but generally, her fictive skills are strong enough to add an air of plausibility to the events of the novel.

Deloria's purpose is to provide a picture of the Siouan kinship network, or *tiyospaye*, which governs every part of their society. In order to present the way the society can work smoothly and flawlessly, all of the main characters exhibit exemplary behavior and are therefore rather uninteresting from a narrative point of view. Deloria does include minor characters who violate the *tiyospaye* and provide some narrative interest. Waterlily's biological father, Star Elk, is such a character; so, too, is her "loud and bold" cousin Alila.

Waterlily is the story of the title character from birth to her adulthood. She is the daughter of Blue Bird, a young girl who makes an unwise choice in consenting to marry Star Elk. Star Elk abandons the young family, and Blue Bird and Waterlily must find their security in the *tiyospaye*. Blue Bird remarries a responsible young widower, Rainbow, and afterward their family is happy and respected. Waterlily grows up witnessing and participating in all of the daily and seasonal behaviors of the Sioux. Through her experiences we learn of the buffalo hunt and the warrior societies of the Siouan men, but the novel primarily focuses on the ways of women. The novel instructs the reader on child-rearing strategies and food gathering and preparation but, more importantly, focuses on the social relationships between members of a *tiyospaye*. Though Deloria subordinates fictional purposes to ethnographic ones, the reader does come to care about Waterlily and the trials of her life. She marries and within the first year loses her husband to smallpox; she bears her first child alone, but remarries quite happily. Though largely a static character, near the end of the novel, Waterlily does become reflective and shows signs of growth.

In embedding cultural data in a novel, Deloria attempts the same feat as does Mourning Dove in her novel *Cogewea, the Half-Blood* (1927, 1981), but with much greater success. (Deloria 1988; DeMallie 1988)

See also *Cogewea, the Half-Blood: A Depiction of the Great Montana Cattle Range*; Deloria, Ella Cara

The Way to Rainy Mountain

The Way to Rainy Mountain (1969) is a mixed-genre volume by N. Scott Momaday that embodies a strongly poetic voice telling a personal, historical, and cultural memoir. The volume is a collection of 24 story groups (called *triads* by Matthias Schubnell), which are arranged on facing pages and require the reader to make associative connections between the three in order to come to some understanding of the text. The text is framed by two poems, "Headwaters" at the beginning and "Rainy Mountain Cemetery" at the end. There is a second, interior framing of a prologue with introduction and an epilogue at the closing. Within the frames are the story groups. Each grouping contains three voices, which Momaday has called "historical, personal as well as cultural."

In his acknowledgments, Momaday thanks his "kinsman who willingly recounted to me the tribal history and literature which informs this book." Momaday takes the tribal history and literature of the Kiowa people and joins it with his own personal accounts and remembrances in an attempt to enter into his cultural past, as well as to let the cultural past seep into him. The product is both a highly intense and intimate picture of a man defined and shaped by his culture and a glimpse into the Kiowa culture.

As indicated by the title, the story is of a journey, of the way to Rainy Mountain. Fundamental to the understanding of the text is the information about the Kiowa people given in the introduction. They migrated from the "high country in western Montana nearly three centuries ago" and made their way to the southern plains of Oklahoma, to Rainy Mountain, where Momaday's grandmother still lived in his lifetime. It is the occasion of her death that brings Momaday back to Rainy Mountain once more. The journey is circular, for not only does Momaday return to Rainy Mountain, but he traces the migration route of his ancestors from Montana to Oklahoma, and the text reflects both this geographical journey as well as the origin of the Kiowa people and the transformative genesis of their own cultural identity. For in migrating from the high mountain country of Montana to the open and sunbaked plains of Oklahoma, they acquired a new idea of themselves. As Momaday says, "They had conceived a good idea of themselves; they had dared to imagine and determine who they were." Along the way they also acquired "horses, the sun dance religion, and a certain love and possession of the prairies."

There is a deliberate artfulness to the physical presentation of the text. With the line drawings by Momaday's father, Al Momaday, and the different typefaces, the book requires a visual reading as well as a literary one. Each triad is purposefully arranged on facing pages. The cultural, or mythic, voice is always given first, on the left-hand side of the page. On the right-hand page, the historical voice is at the top of the page and, following some white space, is the third, and personal, voice. When the book is closed, it is almost as if the three voices are in dialogue with each other. And indeed, a responsible reading of the text asks the reader to let the three voices interact with one another. The amount of white space suggests a simplicity that is deceptive. For just as there is meaning in silence, there seems to be meaning in the absence of text as well as in its presence. Momaday says that when his step-great-grandfather would tell a story, "he began by being quiet." The quiet that surrounds a story in the oral tradition is full of the unspoken contexts that each listener brings to the experience and of the cultural context that surrounds the story. And so, the white spaces in Momaday's text ask the reader to supply context and associative meaning as well.

The 24 triads are divided into three groups, which Momaday subtitles "The Setting Out," "The Going On," and "The Closing In." In the first grouping, the mythic stories are all from the distant past. The first one relates the Kiowa origin myth, the emergence into the world through a hollow log. Other mythic passages tell of the birth of the sun's son, of his adventures, of the trouble his grandmother has controlling him and teaching him necessary survival skills, and of the transformation of the boy into twins and their adventures. In "The Going On," the mythic passages are more particular to the existence of the Kiowas once they became people of the sun and of the plains. By the last section, "The Closing In," the mythic passages are dominated by Mammedaty and Aho, Momaday's paternal grandparents. They have become mythologized and have entered into the Kiowa cultural ethos. The historical sections give useful dates and events concerning the Kiowas and even include some selections from the work of nineteenth-century anthropologist James Mooney. Throughout the volume, the personal sections are marked by a quiet and meditative voice that provides poetic resonance to the text.

The story of Momaday's grandmother in the introduction will be familiar to readers of his novel, *House Made of Dawn*. Her story is given there to the character Tosamah, and he recounts it as his grandmother's story. The epilogue of *The Way to Rainy Mountain* is remarkable for its revelation of another Kiowa elder, Ko-sahn, who is Momaday's last tenuous connection to his Kiowa past. (Jaskowski 1988; McAllister 1978b; Momaday 1976; Schubnell 1988)

See also Aho; *House Made of Dawn*; Ko-sahn; Mammedaty; Momaday, N. Scott; *The Names*.

Weasel Tail, Wilson

Wilson Weasel Tail is a character in Leslie Marmon Silko's *Almanac of the Dead* (1991). He is a Lakota man who dropped out of the third year of law school at the University of California at Los Angeles "to devote himself to poetry." He appears at the International Holistic Healers Convention in Tucson and advocates peaceful revolution, though he issues a stern message to the U.S. government: "Give back what you have stolen or else as a people you will continue your self-destruction." He and the Barefoot Hopi are the main attractions at the convention.

In the early days of his activism, he knew Lecha, the keeper of the almanac of the title, on the TV talk-show circuit. After Lecha's twin sister Zeta's ranch is raided by the police, Lecha and Seese leave Tucson and go to South Dakota to join Weasel Tail.

See also *Almanac of the Dead*; The Barefoot Hopi; Lecha; Seese.

Welch, James

Blackfeet on his father's side of the family and Gros Ventre on his mother's, James Welch was born in 1940 in Browning, Montana. He attended Blackfeet and Fort Belknap reservation schools; he later attended Northern Montana College and Minnesota University and received a bachelor's degree from the University of Montana. He entered a master of fine arts degree program at the University of Montana and studied with Richard Hugo, from whom he learned much about writing. Welch says, "He really taught me how to write. He taught me how to be economical with language, how to be evocative. He taught me you can write about the country you come from." After writing poetry "exclusively for seven or eight years," Welch turned his attention toward fiction and his first novel, *Winter in the Blood*. Once he started writing novels, "feeling [his] way around" in the genre, Welch decided to continue to write fiction. He says, "I think that I decided I would keep writing novels and see how far that took me. And I'm still writing novels." Welch has now written four novels (*Winter in the Blood, The Death of Jim Loney, Fools Crow,* and *The Indian Lawyer*) in addition to his first volume of poetry, *Riding the Earthboy 40*, published in 1971.

In all of his work, one can see that Welch has taken the encouragement of Richard Hugo to heart. The palette on which Welch sweeps his stories and poems is the Montana plains. "I always thought the Northern Montana plains would be boring to most people," Welch says, "but I found out it isn't." Of course, Welch isn't writing merely about the Montana plains; he is writing about the conditions of the human experience that may be shaped, in part, by the geographical context of one's life but are, more importantly, simply about the struggle to live with love and without it; to live with the specter of guilt and to banish it and survive; and to live in a historical situation that demands extinction of one's culture. These concerns, in fact, become the thematic pegs upon which his novels hang.

Although the northern Montana plains provide the geographical backdrop to Welch's writing, the cultural background is certainly his Blackfeet and Gros Ventre heritage. Even though he did not grow up in a traditional manner, Welch says:

Kind of growing up around the reservations, I just kept my eyes open and my ears open, listened to a lot of stories. You might say my senses were really brought alive by that culture. I learned more about it than I really knew. It was only after I began writing about it that I realized what I had learned. I knew quite a bit, in certain ways, about the Blackfeet and Gros Ventre ways of life.

Welch writes part of his own family's history into his third novel, *Fools Crow*:

My great grandmother lived during the time of the 1860's, and in 1870 when the Massacre on the Marias happened she would have been fourteen or fifteen, and she was in that massacre and she survived. She and a small group of people managed to sneak up the river under a cutbank. That's how they escaped. She is one of the survivors Fools Crow comes upon.

There is a general perception that Welch's fiction is bleak; his use of spare and lean prose may contribute to that notion, as may the apparent desolation of his landscapes. Indeed, the very subject matter of Welch's work makes a certain sense of despair unavoidable. Welch says about *Fools Crow*:

I think that if there is a bleakness about the future in that book, it's because of what I know to be true of reservation life. 1870 for the Blackfeet was probably the end of their way of life as they had lived it. History has proven that once the Indians were put on reservations, their life style diminished quite a bit.

But Welch's prose is also marked by the personal victories achieved by his protagonists and by the resilience and survival of his characters.

Though Welch does not see himself as a militant writer, the ever-present realities of the Indian situation intrude themselves into the foreground of each of his texts. Welch says, "I hope my writing can keep reminding people that there is an Indian situation, problem, or however you want to put it—and that it's still going on." In the meantime, he continues to balance the "contrast between the sense of modern desolation and desperation and the old ways."

Welch has been a visiting professor at University of Washington and Cornell University; he has served on the Montana State Board of Pardons and on the literature panel of the National Endowment for the Arts. He currently lives in Missoula, Montana. (Bruchac 1987; Coltelli 1990; Robbins 1990; Vangen 1994; Witalec 1995)

See also *The Death of Jim Loney; Fools Crow; The Indian Lawyer; Winter in the Blood.*

White Man's Dog

White Man's Dog is the main character in James Welch's *Fools Crow* (1986). He is an unlucky youth who is not looked upon with promise by his family and tribal group. At 18 years of age, he has "three horses and no wives. His animals [are] puny, not a blackhorn runner among them. He [owns] a musket and no powder and his animal helper [is] weak." However, after a successful horse raid into Crow territory, White Man's Dog is honored for his responsible behavior, and he returns to the camp with the wealth of 20 horses, enough to allow him to begin looking for a wife and a lodge of his own. Having been proven worthy in one test, he is given more and more responsibility, and his luck and his public perception change. When Yellow Kidney's wife, Heavy Shield Woman, asks to be the Sacred Vow Woman at the Sun Dance the following summer, assent must be given by all of the bands of the Pikuni. White Man's Dog is chosen to make the journey to all of the camps and present her request. After his return from a successful mission, White Man's Dog is soon married to Red Paint, the daughter of Heavy Shield Woman and Yellow Kidney.

That White Man's Dog has absorbed the ethos of the tribe, which calls for the consideration of the group over any self-aggrandizing behavior, is evident by several of his behaviors. When Yellow Kidney does not return from the Crow raid, his wife and three children are left without a hunter to provide for them. White Man's Dog takes it upon himself to share his kill with them, and he continues to do so when Yellow Kidney returns to the camp mutilated and unable to hunt. He also takes an interest in the healing ceremonies that are performed by his mentor, Mik-api, the "many-faces man."

When the Lone Eaters decide to take revenge on the Crow for the mutilation of Yellow Kidney, they give White Man's Dog the honor of counting first coup on Bull Shield, the Crow leader. Though he is shot, White Man's Dog kills Bull Shield and takes his best buffalo runner horse. He is rewarded with praise from his father: "My fine son, this day you are a brave!" He is also given a new name, "Fools Crow," by Three Bears, the Lone Eater chief.

The growth of White Man's Dog (hereafter Fools Crow) is perhaps best noted through the series of visions that he has and how he chooses to respond to them. The first of his visions

comes while he is on the raiding party to the Crow. For three nights running, he dreams he is in an enemy camp and is beckoned into a lodge by a black dog. In the lodge he sees several bodies around the perimeter and realizes that they are naked girls, all with a look of desire in their eyes. A white-faced girl rises and holds out her arms to him, and he moves toward her. At this point, he awakens. He tells no one of his dream, and not until Yellow Kidney returns to camp pockmarked and mutilated does he realize what his dream meant. He recognizes that it was a warning of the events that were to play out in the life of Yellow Kidney, and that if he had told his dream, he could have diffused its power. Because he didn't, he feels a measure of responsibility for the fate of Yellow Kidney.

Another dream that Fools Crow has is significantly paired to a dream of Mik-api's. Mik-api has a dream in which Raven tells him:

"I understand you now have a helper who is both strong and true of heart. It will take such a man to release our four-legged brother. . . . If you will send this young man, I will teach him how to use this creature's power, for in truth only the real-bear is a stronger power animal."

On the strength of Mik-api's dream, Fools Crow leaves camp in search of an animal caught in a trap. He finds a wolverine just where he was directed to look and releases him. Raven comes to him and tells him to sleep on his left side and think of what happened on that day. Then the power of the Skunk Bear (wolverine) will be his. Raven continues, "You will fear nothing, and you will have many horses and wives. But you must not abuse this power, and you must listen to Mik-api. . . ." Fools Crow obeys the instructions given to him, and the next time his power animal is caught in a trap, the dream comes directly to him. The dream comes to him on the night that he has danced the Sun Dance, and, in his altered state, Fools Crow releases the animal in his dream. Given that the line between the actual and spiritual worlds is per-

A painting of a Ute Sun Dance Ceremony on buckskin ca. 1880–1890; the Blackfeet counterpart figures prominently in James Welch's Fools Crow. *(Colorado Historical Society)*

meable in most Native American cultures, the spiritual act that Fools Crow performs is just as real and efficacious as the previous physical act. This time, Fools Crow is given a "slender white stone" and a power song by the wolverine. The wolverine tells Fools Crow, "You sing that loudly and boldly and you will never want for power."

In that same dream, Kills-close-to-the-lake comes to Fools Crow and tells him that his desire for her is not inappropriate in the world of dreams. He later learns that during the Sun Dance, she sacrificed her little finger and made a vow. She too has had a dream of the wolverine, who has warned her of the danger of her desires. Uncertain of how it happened but sure that it had, Fools Crow thinks that Wolverine "had cleansed both him and Kills-close-to-the-lake." Freed by his dream of the distraction of his father's third wife, Fools Crow can settle into the pattern of responsibility that calls to him.

Another time, in a waking dream or vision, Fools Crow is sought out by Raven, who tells him of an evil that has come to the Backbone (Rocky Mountains). There is a white man who kills for the sport of killing and who devalues the animals by giving no useful purpose for their deaths. Raven asks Fools Crow to go kill the white man who is mercilessly killing the animals. Fools Crow does as he is requested, and when he returns to the camp of the Lone Eaters, he tells the council of his actions. His behavior is respected by the elders, though they caution him to kill no more white men because it will bring serious retribution to the Pikuni. The nature of Fools Crow's action is in direct opposition to the killing of white men by Owl Child. Owl Child kills out of anger and vengeance; Fools Crow kills to protect the animal kingdom when it is in danger. Again, Fools Crow shows his connection to the larger community; he does not act to aggregate honors or draw attention to himself.

Fools Crow's final dream/vision is of epic proportions. The dream is initiated by Nitsokan, the dream helper, who instructs Fools Crow to make a journey of seven sleeps. He enters the mythic world of the Pikunis when he dreams of So-at-sa-ki, or Feather Woman. After a lengthy period of waiting, Feather Woman reveals who she is and tells her story. She paints designs on a yellow skin that tells the future of the Pikuni people. At first Fools Crow is unable to see the designs, but then they come clear:

> He was powerless to keep from seeing, and so he saw inside the lodges and he saw the agony of the sick ones, the grief of the mothers and fathers, the children, the old ones. And he saw the bundled bodies of the dead, slung across the painted horses being led from the camp. He saw inside the lodges of all the Pikunis and he saw suffering and crying and wailing. He saw mothers mutilate themselves, men rush from lodge to lodge, clutching their young ones, the elders sending up their futile prayers.

Fools Crow's despair is deep, for he realizes that he has seen the fate of his people unfold before him, and he knows that he is powerless to change it. Feather Woman tells him that though he cannot change the events, he can do "much good" for his people. She says, "You can prepare them for the times to come. If they make peace within themselves, they will live a good life in the Sand Hills [afterlife]." She continues, "Much will be lost to them, but they will know the way it was. The stories will be handed down, and they will see that their people were proud and lived in accordance with the Below Ones, the Underwater People—and the Above Ones."

When Fools Crow leaves the dream world of Feather Woman, he starts to see the truth of her revelations at once. He comes upon a group of fleeing Pikunis who have survived the massacre of Heavy Runner's band. At the camp of the Lone Eaters, smallpox is devastating his own people. And yet, the novel ends on a note of hope, for Fools Crow has believed Feather

Woman—the *stories* will endure. (Ballard 1991; Barry 1991–1992; Owens 1992a)

> **See also** Fast Horse; Feather Woman; *Fools Crow*; Heavy Runner; Heavy Shield Woman; Kills-close-to-the-lake; Mik-api; Owl Child; Red Paint; Rides-at-the-door; Three Bears; Yellow Kidney.

Whiteman, Roberta Hill

An Oneida poet born in 1947, Whiteman grew up near Green Bay and Oneida, Wisconsin. She earned a bachelor's degree from the University of Wisconsin, a master of fine arts degree from the University of Montana, and a doctoral degree from the University of Minnesota and has taught at the University of Wisconsin at Eau Claire. Whiteman gained recognition for her strong volume, *Star Quilt* (1984), which is about the pain and dislocations of reservation life, the bonds of family, and the strength of love. In the title poem, "Star Quilt," the poet asks the quilt to "anoint" her and her lover "with grass and twilight air, / so we may embrace, two bitter roots / pushing back into the dust." In "In the Longhouse, Oneida Museum," the poet laments that the longhouse, the central communal dwelling of the Iroquoian peoples, has been turned into a museum. She writes, "House of five fires, they take you for a tomb, / but I know better. When desolation comes, / I'll hide your ridgepole in my spine." Her work is frequently anthologized and is included in *The Norton Anthology of Modern Poetry*.

Whiteman's mother died when she was a young girl, but she remembers her grandmother telling stories and leaving the family a modest but influential set of books. Whiteman found her center in reading and writing at an early age. She says that her writing tries to "just look at life, to appreciate life, its mystery." (Ruoff 1990; Whiteman 1984; Whiteman 1987; Wilson 1994a; Witalec 1995)

Wild Harvest

John Milton Oskison's *Wild Harvest* (1925) is a prairie romance, replete with gunplay, murder, bank robbers, Texas longhorns, bootleg liquor, and the requisite two kinds of women. There is Nan Forest, the pure, innocent young woman of the land, and the full-lipped, scheming seductress, Ruby Engel. In short, the book has all the stuff of a western melodrama. It has the stylized inflamed rhetoric of the melodrama, the predictability of plot, and the usual cast of stock characters. But the book is interesting for its position on the Indian question in the then-developing "Indian territory."

The book opens with Nan Forest protesting as the "fumbling fingers of a July dawn first touched her face." But that is the last protest of the novel from the young protagonist. She is soon provided with ample motivation to rise out of bed each day and conquer every farm girl chore from shelling corn and raking hay to baking pies and cakes for threshing crews to rescuing her father's farm from years of neglect. She is staying with her loving aunt Susan and uncle Billy Dines, while her hapless father travels to Texas to bring back 200 head of longhorns that will secure the family's fortunes. There is little hope in the family, or the community at large, save in Nan, that Chester Forest will make a successful journey to Texas and back with the longhorns. Sam Davis, a ranchhand on Billy Dines's place, vows that he can eat all that Forest brings back "for breakfast."

Chester Forest has come to Indian territory just three years ago with his frail wife and daughter Nan. Within the first year, his wife dies, and it is Nan who becomes the parent in the small family. She must remind her father to put his book down and do his chores while she makes the evening meal. A genial man, Forest is lackluster in his work habits, long on dreaming and short on work. He is greatly influenced by dime novels with such lurid titles as "Hell on Wheels; or the Terror of Fiddler's Gulch." In his mythologizing of the West, he seems of a piece with the Swede in Stephen Crane's "The Blue Hotel." When Forest comes back from Texas, he is without the cattle and furtively on the run for the supposed murder of an unarmed man. His capture and removal back to Texas to stand trial for the shooting further motivate Nan to

make a go of the leased land they are farming. She takes hold of the hay harvest with the intention of making enough money to help her father with legal fees. She is helped in the endeavor by her uncle Billy Dines and his ranchhands, and the hay they put up is later sold to a Texas rancher, Gabe Horner, who is moving herds of cattle northward.

Nan's dream for an education in St. Louis and then a career as an elocutionist is interrupted by her father's troubles. She does enter the New Academy in a nearby town, where she studies throughout the week, but returns weekends to the homestead to work. Meanwhile, her father stands trial in Fort Tyler, Texas, and, at the request of Mr. Kearns, Forest's lawyer, Nan goes to Texas for the trial. In an overblown and sentimental courtroom scene, Kearns exploits the presence of Nan in an attempt to sway the jury. The tactic is only partially successful, and the jury is hung.

While in Fort Tyler, Nan meets a beautiful young widow, Julia Ellery, who has taken an interest in her father. In her concern over her father, however, Nan is oblivious to the mutual affection between the two. It takes a second trial before Forest is acquitted, and when he does return home, it is with Julia Ellery as his wife.

All the while the 15-year-old girl is maturing, and those in the community are noticing it. She soon becomes the object of interest for several young men. The novel chronicles the tangled affections of Nan for Tom Winger, the quiet, steady cowboy; for Harvey Stokes, the hardworking but hot-tempered and possessive farmer; and for the dashing Jack Hayes, a "reformed" bootlegger who is later revealed to be a part of a bank-robbing gang. Each of the budding love interests is subject to the interference of Ruby Engel, a neighbor girl who is known as "too wise" in the ways of men. With the predictability of a Western, Tom emerges as the victorious suitor, but not without the disposal of the other two. Jack Hayes is sent to prison for life for his part in the bank robbery, and Harvey Stokes is accidentally shot and killed in a lover's quarrel. Nan and Tom marry, and Ruby Engel—having lost all chance of a relationship with any of the three men—moves to Denver. Tom gains a herd of his own and builds a home for his new wife, and the two live happily ever after.

Although *Wild Harvest* is a pleasant enough read, it lacks the complexity and sophistication of later Native American novels; neither does it compare with novels by Oskison's contemporaries, such as William Faulkner or Willa Cather. But it is significant in the history of the Native American novel, for although the Cherokee Oskison writes a novel with white main characters, he does address Indian issues. It seems clear that Oskison is writing for a white audience, and he attempts to show the "progressiveness" of the Indian in the novel. That Oskison is committed to assimilation as a partial solution to the "Indian problem" also seems obvious in *Wild Harvest*. (Larson 1978; Oskison 1925)

> See also Davis, Sam; Dines, Billy and Susan; Engel, Ruby; Forest, Nancy; Oskison, John Milton; Stokes, Harvey; Winger, Tom.

Wilson, Jack

In Sherman Alexie's *Indian Killer* (1996), Jack Wilson "grew up white and orphaned in Seattle" and always dreamed of being Indian. By high school, he decides that he is Indian and claims a genealogical connection to Red Fox, a Shilshomish Indian. He becomes a police officer, and in his rookie year, he establishes a tenuous relationship with a homeless Indian woman, Beautiful Mary. One night, Wilson finds Mary raped and murdered. Because Mary was "a visible member of the homeless community," Wilson is surprised that the police do not work aggressively on the case. A detective tells him the case is "low priority" because "one dead Indian don't add up to much. . . . You ask me, it's pest control." Wilson looks into the case himself and assists in an arrest. His identification with all things Indian grows, and after a career in homicide, a knee injury, and a desk job, he finally retires and writes books about a "practicing medicine man and private detective in Seattle." His fictional detective is Aristotle

Little Hawk, "the very last Shilshomish Indian." Wilson has some measure of success with his first two books and gets an agent, a contract for a third novel, and a new truck that he outfits with vanity plates that read "SHAMAN."

Wilson gets his ideas going by sniffing around his old precinct. There he learns the latest on the killing of Justin Summers, a white man who was scalped and on whom the killer left two owl feathers, "like a signature or something." The officer tells Wilson that the police are calling the murderer the "Indian Killer," and the idea becomes the kernel of his third book, *Indian Killer*. On the night that he gives a reading and discusses his work-in-progress at the Elliott Bay Book Company, Marie Polatkin and other Indians protest his reading with signs saying, "Wilson is a fraud" and "Only Indians should tell Indian stories." That same night Marie Polatkin and John Smith follow Wilson home and confront him; when Wilson sees John Smith, he is struck that John is the living model of his fictional detective, Aristotle Little Hawk. Thus begins his fascination with Smith.

John Smith and Jack Wilson are mirror images of one another. John is an Indian who is raised by whites, who doesn't know his specific tribal heritage, and who feels cut off from his heritage. Jack Wilson is a white man who claims he is an Indian, who imaginatively reconstructs his own history. Neither has access to the Indianness they both long for. Wilson is a white man with an Indian name ("Jack Wilson" is the name given by whites to the Paiute messiah, Wovoka), and John Smith is an Indian with a white man's name.

Wilson intensifies his work on his book and focuses on John Smith as the killer. One night John Smith finds Wilson in his truck, hits him on the head, and drives him to the last skyscraper being built in Seattle. John ties Wilson to the wall and waits for him to come to. He puts Wilson's pistol to Wilson's head but doesn't shoot. Instead, he takes a dull knife and places it to Wilson's throat and imagines killing him and disposing of the body. John cuts Wilson across his eye and face and pleads, "Please, let me, let us have our own pain." Before walking off the edge of the building, John tells Wilson, "You're not innocent." Wilson survives the attack and finishes his book, which claims that John Smith is the Indian Killer. (Alexie 1996)

See also *Indian Killer*; Polatkin, Marie; Smith, John; Smith, Olivia and Daniel.

Wind Soldier, Calvin

Calvin Wind Soldier is a character in Susan Power's 1994 novel, *The Grass Dancer,* who is acted upon by outside forces that dangerously disrupt his life. Before he goes to fight in Korea, his father requests that he make a vision quest and seek the protection of his ancestors. Calvin reluctantly honors his father's wish and is warned in his vision by the spirit of Red Dress that Anna Thunder will come after him. He thinks little of the warning at the time.

He returns from Korea, "haunted by the Silver Star and what he had done to merit the award." He drinks heavily for a while, until he falls in love with Lydia Many Wounds and marries her. He quits drinking, gets a job with the tribal police, and builds a nice house for his wife. Back home, the threat of Anna Thunder seems more likely, and he goes to Herod Small War and asks him to make a protective belt of snakeskin. Calvin reasons that the snake is favored by Red Dress, and if her descendant comes to bother him, she cannot "get far with her pranks" because "it would be like crushing her own spirit."

Calvin is only partially right; the snakeskin belt does provide direct protection from Anna, but she manages to harm him by indirection. She puts a spell on him and his sister-in-law Evelyn that causes them to commit adultery and have a son. Though he and Lydia raise the son as their own, the affair creates much pain, for Lydia especially. One night when the child is fussy, Lydia screams in frustration for Calvin to take him for a drive. Both are killed by a drunk driver, and Lydia is left to bear the guilt and, one month later, Calvin's second son, Harley Wind Soldier. (Power 1994)

See also *The Grass Dancer*; Many Wounds, Evelyn; Red Dress; Small War, Herod; Thunder, Anna (Mercury); Wind Soldier, Harley; Wind Soldier, Lydia.

Wind Soldier, Harley

In Susan Power's novel, *The Grass Dancer* (1994), Harley Wind Soldier is a character who struggles to understand his place in the world. He was born four weeks after his father and brother Duane were killed in a car accident, and his mother, Lydia, has not spoken since. Harley understands her silence as "an empty space" between the two of them, an indication that "she fed [Duane] his brother's soul, forced it between stitched lips." As a result, he feels a "black, empty hole squeezed in his chest between heart and lungs." As a child he always draws pictures of himself that include a "black spot on his torso" to indicate the emptiness; in his young adulthood, his emptiness is manifested in his black-and-white beaded powwow regalia and his "painted tears from forehead to chin."

Harley's healing begins when he is 17 and meets Pumpkin, a grass dancer who is on the powwow trail before going to Stanford in the fall. Pumpkin has an intuitive knowledge of his inarticulate pain and tells him, "I'm your friend now. I have plenty of soul to spare. I'm rubbing it into you right now." Though she promises that he "won't be alone now," Pumpkin is killed in a car wreck on her way to the next powwow. Harley feels empty again.

In spite of his perceived emptiness, Harley has "one firm gift": his imagination. As a young man, he is still "wholly unaware of how remarkable his vision [is]." His gift is first apparent when Harley is only five years old and his grandmother is dying. She moves from life to death just as Neil Armstrong and Buzz Aldrin are walking on the moon. Harley watches the television and sees "his grandmother's figure emerging on the screen, dancing toward him from the far horizon behind the astronauts." When she reaches the Sea of Tranquillity, she feels Harley's presence and calls to him with her spirit, "*Takoja. Look at me, look at the magic. There is still magic in the world.*"

In the year that follows Pumpkin's death, Harley's struggle to maintain personal balance reaches its nadir when he appears at a rodeo drunk. His mentor, Herod Small War, steps in and starts Harley on his recovery. After a purifying sweat bath, Harley is ready for the *hanbdec'eya*, a vision quest. He goes to the "same deep pit his father had occupied thirty years before" and awaits his vision. There he sees and is encouraged by his grandmother, his father and brother, his ancestor Ghost Horse, and finally, Red Dress. Red Dress tells him that the grass on his grass dance costume represents "the long hair of our adversaries." She continues, "So when you move through those old steps, remember that you are dancing a rebellion." At the end of his four days, his friends come to the vision pit singing an honor song, but Harley hears his own voice singing too, "rising above the rest." (Power 1994; Thornton 1994)

> See also *The Grass Dancer*; Many Wounds, Margaret; Pumpkin; Red Dress; Small War, Herod; Wind Soldier, Calvin; Wind Soldier, Lydia.

Wind Soldier, Lydia

A character in Susan Power's novel *The Grass Dancer* (1994), Lydia Wind Soldier has refused to speak a word to anyone in the 17 years since the accident that killed her husband and his son. The twin sister to Evelyn (Evie) Many Wounds, Lydia has always been "the good daughter, sweet-tempered and incurious, never dreaming of taking flight." After graduating from high school, Lydia takes a job working in the school kitchen as assistant to the cook. One night they work late, decorating Valentine cookies, and on the way home, she nearly runs over a man in the road. It is the drunken Calvin Wind Soldier, passed out in the road. Lydia takes him to his home and spends the night thawing him out. Two months later, she marries a reformed and industrious Calvin. He builds Lydia a new house, where she is "greedy not for things, but rather order."

A year after marrying Calvin, Lydia has a dream in which Anna Thunder poses as Red Dress. Lydia is alert to Anna's designs on Calvin, and when Anna comes to their home a week later to put a spell on Calvin, Herod Small War is there, ready to counteract her with his own powers. Thwarted in her direct attempt to have

Calvin, Anna chooses a route of indirection. She puts a spell on the bed of Calvin and of his sister-in-law, Evie. The two unwillingly fall into an adulterous affair, which produces a son, Duane. Though Lydia knows that her husband and twin sister "had come together as a result of sinister medicine," she feels "as if the veins had been stripped from [her] arms, or [her] hair was lit, burning to the roots." She loses her "sense of smell and the ability to taste" but nonetheless takes in Duane as her own child when Evie refuses to care for him.

A month before her own son is born, Duane develops a hacking cough and is very fussy. Stressed and finally impatient, Lydia shouts to Calvin, "Please take your son and get out of my hair." When they are killed in a car wreck, Lydia stops speaking, fearful of the power of her words: "My throat burned and my tongue swelled. They said a drunk driver was responsible for the tragedy, but I knew it was my anger and the terrible power of my voice." From then on, Lydia thinks of herself as "Ini Naon Win. Silent Woman."

Her 17 years of self-imposed silence have a profound effect on her son Harley. In an effort to speak to her son without words, she works for several years on a traditional Dakota dress. Lydia "would never use her voice to tell Harley what he needed to hear. She would offer a story he could read with his eyes." When he reads the story of her dress, Lydia believes Harley "will finally know me and understand where he comes from." (Power 1994)

> See also *The Grass Dancer*; Many Wounds, Evelyn; Many Wounds, Margaret; Red Dress; Small War, Herod; Thunder, Anna (Mercury); Wind Soldier, Calvin; Wind Soldier, Harley.

Windzer, Challenge

Challenge Windzer is the main character in John Joseph Mathews's 1934 novel, *Sundown*. Though he was born at a time when the "god of the great Osages was still dominant over the wild prairie and the blackjack hills," he is a character who feels intense dislocation from his Osage culture. In naming him, his father says, "He shall be a challenge to the dis-inheritors of his people," but that prophecy does not come true.

Chal's childhood is one of both "contemplation and action." He has an artist's sensitivity to language and a strong imagination. He often daydreams that he is an animal—a coyote, a hawk, "an indefinite animal in a snug den under the dripping boughs of a tree." He experiences a painful longing to fly, "like the turkey vulture and the hawk," and has a "hopeless feeling of inferiority in being earthbound." He plays war as a child, staging battles between the hated English and the Americans. Sometimes he leads charges of "Osages and Sioux against the mythical tyranny of an England who was taking Indian land." Interestingly enough, he does not acknowledge that the Americans are taking Indian land even though the Osage lands are being aggressively, and often illegally, grasped by whites.

During Chal's childhood, his family is visited by a cousin who gives the boy some Sunday School picture cards. Chal is unnerved by the pictures of the Roman soldier thrusting a spear in the side of Christ. In a protective gesture toward the innocent Christ, Chal cuts the cruel soldiers from the picture with a butcher knife. His cousin Ellen catches him and explodes, "Little savage!" Ironically, the "little savage" is more moved by the cruelty of the soldiers and perhaps the very idea of crucifixion than his pious cousin Ellen.

Chal's school experiences provoke more uncertainties in the young boy. His teacher comes to Indian Territory "to teach little Indian minds. To see them open like flowers on their own beautiful prairie." Not a month later, though, the Quaker teacher abandons her sentimentalized version of Indians to a patronizing racism.

On the playground, other children bully him and call him "a little white gurl." Chal feels helpless to address the attacks until he remembers curse words that he has heard a freighter use. He feels the words "were mysteriously forceful and could vindicate him." As he grows, many of Chal's experiences continue to focus on language. He first imagines that the

"guv'mint" is a "great, bearded patriarch somewhere among the clouds, with outspread arms," but later feels that it "would be better to avoid it, as one might avoid the giant which the little white boy, Jack, had killed." When he hears the word "civilization," he gets the idea "that civilization was feminine . . . the most delicate white woman he could imagine; a composite of all the white women he had seen."

All the while that Chal is growing up, he feels a pull to his Osage heritage that manifests itself as an inarticulate pain. He enacts behaviors of the Osage before they became "civilized": he dances naked in a storm, singing war songs; he rides and swims until he is physically exhausted; once he even wears an eagle feather in his hair and paints his face, but is "so mortified that he could scarcely bathe the paint off fast enough," afraid that a cowboy would see him on the prairie. But his efforts at reconnecting to his Indian background cannot secure his identity.

When Chal enters college with his two traditional friends, Sun-on-His-Wings and Running Elk, he immediately recognizes that they will not fit into the college culture and that if he is to do so, it must be at the price of turning his back on them. In taking this first step at compromising his already unstable identity, Chal initiates a pattern of denials that soon leave him thoroughly decentered. Unable to balance his own identity and the expectations and prejudices that his friends have because he is an Indian, he finally utters, "I wish I didn't have a drop of God damn' Indian blood in my veins."

The advent of the war gives Chal a chance to escape his college life as well as live his dream of flying. He enlists and becomes a pilot. But all the while, he grows further and further estranged from his background. He is contemptuous of his family and friends and is happy to feel "separated by a great abyss from Sun-on-His-Wings and Running Elk, and from the village with the people moving among the lodges."

While in training, Chal develops a relationship with a married white woman. When she asks him, "Are you Spanish or something?" he agrees. Still, for all his attempts to deny his

Osage heritage, he cannot help but feel a superiority to white men. Once on a night flying mission, he looks below and thinks of "the millions of people below him as white men" and cannot suppress a smug smile.

Chal is still in the military when his father is killed, but soon after, he resigns his commission and returns home. Without any sense of direction and with plenty of inheritance and oil money, Chal flounders back home. He falls in with a rough crowd and drinks and idles away most of his days. Soon it is years that are passing, but Chal does little except "ride around in his long, powerful red roadster." One night, when he reaches a very low point, Chal dances in an attempt to reconnect to experiences from his childhood when he felt most Indian. The dance is a meaningless frenzy, though, which leads not to reconnection but to inefficacious cursing.

By the end of the novel, Chal is still inarticulate and locked in stasis. In a confrontation with his mother, he resents her intrusion and boastfully tells her that he will go to Harvard Law School and become an orator. But he then falls asleep, and it is uncertain whether he will ever move beyond his present state. (Hunter 1982a; Hunter 1982b; Mathews 1934, 1988; Owens 1992a)

See also Mathews, John Joseph; *Sundown*; Windzer, John.

Windzer, John

John Windzer is the father of the protagonist, Chal Windzer, in John Joseph Mathews's 1934 novel *Sundown*. He is a mixed-blood Osage who identifies more with his white heritage than with his Indian ancestors. He belongs to the group of progressives who want to assimilate into white culture rather than hold on to traditional ways. For instance, the traditional Osages want to maintain community ownership of their land, and they resist the movement toward allotment. Windzer is anxious for the land to be allotted to individuals so that the old Indian Agency might develop into a town. He is "almost continually thrilled" with the "atmosphere

of growth and progress." He serves on the council that pushes for and achieves allotment; only later when he has made a trip to Washington to discuss oil leases does Windzer realize that perhaps he has made a mistake.

Even though John Windzer embraces the new ways, he still does retain a slender thread of connection to his Osage heritage. Every night he would, "Indian-like, go out and look at the heavens before going to bed." But his connection to his Osage heritage is not strong enough to ground him or his son. When he is killed in a robbery, he is still a deeply divided character. (Hunter 1982a; Hunter 1982b; Mathews 1934, 1988; Owens 1992a)

See also Mathews, John Joseph; *Sundown*; Windzer, Challenge.

Winger, Tom

In John Milton Oskison's *Wild Harvest* (1925), Tom Winger is the cowboy suitor of the main character, Nan Forest. He works for Gabe Horner, a prominent cattleman from Texas. He is responsible and early recognizes his attraction to Nan. He grows confused when Ruby Engel tries to entrap his affections as a result of her jealousy of Nan. As a result of his flirtation with Ruby, he loses Nan to Harvey Stokes. In spite of his regret over his loss, he helps save Harvey from Buster Hayes. In the shootout between Hayes and Tom and his friends, Tom is shot in the arm. After the shoot-out, Nan recognizes that her earlier affections for Tom were genuine, and they marry. (Oskison 1925)

See also Engel, Ruby; Forest, Nancy; Stokes, Harvey; *Wild Harvest*.

Winter in the Blood

Winter in the Blood (1974, 1986), the first novel of Blackfeet/Gros Ventre writer James Welch, is the story of a nameless narrator and his quest for identity. When the novel opens, the narrator feels "as distant from [him]self as a hawk from the moon." The action begins when the narrator goes after his girlfriend who has left him. However, the narrator's fundamental problem is not merely a broken relationship with his girlfriend; he is more seriously disconnected from himself and his world as a result of the untimely deaths of his brother and father.

The novel opens with his return to his mother's home to find that the woman whom he had brought home some weeks earlier and whom his family believed to be his wife has disappeared with his razor and gun. The main object of the narrator as he goes in search of his razor and gun is not his possessions or even a restored relationship with Agnes; the necessary quest is an inward and backward one. The narrator must go inward to find who he was before he assumed unnecessary guilt over his brother Mose's death. He must go backward to understand and claim his heritage as the grandson of two extraordinary characters.

In speaking of Agnes, the narrator says, "The memory was more real than the experience." That condition is one that is present in all of his relationships, but the narrator has encouraged memories that do not square with reality and that, inevitably, become tyrannical. The journey of the narrator is to remember and then correct his memories. His mother, Teresa, starts the narrator on his journey by forcing him to realize the truth about the death of Amos, the duck. On his own, the narrator must remember and reconcile himself to the death of his brother Mose. He must relive the accident in its most painful detail in order to understand that Mose's death was not his fault.

Prompted by his mother to seek Agnes, the narrator halfheartedly goes into town. There he runs into a surrealistic character, the Airplane Man, who involves him in a series of adventures that further dislocate him from any sense of reality. It is only in his return home that he begins to find the answers that will sever him from his self-described fate as a "servant to the memory of death." He visits Yellow Calf and realizes in a moment of epiphany that Yellow Calf is his own grandfather. The knowledge causes him to reevaluate both his grandmother and mother. After his visit with Yellow Calf, he goes back to his mother's home, where he finds a cow stuck in a slough. With Bird, the horse,

he tries to save the cow; the scene is complicated for the narrator by his memory of the cow that precipitated the stampede that resulted in the death of Mose. Though he is unable to save the cow, he breaks through the frozen emotional state that has kept him in stasis for years. As he stands in a healing rain, he thinks, "Some people will never know how pleasant it is to be distant in a clean rain, the driving rain of a summer storm. It's not like you'd expect, nothing like you'd expect." The winter in his blood is thawed. (Barnett 1978; Owens 1992a; Velie 1994; Welch 1974, 1986)

See also The Airplane Man; Amos; Bird; First Raise, John; First Raise, Teresa; Lame Bull; Malvina; Mose; Welch, James; Yellow Calf.

Wissakodewinini, Pio

Pio Wissakodewinini is a "Parawoman mixed-blood mammoth clown" in Gerald Vizenor's *Bearheart: The Heirship Chronicles* (1978, 1990). When he was male, Pio was convicted of the rape of two white women. Though he denied the crime, he was forced to become a woman through hormone treatments. When the economic conditions went sour, there was not enough federal money to continue his hormone treatments, and he now searches for "a special tribal herb which would bring back to him her new woman dreams and voices." Ashamed of his "visible decline as a woman," he joins the pilgrim band. He becomes an important member of the group, helping them to gain entrance into the gambler's trailer in What Cheer, Iowa, and to liberate the witches in Ponca City.

Before Bishop Omax Parasimo is killed, he gives Pio his three metamasks; Pio is much relieved to once again be able to speak through a woman's persona. (Vizenor 1978, 1990)

See also *Bearheart: The Heirship Chronicles*; Parasimo, Bishop Omax.

Witchery

In Leslie Marmon Silko's *Ceremony* (1977, 1986), an interpolated mythic passage relates the story of the beginning of witchery. Witches from all over the world gather in a great contest of "dark things." After all have shown charms or powers, a final witch emerges from the shadows and only speaks a story. Amid the laughter of the others present, the witch warns that "as I tell the story / it will begin to happen." The telling of the story sets into motion the creation of a race of white people, a people of fear who are separated from the earth. The fearfulness of this race makes them easy prey to the powers of the witchery, and they become destroyers who kill or colonize all that they encounter. They believe the lie of violence and conquest, but in the process of destroying others, they also destroy themselves and the earth.

The power of witchery is unleashed with renewed force on the Laguna reservation, with the nearby atomic testing at White Sands and later, with the return of the veterans from World War II. Emo, Leroy, Harley, and Pinkie are consumed by the witchery, though Tayo resists it and even counters it with Betonie's ceremony, so that the penultimate page of the book declares in a fourfold chant, "It is dead for now." (Allen 1986; Lincoln 1983; Mitchell 1979; Owens 1992a; St. Andrews 1988)

See also Betonie; *Ceremony*; Emo; Harley; Ku'oosh; Silko, Leslie Marmon; Tayo.

The Woman Who Owned the Shadows

Paula Gunn Allen's *The Woman Who Owned the Shadows* (1983) is a novel of discovery and growth. The main character, Ephanie Atencio, is a young woman of Guadalupe Indian and white heritage who is seeking to understand whom she has become and the circumstances that determined her identity. The novel is a pastiche of literary techniques, including myth, letters, therapist's reports, and stream of consciousness. The story chronicles the experiences of Ephanie from her childhood relationship with her girlfriend, Elena, their growing awareness that they are falling in love, their first expressions of lesbian love, and Elena's withdrawal from the relationship. This loss, along with a remembered fall from an apple tree, is at the center of Ephanie's development and personal-

ity. The fall from the tree marks the movement from innocence to experience for Ephanie. Before she fell, she was at ease with her body; it willingly joined her spirit in adventures. But after the fall, Ephanie grows reserved and no longer trusting of the impulses "from the sweet spring of her own being."

The novel relates Ephanie's failed relationships with men. Her first marriage ends in divorce, and she is comforted and looked after by her cousin Stephen. Her two children are largely taken care of by her mother, and Ephanie has a period of freedom in which to find herself. She is betrayed by Stephen, though, when he has sex with her. Against her best instincts, she later marries a second-generation Japanese man, Thomas Yoshuri. The marriage ends in divorce after the birth of their twin sons, one of whom dies. The baby dies on a night that the parents decide to let him cry for a while, and the guilt and pain of his death last a long time. Though Ephanie suffers a mental breakdown and nearly commits suicide, in her growing friendship with a woman named Teresa and in her repository of cultural myth, she does have constants in her life.

Shadows play an important part in the novel. Allen describes the shadows as a positive thing, a metaphor for being mixed-blood. That the novel is entitled *The Woman Who Owned the Shadows* is significant, for it suggests that Ephanie finally comes to a place of ownership over her identity.

The Woman Who Owned the Shadows has many of the faults of a first novel, but nonetheless Allen's story of a young woman who locates her own self amid the clamorous voices of racism and sexism has merit. (Allen 1983a; Allen 1986; Allen 1987b; Hoffman 1984; Van Dyke 1990)

See also Allen, Paula Gunn.

Woven Stone

Simon Ortiz's volume *Woven Stone* (1992) is a collection of three of his earlier volumes that are out of print, *Going for the Rain* (1976), *A Good Journey* (1977), and *Fight Back: For the*

Sake of the People, for the Sake of the Land (1980). Ortiz includes a lengthy prose introduction that presents his thoughts on language, poetry, the oral tradition, and his own experiences growing up as a "child of colonialism."

Going for the Rain focuses on family, the land, a respect for all life, and the power of language. One poem in which all of these themes unite is "My Father's Song." As a boy, the poet and his father are planting corn, and they uncover the burrow of a mouse. The poet remembers: "I remember the very softness / of cool and warm sand and tiny alive / mice and my father saying things."

"Travels in the South" is a poetic rendering of Ortiz's desire to counter the myth of the vanishing Indian. He travels across the South, visiting Indians as he finds them. His journey not only proves the existence of Indians but also highlights the continuing belief in the myth of their disappearance by those who chose to ignore the presence of Indians, either historical or present. He is told by a park ranger, "'This place is noted for the Indians / that don't live here anymore.' / He didn't know who they used to be."

In *A Good Journey*, Ortiz makes an effort "to achieve the direct impact that spoken narrative has." He wants the reader-listener to assume "as much responsibility and commitment to poetic effect as the poet." This volume begins as *Going for the Rain* does, with a poem about Coyote, the trickster figure. Coyote gets into trouble but always bounces back. "Don't worry," the poet says. "He'll be back."

This volume also celebrates the ties to family and earth. In "Speaking," the poet introduces his son to the crickets, cicadas, and ants. As the son "murmurs infant words," the poet watches the "Tree leaves tremble. / They list to this boy / speaking for me."

In *Fight Back*, Ortiz moves to a more overtly political posture. Many of the poems focus on the uranium mines and the exploitation of Indian workers in the American Southwest. The second half of the volume moves to a blend of prose and poetry in which Ortiz gives a history of his home, Acoma Pueblo, and then continues to address the issues of exploitation. He writes:

> Only when the people of this nation, not just Indian people, fight for what is just and good for all life, will we know life and its continuance. And when we fight, and fight back those who are bent on destruction of land and people, we will win. We will win.

Woven Stone is too rich a volume to condense into summary remarks. Each section, each poem needs to be read and spoken and held in the mouth. Ortiz does achieve his goal of involving the reader in the oral nature of poetry. (Ortiz 1992; Wiget 1986)

See also Ortiz, Simon.

Y

Yellow Calf

In James Welch's *Winter in the Blood* (1974), Yellow Calf is a character who holds information that will secure the narrator's identity. He is a blind old man who is viewed with suspicion by the community. The narrator remembers that his father used to take him to visit Yellow Calf, but the motive or particulars of the visits are lost to him.

Yellow Calf is in tune with nature in a way that the narrator is not. He says that he speaks with the deer, and they have told him that they are not happy: "They are not happy with the way things are. They know what a bad time it is. They can tell by the moon when the world is cockeyed." By the end of the novel, the narrator learns that Yellow Calf is his own grandfather, the father of his mother and the hunter who saved his grandmother from starvation in the winter the Blackfeet died. The information provides the narrator with a place of stability and cultural identification that greatly assists him in coming to some sense of who he is. (Ballard 1991–1992; Owens 1992a; Ruoff 1978)

See also First Raise, John; Nameless Narrator; *Winter in the Blood.*

Yellow Kidney

In James Welch's 1986 novel, *Fools Crow*, Yellow Kidney is a respected warrior of the Lone Eaters band. He takes White Man's Dog, Fast Horse, and a group of young men on their first horse-taking raid. When Fast Horse boasts in the Crow camp and alerts the enemy, it is Yellow Kidney who suffers the consequences. He flees capture and enters a lodge, where he finds several young women. He hides under the robe of one of the girls and soon finds his passion stirred by her body. He enters her and realizes, to his horror, that the girl is in the late stages of smallpox. To his credit, Yellow Kidney later acknowledges that he was wrong to take advantage of the girl:

I had broken one of the simplest decencies by which people live. In fornicating with the dying girl, I had taken her honor, her opportunity to die virtuously. I had taken the path traveled only by the meanest of scavengers.

He flees the lodge of the dying young women and is captured by the Crows. Bull Shield, the

Crow chief, is merciless with him, and cuts his fingers off as an example to the Pikuni. Yellow Kidney is tied to a scrawny horse and sent out into a snowstorm, but he eventually finds his way back to the camp of the Lone Eaters.

Yellow Kidney finds it extremely difficult to adjust to his new life situation. He is no longer the respected warrior and hunter who provides for his family; he has become an object of pity. He does not reestablish relationships with his wife or children, and he passes his days in self-pity. Heavy Shield Woman and Mik-api long to help him but realize that unless he has the willingness to be helped, no healing ceremony will be effective. Yellow Kidney finally decides his usefulness is over, and he leaves the camp to seek his death. On his journey to the camp of the Spotted Horse People (Cheyenne), though, Yellow Kidney comes to realize that he still does have capabilities, that "he could do things if he did them deliberately and without haste." Six days away from the quiet pity of his own lodge, he "changed his thinking about himself." He believed that he could go back to his wife and children and live a useful life. As he seeks shelter from a blizzard in an old war lodge, he determines to live to see his grandson, and he wants to name him Yellow Calf.

In perhaps one of the more predictable ironies of the novel, Yellow Kidney is killed before he can return home. A white settler who is still stinging from the brutal treatment of his rancher friends longs for vengeance. His friend, Frank Standley, has been killed, and Standley's wife has been beaten and raped by Owl Child and his gang. "I want to kill an Indian," the settler thinks as he seeks shelter from a storm in a war lodge. Yellow Kidney is the unlucky recipient of the settler's rage. (Ballard 1991; Barry 1991–1992; Murphree 1994; Owens 1992a)

See also Fast Horse; *Fools Crow*; Heavy Shield Woman; Mik-api; White Man's Dog.

A Yellow Raft in Blue Water

This 1987 first novel by Michael Dorris features the narrative voices of three generations of women. All narrations are in the first person, and Dorris does a remarkable job of capturing the voices of three very different women. The first voice is Rayona Taylor, a 15-year-old girl who has largely had to make her own way in the difficult landscape of her parents' dysfunctional marriage. Her mother, Christine Taylor, is the second voice, and her narration goes a significant way toward mitigating the damage done to her character by Rayona's account. The third and final account is the voice of Aunt Ida, the woman who raised Christine and whom Christine believes to be her mother. Again, the revelations of another narrator answer the nagging questions, address the stated and implied blame, and present a more generous delineation of character than that which is given by the voices of the first two women. It is not that Rayona and Christine are malicious; rather, they are ignorant of all the threads that contribute to the construction of their life tapestry.

The novel opens with all the ingredients of a tragedy. Christine is sick in a Seattle hospital and decides that her life is worthless, that she would be better off dead. She tells Rayona, "We're broke. We owe two months back rent on that lousy apartment. My unemployment is expired and I'm tired of finding two-bit jobs. I'm past forty years old and my husband wants to ditch me and marry some Arletta." Christine leaves the hospital, planning to commit suicide in a park in Tacoma where she and her husband, Elgin, fell in love and conceived Rayona. Rayona is able to convince her to abandon the plan, and they decide to go to Christine's home on the reservation in Montana.

The return home is risky for Christine. She has not been home since the funeral of her brother, Lee, over a dozen years ago, and she and Aunt Ida have never been on good terms. One of their points of contention is that her mother has always insisted on being called "Aunt Ida," and Christine understands that as a deliberate distancing and rejection. Christine and Rayona arrive at the reservation, and within ten minutes, Christine and Aunt Ida are at odds. Christine leaves in a huff, abandoning Rayona to a grandmother she barely knows. It is not until Father Hurlburt, the parish priest, comes to visit that Rayona learns that her mother is not back in Seattle but living on the reservation with an old acquaintance named Dayton Nickles. Father Hurlburt arranges for Rayona to meet other young people and the priest in charge of the God Squad, Father Tom Novak.

As a mixed-blood Indian and African American and as the daughter of Christine, Rayona finds it difficult to fit in on the reservation. Though Father Tom is the "last one on the reservation" that Rayona wants to be friends with, it is clear that he has made her his "special project." He arranges to take her to Helena to the "Teens for Christ Jamboree" and on the drive pushes her to discuss sexual issues. When they stop for a break at Bearpaw Lake State Park and take a swim, Father Tom gropes Rayona. In his eagerness to protect himself should anyone find out, Father Tom is more than happy to abort the Teens for Christ Jamboree and put Rayona on a bus straight back to Seattle, where she has told him her father lives.

Rayona's desire to leave the reservation is fueled by more than Father Tom's attack. Her mother has never established contact with her since leaving her at Aunt Ida's, but just days before the trip to the jamboree, Christine did go back to Ida's to pick up a package of medicine that had been delivered to her there. Rayona doesn't know that Christine is dangerously ill and that she is avoiding her daughter, not because she doesn't love her but to protect Rayona from her imminent death. The experience with Father Tom and this second apparent rejection by her mother convince Rayona to make her own way in the world. She does not go back to Seattle to a father who has never taken much interest in her; instead, she stays at Bearpaw Lake State Park and gets a job with the cleanup crew. She makes friends there with a childless couple, Evelyn and Sky Dial, though she lies to them about her family. As the summer and their friendship progress, Rayona shares her recent history. Rayona suspects that her mother will be at the Fourth of July rodeo in Havre, Montana, and Evelyn and Sky take her there to be reunited with her family.

Christine opens her narrative by describing herself as "the bastard daughter of a woman who wouldn't even admit she was my mother and the fat sister of the prettiest boy that ever lived." Her life is defined by these two relationships, and in each of them she sees herself as lacking. When her brother Lee George becomes best friends with Dayton Nickles, Christine tries to interrupt the relationship, certain that she is losing Lee. When Lee graduates from high school, Christine shames him into going into the military even though he is politically opposed to the Vietnam War. And when Lee is killed in Vietnam, Christine is held responsible by the silent and disapproving community. By that time, Christine has moved to Seattle, married, and had a child. But her marriage to Elgin Taylor is in trouble from the start. They cannot maintain a stable and committed relationship, and Christine raises Rayona largely by herself.

In her narrative, Christine also reveals the event that caused her to lose her faith. When she was 15 years old, the nuns at her school told of the letter given to Lucy of Fatima by the Blessed Virgin that supposedly predicted either the conversion of communist Russia or the end of the world. Christine declines the first party invitation she has ever received so she can be prepared for the end of the world on New Year's Eve. When nothing happens, Christine feels she has been duped by the nuns and by God.

The third narrative, Ida George's, is the most moving and most authentic. Her account is not cluttered with the popular culture of Rayona's or the tangled self-absorption and victimhood of Christine's. Her story cuts to the heart of human sacrifice and suffering. Her life is determined by choices she made as a young woman, and the life that unfolds before her turns out to be almost more than she can bear.

Ida begins her story with the declaration, "I never grew up, but I got old." Certainly Ida does forfeit her young life, when at age 18, she is asked by her father to take responsibility for the illegitimate baby that is born to him and his sister-in-law. The story begins with the illness of Ida's mother and the arrival of her sister Clara. Clara is to nurse her sister and help with the household, but she and Ida's father begin a relationship that results in her pregnancy. With Ida's agreement, the family decides to send Clara and Ida to Denver during the pregnancy and to say that the baby is Ida's when they return. The agreement becomes burdensome in ways that Ida did not anticipate. She grows to love Christine and is alarmed when Clara tries to take the baby away. Father Hurlburt joins Ida in securing a birth certificate that says she is Christine's mother. Ida's love for Christine is always overshadowed by her fear that Clara will return and secure her affections.

Later Ida comes to love Willard Pretty Dog and has a son by him. Pretty Dog does not understand or value Ida, thinking of her only as a dutiful and unintelligent drudge. In one of her first acts of self-assertion, Ida separates herself from Pretty Dog's condescension and raises her two children alone. She never tells either Christine or Lee the circumstances of their origins, and Christine, especially, is always troubled by what she perceives as Ida's preference for Lee. In actuality, Ida loves both of the children but cannot bear to speak her love aloud for fear that she will lose them.

For all the misunderstandings of the three women, the novel ends on a note of promise. Ida and Christine have a moment of reconciliation and a shared anxiety over Rayona's absence. And there is every indication that Ida will share the secrets of two generations with Rayona. Dorris's narrative comes to us with the faintness of an echo, and the reader's journey through the generations of three fascinating women is the journey back to the origin of the voice. (Broyard 1987; Dorris 1987; Owens 1992a)

See also Cree, Kennedy (Foxy); Dial, Evelyn and Sky; Dorris, Michael; Father Hurlburt; Father Tom Novak; George, Ida; George, Lee; Nickles, Dayton; Pretty Dog, Willard; Taylor, Christine; Taylor, Elgin; Taylor, Rayona; *A Yellow Raft in Blue Water*.

Yoeme

Yoeme is a character in Leslie Marmon Silko's *Almanac of the Dead* (1991). She is the grand-mother of the twins, Lecha and Zeta. A Yaqui Indian, she married Guzman, the white man who came to their village to exploit the people, land, and natural resources. Yoeme married him not out of love, but to safeguard the agreements the encroaching white men had made with her community. Cryptic family stories about her center around cottonwood trees, and she tells the full story to her granddaughters. Her husband used Indian slave labor to transport cottonwood trees hundreds of miles so that they might be transplanted around his plantation and mines. The trees were watered and cared for better than the slaves who were responsible for them. One day Yoeme returned home to see the bodies of her clanspeople hanging from the trees. Determined that Guzman would kill no more Indians, Yoeme ordered three gardeners to cut all the trees they could and girdle the rest so that they would soon die too. She then took the silver from under Guzman's bed and fled to the mountains. She left behind the seven children she had borne Guzman, for they all showed signs of his moral weaknesses. From time to time she returned to see if she had gained any grandchildren that "might have turned out human." On one such trip, she recognizes that Lecha and Zeta are such children. She stays and begins their instruction. Later, it is to these twins that Yoeme gives the gift of stories and of the sacred notebooks that chronicle the history of their people.

Always a revolutionary, Yoeme has had a bounty placed on her scalp by the Mexican government. Once she was captured and scheduled to be hanged, but an influenza epidemic rendered her captors too ill to carry out the sentence. She was freed by clanspeople, and her legendary status only increased throughout the years. Yoeme steadfastly believes that the "almanac had living power within it, a power that would bring all the tribal people of the Americas together to retake the land." According to her, the earth will continue in spite of what people do to it, but the "humans might not survive." (Silko 1991)

See also *Almanac of the Dead*; Lecha; Zeta.

Zeta

Zeta is a character in Leslie Marmon Silko's *Almanac of the Dead* (1991). She and her twin sister Lecha arrived in Tucson at age 14 when their mother died and they were sent to their father. Their parents separated when the girls were only four years old, and they had never really known their German geologist father, who was already 60 when they were born. He sent Zeta and Lecha to El Paso to a school run by nuns, and then he died in the hotel room where he met them. He left them the ranch that Zeta uses as her base of operations for her smuggling business. Her partner in the operation is her nephew Ferro, whom she has raised since Lecha abandoned him at one week old.

Zeta works for a time with Mexico Tours and its owner, Mr. Coco. She learns the business from him and then leaves him as soon as she is able to start her own business, but not before he uses her sexually and gives her a sense of power that comes from having control over men through her body. She takes his smuggling business a step further and moves from the fake Rolexes and pottery he takes across the border in a tour bus to artifacts of all kinds, including figurines, carved stone, jade axes, and knives. Soon she begins smuggling drugs and weapons as well.

Yoeme does not approve of Zeta's smuggling business, for she sees it as one more example of the exploitation of the people she is hoping to free from capitalistic oppressors. In response, Zeta becomes proficient at mocking Yoeme's theories about the illegality of European governments in the Americas. Despite their fundamental differences, Zeta takes seriously her responsibility of transcribing the one section of the almanac that Yoeme has given her.

Zeta calls herself "an enemy of the United States government." Near the end of the book, she kills the racist arms dealer, Greenlee, and gathers data from his office to aid Awa Gee in his computer shutdown of electricity to the United States. (Silko 1991)

See also *Almanac of the Dead*; Calabazas; Ferro; Lecha; Yoeme.

Zitkala-Ša

A Yankton Sioux, Zitkala-Ša was born on the Yankton reservation in South Dakota on February 22, 1876, as Gertrude Simmons. Gertrude's father was a white man named Felker who deserted the family before her birth; her mother gave her the last name of her second husband, Simmons. Her early childhood was spent on the reservation with her mother and

Gertrude Bonnin, or Zitkala-Ša, appearing in the front row, holding her hat, with fellow members of the Society of American Indians on the steps of the Carnegie Library in Cedar Rapids, 29 September 1916. (Reproduced from The Quarterly Journal of the Society of American Indians, *Vol. IV, No. 3, July–September, 1916)*

seems to have been happy. At age eight, how-ever, young Gertrude was encouraged by mis-sionaries to seek an education at White's Manual Institute in Wabash, Indiana. She left the res-ervation, and in doing so, left a way of life for-ever behind her. Three years later, when she was allowed home for her first visit, she already felt the tensions created and exacerbated by assimi-lation into the culture and religion of the white world. After four years back in the West—in-cluding a one-year enrollment at the Santee Normal Training School in Nebraska— Simmons returned east to White's until 1895 and later attended Earlham College in Rich-mond, Indiana, where she studied for two more years. Her time at Earlham was a mixture of professional success and personal humiliation. She polished her skills in oratory, poetry, and music, but she was never truly free from racial

discrimination. In the Indiana State Oratorical Contest of 1896, in which she won second prize, Simmons endured the presence of an inflammatory banner on which was emblazoned the word "squaw" and an uncharitable image of herself.

After leaving Earlham, Simmons went to work at the Carlisle Indian Industrial School in Carlisle, Pennsylvania, in 1898, where she taught and played in the orchestra. During her years at Carlisle, Simmons started writing au-tobiographical essays, which were published under her new, self-given name, Zitkala-Ša (Lakota for "Red Bird"), in leading American magazines, including *Harper's Magazine* and *Atlantic Monthly*. The stories were later collected in the volume *American Indian Stories* and were published in 1921. She also wrote down many legends she had heard in her childhood, and these were published in 1901 as *Old Indian Legends.*

Her increasing criticism of the policy of assimilation of the Indians flew in the face of Carlisle ideology, and when she left there in 1902, it was to return to the Yankton reservation to gather more stories from her culture. That year also saw her marriage to Raymond T. Bonnin, another Yankton Sioux, who worked with the Indian Service (a precursor to the Bureau of Indian Affairs). In that year they were assigned to the Uintah Ouray Ute Agency in Duchesne, Utah, where they lived and worked until 1916, when they moved to Washington, D.C.

After her marriage to Bonnin, Zitkala-Ša did not write any longer, excepting her collaboration with William Hanson of Brigham Young University in the production of an opera featuring native melodies, called *The Sun Dance Opera.* The show had several successful productions in Utah and later was selected by the New York Light Opera Guild for production in New York City in 1938.

The Bonnins had one son, Raymond Ohiya, born in 1903. During the years the Bonnins spent in Utah, Zitkala-Ša devoted her attention to political matters of interest to the Native American communities. She became affiliated with the Society of American Indians (SAI) and was elected secretary of the organization in 1916. The new position took her and her family to Washington, D.C., where she and her husband continued to be involved in lobbying for rights of Native Americans for many years. In 1926, she and her husband formed the National Congress of American Indians (NCAI), of which she was the single president until her death in 1938. (Fisher 1985; Hafen 1996; Krupat 1994; Picotte 1985)

See also *American Indian Stories.*

Bibliography

Alexie, Sherman. *The Business of Fancydancing.* Brooklyn: Hanging Loose Press, 1992.

———. *Indian Killer.* New York: Atlantic Monthly Press, 1996.

———. *The Lone Ranger and Tonto Fistfight in Heaven.* 1993. New York: HarperPerennial, 1994.

———. *Reservation Blues.* New York: Warner Books, 1995.

Allen, Paula Gunn. "The Autobiography of a Confluence." In Brian Swann and Arnold Krupat, eds., *I Tell You Now: Autobiographical Essays by Native American Writers.* Lincoln: University of Nebraska Press, 1987a, pp. 141–154.

———. "I Climb the Mesas in My Dreams." In Joseph Bruchac, ed., *Survival This Way: Interviews with American Indian Poets.* Tucson: University of Arizona Press, 1987b, pp. 1–21.

———. Interview. In William Balassi, John F. Crawford, and Annie O. Eysturoy, eds., *This Is about Vision: Interviews with Southwestern Writers.* Albuquerque: University of New Mexico Press, 1990a, pp. 95–107.

———. Interview. In Laura Coltelli, ed., *Winged Words: American Indian Writers Speak.* Lincoln: University of Nebraska Press, 1990b, pp. 11–39.

———. "The Psychological Landscape of *Ceremony.*" *American Indian Quarterly* 5 (1979): 7–12.

———. *The Sacred Hoop: Recovering the Feminine in American Indian Traditions.* Boston: Beacon Press, 1986.

———. *The Woman Who Owned the Shadows.* San Francisco: Spinsters' Ink, 1983a.

Allen, Paula Gunn, ed. *Studies in American Indian Literature.* New York: MLA, 1983b.

Apess, William. *The Experiences of Five Christian Indians of the Pequot Tribe.* Boston: James B. Dow, 1833.

Babcock, Barbara, and Jay Cox. "The Native American Trickster." In Andrew Wiget, ed., *Dictionary of Native American Literature.* New York: Garland Publishing, 1994, pp. 99–105.

Bak, Hans. "Toward a Native American 'Realism': The Amphibious Fiction of Louise Erdrich." In Kristiaan Versluys, ed., *Neo-Realism in Contemporary American Fiction.* Amsterdam: Rodopi, 1992.

Balassi, William, John F. Crawford, and Annie O. Eysturoy, eds. *This Is about Vision: Interviews with Southwestern Writers.* Albuquerque: University of New Mexico Press, 1990.

Ballard, Charles G. "The Question of Survival in *Fools Crow.*" *North Dakota Quarterly* 59 (1991): 251–259.

———. "The Theme of the Helping Hand in *Winter in the Blood.*" *MELUS* 17 (1991–1992): 63–74.

Ballinger, Franchot. "Carter Revard." In Andrew Wiget, ed., *Dictionary of Native American Literature.* New York: Garland Publishing, 1994, pp. 491–494.

Barnes, Jim. "On Native Ground." In Brian Swann and Arnold Krupat, eds., *I Tell You Now: Autobiographical Essays by Native American Writers.* Lincoln: University of Nebraska Press, 1987, pp. 85–97.

Barnett, Louise K. "Alienation and Ritual in *Winter in the Blood.*" *American Indian Quarterly* 4 (1978): 123–130.

Barry, Nora. "'A Myth to Be Alive': James Welch's *Fools Crow.*" *MELUS* 17 (1991–1992): 3–20.

Barry, Nora, and Mary Prescott. "The Triumph of the Brave: *Love Medicine's* Holistic Vision." *Critique: Studies in Modern Fiction* 30, no. 2 (1989): 123–138.

Bear Don't Walk, Scott. "McNickle, D'Arcy." In Frederick E. Hoxie, ed., *Encyclopedia of North American Indians.* Boston: Houghton Mifflin, 1996, pp. 369–370.

Bell, Betty Louise. *Faces in the Moon.* Norman: University of Oklahoma Press, 1994.

Bell, Robert C. "Circular Design in *Ceremony.*" *American Indian Quarterly* 5 (1979): 47–62.

Bird, Gloria. "Searching for Evidence of Colonialism at Work: A Reading of Louise Erdrich's *Tracks.*" *Wicazo Sa Review* 8, no. 2 (1992): 40–47.

Blaeser, Kimberly M. *Trailing You.* New York: Greenfield Review Press, 1994.

Bovey, Seth. "Whitehorns and Blackhorns: Images of Cattle Ranching in the Novels of James Welch." *South Dakota Review* 29 (1991): 129–139.

Brave Bird, Mary, with Richard Erdoes. *Ohitika Woman.* New York: Grove Press, 1993. New York: HarperPerennial, 1994.

Brown, Alanna K. "Mourning Dove." In Andrew Wiget, ed., *Dictionary of Native American Literature.* New York: Garland Publishing, 1994, pp. 259–264.

Broyard, Anatole. "Eccentricity Was All They Could Afford." Review of *A Yellow Raft in Blue Water,* by Michael Dorris. *New York Times Book Review,* 7 June 1987, p. 7.

Bruchac, Joseph. "Notes of a Translator's Son." In Brian Swann and Arnold Krupat, eds., *I Tell You Now: Autobiographical Essays by Native American Writers.* Lincoln: University of Nebraska Press, 1987a, pp. 195–205.

Bruchac, Joseph, ed. *Survival This Way: Interviews with American Indian Poets.* Tucson: University of Arizona Press, 1987b.

Brumble, H. David III. *American Indian Autobiography.* Berkeley: University of California Press, 1988.

Brumble, H. David III, and Arnold Krupat. "Autobiography." In Andrew Wiget, ed., *Dictionary of Native American Literature.* New York: Garland Publishing, 1994, pp. 175–183.

Catt, Catherine M. "Ancient Myth in Modern America: The Trickster in the Fiction of Louise Erdrich." *Platte Valley Review* 19, no. 1 (1991): 71–81.

Chavkin, Allan, and Nancy Feyl Chavkin. "An Interview with Michael Dorris." In Chavkin and Chavkin, eds., *Conversations with Louise Erdrich and Michael Dorris.* Jackson: University Press of Mississippi, 1994a, pp. 184–219.

Chavkin, Allan, and Nancy Feyl Chavkin, eds. *Conversations with Louise Erdrich and Michael Dorris.* Jackson: University Press of Mississippi, 1994b.

Cheuse, Alan. "Dead Reckoning." Review of *Almanac of the Dead* by Leslie Marmon Silko. *Chicago Tribune—Books,* 1 December 1991, p. 3.

Child, Brenda J. "Boarding Schools." In Frederick E. Hoxie, ed., *Encyclopedia of North American Indians.* Boston: Houghton Mifflin, 1996, pp. 78–80.

Childress, Mark. "A Gathering of Widows." *New York Times Book Review* 101 (12 May 1996): 10, 11.

Coltelli, Laura. *Winged Words: American Indian Writers Speak.* Lincoln: University of Nebraska Press, 1990.

Contemporary Authors. Vol. 136. Detroit: Gale Research, 1992a.

———. Vol. 137. Detroit: Gale Research, 1992b.

———. Vol. 145. Detroit: Gale Research, 1995a.

———. Vol. 146. Detroit: Gale Research, 1995b.

————. Vol. 147. Detroit: Gale Research, 1995c.

————, *New Revision Series*. Vol. 47. Detroit: Gale Research, 1995c.

Cook-Lynn, Elizabeth. Review of *The Broken Cord* by Michael Dorris. *Wicazo Sa Review* 5, no. 2 (1989): 42–45.

————. "You May Consider Speaking about Your Art . . ." In Brian Swann and Arnold Krupat, eds., *I Tell You Now: Autobiographical Essays by Native American Writers*. Lincoln: University of Nebraska Press, 1987, pp. 55–63.

Copway, George. *The Life, History, and Travels of Kah-ge-ga-gah-bowh (George Copway), A Young Indian Chief of the Ojebwa Nation, A Convert to the Christian Faith, and a Missionary to His People for Twelve Years*. Albany, NY: Weed and Parsons, 1847.

————. *The Traditional History and Characteristic Sketches of the Ojibway Nation*. London: Charles Gilpin, 1850.

Crawford, John, and Patricia Clark Smith. "Joy Harjo." In William Balassi, John F. Crawford, and Annie O. Eysturoy, eds., *This Is about Vision: Interviews with Southwestern Writers*. Albuquerque: University of New Mexico Press, 1990, pp. 171–179.

Croft, Georgia. "Something Ventured." In Allan Chavkin and Nancy Feyl Chavkin, eds., *Conversations with Louise Erdrich and Michael Dorris*. Jackson: University Press of Mississippi, 1994, pp. 86–93.

Crow Dog, Mary, with Richard Erdoes. *Lakota Woman*. 1990. New York: HarperPerennial, 1991.

Cutter, Martha J. "Zitkala-Ša's Autobiographical Writings: The Problems of a Canonical Search for Language and Identity." *MELUS* 19 (1994): 31–44.

Dannenberg, Anne Marie. "'Where, Then, Shall We Place the Hero of the Wilderness?' William Apess's *Eulogy on King Philip* and Doctrines of Racial Destiny." In Helen Jaskoski, ed., *Early Native American Writing: New Critical Essays*. Cambridge: Cambridge University Press, 1996, pp. 66–82.

Deloria, Ella Cara. *Waterlily*. Lincoln: University of Nebraska Press, 1988.

Deloria, Philip J. "Deloria, Ella (Anpetu Waste)." In Frederick E. Hoxie, ed., *Encyclopedia of North American Indians*. Boston: Houghton Mifflin, 1996, pp. 159–161.

Deloria, Vine, Jr. Introduction. In John Neihardt, ed., *Black Elk Speaks*. 1932. Lincoln: University of Nebraska Press, 1988, pp. xi–xiv.

DeMallie, Raymond J. Afterword. In Ella Cara Deloria, *Waterlily*. Lincoln: University of Nebraska Press, 1988, pp. 233–244.

DeMallie, Raymond J., ed. *The Sixth Grandfather: Black Elk's Teachings Given to John G. Neihardt*. Foreword by Hilda Neihardt Petri. Lincoln: University of Nebraska Press, 1984.

Dorris, Michael. "A Dynamic First Effort That Proves to Be the Real Thing." Review of *The Grass Dancer* by Susan Power. *Los Angeles Times*, 4 August 1994, p. E7.

————. *A Yellow Raft in Blue Water*. New York: Henry Holt, 1987.

Dyk, Walter. Preface. In Walter Dyk, recorder, *Left Handed, Son of Old Man Hat: A Navajo Autobiography*. 1938. Lincoln: University of Nebraska Press, 1995.

Eastman, Charles A. *Indian Boyhood*. 1902. New York: Dover, 1971.

————. *The Soul of the Indian*. 1911. Lincoln: University of Nebraska Press, 1980.

Elliott, Michael. "'This Indian Bait': Samson Occom and the Voice of Liminality." *Early American Literature* 29 (1994): 233–253.

Erdrich, Louise. *The Antelope Wife*. New York: HarperFlamingo/HarperCollins, 1998.

————. *The Beet Queen*. New York: Henry Holt, 1986.

————. *The Bingo Palace*. New York: Harper-Collins, 1994.

————. "Interview with Louise Erdrich." By Jan George. *North Dakota Quarterly* 53 (1985): 240–246.

————. *Jacklight*. New York: Henry Holt, 1984.

————. "Louise Erdrich and Michael Dorris: A Marriage of Minds." By Michael Schumacher. *Writer's Digest* (June 1991): 28.

————. *Love Medicine: The New and Expanded Version*. New York: Henry Holt, 1993. (First published in 1984.)

———. *Tales of Burning Love*. New York: HarperCollins, 1996.

———. *Tracks*. New York: Henry Holt, 1988.

———. "Whatever Is Really Yours: An Interview with Louise Erdrich." In Joseph Bruchac, ed., *Survival This Way: Interviews with American Indian Poets*. Tucson: University of Arizona Press, 1987, pp. 73–86.

Evers, Larry. "Cycles of Appreciation." In Paula Gunn Allen, ed., *Studies in American Indian Literature*. New York: MLA, 1983, pp. 23–32.

Evers, Lawrence J. "Words and Place: A Reading of *House Made of Dawn*. In Andrew Wiget, ed., *Critical Essays on Native American Literature*. Boston: G. K. Hall, 1985, pp. 211–230.

Fewkes, J. Walter. "Report of the Chief." Fortieth Annual Report of the Bureau of American Ethnology. Washington, D.C.: Smithsonian Institution, 1925, pp. 1–20.

Fisher, Dexter. Foreword. In Zitkala-Ša, *American Indian Stories*. Lincoln: University of Nebraska Press, 1985.

———. Introduction. In Mourning Dove, *Cogewea, the Half Blood: A Depiction of the Great Montana Cattle Range*. 1927. Lincoln: University of Nebraska Press, 1981.

———. *The Third Woman: Minority Women Writers of the United States*. Boston: Houghton Mifflin, 1980.

Flavin, James. "The Novel as Performance: Communication in Louise Erdrich's *Tracks*." *Studies in American Indian Literatures* 3, no. 4 (1991): 1–12.

Flavin, Louise. "Louise Erdrich's *Love Medicine*: Loving over Time and Distance." *Critique: Studies in Modern Fiction* 31 (1989): 55–64.

Furman, Jan. Review of *Other Destinies: Understanding the Native American Novel* by Louis Owens. *American Literature* 66 (1994): 202–203.

Geiogamah, Hanay. *New Native American Drama: Three Plays*. Norman: University of Oklahoma Press, 1980.

"Ghost Dance." In Frederick E. Hoxie, ed., *Encyclopedia of North American Indians*. Boston: Houghton Mifflin, 1996, p. 223.

Givens, Bettye. "Interview: N. Scott Momaday— A Slant of Light." *MELUS* 12 (1985): 79–87.

Glancy, Diane. *Claiming Breath*. Lincoln: University of Nebraska Press, 1992.

———. "The Cold-and-Hunger Dance." *Contemporary Authors Autobiography Series*. Vol. 24. Detroit: Gale Research, 1996, pp. 199–215.

———. "Two Dresses." In Brian Swann and Arnold Krupat, eds., *I Tell You Now: Autobiographical Essays by Native American Writers*. Lincoln: University of Nebraska Press, 1987, pp. 167–183.

Gleason, William. "'Her Laugh an Ace': The Function of Humor in Louise Erdrich's *Love Medicine*." *American Indian Culture and Research Journal* 11, no. 3 (1987): 51–73.

Gustafson, Sandra. "Nations of Israelites: Prophecy and Cultural Autonomy in the Writings of William Apess." *Religion and Literature* 26 (1994): 31–53.

Hafen, P. Jane. "Zitkala-Ša." In Frederick E. Hoxie, ed., *Encyclopedia of North American Indians*. Boston: Houghton Mifflin, 1996.

Hans, Birgit. "(William) D'Arcy McNickle." In Andrew Wiget, ed., *Dictionary of Native American Literature*. New York: Garland Publishing, 1994, pp. 251–258.

Hanson, Elizabeth I. *Forever There: Race and Gender in Contemporary Native American Fiction*. New York: Peter Lang, 1989.

Harjo, Joy. "Ordinary Spirit." In Brian Swann and Arnold Krupat, eds., *I Tell You Now: Autobiographical Essays by Native American Writers*. Lincoln: University of Nebraska Press, 1987, pp. 263–270.

———. *She Had Some Horses*. New York: Thunder's Mouth Press, 1983.

Henry, Gordon D., Jr. *The Light People*. Norman: University of Oklahoma Press, 1994.

Herzog, Kristin. "Thinking Woman and Feeling Man: Gender in Silko's *Ceremony*." *MELUS* 12 (1985): 25–36.

Hirsch, Bernard A. "Self-Hatred and Spiritual Corruption in *House Made of Dawn*." *Western American Literature* 17 (1983): 307–320.

———. "'The Telling Which Continues': Oral Tradition and the Written Word in Leslie Marmon Silko's *Storyteller*." *American Indian Quarterly* 12, no. 1 (1988): 1–26.

Hittman, Michael. "Wovoka (Jack Wilson)." In Frederick E. Hoxie, ed., *Encyclopedia of North American Indians*. Boston: Houghton Mifflin, 1996, pp. 700–702.

Hoefel, Roseanne. "Gendered Cartography: Mapping the Mind of Female Characters in D'Arcy McNickle's *The Surrounded*." *SAIL: Studies in American Indian Literatures*, 2d ser. 10 (1998): 45–64.

Hoffman, Alice. "Ephanie's Ghosts." *The New York Times Book Review*, 3 June 1984, p. 18.

Hogan, Linda. Interview. In Laura Coltelli, ed., *Winged Words: American Indian Writers Speak*. Lincoln: University of Nebraska Press, 1990a, pp. 71–86.

———. *Mean Spirit*. New York: Atheneum, 1990b.

———. "To Take Care of Life." In Joseph Bruchac, ed., *Survival This Way: Interviews with American Indian Poets*. Tucson: University of Arizona Press, 1987a, pp. 119–133.

———. "The Two Lives." In Brian Swann and Arnold Krupat, eds., *I Tell You Now: Autobiographical Essays by Native American Writers*. Lincoln: University of Nebraska Press, 1987b, pp. 231–249.

Holton, Robert. "The Politics of Point of View: Representing History in Mourning Dove's *Cogewea* and D'Arcy McNickle's *The Surrounded*." *SAIL: Studies in American Indian Literatures*, 2d ser. 9 (1997): 69–80.

Hoxie, Frederick E., ed. *Encyclopedia of North American Indians*. Boston: Houghton Mifflin, 1996.

Hunt, John. "John Joseph Mathews." In Frederick E. Hoxie, ed., *Encyclopedia of North American Indians*. Boston: Houghton Mifflin, 1996, pp. 363–365.

Hunter, Carol. "The Historical Context in John Joseph Mathews' *Sundown*." *MELUS* 9 (1982a): 61–72.

———. "The Protagonist as a Mixed-Blood in John Joseph Mathews' Novel: *Sundown*." *American Indian Quarterly* 6 (1982b): 319–337.

Huntsman, Jeffrey. Introduction. In Hanay Geiogamah, *New Native American Drama: Three Plays*. Norman: University of Oklahoma Press, 1980, pp. ix–xxiv.

Hylton, Marion W. "On a Trail of Pollen: Momaday's *House Made of Dawn*." *Critique: Studies in Modern Fiction* 14 (1972): 60–69.

Jahner, Elaine. "An Act of Attention: Event Structure in *Ceremony*." *American Indian Quarterly* 5 (1979): 37–46.

———. "The Novel and Oral Tradition: An Interview with Leslie Marmon Silko." *Book Forum* 5, no. 3 (1981): 383–388.

Jaimes, M. Annette. "The Disharmonic Convergence." Review of *Almanac of the Dead* by Leslie Marmon Silko. *The Bloomsbury Review*, April–May 1992, p. 5.

Janke, Ronald A. "Population, Reservations, and Federal Indian Policy." In Andrew Wiget, ed., *Dictionary of Native American Literature*. New York: Garland Publishing, 1994, pp. 155–173.

Jaskoski, Helen. "Image and Silence." In Kenneth M. Roemer, ed., *Approaches to Teaching Momaday's The Way to Rainy Mountain*. New York: MLA, 1988, pp. 69–77.

———. "A *MELUS* Interview: Joy Harjo." *MELUS* 16 (1989–1990): 5–13.

Johnson, Sue M. "Hanay Geiogamah." In Andrew Wiget, ed., *Dictionary of Native American Literature*. New York: Garland Publishing, 1994, pp. 431–435.

King, Tom. "A *MELUS* Interview: N. Scott Momaday—Literature and the Native Writer." *MELUS* 10 (1983): 66–72.

Krupat, Arnold. Review of *Other Destinies: Understanding the Native American Novel* by Louis Owens. *Journal of American History* 80 (1993): 1089–1090.

———. *The Turn to the Native: Studies in Criticism and Culture*. Lincoln: University of Nebraska Press, 1996.

Krupat, Arnold, ed. *Native American Autobiography: An Anthology*. Madison: University of Wisconsin Press, 1994.

Lame Deer, John (Fire), and Richard Erdoes. *Lame Deer, Seeker of Visions: The Life of a Sioux Medicine Man*. New York: Simon and Schuster, 1972.

Larson, Charles R. *American Indian Fiction*. Albuquerque: University of New Mexico Press, 1978.

———. "The Jungles of the Mind." Review of *Ceremony* by Leslie Marmon Silko. *Washington Post*, 24 April 1977, p. E4.

Left Handed, with Walter Dyk. *Left Handed, Son of Old Man Hat: A Navajo Autobiography*. Foreword by Edward Sapir. 1938. Lincoln: University of Nebraska Press, 1995.

Lerner, Andrea. "Joseph Bruchac." In Andrew Wiget, ed., *Dictionary of Native American Literature*. New York: Garland Publishing, 1994, pp. 401–405.

Lincoln, Kenneth. *Native American Renaissance*. Berkeley: University of California Press, 1983.

Littlefield, Daniel F., Jr., and James W. Parins. "Short Fiction Writers of the Indian Territory." *American Studies* 23 (1982): 23–38.

Lone Hill, Karen D. "Black Elk." In Frederick E. Hoxie, ed., *Encyclopedia of North American Indians*. Boston: Houghton Mifflin, 1996, pp. 73–74.

Lyman, Rich. "Writer Who Committed Suicide Was Under Investigation on Sexual Abuse Charge." *New York Times*, 16 April 1997, p. A12.

MacShane, Frank. "American Indians, Peruvian Jews: *Ceremony*." Review of *Ceremony* by Leslie Marmon Silko. *The New York Times Book Review*, 12 June 1977, pp. 15, 33.

Markowitz, Harvey. "Standing Bear, Luther." In Frederick E. Hoxie, ed., *Encyclopedia of North American Indians*. Boston: Houghton Mifflin, 1996, pp. 607–608.

Mathews, John Joseph. *Sundown*. 1934. Norman: University of Oklahoma Press, 1988.

McAllister, Harold S. "Incarnate Grace and the Paths of Salvation in *House Made of Dawn*." *South Dakota Review* 12 (1974): 115–125.

McAllister, Mick. "The Names." *Southern Review* no. 14 (1978a): 387.

———. "The Topology of Remembrance in *The Way to Rainy Mountain*." *Denver Quarterly* 12, no. 4 (1978b): 19–31.

McClure, Andrew. "Liberation and Identity: Bearing the Heart of *The Heirship Chronicles*." *SAIL: Studies in American Indian Literatures*, 2nd ser. 9 (1997): 47–59.

McFarland, Ron, ed. *James Welch*. Lewiston, Idaho: Confluence Press, 1986.

McFarland, Ron, and M. K. Browning. "An Interview with James Welch." In Ron McFarland, ed., *James Welch*. Lewiston, Idaho: Confluence Press, 1986, pp. 1–19.

McKenzie, James. "Lipsha's Good Road Home: The Revival of Chippewa Culture in *Love Medicine*." *American Indian Culture and Research Journal* 10, no. 3 (1986): 53–63.

McNickle, D'Arcy. *The Surrounded*. 1936. Albuquerque: University of New Mexico Press, 1978.

Medicine, Bea. "Ella C. Deloria: The Emic Voice." *MELUS* 7, no. 4 (1980): 23–30.

Mee, Charles L., Jr. *The Genius of the People*. New York: Harper and Row, 1987.

Meisenhelder, Susan. "Race and Gender in Louise Erdrich's *The Beet Queen*." *ARIEL: A Review of International English Literature* 25 (1994): 45–57.

Miller, Carol. "The Story Is Brimming Around: An Interview with Linda Hogan." *Studies in American Indian Literatures* 2 (1990): 1–9.

Miller, David Reed. "Eastman, Charles (Ohiyesa)." In Frederick E. Hoxie, ed., *Encyclopedia of North American Indians*. Boston: Houghton Mifflin, 1996, pp. 175–176.

Miller, Jay. Introduction. In Mourning Dove, *Coyote Stories*. 1933. Lincoln: University of Nebraska Press, 1990a, pp. v–xvii.

———. Introduction. In Jay Miller, ed., *Mourning Dove: A Salishan Autobiography*. Lincoln: University of Nebraska Press, 1990b, pp. xi–xxxix.

Mitchell, Carol. "*Ceremony* as Ritual." *American Indian Quarterly* 5 (1979): 27–35.

Momaday, N. Scott. *The Ancient Child*. New York: Doubleday, 1989.

———. *House Made of Dawn*. New York: Harper and Row, 1968.

———. Interview with Louis Owens. In William Balassi, John F. Crawford, and Annie O. Eysturoy, eds., *This Is about Vision: Interviews with Southwestern Writers*. Albuquerque: University of New Mexico Press, 1990, pp. 59–68.

———. *The Names: A Memoir*. Tucson: University of Arizona Press, 1976.

———. *The Way to Rainy Mountain.* Albuquerque: University of New Mexico Press, 1969.

Monsma, Bradley John. "Liminal Landscapes: Motion, Perspective, and Place in Gerald Vizenor's Fiction." *SAIL: Studies in American Indian Literatures,* 2nd ser. 9 (1997): 60–72.

Mourning Dove. *Cogewea, the Half-Blood: A Depiction of the Great Montana Cattle Range.* 1927. Lincoln: University of Nebraska Press, 1981.

———. *Coyote Stories.* Ed. Heister Dean Guie. 1933. Lincoln: University of Nebraska Press, 1990a.

———. *Mourning Dove: A Salishan Autobiography.* Ed. Jay Miller. Lincoln: University of Nebraska Press, 1990b.

Murphree, Bruce. "Welch's *Fools Crow.*" *Explicator* 52 (1994): 186–187.

Neihardt, John, ed. *Black Elk Speaks.* 1932. Lincoln: University of Nebraska Press, 1988.

Nelson, Robert M. "Place and Vision: The Function of Landscape in *Ceremony.*" *Journal of the Southwest* 30, no. 3 (1988): 281–316.

———. "Simon J. Ortiz." In Andrew Wiget, ed., *Dictionary of Native American Literature.* New York: Garland Publishing, 1994, pp. 483–489.

Niatum, Duane, ed. *Harper's Anthology of 20th Century Native American Poetry.* San Francisco: Harper and Row, 1988.

Niemann, Linda. "Healing History." Review of *The Grass Dancer* by Susan Power. *The Women's Review of Books,* 4 January 1995, p. 23.

Occom, Samson. *A Sermon Preached at the Execution of Moses Paul, an Indian Who Was Executed at New Haven, on the 2d of September 1772.* Bennington: William Watson, 1772.

O'Connell, Barry. "Apess, William." In Frederick E. Hoxie, ed., *Encyclopedia of North American Indians.* Boston: Houghton Mifflin, 1996, pp. 30–31.

Oleson, Carole. "The Remembered Earth: Momaday's *House Made of Dawn.*" *South Dakota Review* 11 (1973): 59–78.

Ortiz, Simon J. "The Language We Know." In Brian Swann and Arnold Krupat, eds., *I Tell You Now: Autobiographical Essays by Native American Writers.* Lincoln: University of Nebraska Press, 1987a, pp. 187–194.

———. "The Story Never Ends." In Joseph Bruchac, ed., *Survival This Way: Interviews with American Indian Poets.* Tucson: University of Arizona Press, 1987b, pp. 211–229.

———. *Woven Stone.* Tucson: University of Arizona Press, 1992.

Oskison, John Milton. *Black Jack Davy.* New York: Appleton, 1926.

———. *Brothers Three.* New York: Macmillan, 1935.

———. *Wild Harvest: A Novel of Transition Days in Oklahoma.* New York: Appleton, 1925.

Owens, Louis. *Bone Game.* Norman: University of Oklahoma Press, 1994.

———. *Other Destinies: Understanding the American Indian Novel.* Norman: University of Oklahoma Press, 1992a.

———. *The Sharpest Sight.* Norman: University of Oklahoma Press, 1992b.

Parins, James W. "Elias Boudinot." In Andrew Wiget, ed., *Dictionary of Native American Literature.* New York: Garland Publishing, 1994, pp. 217–219.

Parker, Dorothy R. *Singing an Indian Song: A Biography of D'Arcy McNickle.* Lincoln: University of Nebraska Press, 1992.

Parker, Robert Dale. "Who Shot the Sheriff: Storytelling, Indian Identity, and the Marketplace of Masculinity in D'Arcy McNickle's *The Surrounded.*" *Modern Fiction Studies* 43 (1997): 898–932.

Passaro, Vince. "Tales from a Literary Marriage." In Allan Chavkin and Nancy Feyl Chavkin, eds., *Conversations with Louise Erdrich and Michael Dorris.* Jackson: University Press of Mississippi, 1994, pp. 157–167.

Penn, William S. *The Absence of Angels.* Sag Harbor, NY: Permanent Press, 1994.

Perdue, Theda. "Boudinot, Elias." In Frederick E. Hoxie, ed., *Encyclopedia of North American Indians.* Boston: Houghton Mifflin, 1996, pp. 80–82.

Peyer, Bernd C. "Charles Alexander Eastman." In Andrew Wiget, ed., *Dictionary of Native American Literature.* New York: Garland Publishing, 1994a, pp. 231–237.

———. "Samson Occom." In Andrew Wiget, ed., *Dictionary of Native American Literature*. New York: Garland Publishing, 1994b, pp. 265–269.

———. "William Apess." In Andrew Wiget, ed., *Dictionary of Native American Literature*. New York: Garland Publishing, 1994c, pp. 207–209.

Picotte, Agnes M. Biographical Sketch of the Author. In Ella Cara Deloria, *Waterlily*. Lincoln: University of Nebraska Press, 1988.

———. Foreword. In Zitkala-Ša, *Old Indian Legends*. Lincoln: University of Nebraska Press, 1985.

Pollitt, Katha. "A New Assault on Feminism." Review of *The Broken Cord* by Michael Dorris. *The Nation*, 26 March 1990, p. 409.

Power, Susan. *The Grass Dancer*. New York: G. P. Putnam's Sons, 1994.

Prucha, Francis Paul. *Documents of United States Indian Policy*. 2nd ed. Lincoln: University of Nebraska Press, 1990.

Purdy, John. "Crossroads: A Conversation with Sherman Alexie." *SAIL: Studies in American Indian Literatures*, 2d ser. 9 (1997): 1–18.

Rainwater, Catherine. "Reading between Worlds: Narrativity in the Fiction of Louise Erdrich." *American Literature* 62 (1990): 405–422.

Raymond, Michael W. "Tai-Me, Christ, and the Machine: Affirmation through Mythic Pluralism in *House Made of Dawn*." *Studies in American Fiction* 11 (1983): 61–71.

Rayson, Ann. "Shifting Identity in the Work of Louise Erdrich and Michael Dorris." *Studies in American Indian Literature* 3 (1991): 27–36.

Revard, Carter. "Walking among the Stars." In Brian Swann and Arnold Krupat, eds., *I Tell You Now: Autobiographical Essays by Native American Writers*. Lincoln: University of Nebraska Press, 1987, pp. 65–84.

Rice, Julian. "Black Elk." In Andrew Wiget, ed., *Dictionary of Native American Literature*. New York: Garland Publishing, 1994, pp. 211–216.

Ridge, John Rollin. *The Life and Adventures of Joaquín Murieta, the Celebrated California Bandit*. 1854. Introduction by Joseph Henry Jackson. Norman: University of Oklahoma Press, 1977.

———. *Poems*. San Francisco: Payot, 1868.

Rigel-Cellard, Bernadette. "Doubling in Gerald Vizenor's *Bearheart*: The Pilgrimage Strategy or Bunyan Revisited." *SAIL: Studies in American Indian Literatures*, 2d ser. 9 (1997): 93–114.

Robbins, Kenn. "A Conversation with James Welch." *South Dakota Review* 28 (1990): 103–110.

Robins, Barbara K. "Michael (Anthony) Dorris." In Andrew Wiget, ed., *Dictionary of Native American Literature*. New York: Garland Publishing, 1994, pp. 417–422.

Ronnow, Gretchen. "John Milton Oskison." In Andrew Wiget, ed., *Dictionary of Native American Literature*. New York: Garland Publishing, 1994, pp. 271–275.

———. "Tayo, Death, and Desire: A Lacanian Reading of *Ceremony*." In Gerald Vizenor, ed., *Narrative Chance: Postmodern Discourse on Native American Literatures*. Albuquerque: University of New Mexico Press, 1989, pp. 69–89.

Rose, Wendy. "The Bones Are Alive." In Joseph Bruchac, ed., *Survival This Way: Interviews with American Indian Poets*. Tucson: University of Arizona Press, 1987, pp. 249–269.

———. Interview. In Laura Coltelli, ed., *Winged Words*. Lincoln: University of Nebraska Press, 1990, pp. 121–133.

Ruoff, A. LaVonne Brown. "Alienation and the Female Principle in *Winter in the Blood*. *American Indian Quarterly* 4 (1978a): 107–122.

———. *American Indian Literatures: An Introduction, Bibliographic Review, and Selected Bibliography*. New York: MLA, 1990.

———. "George Copway." In Andrew Wiget, ed., *Dictionary of Native American Literature*. New York: Garland Publishing, 1994, pp. 225–230.

———. "Introduction: Samson Occom's *Sermon Preached . . . at the Execution of Moses Paul*." *SAIL: Studies in American Indian Literature*, 2nd ser. 4 (1992): 75–81.

———. "Old Traditions and New Forms." In Paula Gunn Allen, ed., *Studies in American Indian Literature: Critical Essays and Course Designs*. New York: MLA, 1983, pp. 147–168.

————. "Ritual and Renewal: Keres Traditions in the Short Fiction of Leslie Silko." *MELUS* 5 (1978b): 2–17.

Ruppert, James. *Mediation in Contemporary Native American Fiction*. Norman: University of Oklahoma Press, 1995.

————. "Paula Gunn Allen." In Andrew Wiget, ed., *Dictionary of Native American Literature*. New York: Garland Publishing, 1994, pp. 395–399.

————. "The Reader's Lessons in *Ceremony*." *The Arizona Quarterly* 44 (1988): 78–85.

Sands, Kathleen. "*The Death of Jim Loney*: Indian or Not?" In Ron McFarland, ed., *James Welch*. Lewiston, Idaho: Confluence Press, 1986, pp. 127–133.

Sands, Kathleen M. "Alienation and Broken Narrative in *Winter in the Blood*." *American Indian Quarterly* 4 (1978): 97–105.

Sands, Kathleen Mullen. "Closing the Distance: Critic, Reader and the Works of James Welch." *MELUS* 14 (1987): 73–85.

Sarris, Greg. *Grand Avenue: A Novel in Stories*. New York: Hyperion, 1994. New York: Penguin, 1995.

Scarberry, Susan J. "Memory as Medicine: The Power of Recollection in *Ceremony*." *American Indian Quarterly* 5 (1979): 19–26.

Scheckter, John. "James Welch: Settling Up on the Reservation." *South Dakota Review* 24, no. 2 (1986): 7–19.

Schneider, Alison. "Words as Medicine: Professor Writes of Urban Indians from the Heart." *The Chronicle of Higher Education,* 19 July 1996, p. B4.

Scholer, Bo. Review of *The Sun Is Not Merciful* by Anna Lee Walters. *American Indian Quarterly* 10 (1986): 171–173.

Schubnell, Matthias. *N. Scott Momaday: The Cultural and Literary Background*. Norman: University of Oklahoma Press, 1985.

————. "Tribal Identity and the Imagination." In Kenneth M. Roemer, ed., *Approaches to Teaching Momaday's* The Way to Rainy Mountain. New York: MLA, 1988, pp. 24–31.

Schultz, Lydia A. "Fragments and Ojibwe Stories: Narrative Strategies in Louise Erdrich's *Love Medicine*." *College Literature* 18 (1991): 80–95.

Schumacher, Michael. "Louise Erdrich and Michael Dorris: A Marriage of Minds." In Allan Chavkin and Nancy Feyl Chavkin, eds., *Conversations with Louise Erdrich and Michael Dorris*. Jackson: University Press of Mississippi, 1994, pp. 173–183.

Sergi, Jennifer. "Storytelling: Tradition and Preservation in Louise Erdrich's *Tracks*." *World Literature Today* 66 (1992): 279–282.

Silko, Leslie Marmon. *Almanac of the Dead*. New York: Simon and Schuster, 1991.

————. *Ceremony*. New York: Viking, 1977. New York: Penguin, 1986.

————. *Storyteller*. New York: Arcade Publishing, 1981.

————. *Yellow Woman and a Beauty of the Spirit*. New York: Simon and Schuster, 1996.

Smith, Donald B. "George Copway." In Frederick E. Hoxie, ed., *Encyclopedia of North American Indians*. Boston: Houghton Mifflin, 1996, pp. 134–135.

————. "The Life of George Copway or Kah-ge-ga-gah-bowh (1818–1869)—and a Review of His Writings." *Journal of Canadian Studies* 23, no. 3 (1988): 5–38.

Smith, Jeanne. "Transpersonal Selfhood: The Boundaries of Identity in Louise Erdrich's *Love Medicine*." *SAIL: Studies in American Indian Literatures* 3, no. 4 (1991): 13–26.

St. Andrews, B. A. "Healing the Witching: Medicine in Silko's *Ceremony*." *ARQ* 44, no. 1 (Spring 1988): 86–94.

Standing Bear, Luther. *My Indian Boyhood*. 1931. Lincoln: University of Nebraska Press, 1988.

————. *My People, the Sioux*. Ed. E. A. Brinninstool. 1928. Lincoln: University of Nebraska Press, 1975.

Streitfeld, David. "The Writer's Cloudy Final Chapter: Michael Dorris Suicide Stuns Literary Community." *Washington Post,* 15 April 1997a, p. D1.

————. "Writer Was Suspected of Child Abuse: Probe Ends with Michael Dorris Suicide." *Washington Post,* 16 April 1997b, D1.

Stripes, James D. "The Problem(s) of (Anishinaabe) History in the Fiction of Louise Erdrich: Voices and Contexts." *Wicazo Sa Review* 7, no. 2 (1991): 26–33.

Strong, John A. "Occum, Samson." In Frederick E. Hoxie, ed., *Encyclopedia of North American Indians.* Boston: Houghton Mifflin, 1996, pp. 434–436.

Swan, Edith. "Feminine Perspectives at Laguna Pueblo: Silko's *Ceremony.*" *Tulsa Studies in Women's Literature* 11 (1992): 309–327.

———. "Laguna Prototypes of Manhood in *Ceremony.*" *MELUS* 17 (1991–1992): 39–61.

———. "Laguna Symbolic Geography and Silko's *Ceremony.*" *American Indian Quarterly* 12, no. 3 (1988): 229–249.

Swann, Brian, and Arnold Krupat. *I Tell You Now: Autobiographical Essays by Native American Writers.* Lincoln: University of Nebraska Press, 1987.

Tallent, Elizabeth. "Storytelling with a Vengeance." Review of *Almanac of the Dead* by Leslie Marmon Silko. *The New York Times Book Review,* 22 December 1991, p. 6.

TallMountain, Mary. "You *Can* Go Home Again: A Sequence." In Brian Swann and Arnold Krupat, eds., *I Tell You Now: Autobiographical Essays by Native American Writers.* Lincoln: University of Nebraska Press, 1987, pp. 1–13.

Tapahonso, Luci. *Sáanii Dahataał: The Women Are Singing.* Tucson: University of Arizona Press, 1993.

"Termination." In Frederick E. Hoxie, ed., *Encyclopedia of North American Indians.* Boston: Houghton Mifflin, 1996, p. 625.

Thackeray, William W. "Animal Allies and Transformers in *Winter in the Blood.*" *MELUS* 12 (1985): 37–64.

Thornton, Lawrence. "The Grandmother in the Moon." Review of *The Grass Dancer* by Susan Power. *The New York Times Book Review,* 21 August 1994, p. 7.

Towery, Margie. "Continuity and Connection: Characters in Louise Erdrich's Fiction." *American Indian Culture and Research Journal* 16, no. 4 (1992): 99–122.

Underhill, Ruth. "The Autobiography of a Papago Woman." *Memoirs of the American Anthropological Association* 46 (1936): 1–64.

Van Dyke, Annette. "The Journey Back to Female Roots: A Laguna Pueblo Model." In Karla Jay and Joanne Glasgow, eds., *Lesbian Texts and Contexts: Radical Revisions.* New York: New York University Press, 1990, pp. 339–354.

Vangen, Kathryn S. "James Welch." In Andrew Wiget, ed., *Dictionary of Native American Literature.* New York: Garland Publishing, 1994, pp. 531–537.

Vecsey, Christopher. *Traditional Ojibwa Religion and Its Historical Changes.* Philadelphia: American Philosophical Society, 1983.

Velie, Alan R. *Four American Indian Literary Masters: N. Scott Momaday, James Welch, Leslie Marmon Silko, and Gerald Vizenor.* Norman: University of Oklahoma Press, 1982.

———. "Gerald Vizenor." In Andrew Wiget, ed., *Dictionary of Native American Literature.* New York: Garland Publishing, 1994a, pp. 519–525.

———. "Gerald Vizenor's Indian Gothic." *MELUS* 17 (Spring 1992): 75–85.

———. "The Return of the Native: The Renaissance of Tribal Religions as Reflected in the Fiction of N. Scott Momaday." *Religion and Literature* 26 (1994b): 135–145.

———. "*Winter in the Blood* as Comic Novel." *American Indian Quarterly* 4 (1978): 141–147.

Vizenor, Gerald. *Bearheart: The Heirship Chronicles.* Minneapolis: University of Minnesota Press, 1990. First published as *Darkness in Saint Louis Bearheart* by Truck Press in 1978.

———. "Follow the Trickroutes." In Joseph Bruchac, ed., *Survival This Way: Interviews with American Indian Poets.* Tucson: University of Arizona Press, 1987, pp. 287–310.

———. Interview. In Laura Coltelli, ed., *Winged Words: American Indian Writers Speak.* Lincoln: University of Nebraska Press, 1990, pp. 155–182.

Vizenor, Gerald, ed. *Narrative Chance: Postmodern Discourse on Native American Literatures.* Albuquerque: University of New Mexico Press, 1989.

Walker, Victoria. "A Note on Narrative Perspective in *Tracks.*" *SAIL: Studies in American Indian Literatures* 3, no. 4 (1991): 37–40.

Walsh, Dennis M., and Ann Braley. "The Indianness of Louise Erdrich's *The Beet Queen*: Latency as Presence." *American Indian Culture and Research Journal* 18, no. 3 (1994): 1–17.

Weiler, Dagmar. "N. Scott Momaday: Storyteller." *Journal of Ethnic Studies* 16 (1988): 118–126.

Welch, James. *The Death of Jim Loney.* Harper and Row, 1979. New York: Penguin, 1987.

———. *Fools Crow.* Viking, 1986. New York: Penguin, 1987.

———. *The Indian Lawyer.* 1990. New York: Penguin, 1991.

———. *Winter in the Blood.* New York: Harper and Row, 1974. New York: Penguin, 1986.

Westrum, Dexter. "Transcendental Survival: The Way the Bird Works in *The Death of Jim Loney.*" In Ron McFarland, ed., *James Welch.* Lewiston, Idaho: Confluence Press, 1986, pp. 139–146.

Whiteman, Roberta Hill. "Massaging the Earth." In Joseph Bruchac, ed., *Survival This Way: Interviews with American Indian Poets.* Tucson: University of Arizona Press, 1987, pp. 323–335.

———. *Star Quilt.* Minneapolis: Holy Cow! Press, 1984.

Whitson, Kathy J. "Louise Erdrich's *Love Medicine* and *Tracks*: A Culturalist Approach." Ph.D. diss., University of Missouri, 1993.

Wiget, Andrew. *Native American Literature.* Boston: Twayne Publishers, 1985.

———. *Simon Ortiz.* Boise: Boise State University Press, 1986.

Wiget, Andrew, ed. *Dictionary of Native American Literature.* New York: Garland Publishing, 1994.

Wilson, Norma C. "Roberta Hill Whiteman." In Andrew Wiget, ed., *Dictionary of Native American Literature.* New York: Garland Publishing, 1994a, pp. 539–543.

———. "Wendy Rose." In Andrew Wiget, ed., *Dictionary of Native American Literature.* New York: Garland Publishing, 1994b, pp. 495–498.

Wilson, Terry P. "John Joseph Mathews." In Andrew Wiget, ed., *Dictionary of Native American Literature.* New York: Garland Publishing, 1994, pp. 245–249.

Witalec, Janet, ed. *Smoke Rising: The Native North American Literary Companion.* Detroit: Visible Ink Press, 1995.

Wong, Hertha Dawn. "Adoptive Mothers and Thrown-Away Children in the Novels of Louise Erdrich." In Brenda O. Daly and Maureen T. Reddy, eds., *Narrating Mothers: Theorizing Maternal Subjectives.* Knoxville: University of Tennessee Press, 1991, pp. 174–192.

———. "An Interview with Louise Erdrich and Michael Dorris." In Allan Chavkin and Nancy Feyl Chavkin, eds., *Conversations with Louise Erdrich and Michael Dorris.* Jackson: University Press of Mississippi, 1994, pp. 30–53.

———. *Sending My Heart Back across the Years: Tradition and Innovation in Native American Autobiography.* New York: Oxford University Press, 1992.

Woodard, Charles L. *Ancestral Voice: Conversations with N. Scott Momaday.* Lincoln: University of Nebraska Press, 1989.

Zitkala-Ša. *American Indian Stories.* 1921. Introduction by Dexter Fisher. Lincoln: University of Nebraska Press, 1985.

———. *Old Indian Legends.* 1901. Lincoln: University of Nebraska Press, 1985.

Index